Best of the Journals in
Rhetoric and Composition

Best of the Journals in Rhetoric and Composition
SERIES EDITOR: STEVE PARKS

Each year, a team of editors selects the best work published in the independent journals in the field of Rhetoric and Composition, following a competitive review process involving journal editors and publishers. For additional information about the series, see http://www.parlorpress.com/bestofrhetcomp.

BEST OF THE JOURNALS IN RHETORIC AND COMPOSITION

2015-2016

Edited by Steve Parks, Brian Bailie, Romeo Garcia, Adela Licona, Kate Navickas, and David Blakesley

Parlor Press
Anderson, South Carolina
www.parlorpress.com

Parlor Press LLC, Anderson, South Carolina, USA

© 2017 by Parlor Press. Individual essays in this book have been reprinted with permission of the respective copyright owners.
All rights reserved.
Printed in the United States of America

S A N: 2 5 4 - 8 8 7 9

ISSN 2327-4778 (print)
ISSN 2327-4786 (online)

978-1-60235-989-5 (paperback)
978-1-60235-990-1 (Adobe eBook)
978-1-60235-991-8 (ePub)
978-1-60235-992-5 (iBook)
978-1-60235-993-2 (Kindle)

1 2 3 4 5

Cover design by David Blakesley.
Printed on acid-free paper.

Parlor Press, LLC is an independent publisher of scholarly and trade titles in print and multimedia formats. This book is available in paper and digital formats from Parlor Press on the World Wide Web at http://www.parlorpress.com or through online and brick-and-mortar bookstores. For submission information or to find out about Parlor Press publications, write to Parlor Press, 3015 Brackenberry Drive, Anderson, South Carolina, 29621, or email editor@parlorpress.com.

Contents

Introduction   *vii*
   Romeo Garcia, Adela Licona, and Kate Navickas

Home and Community-Based Knowledge Making as Responsive Pedagogies

BASIC WRITING EJOURNAL

1 Basic Writing Through the Back Door: Community-Engaged Courses in the Rush-to-Credit Age   *3*
   Cori Brewster

JOURNAL OF TEACHING WRITING

2 Mapping Students' Funds of Knowledge in the First-Year Writing Classroom   *21*
   Genesea M. Carter

REFLECTIONS

3 Why Study Disability? Lessons Learned from a Community Writing Project   *47*
   Annika Konrad

COMMUNITY LITERACY JOURNAL

4 Poetic Signs of Third Place: A Case Study of Student-Driven Imitation in a Shelter for Young Homeless People in Copenhagen   *61*
   Christina Matthiesen

Multimodalities and Multiply-Situated Subjects: Decenterings in and beyond the Classroom

COMPOSITION FORUM

5 Multimodality, Translingualism, and Rhetorical Genre Studies   *85*
   Laura Gonzales

JOURNAL OF SECOND LANGUAGE WRITING

6 L2 Student–U.S. Professor Interactions Through Disciplinary Writing Assignments: An Activity Theory Perspective   *121*
   Mayumi Fujioka

WLN: A JOURNAL OF WRITING CENTER SCHOLARSHIP
7 Student Perceptions of Intellectual Engagement in the Writing Center: Cognitive Challenge, Tutor Involvement, and Productive Sessions   *159*
   Pamela Bromley, Eliana Schonberg, and Kara Northway

ACROSS THE DISCIPLINES
8 Instructor Feedback in Upper-Division Biology Courses: Moving from Spelling and Syntax to Scientific Discourse   *169*
   Erika Amethyst Szymanski

Sound and Sensual Knowledges as Affective Circulations

HARLOT
9 Emoji, Emoji, What for Art Thou?   *191*
   Lisa Lebduska

ENCULTURATION
10 Listening to the Sonic Archive: Rhetoric, Representation, and Race in the Lomax Prison Recordings   *215*
   Jonathan W. Stone

Research, Writing, Teaching, Mentoring & Administration in Rhetoric and Composition: A Call for Rigorous Intersectionality

PRESENT TENSE
11 An Annotated Bibliography of LGBTQ Rhetorics   *249*
   Matthew B. Cox and Michael J. Faris

COMPOSITION STUDIES
12 A Plea for Critical Race Theory Counterstory: Stock Story versus Counterstory Dialogues Concerning Alejandra's "Fit" in the Academy   *263*
   Aja Y. Martinez

LITERACY IN COMPOSITION STUDIES
13 Teaching While Black: Witnessing and Countering Disciplinary Whiteness, Racial Violence, and University Race-Management   *291*
   Carmen Kynard

About the Editors   *317*

Introduction

Romeo Garcia, Adela Licona, and Kate Navickas

This collection of articles from thirteen independent journals in rhetoric and composition reflects a still-growing interest and commitment to diverse scholarly pursuits and areas of research. In coming together to serve as editors of this collection, we share an interest in the articulation of diverse knowledge domains and recognize the enormous value of well-informed, cross-disciplinary and responsive pedagogies, theories, and research. As the field continues to grow and diversify, many scholars are reflecting on the work accomplished and the work left-to-be-done. With diverse research agendas and methodologies, the authors in this collection demonstrate discernment for "work" in ethical and socially responsible ways. In part, the research questions and scholarly conversations in each of the thirteen articles reveals an engaged interest in changing social, economic, and political environments. Collectively, these works offer insights into a changing vision of what rhetoric and composition pedagogies are, where they are undertaken and encountered, and what they can achieve.

As editors of this collection, the challenging, yet exciting task for us has been delineating a vision of responsive works that simultaneously and thoughtfully engage literacies, rhetorics, and multiply-situated subjectivities. Among these articles, we have identified four sections: 1) knowledge and meaning-making, 2) multimodalities and multiply-situated subjects, 3) sound and sensual knowledges, and 4) rigorous intersectionality. While we have grouped these articles according to themes meaningful to us, we encourage readers to read across sections to create their own connections. In this collection, some of the articles ask us to consider how to respectfully and reciprocally draw from community-based knowledges and meaning-making practices, while others offer critical insight into the innovative and meaningful engagements with multiplicity to include multiply-situated subjects and multimodalities. There are also essays here that move us from the sight-centered to the sonic, to sensual knowledges, and the affective realm. The authors share pedagogies and practices that not only decenter the teacher as the center of knowledge-production but also decenter normative subjectivities, dominant languages, and ways of understanding the various sites of our work. We believe decentering is at the heart of these works.

We acknowledge and appreciate the risks independent journals take in publishing innovative work that attends to non-dominant knowledge productions and producers, especially in these times of heightened nationalism, nativism, and all forms of bigotry. As editors, we'd like to continue the worlds-making we see these authors calling for by further seeking work that thoughtfully includes and meaningfully considers trans* perspectives, Indigenous and Native knowledges, and local and decolonial frameworks and action. We call on those who come next--editors, writers, thinkers, and teachers--to invest in work that is rigorously and robustly intersectional.

Home and Community-Based Knowledge Making as Responsive Pedagogies

The field continues to ask and attend to how the pedagogical situation of a composition classroom can draw upon and extrapolate from community-based meaning and knowledge making practices to develop enriched pedagogical frameworks and practices. The articles in this section provide critical insight on the challenges of designing curricula, the strategic ways students can navigate discourse communities, the life lessons to be learned, and the possibilities of place-based and third-space practices.

In, "Basic Writing through the Back Door: Community-Engaged Courses in the Rush-to-Credit Age," from the *Basic Writing E-Journal*, Cori Brewster attends to the entanglements of public writing, service learning, and the politics of access, retention and success. Brewster reflects on her teaching experience with two three-week courses for rural high school students. In the "rush-to-credit" age, Brewster notes, the allotted three-week time frame became a matter of ethical concern and social responsibility. Curriculum design was a challenge because of the tension between preparing students for success and compressing student's opportunities to learn. Responding to this tension, Brewster created a "project-oriented" public writing course on food stories ranging from a food literacy narrative to interview-based research. Although a success, Brewster asks us to consider whether any of this public work has any bearing on student success and retention beyond this one course. Brewster maintains that there is much lost with "quick-credentialing" efforts and advocates for curricular decisions that aim more at "preparing students not just to start college but to stay" (18-19).

The concern of preparing students beyond the point of access into higher education is addressed by Genesea Carter in, "Mapping Students' Funds of Knowledge in the First-Year Writing Classroom," from the *Journal of Teaching Writing*. For Carter, this concern begins with first-year students transitioning from high school to college and learning how to "adapt" to new discourse communities in and across campus. Through research on discourse communities and community literacies, Carter explores the intersectional possibilities of students' Funds of Knowledge (FoK) and a discourse community framework. Carter works to develop a multi-modal approach to actualize such possibilities by "empowering" students, "validating their home knowledge while teaching them how to be members of multiple communities" (27). Carter's digital literacy map assignment introduces students to discourse community concepts, which asks them to map and trace literacy practices in visual representations, create a profile of these representations in places, and present a public service announcement. Demonstrating the importance of membership, literacy sponsors, and awareness, Carter sees her own classroom as a discourse community and sees the classroom as the opportune space to situate lived experiences and knowledges.

From *Reflections*, Annika Konrad's "Why Study Disability? Lessons Learned from a Community Writing Project," is one case in point of the lessons to be learned in community-based writing projects. Konrad, a writing instructor and visually impaired person, reflects on creating a community writing project around disabilities, specifically, the blind and/or visually impaired. Konrad quickly realizes that her expectations and assumptions in providing writing instruction at the university level does not simply translate into diverse spaces such as those occupied with the rhetoric of disability. Konrad notes, "I soon realized that I would need to adapt my agenda, on both a conceptual and logistical level" (126). Konrad recounts how through the experience of the class, they all discovered how to "tell" a story from a positionality of disability, how to narrate and communicate disability. Ultimately, Konrad learns to re-imagine what it means to tell a powerful story and what it means to respect desires and intentions even as it rubs against assumptions of agency and predispositions of writing instruction.

In the *Community Literacy Journal*, Christina Matthiesen's "Poetic Signs of Third Place: A Case Study of Student-Driven Imitation in a Shelter for Young Homeless People in Copenhagen," offers an action-research oriented case study of listening to young homeless people and their meaning-making practices in the shelters of Copenhagen. Interested in Quintilian's notion of imitation and Ray Oldenburg's idea of third place, Matthiesen explores intersectional possibilities of the classical rhetorical tradition and community literacy projects. Working to re-orient imitation as a "process" that combines experiences and reflective practices within the decision-making of the learner, Matthiesen premises imitation with dialogism and critical thinking to support student-driven imitation exercises. Matthiesen notes student-driven imitation, as a literate practice, "seeks to promote independence, confidence, and a sense of agency" (2), while linking the private and public spheres (8). Matthiesen finds that poetry is the preferred genre for creating a dialogic space, where the youth interactionally participated in shaping their language and expressions through the strategy of imitation, thus, highlighting a rhetorical dimension. Ultimately, Matthiesen questions the efficacy and value of working from the notion of third place.

Multimodalities & Multiply-Situated Subjects: Decenterings In & Beyond the Classroom

This section draws together a set of essays that are at once keenly analytical and eloquently descriptive. Each essay, written solo or in collaboration, meaningfully engages in asset-driven approaches, especially to L2 student knowledges and interests, and each is attentive to multiplicities in ways that will enrich classroom and mentoring practices as well as translingual, cross-cultural, and even transnational research designs and endeavors. These four essays call readers to be attentive to distinct literacies and histories and to diverse knowledge domains as sites of rich possibilities.

Laura Gonzales's chapter, "Multimodality, Translingualism, and Rhetorical Genre Studies," approaches L2 students as sophisticated readers, thinkers, and writers of layered meaning-making and of multimodal compositions and communications. Her meticulous research reveals L2 learners as students whose complex abilities to layer modes and meanings in their translanguaging practices displays rhetorical ingenuity with particular implications for rhetorical genre studies. Translingualism, in Gonzales' work, moves beyond a definition grounded exclusively in linguistic histories or practices to a more capacious engagement with the concept as a framework for comprehending the "fluidity of modalities and languages," and the crisscrossing of languages, as assets that allow for a deeper understanding and appreciation for the multiple ways students make meaning of and through the composing processes and practices. We recognize the composing practices that Gonzales so carefully details as those of multiply-situated subjects whose multiplicities have been similarly illuminated through women-of-color feminisms. While intellectually related projects, Gonzales' work here is clearly focused on students' linguistic repertoires and in their approaches to and innovations with multimodal composition.

In keeping with Gonzales's asset-driven approach to L2 students, Miyumi Fujioka also concludes that L2 learners can well inform multi-directional teaching and learning practices through a demonstrated understanding of the possibility for reciprocity between learner-teachers and teacher-learners. Fujioka's "L2 student- U.S. Professor Interactions Through Disciplinary Writing Assignments: An Activity Theory Perspective" offers a refreshing focus on graduate–level L2 writing studies and disciplinary socializations. The focus of Fujiok'a study shifts from "a unidirectional trajectory in which novices become experts" to one that considers the multi-directionality of both the teaching and the learning process, such that novices have something to learn and something to teach. To "understand concurrent and multi-directional learning between the student and the professor, who mutually shaped and influenced each other's writing and teaching practices," each assignment analyzed here is treated as an activity system (40). New insights into writing practices, including for new professors, emerge in this study to demonstrate a responsive pedagogy and the mutli-directional learning that can happen "between the student and the professor, who mutually shaped and influenced each other's writing and teaching practices" (40).

In "Student Perceptions of Intellectual Engagement in the Writing Center: Cognitive Challenge, Tutor Involvement, and Productive Sessions," Pamela Bromley, Kara Northway and Eliana Schonberg share their findings from a three-school empirical study of student engagement during writing center tutoring sessions. Findings on engagement exemplify "one way that writing center missions dovetail with institutional missions—an expectation sometimes difficult for centers to make explicit" (6). By collating students' definitions of intellectual engagement, they found two categories: cognitive challenge and tutor collaboration (3). They equate cognitive challenge with higher-order thinking that occurs not just through challenging content, but through the actual social and collaborative exchange that takes place with the tutor. They link intellectual engagement with productive tutoring sessions, noting that almost all (99-100%) of the students who found a session to be intellectually engaging also found the session to be productive, whereas students were much less likely to find sessions productive if they were not also intellectually stimulating (4). Bromley et al. argue that these findings have implications for tutor training and, perhaps more importantly, for the institutional promotion of writing center work as more than just one-way support services--but as an extension of the intellectual work students do in the classroom.

Erika Amethyst Szymanski's chapter, "Instructor Feedback in Upper-Division Biology Courses: Moving from Spelling and Syntax to Scientific Discourse," is based on a limited study on a university campus with "a long-standing and well-regarded culture of writing but no formal WAC program independent of the general university writing program." Symanski considers current practices in teaching writing to science majors with an interest in instructor feedback on student writing within biology and science. A majority of professors in the first part of her study were revealed to focus their writing feedback on lower-order concerns, whereas a minority of professors focused feedback on how students could better enact the disciplinary writing conventions of the scientific genres. In the second part of her study, Szymanski interviews these professors. In support of much rhetorical genre studies research, she finds feedback that directs students to the scientific discourses and purposes of the disciplinary genres is most productive in helping students to understand writing in the sciences.

The Sonic and the Emotive: Sensual Knowledges as Affective Circulations

In this section, two authors consider how to expand and re-attune rhetorical theory to consider affective, symbolic and material means, values, and circulations of rhetoric. The two articles illustrate an ethics of listening to material objects (emojis) and things (archives of sound and voice) as they emerge from historical, economic, cultural and material contexts. While the scope of their rhetorical work differ, both authors imagine rhetorical practices occurring in and across the sensorium, furthering the scope of rhetoric itself.

In "Emoji, Emoji, What for Art Thou?," Lisa Lebduska playfully counters those who attack emojis as the death of language. Noting their birth by Carnegie Mellon researchers in 1982 via the iconic :) emoji, Lebduska offers a history of emojis that connects this contemporary visual shorthand to earlier visual communication systems like petrographs, pictographs, and cuneiform. She traces the emergence of emojis as a means of making communication faster and cheaper as similar to other communication technology innovations like the telegraph and shorthand. Lebduska advocates for understanding the emoji as a form of communication that is, perhaps surprisingly, not new, and materially, culturally, and contextually bound. She grapples with the tension that emojis are paradoxically both transparent in their intended meaning (making communication across languages easier and more accessible) and mysterious, murky, and context-dependent--characteristics eerily similar to alphabetic language. Lebduska offers us a multitude of ways to understand emojis: through literacy, alphabetic communication, and technological access and circulation; via contemporary evolutions in emojis that have accounted for racial diversity, emoji literature, and emoji art; and through disciplinary investigations into emojis as visual rhetorics and multimodal communication. Her work challenges us to take seriously the complex ways that emojis, and other visual rhetorics, shape meaning-making.

Jonathan Stone's essay, "Listening to the Sonic Archives: Rhetoric, Representation, and Race in the Lomax Prison Recordings," joins a scholarly conversation of sonic boom, a sustained attention to sound as integral to rhetorical studies—sonic rhetoric. His essay is situated within this notion of sonic archives, specifically, that of musical artifacts such as prison recordings, with a focus on how sonic rhetoric nuances understanding of cultural history and historiography. Stone asks readers to "listen" to the sonic rhetoric of four prison recordings and how the black experience is articulated as dissonance and agency through historical and symbolic sonic renderings. The meshing of the "ontic" and the "symbolic" illuminates a meshing of personal and communal signifying meaning making practices and elements. This, Stone argues, ties into the (re)inventional practices of Black culture, giving way to various possibilities for understanding cultural formation and difference. Some of these possibilities include listening to how these recordings stand as vernacular discourse meant to create change within racial relations and racial difference.

Research, Writing, Teaching, Mentoring & Administration in Rhetoric and Composition: A Call for Rigorous Intersectionality

We understand it as especially urgent now in the face of the most recent national election in the U.S. to teach, write, research, and mentor without the mandate for extraction or conquest. We, therefore, end with a call for a full turn toward rigorous intersectionality taken in order to attend to the effects of settler state governances and to the present and undeniable re-entrenchment of institutionalized systems, structures, and practices of everyday racism, bigotry, and inequality that we are facing in the U.S. and transnationally. We see this turn as having been initiated through recent keynote addresses, in which CCCC Chair scholars such as Joyce Carter and Adam Banks urged the field towards what we name here rigorous and robust intersectional inquiries and engagements in our thinking, research, writing, teaching, and mentoring. The articles in this section lead the way in making the turn we call for here by offering a powerful reminder that the work is not done yet, especially in terms of radical intersectionality. Even more so, these three articles suggest that this internal narrative of the social progressiveness of the field may allow us to ignore social inequalities and institutionalized racism that happens right here--in rhetoric and composition.

In the *Present Tense* winning article, "An Annotated Bibliography of LGBTQ Rhetorics," Matthew Cox and Michael Faris offer a bibliography that highlights LGBTQ work by rhetorical scholars through both a thematic and chronological lens. In their opening statement, they offer queer theory as a methodological approach and emphasize rhetorical content on the study of sexuality and rhetoric. As editors, we would add the significance of Teresa de Lauretis in introducing the very phrase "queer theory." Although not canonical, Cox and Farris put together a bibliography that is in-progress and meant to be a generative tool to "challenge the field in terms of methods, methodologies, epistemologies, and modes of publishing—digital and print" (7). They urge us to be more invested in, conversant in, and supportive of work that considers sexuality and rhetoric and queers heteronormative ways of knowing and doing. As they suggest, "Rhetoric studies seemed incredibly straight. And, in many ways, it still does. Graduate students are often encouraged to study heteronormative theory and, we might say, are trained to identify with it" (2).

In "A Plea for Critical Race Theory Counterstory," Aja Martinez tells a stock story and a counterstory about the place of Latin@s in higher education in order to showcase the value of counterstory as a method for rhetoric and composition that centers marginalized stories and institutional and disciplinary racism. Drawing from critical race theory, especially Richard Delgado, Martinez explains the normalization of stock stories, those told by dominant groups and privileged people, to create a homogenized and white narrative of reality that continues to marginalize the everyday experiences of people of color. As Martinez writes, counterstory functions as a method for "marginalized people to intervene in research methods that would form master narratives based on ignorance and on assumptions about minoritized peoples" (53). Citing the very low, almost non-existent, statistics of Chican@s and even Latin@s at all stages in the educational pipeline, Martinez goes onto share a stock story and a counterstory on a relevant educational moment in the life of Alejandra. Juxtaposed, the two stories highlight the ways that narrative counterstories expose racism and more complex understandings of situations. Martinez hopes this particular stock and counterstory set will raise awareness of the issues facing Latin@s, Chican@s and other marginalized graduate students in higher education, will foster more critical conversations around mentoring and supporting marginalized students in graduate work, and will encourage future research that uses CRT to theorize new counterstories.

In "Teaching While Black: Witnessing and Countering Disciplinary Whiteness, Racial Violence, and University Race-Management,"

Carmen Kynard powerfully calls out the ways in which institutions and the field of rhetoric and composition, in particular, continue to systematically value and enforce white supremacist cultural logics, thus enacting daily acts of racial violence that mirror the racial violence academic scholars and departments claim to study. Throughout the essay, Kynard shares a number of personal stories of daily racism that targets both her, her work, and students at her institutions. While she theorizes these experiences, they also function to highlight the daily ubiquity of racial violence leveled against faculty and students of color at all institutions of higher education. She is clear that these narratives are not single or exemplary, not racism over there, but rather the result of a disciplinary (and academic) system that reproduces and validates white cultural logics and racism. Kynard's stories and argument works as a gut-check to white scholars and those claiming allyship, and, an affirmation of the obvious state of affairs to academics of color and those fighting daily acts of racism at their home institutions. As Kynard makes clear, anti-racist ideologies are only as powerful as the ways they are practiced and used to fight real, everyday racial violence.

A Note on the Selection Process

This year, the 13 winning journal articles were selected by an extensive national set of 22 reading groups from 19 different universities. The reading groups that participated included composition graduate seminars, independent graduate student groups, and professional development faculty groups. The process began with the submission of 24 articles by 13 different independent journals in Rhetoric and Composition. The participating journals met with their editorial boards to determine their highest quality articles and then sent us one or two, depending on each journal's discussion regarding article quality and availability from the previous year. Then, we sent the articles to the reading groups with the following broad criteria:

- Article demonstrates a broad sense of the discipline, demonstrating the ability to explain how its specific focus in a sub-disciplinary area addresses broader concerns in the field.
- Article makes original contributions to the field, expanding or rearticulating central premises.

- Article is written in a style which, while based in the discipline, attempts to engage with a wider audience or concerns a wider audience.

Reading groups had a semester to read the articles and use our broad criteria as a starting point for their own rich discussions around research, pedagogy, and issues that are central to the work of the discipline. Each group sent us back their reports, which often involved various charts and in-depth rationales for their group's rankings. From the rankings reports, as an editorial team, we reviewed rationales and tallied the votes. Although the tallying process may seem fairly straightforward, many groups shared their misgivings in selecting one article over another from specific journals. These ties were determined based on comparing the larger response to the specific articles across the groups; but, importantly, we believe the ties represent the vitality and strength of the research and writing that the independent journals of rhetoric and composition consistently publish.

We are extremely grateful, then, to those who volunteered to organize faculty and graduate student readings groups and to use their classes to review and rank the submitted articles. Indeed, the work of the *Best of Independent Rhetoric and Composition Journals* collections depends on the thoughtful insights, commitment, and collaboration of all of our associate editors. Thank you, for all of your efforts and contributions:

Kristi Costello, Arkansas State University
Airek Beauchamp, Arkansas State University
Kerri Bennett, Arkansas State University
Jake Buechler, Arkansas State University
Justin Cook, Arkansas State University
Brennah Hutchison, Arkansas State University
Leslie Reed, Arkansas State University
Roy Tanksley, Arkansas State University
Dylan Travis, Arkansas State University
Stephen Turner, Arkansas State University

Chloe del los Reyes, California State University at San Bernardino
Joseph Farago-Spencer, California State University at San Bernardino
Ashley Hamilton, California State University at San Bernardino

Brandon Koepp, California State University at San Bernardino
Briana Lafond, California State University at San Bernardino
Pamela Portenstein, California State University at San Bernardino
Cindy Ragio, California State University at San Bernardino
Patricia Ric'e-Daniels, California State University at San Bernardino
Joseph Whatford, California State University at San Bernardino

Dan Lawson, Central Michigan University
Lori Rogers, Central Michigan University
Steve Bailey, Central Michigan University
Emily Pioszak, Central Michigan University
Elizabeth Bauer, Central Michigan University

Michael Klein, James Madison University
Cynthia J. Allen
Kevin Jefferson
Michael J. Klein
Cynthia Martin
Karen McDonnell

Kristi Shackelford, James Madison University
Rudy Barrett, James Madison University
Emily Bennett, James Madison University
Hannah Berge, James Madison University
Emily Diamond, James Madison University
Juliana Garabedian, James Madison University
Mackenzie Kelley, James Madison University
Emily Kohl, James Madison University
Allison Michelli, James Madison University
Madiha Patel, James Madison University
Alys Sink, James Madison University

Amy Lynch Biniek, Kutztown University
Amanda Morris, Kutztown University
Patricia Pytleski, Kutztown University
Kristina Fennelly, Kutztown University
Robert Moe Folk, Kutztown University

Elizabeth Saur, Miami University of Ohio

Jonathan Rylander, Miami University of Ohio
Enrique Paz, Miami University of Ohio
Kyle Larson, Miami University of Ohio
Ryan Vingum, Miami University of Ohio

Laura Gonzales, Michigan State University
Phil Bratta, Michigan State University
Mirabeth Braude, Michigan State University
Lauren Brentnell, Michigan State University
Victor Del Hierro, Michigan State University
Elise Dixon, Michigan State University
Hannah Espinoza, Michigan State University
Kate Firestone, Michigan State University
Bree Gannon, Michigan State University
Matthew Gomes, Michigan State University
Maria Novotny, Michigan State University
Sarah Prielipp, Michigan State University
Erin Schaefer, Michigan State University

Chen Chen, North Carolina State University
Jenn Bedard, North Carolina State University
Desiree Dighton, North Carolina State University
Meridith Reed, North Carolina State University
Gwendolynne Reid, North Carolina State University
Abigail Browning, North Carolina State University
Kendra Andrews, North Carolina State University

Kyle R. King, Penn State University
Kristin Mathe Coletta, Penn State University
Samantha Dickinson, Penn State University
David Dzikowski, Penn State University
Benjamin Firgens, Penn State University
Emily Hobbs, Penn State University
Chenchen Huang, Penn State University
Joshua Kim, Penn State University
Mudiwa Pettus, Penn State University
Shannon M. Stimpson, Penn State University

Michelle McMullin, Purdue University

Rachel Atherton, Purdue University
Elizabeth A Geib, Purdue University
Joseph Forte, Purdue University
Lindsey M Macdonald, Purdue University
Michelle McMullin, Purdue University
Devon S Cook, Purdue University

Susan Wolff Murphy, Texas A&M University-Corpus Christi
Shelly Fox, Texas A&M University-Corpus Christi
Monzeratt Silgero, Texas A&M University-Corpus Christi
Jimena Burnett, Texas A&M University-Corpus Christi
Traci Vega, Texas A&M University-Corpus Christi

Susan Garza, Texas A&M University-Corpus Christi
Abdullah Alalawi, Texas A&M University-Corpus Christi
Marnie Cannon, Texas A&M University-Corpus Christi
Margaret Everett-Garcia, Texas A&M University-Corpus Christi
Bernadette Flores, Texas A&M University-Corpus Christi
Hector Galvan, Texas A&M University-Corpus Christi
Mary Gonzalez, Texas A&M University-Corpus Christi
Ryan Hagen, Texas A&M University-Corpus Christi
Erin Kinsey, Texas A&M University-Corpus Christi
Nick Martinez, Texas A&M University-Corpus Christi
Elizabeth Mock, Texas A&M University-Corpus Christi
Yadira Uhlig, Texas A&M University-Corpus Christi

Carrie Leverenz, Texas Christian University
Tim Ballingall, Texas Christian University
Rachel Chapman, Texas Christian University
Ashley Hughes, Texas Christian University
Jessica Menkin, Texas Christian University
Heidi Nobles, Texas Christian University
Kassia Waggoner, Texas Christian University

Joanne Matson, University of Arkansas at Little Rock
Ian Bennett, University of Arkansas at Little Rock
Haylee Lindemann, University of Arkansas at Little Rock
Wendy McCloud, University of Arkansas at Little Rock
Stephanie Rice, University of Arkansas at Little Rock

Daniel Spillers, University of Arkansas at Little Rock
Heather Tolliver, University of Arkansas at Little Rock

Al Harahap, University of Arizona
Mark Blaauw-Hara, North Central Michigan College
Brent Chappelow, Arizona State University
Brandon Fralix, Bloomfield College
Barbara L'Eplattenier, University of Arkansas—Little Rock
Rochelle Rodrigo, University of Arizona
Virginia Schwarz, University of Wisconsin—Madison

Angelia Giannone, University of Arizona
Al Harahap, University of Arizona
Brian Hendrickson, University of New Mexico
Karen Lunsford, University of California—Santa Barbara
Dan Melzer, University of California—Davis
Laurie Pinkert, University of Central Florida

Iris Ruiz, University of California, Merced
Maria Astorga, University of California, Merced
Jeffrey Ball, University of California, Merced
Alexander Biwald, University of California, Merced
Jasmin Hinojosa, University of California, Merced
Shumpei Kuwana, University of California, Merced
David Badillo, University of California, Merced
Alina Leon, University of California, Merced
Stephanie Maldonado, University of California, Merced
Iliana Rosales, University of California, Merced
Lucero Soto, University of California, Merced
Anthony Spinks, University of California, Merced
Jahmeel Walker, University of California, Merced

Sana Clason, University of Cincinnati, Blue Ash College
Neely McLaughlin, University of Cincinnati, Blue Ash College
Claudia Skutar, University of Cincinnati, Blue Ash College
Anna Bogen, University of Cincinnati, Blue Ash College
Kevin Oberlin, University of Cincinnati, Blue Ash College
Brian Bailie, University of Cincinnati, Blue Ash College

Risa Applegarth, University of North Carolina at Greensboro
Carl Schlacte, University of North Carolina at Greensboro
Amy Berrier, University of North Carolina at Greensboro
Stacy Rice, University of North Carolina at Greensboro
Brenta Blevins, University of North Carolina at Greensboro
Kt Leuschen, University of North Carolina at Greensboro

Dan Libertz, University of Pittsburgh
Matt Kelly, University of Pittsburgh
Laura Feibush, University of Pittsburgh
Alex Malanych, University of Pittsburgh

Isabel Baca, University of Texas-El Paso
Jasmine Villa, University of Texas-El Paso
Jennifer Falcon, University of Texas-El Paso
Dali Crnkovic, University of Texas-El Paso
Consuelo Salas, University of Texas-El Paso
Margarita Medina, University of Texas-El Paso

BEST OF THE JOURNALS
RHETORIC AND COMPOSITION

BASIC WRITING eJOURNAL

Basic Writing eJournal is on the Web at https://bwe.ccny.cuny.edu/

As a peer-reviewed, online, open-access journal, *BWe* publishes scholarship on teaching and learning in various basic writing contexts. Since basic writing programs often enroll economically disadvantaged students from diverse backgrounds, these students, their teachers, and the policies that influence their access to higher education are often the focus of this journal. Other key topics of concern to *BWe* readers include curriculum, instructional practice, teacher preparation, program evaluation, and student learning. Additionally, reviews of current scholarly books and textbooks appear regularly in *BWe*. A primary goal of BWe is to provide free online access to basic writing scholarship and publication opportunities for teachers of basic writing.

"Basic Writing through the Back Door: Community-Engaged Courses in the Rush to Credit Age."

While portraying basic writing instruction in a rural environment and in a regional public university, this essay describes a linked, community-engaged writing course, "Field Writing: Food Stories." This course was offered as part of an early college program for rural high school students and demonstrates many of the benefits commonly attributed to public writing and service learning in composition. The course raised important questions about the politics of access and acceleration, and about the role of community-engaged coursework in continuing to protect room in the curriculum for both high school and college writers. These are questions that need should be more frequently asked and answered in our composition scholarship. This essay is particularly well written and is a pleasure to read.

1 Basic Writing Through the Back Door: Community-Engaged Courses in the Rush-to-Credit Age

Cori Brewster

This essay describes a linked, community-engaged writing course, "Field Writing: Food Stories," which was offered as part of an early college program for rural high school students at a regional public university. While demonstrating many of the benefits commonly attributed to public writing and service learning in composition, the course raised important questions about the politics of access and acceleration, and about the role of community-engaged coursework in continuing to protect room in the curriculum for both high school and college writers.

In summer 2013, I was asked to teach two three-week courses for high school students as part of a program on my regional four-year campus promoting rural student access to higher education. Unlike the summer bridge programs for graduating high school seniors offered at many colleges, this program is open to students in tenth through twelfth grades, and unlike Upward Bound and other traditional college prep programs, all classes automatically carry college credit. High school students in the program living on campus are encouraged to take a full load of 12 – 14 quarter credits during each three-week session, and they can enroll in any 100-level course, regardless of grade level and without placement testing or other institutional assessment of their readiness for college work.

Faculty members who taught in the program summers before had expressed concern that students were unevenly prepared for college level courses, that three weeks was too little time to hold even the highest-performing students to the same standards required during the academic year, that students had almost no time outside of class for homework due to the number of credits they were taking and the number of hours they spent each day in class—making it all but impossible to cover the same amount of material or hold them to similar expectations, that student maturity and behavior were sometimes problems, especially in sections in which there were few college students co-enrolled, and, critically, that the lack of placement testing and blanket expectation of college credit set many students up for failure—an especially undesirable outcome in a program intended at least in part to build confidence and encourage students to return after high school to pursue a college degree. I shared all of these concerns, but hoped that by agreeing to teach in the program, which was administered by another academic unit, I would not only have greater access to conversations about program design in the future but also come to those conversations more directly informed.

Writing faculty had agreed several years before that we would not offer required composition classes—either basic or first-year—as part of the summer program because three weeks simply does not provide enough time to read, discuss, draft, reflect, and revise, let alone work recursively through a series of progressively challenging academic reading and writing assignments, as our modified Stretch program had been designed to do. The limited time for tutoring and conferencing outside of class due to students' full schedules also lowered their chances of meeting standard composition course outcomes, reduced already by the decision not to placement test. It seemed irresponsible at best to rush tenth and eleventh-grade students through a curriculum for which they may or may not be ready, leaving instructors either to fail underprepared students at the end of three weeks' time or grant transferable credit that would effectively prevent them from taking first-year writing courses when they did reach college later on.

Concerns like these have become increasingly difficult to voice in this rush-to-credit age, however, in which the rising cost of college and longer average time to degree for students beginning in courses labeled remedial are being used at institutional, state, and national levels to rationalize "accelerating learning" by "eliminating barriers" of all kinds. As Kristine Hansen, Christine Farris, and contributors to *College Credit for Writing in High School* so well document, dual enrollment and early college programs like this one have gained incredible traction over the last decade, with varying regard for quality, student readiness, faculty support, and disciplinary expertise. On our campus, given the choice between offering high school writers courses for college credit or offering them nothing at all, the challenge became how to design curriculum that would better prepare participating students for college and facilitate access without further shorting them educationally—whether by expecting readiness to address at the college level what many had barely encountered in high school, by compressing and rushing students' opportunities to learn, or by granting credit for non-equivalent first-year work that would send them even less well prepared into college at the sophomore level.

It seemed to many faculty that what a summer program for high school students should provide was an opportunity for meaningful practice in writing that was engaging, appropriate, and attainable to students at multiple levels, and that not only anticipated but called consciously upon their wide range of knowledge, experiences, literacies, interests, and skills. Moreover, it seemed to me, to facilitate "access," the program should aim not just to be culturally relevant or culturally explicit (as advocated in different ways, for example, by Bartholomae; Bizzell; Delpit; Adler-Kassner and Harrington; Brooke; and many others), but culturally constitutive, giving students an opportunity to critically engage and actively, discursively co-construct the university and community of which they were becoming a part.

I focus in this article on just one of the two courses I developed in this context, a "project-oriented" public writing class (Mathieu) that I called "Field Writing: Food Stories," and the questions about basic writing, community engagement, and the politics of access it inevitably raised. Linked with an introductory economics course and supported by a last-minute grant from the Oregon Agriculture Foundation, "Field Writing: Food Stories" tasked seventeen high school and two college writers with launching an online archive of stories by and about people from across the food system in northeastern Oregon. To use Thomas Deans' terms, it was a course in "writing about" and "writing for" the community (107-11), while also experimenting with writing *into* the community, even if for just a few weeks. Transcripted as a special topics course, it offered college-level elective credit without promising to substitute for basic writing or first-year composition. By many counts the class was very successful. It clearly illustrated many of the benefits commonly attributed to service-learning in composition, and it was an absolute joy to teach. But as I argue here, it also underscored the importance of fighting to retain a wide range of writing courses for entering college students and continuing to push back against claims that we are providing access while critical opportunities for both high school and college writers to learn and develop are increasingly being cut, compressed, and/or delivered too soon.

The structure of this article reflects in part how conflicted I remain about the class, and in part the multiple tensions at the heart of this special issue of *BWe*, which considers how community and cross-disciplinary collaborations position student writers and the institutions of which both they and we are a part. I start with a detailed description of the "Field Writing" course, illustrating how and why I think this community-engaged model in many ways served this mixed-age group of literacy learners very well. Next, I turn to issues the course surfaced about student development, rhetorical acumen, and time to learn: the reasons I argue

nonetheless against offering credit-bearing writing courses to students still in high school. I close with a series of overlapping questions about the role of community-engaged coursework in composition in the current political and educational context, particularly for basic and developing writers, who continue to deserve more time for more meaningful writing in more places, not less.

"Eastern Oregon Food Stories": Public Writing and the Practice of Engagement

In *Tactics of Hope* and again in "After Tactics, What Comes Next?," Paula Mathieu writes compellingly about starting from a project- rather than a problem-orientation in public writing and service learning classes. As she explains,

> A problem orientation operates from a negative space, in that it seeks to solve a problem, ameliorate a deficit, or fix an injustice. There is a transactional quality to it—if the problem is not solved or the injustice ended, the work will be deemed unsuccessful. . . . A project orientation, however, privileges creation and design. Projects respond to problems but determine

their own length, scope, and parameters, instead of being defined by external parameters. (*Tactics* 50)

Given the very short span of the summer program and what little knowledge I had in advance about who my students would be or what prior literacies and commitments they might bring, my first goal in designing the class was to identify a real-world project that students could work on collaboratively and that addressed a current, multifaceted public issue in which all were likely to have some stake. It was important that the project allow students to write for and about an identifiable local audience who they could get to know and who would be invested in but not overly directive of the project's outcome. To use Mathieu's words, I wanted to "privileg[e] creation and design" (*Tactics* 50)—without making promises that we may be unable to keep, further limiting students' ability to shape the project, or putting them in a position of "servitude," as Don Kraemer and others have objected that service learning courses may do. Instead, I hoped students would come to see themselves as makers through this project, creating something new and of value to themselves as well as to an audience beyond the classroom—while at the same time having an immediate and nuanced context within which to explore issues of audience, ethics, representation, arrangement, development, style, and design.

Inspired in part by digital storytelling projects by the Center for Community Change (http://www.keepingfamiliestogether.net/), the Association of Independents in Radio (http://localore.net/), and Tamera Marko's *Medellin Mi Hogar/ My Home Medellin* (http://medellinmihogar.blogspot.com/), I began that spring by approaching the new and outgoing directors of a grassroots community organization on whose board I served about partnering on a similar project related to local food systems, an area in which the organization has done a great deal of work. Though they were undergoing significant staff turnover and were already pulled in multiple directions, they agreed to host the site and connect me to local producers who might be willing to be interviewed, as well as help identify potential guest speakers or area farms students could visit if we were able to secure funding for off-campus trips.

Food was a familiar enough topic that all students would inevitably enter the class with an array of expertise. It was also complex enough to warrant multiple avenues of investigation, and common, current, and controversial enough to provide multiple opportunities for communicating with and getting to know people both on campus and in the community. More importantly, it mattered. As Eileen Schell has argued, "no matter where one teaches, 'food' is an important issue to raise as it poses questions of globalization, environmental health, personal and societal health, consumer choices, social justice, and contemporary politics" (43); it also "provides a space for fostering the critical consciousness and critical literacy needed to assess and attend to the problematic effects and unequal power relations inherent in globalization. . . " (43).

At the encouragement of my Assistant Dean, the next step was to approach Scott McConnell, a new faculty member in Economics, about the possibility of linking our summer courses. Scott was planning to teach an experimental course in everyday economics, exploring basic economic principles in contexts familiar to high school students. The focus on food systems lent well to his course too, and it made sense to connect the two thematically, whether or not we could find time before the start of summer session to develop common readings or assignments. All students would be enrolled in both classes, scheduled to meet back to back from 1:00 – 5:00 Monday through Friday for the three-week term. This block of time would allow for some flexibility in arranging field trips and would overlap with the Tuesday afternoon Farmer's Market, a 10-minute walk downtown. Fortuitously, the focus on food systems also fit well with a fund established on our campus for courses that engaged students in the study of agriculture. Thanks to the multiple administrators who contacted the foundation and helped rush the proposal through, I learned during the first week of class that my request for field trip and web development funds had been granted. The Oregon Agriculture Foundation would provide up to $1,800 for us to tour area farms, conduct interviews, and hire a professional web designer to consult with the class on designing and managing an online archive.

In the end, nineteen students registered for our linked classes: two college sophomores, two students who had just graduated from nearby high schools, and fifteen sophomores, juniors, and seniors from seven different high schools, several of whom had participated in the summer program before. All of the high school students came from rural, agricultural communities within a few hours' drive from campus, and largely represented the racial and economic makeup of their home communities and schools. Roughly one third of the class identified as

Latina, Hispanic, and/or Mexican American; another third as white or European American; and the remaining third as Native, Asian American, and/or multiracial. Approximately half came from families employed directly in the food industry, as farm laborers, farm owners, bakers, packers, servers, processors, nutritionists, market managers, or cooks, and nearly all had studied different aspects of food and agriculture previously in organizations like 4-H and FFA, in school, or on their own.

Although I had intended to start the class with a number of readings on contemporary food issues, when I sat down to map out the three-week calendar, there was simply not enough time. I began instead by asking students to compose their own food literacy narratives, describing a particular belief they held about food and the experiences that had led them to it. While drafting these first essays, they also worked together to generate a list of possible interview questions about others' food memories and values, focusing on what they would most want to know about people who represented different parts of the food system than themselves. On Thursday of the first week, they tested their questions in practice interviews with volunteers recruited across campus: administrative assistants, the dean of Student Affairs, the marketing director for campus food services (a recent graduate, also from a nearby rural town), the payroll manager, the director of Admissions, academic advisors, Disability Services staff, and representatives of a number of other campus departments. As I had hoped, students returned both more familiar with our small college and surprised at the range of answers their questions had elicited. As one student wrote later, "Doing this research helped me a lot to get out of my shell and think differently about people. I got to see that people are not what I actually thought that they were going to be." Based on their experiences with this first set of interviews, we revised questions together in GoogleDocs, and they were then assigned to interview someone they knew at home over the weekend.

That first Friday we also took our first off-campus trip, visiting a ranch operated by Tony and Andrea Malmberg approximately fifteen miles from campus (www.beyondorganicbeef.com/). Tony introduced students to the principles of holistic management that guide decision-making on the ranch, and Nella Parks, who also farms on the property, showed students the garden, goats, chickens, and pigs, explaining how the methods of raising each were informed by this same philosophy. Students took pictures for the archive and asked questions about both economic and environmental aspects, as well as about the personal experiences that had led Tony, a third-generation cattle rancher, to change his approach so dramatically since first starting out.

During the second week of class, we focused more specifically on the genre of profile writing and the ethics of field research, and walked to the local farmers' market to conduct more interviews. With the permission of the market manager, students interviewed both vendors and customers, their first experience asking complete strangers to participate in the project. While waiting for traffic at the market to pick up, some students also walked the length of the town's main street, requesting permission to interview store owners and customers at a number of downtown shops. Back on campus, we moved to a computer classroom where students began drafting profiles based on the interviews conducted so far. In some cases, students who had interviewed the same person together drafted separate profiles and then compared and merged what they had. In others, they worked together on the same draft from beginning to end, discussing among other things which anecdotes might work well as an opening, which descriptors to put in the nut graf, which direct quotations to use, and how to organize the piece to highlight a central theme. Because most writing had to occur in class due to students' full schedules, I was able to circulate and talk through questions as they came up, providing individualized feedback on successive drafts.

During week three, we took our final trip across town to conduct interviews at the county fair. Students who hadn't yet conducted the minimum number of interviews required were also assigned that week to arrange additional interviews outside of class. On campus, students worked on drafting and revising remaining profiles and designing the online archive to which they would be posted. Because the university's web developer was not available on such short notice, Media Arts and Communication Professor Kevin Roy volunteered to help me set up the initial site and work with the class on brainstorming different design possibilities. Reinforcing earlier discussions of rhetorical concepts, Kevin asked students to think about how they imagined different users would navigate the site, how different hierarchies of information would or would not reflect the kinds of stories they had collected, and what they might consider in terms of color and visual design. He also gave students technical tips on the types of photos to use and where to find additional high resolution images online without violating copyright.

Remaining time was spent fact-checking, peer reviewing, revising, and uploading near- final drafts and images to the archive. Students asked all interviewees whether they wanted to review their profiles before they were posted online, and they spent time that week discussing drafts in person and by email with those who did. When most material had been uploaded, we generated a final list of tasks to be completed, including promoting the archive, editing, developing standard systems for tagging posts, and writing explanatory sections about the project and directions for future visitors to add their own stories. Pairs and small groups took on each of these tasks as the last few writers finished up individual profiles. The final assignment was to write a short evaluation of the class, the finished project, and their own performance. Though the end product is far from perfect by most professional standards, launching "Eastern Oregon Food Stories" (http://eastoregonfood.wordpress.com/) felt like a monumental accomplishment that last day of class, with more than seventy profiles collected and written in just three weeks.

Accounting for Time: Age, Experience, and Rhetorical Acumen

From the outset, my hopes for the course, as Mathieu describes them (*Tactics* 54), had been multiple. I was not disappointed, nor, as far as can be told from informal conversations and course evaluations, were most of the students or the community partners with whom we worked. The project lent well to discussions about rhetorical choices and research ethics, as intended, and was accessible to students with a wide range of writing abilities. By and large, individual pieces achieved their general purpose, and the local audience for and about whom students wrote was both engaged and impressed, with many requests to link to the archive from other sites. While students' levels of investment in the project clearly varied, there was also a much stronger sense of engagement and commitment to drafting, design, and revision overall. Writing about the late nights she spent revising with her roommate during the last week of class, for example, one high school sophomore explained, "We wanted the story to be something the interviewee could be proud of. We were writing about someone else and we wanted them to feel like we represented them well." Other students reported that the public aspects of the project changed the way they thought about audience and the value of engaging people whose experiences differed from their own. As one of the juniors in high school put it, "I want to know what the rest of the world sees. I want to be able to live different lives through others' stories." The sometimes artificial glow of end-of-term reflections notwithstanding, this was a strikingly different perspective on writing and research than was expressed by many at the start of the class.

Without question, any successes that might be attributed to the class depended fundamentally on the participation of people across campus and community who took the students seriously as writers, lent their technical and professional expertise, and exemplified through the diversity of their experiences and perspectives that "food" was in fact an issue worth investigating and writing publicly about. The field trips and interviews with members of the campus and broader community were instrumental in building and immersing students in a social context for writing and in cultivating the sense of efficacy students expressed as writers and learners at the end: what they had done in the class mattered to people outside the classroom; because it mattered, they had invested more of themselves in the project; and because of this investment, they had succeeded in making something of public importance, which many had not imagined themselves capable or part of before. The small size of the class, the opportunities to work together, and the necessity of doing the majority of drafting and revising during class time were no doubt key as well. These conditions provided writers with a wide range of abilities and experience opportunities to problem solve and share ideas with one another at all stages of the project, and allowed me to provide immediate, individualized feedback as questions arose and drafts evolved.

Far more difficult to evaluate, however, is what it might mean to have done any of this at a college level, or whether providing high school students college credit for this three-week course served them well on any measure besides cost. Read against the "WPA Outcomes Statement for First-Year Composition," all students' writing demonstrated some improvement in rhetorical knowledge, processes, and knowledge of conventions, and all students gained more experience composing both collaboratively and publicly in electronic environments. Students clearly also gained more experience in critical thinking, as they wrestled with how to represent others' experiences ethically and effectively online, and were better able to articulate how and why they had made particular rhetorical choices than they were at the beginning of the course. But while most students worked hard, made significant gains, and did an excellent job within the context of the project and this particular course, little of the work would have been considered passing if normed against my program's first-year composition course, and less than half of the students still in high school would likely have met outcomes related to focus and development in our basic writing course, even factoring in the difference in genre and the reduced time for revision.

If the question of credit were simply reduced to form, fluency, or some other ostensibly isolable trait, it might be easy enough to draw the line here: a few of the high school students were performing at the end of three weeks at a "level" comparable to first-year students on my campus, and the rest were not. Some should have received college credit based on work submitted and some should not have. Importantly, though, and especially for the students who had just completed their sophomore and junior years of high school, the difference between writing a focused, well-developed profile for the archive and a more superficial one appeared again and again to have as much to do with age and experience as with technical proficiency—in other words, with the distance between many of my teenage students' lives and literacies and those of the adults whose views and experiences they were trying to represent. High school students' write-ups ranged from the very cursory and general to the more nuanced and reflective, with students often struggling in particular with interviewees' moves from individual anecdotes to the philosophical commitments those anecdotes were meant to illustrate, themselves often based on broader structural and systemic awareness that students had not yet developed. In one instance, students interviewed a university administrator who shared how her mother's inability to afford fresh food when she was growing up had made her particularly sensitive to issues of hunger and food insecurity on campus today. Though the students included several quotations and details from the interview in their profile, their rendering of the larger idea was expressed most completely in the broad closing line, "Powdered eggs and milk might not have been her favorite thing, but it did make a huge impact on her life." No doubt, interviewers of all ages are constrained by their own experiences and level of comfort marshalling others' ideas but the differences in maturity and rhetorical acumen in this case and many others were especially pronounced, raising questions not about the value of the project necessarily, but about granting high school students college credit at this juncture—and suggesting in doing so that they skip first-year coursework and the opportunity to analyze and respond to communicative situations in more nuanced ways when they are a couple of years older as well.

Objections to early college and dual enrollment in composition are commonly made on one or more related grounds: differences in writing contexts between high school and college (see for example Yancey); concerns about the decontextualized, skills-based model of literacy frequently used to rationalize accelerated models (Hansen; Purcell-Gates, Jacobson, and Degener 66); issues of time and the iterative, developmental nature of learning (Joliffe; Taczak and Thelin); and differences in high school and college students' "emotional, social, and cognitive maturity" (National 3). Of these, the roles of time and maturity in students' growth as writers are not only the most difficult to measure, but also likely the most compelling reasons not to proceed. As Barbara Schneider attempts to explain in her study of an early college program that enrolled 14-year-old students in first-year composition, many high school-age students simply lack the "miles on the tires" to perform the depth of analysis expected of their more traditionally college-aged peers (157):

> I am . . . aware that chronology, experience, and guidance all affect maturity, that it develops unevenly over time, and that it can be possessed by a fourteen-year- old in the same measure as an eighteen-year-old or a forty-year-old, for that matter. Statistically, however, we might, upon further study, find a distribution of qualitative and quantitative markers that would indicate that younger students cannot fully integrate and retain the higher-order skills they should acquire in these classes, and we would therefore encourage postponement of college courses until an older age. (159-60)

A 2013 policy brief by the National Council of Teachers of English likewise concludes: "Alternate routes to satisfy first-year writing requirements, such as online courses, test-out options, or dual enrollment coursework, can offer students useful preparation for FYW courses. However, such instruction cannot fully replicate the experiences of FYW because high school students' social and cognitive development is at a different level. . ." (2).

But how to account for these different levels in the classroom, faced with politicians and administrators bent on increasing access by reducing time to degree and lowering costs? What *is* lost when quick-credentialing efforts effectively deny younger and younger students multiple, diverse, iterative opportunities to learn? As I remarked at the beginning, the central challenge in agreeing to teach in the summer program was how to design curriculum that would better prepare participating students for college and facilitate access without further shorting them educationally. This was not a challenge I can claim to have overcome. As difficult as maturity, experience, and rhetorical acumen might be to define or to document, few of the teenage students in this summer class were "college ready" at the start of the course, let alone ready to skip further first-year coursework by the time it was done. Whatever successes I might attribute to this community-engaged model, and however valuable the experience to the wide range of developing writers in my class, for most, perhaps all of the high school students, the course should simply have been offered as college prep, not college credit. Whether or not granting three credits for non-college-level work in one elective class was likely to set any of them up for future failure, it did effectively short them the opportunity to engage in first-year curriculum at an older age. It also lent credence to the idea that writing can and should be "taken care of" early and quickly, and that students neither require nor benefit significantly from practice and instruction in diverse contexts over time.

Adding to my concerns, it turned out that more than half of the high school students in the class had already earned one or two terms of credit for first-year composition through their high schools, meaning that they would not be required to take any additional first-year writing courses in college, and despite the fact that very few demonstrated the rhetorical awareness, development, critical thinking, organization, or knowledge of conventions that would have been expected by my college's writing program. The three-week summer class had not included any practice in academic reading, summary, synthesis, or integration of scholarly sources, but based on conversations in class and writing submitted by some of the same students in my summer literature course, it seems fair to speculate that most were fairly inexperienced in those areas as well. By listing my class as a special topics class rather than as basic writing or first-year composition, I had intended to preserve students' opportunity to take first-year writing classes when they did reach college later on. Instead, this designation ended up creating a little more space in the curriculum for students who had already earned dual credit for composition in high school and would not otherwise have had another first-year writing course available to take.

In the end, of course, I can speak only of my experience in one class on one campus with one particular group of students—and without having set out to study the relationships between age, access, and college writing curricula that continue to trouble me most. Likely, there were many ways the summer program could have been designed differently to mitigate some of the issues raised here: stronger admissions and placement measures, opportunities for younger and lower-performing students to earn high school rather college credit, restrictions on the number of classes high schoolers could take at once, a higher ratio of college to high school students in each class, a longer term. From this narrow vantage, however, both the successes and limitations of my early college class would seem to argue for more, and more diverse, literacy experiences for incoming students, not less, as current efforts to compress and cost-save are aiming toward. More research is clearly needed, as is more meaningful faculty involvement in early and dual credit discussions at program, institution, and policy levels alike.

Basic Writing through the Back Door

Faced in the meantime with how to provide meaningful access to higher education to more students in spite of ongoing efforts to eliminate the time and types of support that basic writing and college composition provide, I find myself asking different, and arguably dirtier, questions about community-engaged coursework than if there were more support for more and broader literacy experiences at this point. How, for example, might the greater rhetorical currency of service-learning and community engagement be used to protect room in the curriculum for incoming college students? How might the amount of time often required for service projects help counter poorly-supported moves toward acceleration and compression? For lack of a better word, how might courses like mine now be backfilled with greater attention to particular academic literacies? To whatever extent "basic writing programs" may "have become expressions of our desire to produce basic writers," as David Bartholomae famously argued ("The Tidy House" 315), students whose experiences in writing have not yet prepared them for those expected in college classrooms will continue to exist (Otte and Mlynarczyk 20-28), as, likely, will those who need more time and practice than some early and dual credit programs have provided them. How might public writing and service-learning courses serve both as the meaningful, deeply contextualized literacy experiences they have the potential to be, and as false fronts of sorts to keep from closing academic gates?

More optimistically, as others have asked, how might community-engaged courses provide opportunities to communicate with broader audiences about the complexities of literacy learning and about the amount of time and practice that both high school and college writers deserve? More pointedly, how do faculty gain greater access to and greater credibility within decision-making contexts, navigating both the micro- and macro-politics of the public and private entities increasingly driving higher education reforms? As Shannon Carter writes, "Overturning the institutional, political, social, and economic infrastructure invested in the autonomous model of literacy requires time, patience, and—above all—diplomacy" (145). The opportunity that collaborative, community-engaged courses provide for a wide range of readers and writers both within and outside the university to learn from each other is of tremendous value. Perhaps the most important question as we write with, for, and ideally *into* communities at this political and economic moment is how to marshal our collective resources to shift the script back from cost savings to value-added. As ever, preparing students not just to start college but to stay and find meaning in the experience requires invoking both public and academic spaces in which all writers are afforded time to learn, make, connect, and become.

Works Cited

Abramsky, Sasha. "John Kitzhaber's Oregon Dream." *The Nation* 10-17 June 2013: 23-26. Print. Adler-Kassner, Linda, and Susanmarie Harrington. *Basic Writing as a Political Act: Public Conversations about Writing and Literacies.* Cresskill, NJ: Hampton, 2002. Print.

Bartholomae, David. "Inventing the University." *Writing on the Margins: Essays on Composition and Teaching.* Boston: Bedford, 2005. 60-85. Print.

—. "The Tidy House: Basic Writing in the American Curriculum." *Writing on the Margins: Essays on Composition and Teaching.* Boston: Bedford, 2005. 312-26. Print.

Bizzell, Patricia. *Academic Discourse and Critical Consciousness.* Pittsburgh: U of Pittsburgh P, 1992. Print.

Brewster, Cori. "Toward a Critical Agricultural Literacy." *Reclaiming the Rural: Essays on Literacy, Rhetoric, and Pedagogy.* Eds. Kim Donehower, Charlotte Hogg, and Eileen E. Schell. Carbondale: Southern Illinois UP, 2012. 34-51. Print.

Brooke, Robert. "Migratory and Regional Identity." *Identity Papers: Literacy and Power in Higher Education.* Ed. Bronwyn T. Williams. Logan, UT: Utah State UP, 2006. 141-153. Print.

Brooke, Robert, ed. *Rural Voices: Place-Conscious Education and the Teaching of Writing.* New York: Teachers College P, 2003. Print.

Carter, Shannon. *The Way Literacy Lives: Rhetorical Dexterity and Basic Writing Instruction.* Albany: State U of New York P, 2008. Print.

Deans, Thomas. "English Studies and Public Service." *Writing and Community Engagement: A Critical Sourcebook.* Eds. Thomas Deans, Barbara Roswell, and Adrian J. Wurr. Boston: Bedford, 2010. 97-116. Print.

Delpit, Lisa. *Other People's Children: Cultural Conflict in the Classroom.* New York: New Press, 1995. Print.

Donehower, Kim, Charlotte Hogg, and Eileen E. Schell. *Rural Literacies.* Carbondale: Southern Illinois UP, 2007. Print.

Fox, Tom. *Defending Access: A Critique of Standards in Higher Education.* Portsmouth: Boynton/Cook, 1999. Print.

Hansen, Kristine, and Christine R. Farris, eds. *College Credit for Writing in High School: The 'Taking Care of' Business.* Urbana: NCTE, 2010. Print.

Hansen, Kristine. "The Composition Marketplace: Shopping for Credit versus Learning to Write." *College Credit for Writing in High School: The 'Taking Care of' Business.* Eds. Kristine Hansen and Christine R. Farris. Urbana: NCTE, 2010. 1-42. Print.

Horner, Bruce. "The WPA as Broker: Globalization and the Composition Program." *Teaching Writing in Globalization: Remapping Disciplinary Work.* Eds. Darin Payne and Daphne Desser. Lanham, MD: Lexington, 2012. 57-78. Print.

Joliffe, David A. "Foreword: Tough Questions for Thoughtful Educators." *College Credit for Writing in High School: The 'Taking Care of' Business.* Eds. Kristine Hansen and Christine R. Farris. Urbana: NCTE, 2010. vii - xxxiii. Print.

Kraemer, Don J. "Servant Class: Basic Writers and Service Learning." *Journal of Basic Writing* 24.2 (2005): 92-109.

Kramer, Mark, and Wendy Call, eds. *Telling True Stories: A Nonfiction Writers' Guide.* New York: Penguin, 2007. Print.

Marko, Tamera. "Alternative Feminist Stories Cross the Colombian-U.S. Border." *Reflections* 12.1 (2012): 9-53. Print.

Mathieu, Paula. "After Tactics, What Comes Next?" *Unsustainable: Reimagining Community Literacy, Public Writing, Service-Learning and the University.* Eds. Jessica Restaino and Laurie JC Cella. Lanham, MD: Lexington, 2013. 17-32. Print.

—. *Tactics of Hope: The Public Turn in English Composition.* Portsmouth, NH: Boynton, 2005. Print.

National Council of Teachers of English. "First-Year Writing: What Good Does It Do?" Urbana: NCTE, 2013. Print.

Otte, George, and Rebecca Williams Mlynarczyk. "The Future of Basic Writing." *Journal of Basic Writing* 29.1 (2010): 5-32. Print.

Purcell-Gates, Victoria, Erik Jacobson, and Sophie Degener. *Print Literacy Development: Uniting Cognitive and Social Practice Theories.* Cambridge: Harvard UP, 2004. Print.

Schell, Eileen. "Think Global, Eat Local: Teaching Alternative Agrarian Literacy in a Globalized Age." *Teaching Writing in Globalization: Remapping Disciplinary Work.* Eds. Darin Payne and Daphne Desser. Lanham, MD: Lexington, 2012. 39-56. Print.

Schneider, Barbara. "Early College High Schools: Double-Time." *College Credit for Writing in High School: The 'Taking Care of' Business.* Eds. Kristine Hansen and Christine R. Farris. Urbana: NCTE, 2010. 141 - 164. Print.

Taczak, Kara, and William Thelin. "(Re)Envisioning the Divide: The Impact of College Courses on High School Students." *Teaching English in the Two-Year College* 37.1 (2009): 7-23. Print.

Thelin, William, and Kara Taczak. "(Re)Envisioning the Divide: Juliet Five Years Later." *Teaching English in the Two-Year College* 41.1 (2013): 6-19. Print.

Tinberg, Howard, and Jean-Paul Nadeau. "Contesting the Space between High School and College in the Era of Dual-Enrollment." *College Composition and Communication* 62.4 (2011): 704-725. Print.

"WPA Outcomes Statement for First-Year Composition." Council of Writing Program Administrators, 17 Jul. 2014. Web. 11 Aug. 2014.

Yancey, Kathleen Blake. "Delivering College Composition into the Future." *Delivering College Composition: The Fifth Canon.* Portsmouth, NH: Boynton/Cook, 2006. 199-210. Print.

Notes

I owe many thanks to the students, faculty, staff, administrators, and community members who contributed their time and talents to the "Eastern Oregon Food Stories" project, and to the Oregon Agriculture Foundation for their encouragement and financial support. All student work is quoted here by permission.

Cori Brewster is an associate professor of writing and rhetoric at Eastern Oregon University. Her current work focuses on rural literacy sponsorship, community-based learning, and the rhetorics of race and gender in agricultural movements.

JOURNAL OF TEACHING WRITING

Journal of Teaching Writing is on the Web at http://journals.iupui.edu/index.php/teachingwriting

Now in its thirty-fifth year of publication, the Journal of Teaching Writing (JTW) is the only national, refereed journal devoted to the teaching of writing at all academic levels, from preschool to the university, and in all subject areas of the curriculum. It publishes articles, reviews of books and pedagogical websites, and professional announcements. JTW's Editorial Board, which is composed of distinguished teachers and writers from all educational levels and geographic regions of the U.S., functions as a review team, reading and responding to submissions. With its editors and Editorial Board, the Journal aims to demystify the editorial review process and model the teaching of writing as a process of reflection and revision. Back issues can be downloaded free at http://journals.iupui.edu/index.php/teachingwriting.

"Mapping Students' Funds of Knowledge in the First-Year Writing Classroom"

In "Mapping Students' Funds of Knowledge in the First-Year Writing Classroom," Genesea M. Carter draws on anthropological and ethnographic research in designing a multi-modal assignment in first-year writing that (1) eases students' transition into college and (2) prepares them for success in their social, professional, and academic communities. Carter's approach taps students' pre-existing knowledge of home and community literacies, and then explores their developing knowledge of the discourse communities they inhabit as college students. Grounded in theory, the digital literacy map assignment is innovative, student-centered, and technological, and it is sufficiently detailed to engage classroom teachers in rethinking their pedagogy for today's diverse students.

2 Mapping Students' Funds of Knowledge in the First-Year Writing Classroom

Genesea M. Carter

> I am literate in the language of
> Soccer
> English
> social medias.
> Making breakfast
> Teaching children
> Running
> Track
> How to drive a car
> Change my oil
> Eating
>
> — Thomas,[1] first-semester freshman, English 101

Every student who enters the classroom is literate in multiple ways. For Thomas, one of my English 101 students from the fall of 2013, his literacies empower him to engage with the world socially and practically. Literacy allows people to share knowledge and resources within and between communities. Ethnographer Luis C. Moll believes that "[w]e must think of literacy (or literacies) as particular ways of *using* language for a variety of purposes, as a sociocultural practice with intellectual significance" ("Literacy Research" 237, emphasis in the original). In the National Council of Teachers of English's (NCTE) Position Statement on 21st Century Literacies, the authors concur that literacies extend a user's world. Literacies "are inextricably linked with particular histories, life possibilities, and social trajectories of individuals and groups," they write (n.p.). Complementing Moll and NCTE's definitions, Carmen I. Mercado defines literacy "as a sense-making practice [which] is an ongoing quest to understand, through multiple symbolic media or multiple literacies, information that enables us to act on the world" (242). I adopt all three definitions of literacy in this article, but Mercado's definition provides writing instructors with a tool that can help students transition to academia more effectively.

While the literacies students bring with them into the classroom are diverse and sophisticated, like Thomas' literacies, they do not always translate into academic success. Compositionists Patricia Bizzell, Eli Goldblatt, Mike Rose, and Victor Villanueva, among others, have written about how student success, particularly with underprepared or underrepresented student populations, is dependent upon familiarity with academic literacies. As a result, successful "insider" integration into academia means that students learn the literacies of academic and professional discourse communities. Although students bring pre-existing academic literacies with them to college, they still experience difficulties with their transition into academia (see De Oliveira and Silva; Fromme, Corbin, and Kruse; Joliffe and Harl; and Smith and Zhang).

Concerned with first-year students' transition from high school to college, I take a multi-modal approach in English 101 to teach them how to adapt to the variety of discourse communities on campus. During the semester, students create a digital literacy map, a profile of a place, and a public service announcement. The central theme tying these assignments together is the discourse community concept, a vital factor in students' transition. While students must learn how to adapt to new discourse communities, they must feel supported, valued, and respected within the classroom. In a time of adjustment, their success will depend on how welcomed they feel by their classmates and instructors. Therefore, I dovetail students' Funds of Knowledge (FoK) with the discourse community framework as a method for valuing students' knowledge while teaching them how to adapt to campus. The concept of FoK is traditionally defined as the cultural, social, and subject knowledge people learn within their home communities, such as cooking, farming, or repair. However, it has likewise come to include the social relationships and literacies that allow people to exchange information and knowledge within their own discourse communities (Moll et al. "Funds of Knowledge for Teaching" 85). FoK, as I conceive of it, serves as an overarching umbrella in which students' pre-existing knowledge about community membership and literacies reside. FoK complements Patricia Bizzell's recommendation to investigate and celebrate "the relationship between the academic discourse community and the communities from which [our] students come" (108). FoK scholarship, like the best practices of composition pedagogy, illustrates how instructors can empower students by validating their home knowledge while teaching them how to be members of multiple communities.

In this article, I share with *Journal of Teaching Writing* readers how they can support students' pre-existing knowledge through a digital literacy map assignment. This assignment requires students to visually plot out four of their discourse communities and the accompanying literacies of those communities. Explicitly, the literacy map is meant to introduce students to discourse community concepts. Implicitly, it supports and celebrates students' FoK, as they draw on their digital- and community-specific knowledge to map their communities.

Since examples of similar literacy maps are difficult to find, I include four representative but different student examples and accompanying reflections from my fall 2013 semester of English 101 at the University of Wisconsin-Stout. These examples highlight three trends that emerged from my students' maps and reflections: (1) they recognize that their social success depends on their insider membership, (2) they understand the importance of having a literacy sponsor as they transition from outsider to insider, (3) and they know that becoming an insider on campus will help them enjoy their time while in college.

Mapping students' lives celebrates the classroom's collective FoK by publicly acknowledging students' expertise. Furthermore, this assignment, like similar assignments that celebrate students' preexisting knowledge, legitimizes the FoK students bring into the classroom. As well, the digital literacy map assignment unearths the kinds of FoK first-year students find valuable: the literacy map gives instructors insight into the communities, literacies, and FoK that are valued by their students. With this knowledge instructors can find ways to better integrate their students' FoK into future classroom activities and assignments, a move that may partially bridge the gap from high school to college.

Funds of Knowledge as Community Currency

The phrase "Funds of Knowledge" (FoK) is attributed to anthropologist Eric R. Wolf's book *Peasants* (1966) in which he highlights the various funds peasants use to engage in social exchange, such as the exchange of ceremonial funds or rent funds. While Wolf does not explicitly define FoK, the term's contemporary rendering derives from his explanation that peasants "exchange their own labor and its products for the culturally defined equivalent goods and services of others" (3). Educational psychologist Linda Hogg explains that Wolf's term "define[s] resources and knowledge that households manipulate to make ends meet in the household economy" (667). Consequently, FoK originally denoted skills and knowledge sets needed for economic, social, and cultural survival or success. Within the last two decades, however, the definition has expanded to "refer both to the content and the social relationships that facilitate the exchange," writes Moll ("Literacy Research" 232). The concept of FoK is an interdisciplinary but useful framework for writing instructors and literacy scholars alike as it frames people's literacy acquisition and application within the context of their home communities. As well, it complements literacy sponsorship scholarship, such as Deborah Brandt's work (2).

The research of anthropologist Carlos G. Vélez-Ibáñez and ethnographer Luis C. Moll in the 1980s and 1990s largely define the FoK scholarship. As colleagues at the University of Arizona, they were sometimes co-collaborators studying FoK in Hispanic and Mexican communities within Tucson, Arizona, and across the border to determine the ways Hispanic and Mexican households created an exchange of knowledge and resources. Vélez-Ibáñez and Moll discovered that Mexican and Hispanic people create home communities that instill functional and cultural literacies within their members to increase cultural and economic stability. These home communities privilege FoK that are often radically different from those FoK valued within the mainstream Western society. As a result, Vélez-Ibáñez and Moll observed, Hispanic and Mexican immigrants faced challenges adapting their literacies to those valued in Arizona. While Vélez-Ibáñez and Moll's scholarship provides a case study of one particular people group, their conclusions can be applied to illustrate the difficulties all people face transitioning into new, unfamiliar discourse communities.

Vélez-Ibáñez's study of border families highlights the reciprocal relationships and roles among Mexicans—for example, one person could serve many roles as an uncle, a soccer coach, and a mechanic—that allow them to politically, socially, and culturally support the needs of their community (29). His research shows how Mexican communities exist within "residentially-based networks with a historical sense of cohort identity" that encourages a sharing of resources and support (32). While not termed by Vélez-Ibáñez, these Mexican and Hispanic households function as discourse communities drawn together by common needs and shared literacies. For these working-class Mexicans, FoK are essential to their economic survival. Evident in Vélez-Ibáñez's scholarship is how FoK acts as currency between community relationships and personal literacy.

While Vélez-Ibáñez's research was an effort to push against ethnocentric clichés (28), Moll, with fellow researchers Cathy Amanti, Deborah Neff, and Norma Gonzáles, wanted to discover the underlying reasons for a "persistently high rate of educational failure" within the Latino populations of Tucson (Moll "Literacy Research" 211). Moll et al. began their research by examining the FoK within Hispanic households hoping to identify fissures that impede Latino students' success. Their findings indicate, in part, that Latino students' educational failure is a result of their difficulty transitioning to the Western school system. Moll notes that students' FoK are often disconnected from their classroom curriculum and activities ("Literacy Research" 216). This results in students feeling isolated and marginalized. In order to help Latino students transition to the mainstream school system, Gonzáles, Moll, and Amanti advocate for including "contextualization" within the classroom, defined as "making meaning and connecting school to students' lives" ("Introduction" 8). Without this connection to students' home communities, instructors—regardless of the student populations they teach—run the risk of alienating their students. Therefore, writing instructors of all types of learners, from novice to expert, may consider using the principles of FoK to support their students' learning.

The Importance of Mapping: Showcasing Students' Lived Experiences

Mapping creates a visual representation of content allowing students to conceive of their FoK in a new way. Nancy Barta-Smith and Danette DiMarco explain, "[T]hrough map literacy, students can learn how to integrate their understanding of reading and writing, steps in the research process, and various knowledge bases" (67). Providing innovative and different methods of conception is vital to developing flexible, creative communicators. Furthermore, mapping out knowledge is one way to celebrate students' contributions and "place" in the world. Barta-Smith and DiMarco iterate, "Everyone is on the map, even the cartographer. No one stands outside" (80). Conceiving of literacy as mappable is "a commitment to viewing literacy as spatially and materially constrained," Erin Penner Gallegos explains, because the literacy map "value[s] the landscape in which each particular writing classroom is situated" ("Mapping Student Literacies" n.p.) Thus, the classroom becomes a discourse community in which students share and respond to each other's FoK. Mapping students' lives teaches students to visualize their place in the world. Additionally, the act of mapping students' FoK validates the knowledge they bring with them into the classroom while situating their lives and experiences into a larger, global context.

In 2011, as a third year doctoral student at the University of New Mexico, I learned about literacy maps from my colleague and friend Gallegos. After talking about our similar challenges in teaching first-year students how to adapt to the writing and reading expectations in English 101, she introduced me to her literacy map assignment in which students map their discourse communities and accompanying literacies. Gallegos invented the assignment "out of [her] concern for making discourse communities more tangible to [her] students, and out of a desire to make [her] class more place-based" (Email correspondence). For Gallegos, the literacy map "encapsulates the belief that literacy, and literacy practices, are inherently tied to the material realities that define the lives of our students prior to and during their brief time in our classrooms" ("Mapping Student Literacies" n.p.). Similarly to Gallegos, my iteration of the literacy map emphasizes the intertwined relationship between discourse community membership and literacy, highlighting how communities use literacies in similar and different ways. Our assignment differs, however, in that Gallegos emphasized the place-based component with an assignment arc that included the literacy map, a literacy narrative, and a disciplinary or professional discourse community profile.

In Gallegos' original conception, students could choose to create their literacy maps as physical documents (on poster board, printed maps, or construction paper) or digitally. In my version, the literacy map is a digital assignment in which students practice digital literacy. My university is a "laptop campus" in which every undergraduate student is issued a laptop, and students carry their laptops with them everywhere; however, they are not given training in how to use the computer programs, unless faculty incorporate it into the coursework. Therefore, even though first-year students have the technology with them on a daily basis, many of them do not know how to use basic functions, such as page numbering in Word. In order to harness students' technological FoK while teaching basic digital literacy, I added the map's digital component. The digital nature of the map allows me to introduce students to basic programs and features on their computers. As well, the digital component becomes a conduit that encourages them to apply their technological FoK to class work—something they often have difficulty doing. In the end, students typically create their maps through a Word document, PowerPoint, Prezi, or some other digital medium. Sometimes there are those students who love to draw and want to create paper maps; therefore, I am always flexible in the format, although all students are required to submit their maps electronically.

Like Gallegos' assignment, my students choose four discourse communities in which they are insiders, and they must show a visual relationship between the communities' literacies. Each map must include a map key that helps readers navigate the content and design elements. Finally, to visually illustrate the relationships between communities and literacies, students are required to use graphics, images, colors, or fonts to make this relationship clear (Appendix A). After submitting the map, students spend ten minutes writing a reflection in-class about what they learned about discourse communities and insider/outsider membership (Appendix B).

After teaching the literacy map for four years, my purpose for the assignment has evolved. Initially, I adopted the literacy map as a way to teach students how to reflect upon and evaluate discourse communities. This, I figured, was the first step in their transition into academia. However, I have since learned that students have difficulty with this connection. Either they do not know how their FoK can inform academic discourse community membership, or they do not have the language to talk about it, even after several weeks of class discussion. Alternately, the discourse communities they want to talk and write about are those communities they have left behind, or the social communities of which they have recently become members. First-year students are hyper aware of their need to "fit in" with the campus community, and much of their time and effort is spent building a social support system. In fact, many first-year students place more energy into developing relationships than navigating academia. As a result, my scope has shifted from emphasizing the transition to academia to including the entire campus. Broadening this scope allows my students to select the new discourse communities that they feel most comfortable with, such as social, professional, or academic ones.

LITERACY MAPS IN ENGLISH 101 AT THE UNIVERSITY OF WISCONSIN-STOUT

In the fall semester of 2013, I devoted the first three weeks of the semester to the digital literacy map assignment. In the first week, students were assigned readings about discourse communities, such as the "What is a discourse community?" web page from the University of Central Florida and University of Texas—El Paso student Gabriela Andrade's e-portfolio blog. As well, students were encouraged to find web pages themselves that explained the purposes of discourse communities. I coupled online material with textbook readings about rhetorical purpose (audience, purpose, and genre) to teach my students to actively think about their mapping choices and authorial intent. In the second week, students were introduced to how discourse communities shape identities and literacies through readings from Bradford Hall's *Among Cultures*. Additionally, they had a chance to explore online, interactive "Story Maps" created by ArcGIS users. ArcGIS is an application-based geographic information system in which users map stories and content, such as "Boston 911 Calls," "Zoo Babies," or "The Rapid Rise of Farmers' Markets." These Story Maps allow for conversations about design principles, discourse communities, the rhetorical situation, and literacies. In the third week, students began drafting and finalizing their maps. During this week, one class period became a workshop in which I briefly conferenced with each student about his or her map, troubleshooting problems as they arose. Since students' FoK largely informs the mediums they select for their maps, few problems arise. The problems students do encounter are design-related, such as formatting text boxes and graphics. Most students used Word or PowerPoint to create their maps. However, three students—either art students or those who just love to draw—chose to draw or collage their maps, and one student used Prezi.

To bolster students' understanding of the literacy map, we spent nearly every class period in small group and large group discussions with activities that refined students' understanding of the assignment. Because students had their laptops with them, they used their laptops everyday to take notes, define terms, and conduct simple Google searches. While they brought to the classroom FoK about web browsing, online research, and note taking, those FoK needed to be cultivated in many ways. Students needed to learn how to use the internet to define more complicated content, like the terms "discourse communities" and "literacy," or troubleshoot PowerPoint and Word formatting problems. Despite their technological FoK, they rarely took the initiative to use the internet to problem solve, whether in class or out of class. In addition, I integrated students' FoK by creating activities that capitalized upon their knowledge about social groups, such as friend groups from high school, and helped them identify corresponding literacies. We spent time talking about the intricacies of their communities, noting which literacies overlapped or were shared between communities. To draw connections between their lives and the assignment, I regularly called upon individual students to answer questions about their communities and the corresponding literacies. These in-class discussions built friendships between students and provided a forum to showcase their multiplicity of talents, interests, and skills. In the last week of the assignment, students shared their knowledge through peer review and a "museum walk" of the final product, where they walked around and looked at each map on the laptop screens. The peer-on-peer sharing of knowledge empowered students to reflect upon their experiences and knowledge with pride, and they learned to adapt their FoK to support their classmates.

The following four student examples were selected to demonstrate four very different conceptualizations of the literacy map. Despite the differences, one common thread emerges from their maps and reflections. The maps illustrate the FoK students privilege, namely knowledge that allows them to engage socially with the world. In particular, social media and technology are dominant FoK that allow and encourage students to interact within their discourse communities and across communities. Within the corresponding reflections, students identify the importance of their social (friend) communities. As well, they were able to apply discourse community concepts to their new university friend groups. Perhaps most interestingly, the maps and reflections illuminate to what extent friend, family, and workplace communities trump other kinds of communities, like academia.

Amy's literacy map reveals the shared knowledge between her family, lakers (her lake community), jobs, and Facebook communities (see Figure 1). The ways in which she represents similar literacies through colored boxes, such as "texting" and using the "phone" that both connect her family community and jobs community together, showcases how her FoK empowers her to communicate with different groups. Furthermore, her effective uses of colors as a design principle draws readers' eyes to the similarities and differences between her communities' literacies. In another representation of her FoK, Amy's maps her communities using both people and places to represent her communities. This is a more complex perspective of discourse community construction as it highlights that communities can be organized around people or places. Amy's map builds upon my classroom lectures about how discourse communities are organized around groups of people (like a family) or a location (like Facebook).

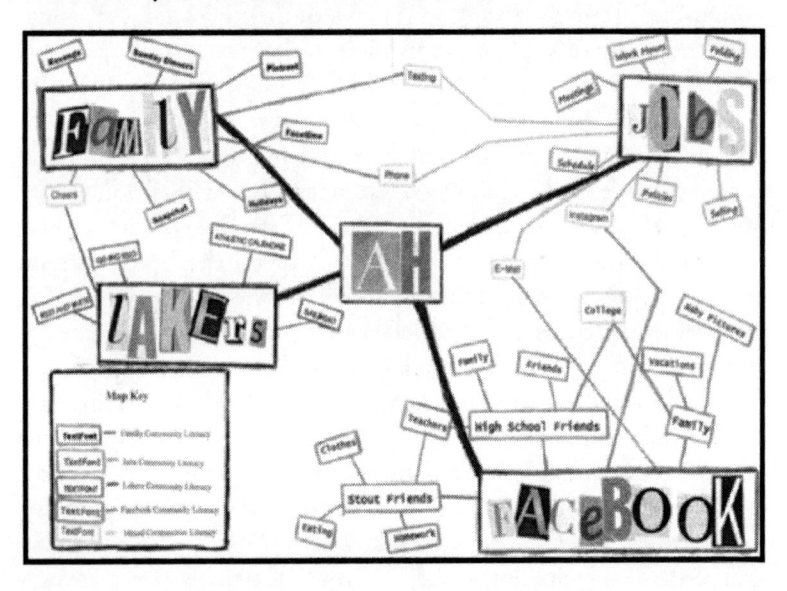

Figure 1. Amy's Literacy Map

In Amy's reflection, she is able to explain that discourse community membership is intimately connected with particular kinds of literacies, a sophisticated connection in only three weeks of class. She writes,

> An insider of a community will most likely know the terms that are used, the language, and communication. Whereas if an outside member were to look into a community that they are not connected to they will have no idea what is going on or what people are talking about.

Even though Amy reflects generally about her understandings of discourse community membership, she articulates more specifically the importance of discourse when adapting to a new environment. Amy's application of her FoK is expected as a new member to the University of Wisconsin-Stout discourse community. She continues,

> These terms can make you more aware of the communities you are in and make you realize what ways to act is okay in a specific community. This can help you transition by giving more information to us as freshman. The way we commuicate with people is a big factor. If I never would have made friends by communicating I would not have any friends which would not have allowed me to part-take in the discourse communites that I am now in on our campus. Communication is also important because if we never communicate with professors when we are confused about something we would never figure out answers.

As a first-semester college student, as all of my students were, Amy is keenly aware of the importance of communication between different groups of people, an important skill if she hopes to be successful at UW-Stout. Even though she was not able to explain how her newfound discourse community and literacy knowledge supports her transition to academia, she focuses on the most important element to her—her social community in college. This is not a surprising point as most first-year students actively build a circle of friends within their first semester. Nevertheless, her ability to recognize that communication is audience-specific is an example of the FoK that she brings into the classroom, a skill learned before coming to college.

In a very different rendering of the literacy map, Tiffany's map represents her discourse communities through the technology that binds them together (see Figure 2). For example, she uses colored circles to represent her communities while using graphics and logos to represent their literacies. For Tiffany to communicate with her communities, she must be literate in social media, like Instagram, Skype, and Snapchat. In an example of the uniqueness of each student's map, Tiffany only includes people-based communities (family, high school friends, neighborhood friends, and online friends). This is a very different approach from Amy, who primarily includes places.

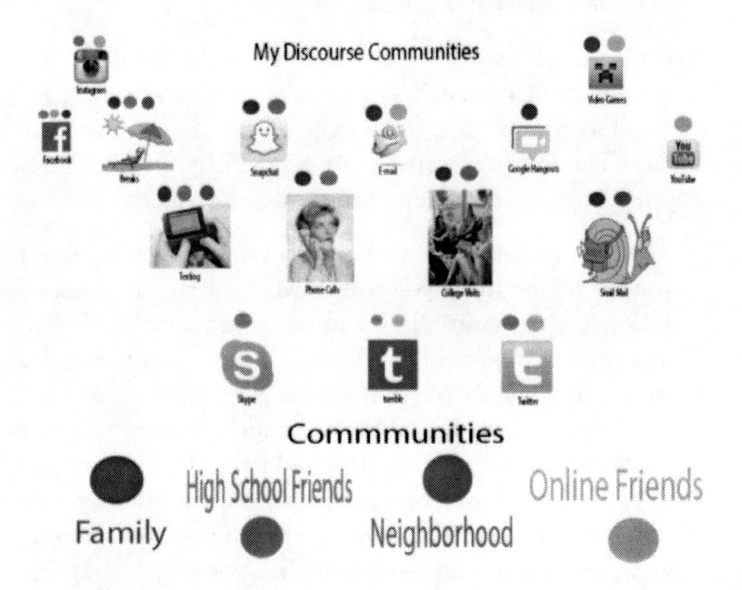

Figure 2. Tiffany's Literacy Map

Applying her digital literacy FoK, Tiffany brings into the classroom her knowledge about effective design, such as her use of white space and balance, which optimally communicates her map's content without overwhelming her readers. Furthermore, her focus on the communication styles used by her communities, predominantly app-based social media and texting, reveals the extent to which being a digital native shapes Tiffany's literacies.

Tiffany's reflection is more specific and shows a complex understanding of how discourse communities affect insider and outsider membership. Responding to the prompt that asks her to consider how her discourse community knowledge can support her transition to become a campus insider, Tiffany explains the importance of a literacy sponsor:

> Discourse communities are a group of people that speak the same language and share a culture with one another. An outsider of the community would, when thrown into the group, be very confused about the things the community does and say. An insider is someone who is part of the community. With an insider's help an outsider can eventually learn and become part of the community. For instance, someone who has no idea about painting getting thrown into a classroom of art students may not understand what acrylic paint is or how to properly use it. But with the students help, this person can become knowledgeable about the discourse community of acrylic painting.

Tiffany's reflection masterfully articulates how academic courses function as individual discourse communities with particular literacies. For students without disciplinary FoK, the transition is more difficult. However, her acrylic paint example illustrates how FoK can be used as currencies of exchange between classmates. Although Tiffany is not an art student, she recognizes the importance of students sharing their disciplinary FoK to help each other transition from outsider to insider. Encouraging students to become FoK sponsors creates a community of sharing and support. Moreover, it may ease students' transition from high school to college.

Greg's literacy map primarily defines discourse community membership through places and events, highlighting the importance his home FoK have upon his identity (see Figure 3). Greg, hailing from Sauk Prairie, Wisconsin, situates all of his communities within that town, a common rendering of many students' literacy maps. Unlike Tiffany's focus on social media and technology, Greg's FoK rests in the events and places that draw the Sauk Prairie community together. For example, he makes connections between the Fourth of July and the Wisconsin River, categorized in the "Special Events" and "Important Places" community, respectively.

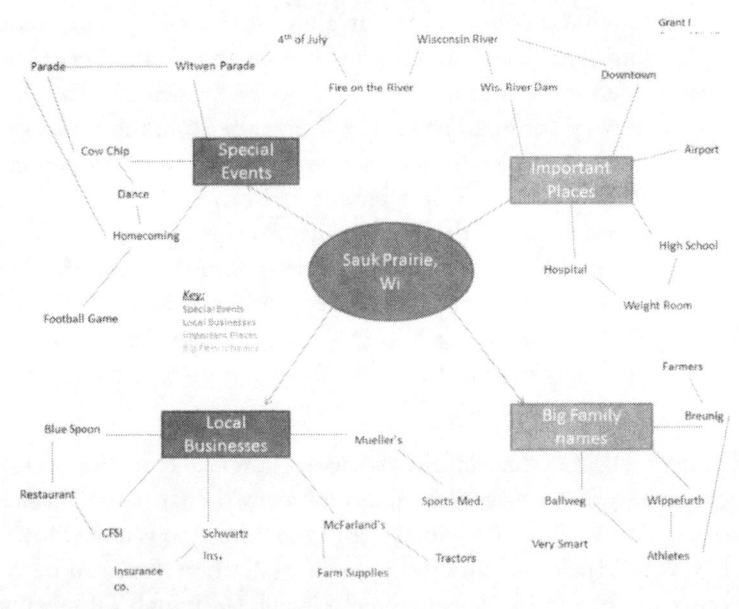

Figure 3. Greg's Literacy Map

In a connection that harkens back to the origins of FoK, Greg's map seems to be informed by an economic framework. Even though his FoK may not be entirely based on economics, the fact that his map represents important places, people, and businesses that contribute to the Sauk Prairie community (and most certainly the economy) shows how people's FoK—even eighteen-year-old students—are affected by the economy around them, as Wolf claimed in the 1960s.

Furthermore, students' social networking FoK emerges from their reflections. Most students' reflections indicate their concern with building a social network at UW-Stout. This fact should not be surprising as most new freshman are more interested in creating a support system and social network than communicating with their instructors or reflecting upon the benefits of their General Education courses. However, they bring similar friendship-specific FoK that affects how they make and maintain friendships; and this is a vital part of campus assimilation and academic success. Greg writes,

> We all belong to thousands of discourse communities, weather it be going to church, liking to draw, a favorite show or favorite food, we all have different passions and knowledge that help us become members of specific communities in the world

today. And here at college with thousands of kids coming together and meet each other for the first time it is important to be able to join the new, and vast amount of communities that surround you and be able to bound and form friendships with the other members of the communities that you belong to. Doing this will help lead you to a better and more enjoyable experience over the next 4 years here at Stout. Becoming a Stout insider is one of the most important thing a new freshmen must due here in their first semester.

For Greg, like other students in the class, navigating discourse community membership can improve their college experience. In the first-year writing classroom, discourse community concepts are an invaluable method to teaching novice writers how to conceive of academia as a community with particular expectations and assumptions. Inexperienced writers, Irene L. Clark explains, must learn to extend perceptions of audience beyond a single person (141). Therefore, capitalizing upon students' FoK to extend their perceptions of audience may make them more effective learners as they transition from high school to college.

Greg's observations show in what ways new students think through the reality of their first semester. At UW-Stout, all first-year students are required to live in campus dorms; as a result, making friends becomes even more important. Without a support system in the first semester, students are less likely to return to campus the spring semester or sophomore year. Another student, Bev, reflects upon the importance of insider membership this way: "*We all want to be a part of the Discourse Community of Stout because otherwise we will feel like we don't belong here and we should've picked a different school to attend.*" And without the right friends, students may take a longer time becoming insiders. Chris affirms this point: "*Becoming more of an insider has helped a ton because I have become friends with some upper classmen who have helped me through some of the first few weeks and always are able to point me in the right direction.*" Greg, Bev, and Chris' wise observations denote the importance of building a community of support. Student-created communities of support can smooth the rough edges of the college transition and increase first-year student retention rates in ways that may not be achieved through adult-orchestrated methods.

Finally, Jeff's map illustrates how his home communities impact his discourse community membership and literacies. Similar to Greg and Tiffany's maps, Jeff's FoK are impacted by the social media, events, and places frequently used by his discourse communities (see Figure 4). His literacy map is equally complex because it includes social media, locations, websites, and interpersonal FoK that allow him to transact with his world. By conceptualizing his literacy map as a map of Wisconsin, Jeff can truly visualize how his communities overlap and interact regardless of time and space. Unlike most of my students' maps, Jeff includes the university and his major as integral facets of his campus discourse community. Because the University of Wisconsin-Stout does not require first-year students to declare majors, most students omitted the academic discourse community from their maps. Jeff's addition of Cross-Media Graphics, his major, on his map is evidence that he is starting to think about academia as its own, unique discourse community.

Jeff's reflection indicates audience awareness FoK, a skill he most likely brought into the classroom with him. He wrote, *"Communication is used throughout each community although the means of communication may vary. You may tweet at some of your friends, but probably not your grandma. Everyone has an identity, and it's the communities that we are apart of that define it and who we are."* Jeff's example illustrates a FoK about communication that will enable him to effectively communicate with the different people around him. Moreover, Jeff's reflection demonstrates a complex understanding of how members' identities are influenced and shaped by their fellow community members. My hope is that he effectively applies this FoK to his communication situations on- and off-campus, in order to increase his personal, professional, and civic success.

As the first assignment of the semester, the digital literacy map gives students language to talk, write, and evaluate the communities around them. With this assignment, I intend to capitalize upon the knowledge students have when they walk into English 101 and start the semester with what they know—their own communities. While the digital literacy map can be taught at any point in the semester, I use it as the first assignment because it teaches students how to visually represent their discourse communities, an easier method of plotting out their communities than the written word. Furthermore, the literacy map provides a visual representation of students' FoK that usually does not emerge from in-class discussions. Finally, this first assignment disarms them, a deliberate rhetorical move that I make to foster course buy-in. First-year students expect "College English" to include essays about literature, and they are quite excited to create something very different from their previous English assignments.

Figure 4. Jeff's Literacy Map

The other two assignments, the profile of a place and the public service announcement (PSA), require students to explore two other new communities, one off-campus and the listeners of a local radio station, respectively. The profile moves students from what they know, their own communities, to a place they do not know, like a coffee shop, park, or church. Through observations and interviews, students learn to articulate how places draw or deter particular discourse communities. The PSA assignment asks students to shift their gaze to another community, the listeners of a local radio station, and to create a research-based PSA for the listening audience. These three assignments build upon students' FoK while intersecting literacy and discourse community concepts, and in all three assignments I empower students to apply their own FoK as they transition from campus outsider to insider.

Recommendations

My students' maps and reflections demonstrate that first-year students know, either implicitly or explicitly, how to apply their FoK to engage with the world around them. This is not surprising as FoK are community-learned. Regardless of where students grew up, they bring into the classroom very similar FoK, as well as personal applications of discourse community scholarship. In following sections, I offer several recommendations for how instructors may want to adapt the digital literacy map to their own students' needs, whether those students are in elementary school or graduate school.

Mapping Academic Communities

For instructors who would like to place an explicit emphasis on supporting their students' transition to the academic discourse community, readers may consider developing a literacy map assignment in which students apply their FoK to map different academic discourse communities that they encounter across campus. This map might plot students' different courses within a semester, requiring an exploration of how literacies are similar or different depending on the academic disciplines. Such an assignment would encourage students to evaluate and assess the academic communities around them, even if they have not declared a major. Additionally, examining academic communities may support students' transition from disciplinary novice to (semi) expert if they learn to find similarities between their academic communities and their own home communities. Furthermore, writing instructors can weave into class discussion or writing assignments questions in which students explore how their academic FoK—from note taking to communicating with instructors—can be applied to different courses and rhetorical situations.

Requiring students to analyze the academic communities around them, regardless of their insider or outsider status, may bridge the gap between students' FoK and the academic literacies they are exposed to. Instructors might consider requiring their students to interview a university professor or professional to learn more about the literacies of that course and discipline. A literacy map with an explicit emphasis on academia could encourage students to "learn to speak our [academics'] language, to speak as we do, to try on the peculiar ways of knowing, selecting, evaluating, reporting, concluding, and arguing," as David Bartholomae has advocated (273). Moreover, the mapping of academic communities may support students' disciplinary inquisitiveness and provide them with the tools to make more informed choices about their professional goals.

Literacy Maps: A Means for Digital Literacy Communication

Although most students are smart device (iPhone, Android, iPod, tablet, etc.) natives, which is a FoK they bring with them to college, they still need guidance communicating in a complex, social, technologically-driven world where audiences and media switch and overlap in a matter of minutes or seconds. Harnessing students' technological skills within the writing classroom teaches them how "to communicate in ways that speech does not," explains Dennis Baron (75). Likewise, Rebecca de Wind Mattingly and Patricia Harkin write,

> Students who don't get enough exercise in paying attention to context and audience in their native forms of computer-enabled writing are more likely to fail to meet the needs of context- and address-sensitive audiences in the types of writing situations encountered in college and the workplace. (16)

Instructors may consider including a digital literacy map within their course curriculum as one method for teaching their students how to navigate the digital literacy landscape. As technology becomes more complex, and technology users develop more sophisticated types of communication, computer-enabled writing is an increasingly important aspect in the writing classroom. The fast-paced society in which our students live means that they must learn to slow down and think about their communicative choices. Without this guidance, students may not learn how to evaluate the data-driven professional and social communities they are exposed to. The literacy map is just one assignment that can be used to teach students how to thoughtfully apply their digital literacy knowledge to a higher stakes situation.

While some of my students enjoyed creating their maps from markers and colored pencils, instructors might consider teaching their students how to use the technologies around them, like Google Maps, Scribble Maps, Odyssey, or ArcGIS, which are four mapmaking websites in which students can create interactive maps. Partnering the digital literacy map with more advanced mapmaking technology can bolster students' dexterity with digital communication while building upon their technology and design savvy. While digital communication is not necessarily "better," it is a medium that students engage with on a daily basis. Writing instructors may want to harness students' preexisting, digital FoK to develop their digital communication dexterity.

CREATING LITERACY AND DISCOURSE COMMUNITY SPONSORS

The physicality of the maps, either on paper or computer laptops, inspires students to present/display their work for other forums. Publicly sharing students' maps, either through museum walks or campus events, teaches students how to assume the role of literacy sponsor while creating work for an audience beyond the instructor. According to Brandt, literacy sponsors are "agents" who are "local or distant, abstract or concrete, who enable, support, teach, model, recruit, regulate, suppress, or withhold literacy and gain advantage by it in some way" (2). Therefore, instructors may want to adopt the literacy map to teach students how to sponsor each other. This sponsorship may take the form of students collaborating on map design, helping each other define community literacies, or sharing how they are applying their FoK to their campus experiences. Moll calls this transmission of knowledge an "activity of sharing" (223). Classroom-based sponsorship through activities of sharing may ease students' transition as they learn to adapt their FoK to support their classmates. Additionally, sharing students' work provides a public forum in which students gain practice creating work for a real-life rhetorical situation.

Fostering a sense of community through sponsorship and sharing is critical to supporting students' transition to the new campus community. Dana L. Mitra notes, "Research in developmental psychology finds agency, belonging and competence to be necessary factors for adolescents to remain motivated in school and to achieve academic success" (655). In addition, Julie Ballantyne's 2009 study at the University of Queensland, St. Lucia, showed that students' sense of belonging was largely connected to their academic success (48). Appreciating and respecting students' FoK, whether through assignments or classroom discussion, are important first steps in helping students envision themselves as contributing members of the academic community. For instructors of peripheral or underrepresented student populations, using the literacy map as a method of sponsorship might be one way to facilitate necessary connections between students' home communities and campus. Framing the literacy map as literacy sponsorship acknowledges that students come to college with sophisticated and complex FoK that can be used to help others succeed; as well, the literacy map assignment presents an opportunity to teach students how to adapt to different discourse communities without losing their senses of self.

The impact of this digital literacy map assignment extends beyond students' abilities to map out their community memberships in a medium where knowledge remains private and static. Instead, the literacy map is a genre that allows for and fosters a community of sharing within the classroom. Like other assignments that support and value students FoK, the literacy map encourages students to share knowledge and experiences without feeling threatened. Brian, another one of my English 101 students, writes in his map reflection, "*I've learned that we as individuals are not alone in a big world. We are apart of multiple groups that we don't even think of...It ends up being like a giant spider web of contacts!*" Thus, the map provides an opportunity for students to give voice to their FoK while recognizing and developing their own network of friends and future colleagues.

The digital literacy map assignment is valuable because it empowers students to think about their FoK as currency and themselves as agents. Once they learn how to harness their currency and agency, they can use their new skills to move within and between communities. Because students already bring some community- and literacy-based FoK into the classroom, the literacy map fosters an explicit awareness that provides students with tools to reflect and act upon their own community memberships, as well as become insiders into the communities they wish to enter. Kelsey reflected, "*I feel that this [literacy map] unit helped me into realizing that everyone was an outsider when they first came here, but slowly transitioning into a college makes me feel like an insider.*" My goal is to impress upon my students that their FoK can contribute to their campus success in ways that do not suppress their pre-college identities. Using the FoK framework as my guide, I am inspired to create assignments that support students as they move between and across discourse communities—a critical skill needed in order to become effective academics, professionals, and citizens.

Note

1. All names have been changed, and students' writing style is unedited.

Works Cited

Ballantyne, Julie. "Valuing Students' Voices: Experiences of First Year Students at a New Campus." *International Journal of Pedagogies and Learning* 7.1 (2012): 41-50. *EBSCO.* Web. 7 March 2013.

Baron, Dennis. "From Pencils to Pixels: The Stages of Literacy Technologies." *Literacy: A Critical Sourcebook.* Eds. Ellen Cushman, Eugene R. Kintgen, Barry M. Kroll, and Mike Rose. Boston and New York: Bedford/St. Martin's, 2001. 70-84. Print.

Bartholomae, David. "Inventing the University." *When a Writer Can't Write: Studies in Writer's Block and Other Composing Problems.* Ed. Mike Rose. New York: The Guilford Press, 1985. 273-285. Print.

Barta-Smith, Nancy, and Danette DiMarco. "Navigating Everyday Literacies: Mapping as a Deep Frame in Teaching Argument." *Teaching English in the Two-Year College* 37.1 (Sept. 2009): 68-83. Web. 12 Feb. 2014.

Brandt, Deborah. *Literacy and Learning: Reflections on Writing, Reading, and Society.* San Francisco: John Wiley & Sons, 2009. Print.

Bizzell, Patricia. *Academic Discourse and Critical Consciousness.* Pittsburgh: University of Pittsburgh Press, 1992. Print.

Clark, Irene L. *Concepts in Writing: Theory and Practice in the Teaching of Writing.* Oxford and New York: Routledge, 2011. Print.

Gallegos, Erin Penner. Email correspondence. 19 Feb. 2015.

—. "Mapping Student Literacies: Reimagining College Writing Instruction within the Literacy Landscape." *Composition Forum* 27 (Spring 2013): n.p. Web. 2 June 2013.

González, Norma, Luis C. Moll, and Cathy Amanti. "Introduction: Theorizing Practices." *Funds of Knowledge: Theorizing Practices in Households, Communities, and Classrooms.* Eds. Norma González, Luis C. Moll, and Cathy Amanti. Mahwah, New Jersey: 2005. 1-28. Print.

Hogg, Linda. "Funds of Knowledge: An Investigation of Coherence within the Literature." *Teaching and Teacher Education* 27 (2011): 666-677. *EBSCO.*Web. 10 May 2012.

Mattingly, Rebecca de Wind, and Patricia Harkin. "A Major in Flexibility." *What We Are Becoming: Developments in Undergraduate Writing Majors.* Eds. Greg A Giberson and Thomas A. Moriarty. Logan: Utah State University Press, 2010. 13-31. Print.

Mercado, Carmen I. "Reflections on the Study of Households in New York City and Long Island: A Different Route, a Common Destination. *Funds of Knowledge: Theorizing Practices in Households, Communities, and Class-*

rooms. Eds. Norma González, Luis C. Moll, and Cathy Amanti. New Jersey: Mahwah, 2005. 233-256. Print.

Mitra, Dana L. "The Significance of Students: Can Increasing 'Student Voice' in Schools Lead to Gains in Youth Development?" *Teachers College Record* 106.4 (April 2004): 651-688. Web. 7 March 2013.

Moll, Luis C. "Literacy Research in Community and Classrooms." *Multidisciplinary Perspectives on Literacy Research*. Ed. Richard Beach. New York: NCTE, 1992. 211-243. *ERIC*. Web. 1 Aug. 2012.

—., Cathy Amanti, Deborah Neff, and Norma González. "Funds of Knowledge for Teaching: Using a Qualitative Approach to Connect Home and Classrooms." *Funds of Knowledge: Theorizing Practices in Households, Communities, and Classrooms*. Eds. Norma González, Luis C. Moll, and Cathy Amanti. New Jersey: Mahwah, 2005. 71-88. Print.

National Council of Teachers of English. "The NCTE Definition of 21st Century Literacies." *NCTE Position Statement*. Feb. 2013. Web. 5 April. 2013.

Vélez-Ibáñez, Carlos G. "Networks of Exchange Among Mexicans in the U.S. and Mexico: Local Level Mediating Reponses to National and International Transformations. *Urban Anthropology and Studies of Cultural Systems and World Economic Development* 17.1 (Spring 1988): 27-51. Web. 1 Aug. 2012.

Wolf, Eric R. *Peasants*. New Jersey: Prentice-Hall, 1966. Print.

Appendix A

Sequence One: Literacy Map Prompt

The Task

In this assignment, you will be presenting information that you are familiar with—your own literacy and discourse communities—in a way that might not be familiar to you: You'll be creating a map.

What is a map? A map is a visual and verbal text that conveys information, often very complex information, to the people who view it. Consider this quote:

Maps are an important source of information from which people form their impressions about places and distributions. Each map is a view of the earth that affects the way people think about the world. Our thoughts about the space in which we live and especially the areas beyond our direct perception are largely influenced by the representations of space that we see, and the way we think about our environment influences the way we act within it.

(Michael Peterson, "Cartography and the Internet: Implications for Modern Cartography")

Purpose
The information that you will convey through your map has to do with your own discourse communities, and the literacy practices of those communities. The map you create will be both personal and public, because it will convey your impression of and interaction with the world(s) that you live, write, and communicate in.

Audience
Your audience for this map is your peers in this class and the rest of the UW-Stout community, including other students, staff, and administrators. Think about how you want these people to understand you and where you come from.

This map is both a geographic (shows relations between places) and a concept (shows relations between ideas) map. *Be creative!*

Literacy Map Guidelines
Your map should be made through one single PowerPoint slide or drawn and scanned document.

When considering how to show relationships between communities, you might want to use an actual map of the city, state, country, or globe to represent how far removed each of your communities is from one another. Or you can design another way to show the relationships and proximities between communities. You should also think about how you might represent the similarity of discourse communities that are not close to one another in real space. For virtual communities, you should think about how to relate them to real communities.

Your map should include
- Your name
- Headings with names of each of four communities
- Names and examples of literacies each community uses
- A map key that helps your readers navigate the document and explains any visual symbols
- Visual relationship between communities (arrows, lines, circles, etc.)
- Visually pleasing design and image choices

Appendix B

Spend ten minutes writing about the following two points. Include specific examples in this reflection.

1. What did you learn over the last few weeks about discourse communities, insider/outsider membership, literacy, communication, and/or identity?

2. How might your new knowledge about the terms and concepts of discourse community, insider/outsider membership, literacy, communication, and/or identity help you transition as a Stout outsider to a Stout insider?

REFLECTIONS

Reflections is on the Web at https://reflectionsjournal.net/

Reflections: A Journal of Public Rhetoric, Civic Writing, and Service Learning, a peer reviewed journal, provides a forum for scholarship on public rhetoric, civic writing, service-learning, and community literacy. Originally founded as a venue for teachers, researchers, students and community partners to share research and discuss the theoretical, political and ethical implications of community-based writing and writing instruction, Reflections publishes a lively collection of scholarship on public rhetoric and civic writing, occasional essays and stories both from and about community writing and literacy projects, interviews with leading workers in the field, and reviews of current scholarship touching on these issues and topics.

"Why Study Disability? Lessons Learned From a Community Writing Project"

The editors of *Reflections* wish to include a submission that is a personal narrative, but one grounded in methodology (Jay Dolmage's) as an opportunity to better understand the rhetorical choices that disabled writers in the community writing project made when discussing and representing disability. The 14.1 issue had a few articles with a strong personal voice, but we believe this one stands out with its meta-analytical response through a blend of narrative and scholarly conversation. Crip theory is grounded in a more narrative scholarly approach that can capture a disability studies lens, and this article does just that with an emphasis in helping readers understand "language and the teaching of writing." We believe an inclusion of this narrative article would be a refreshing and needed addition that demonstrates the importance of the scholarly narrative.

3 Why Study Disability? Lessons Learned from a Community Writing Project

Annika Konrad

For five years of graduate school, I avoided studying disability because I thought it would require confronting the idea that I have a disability. I was first introduced to disability studies during my master's coursework. I mustered the courage to take the course on disability because deep down, I knew that this thing I was calling a "vision problem" or what the doctors told me is a degenerative retinal disease called retinitis pigmentosa, might actually be a "disability." I left the course feeling stimulated but no less intimidated by the idea of looking at myself in the mirror and thinking "disabled." I resolved that my interest in disability studies was purely personal—it would allow me to learn about my own experiences, but I would do it privately, and I would publicly study something more obviously related to my profession as a writing instructor.

Stephanie L. Kerschbaum corroborates this feeling in her recent article "On Rhetorical Agency and Disclosing Disability in Academic Writing." Kerschbaum writes that she, too, resisted suggestions to engage with her own deafness in her scholarship. As Kerschbaum and others have observed, there is a quiet assumption in academics that people who do disability studies either have a disability or are related to someone who does (56). I too made this assumption. I did not want to be doing disability studies just because of my own "vision problem"; I did not want to be seen as doing research that is self-fulfilling; and most of all, I knew that if I did disability studies, then I would really have to come out as "disabled."

Eventually, though, my personal exploration of disability converged with my professional exploration of writing and rhetoric. When I attended a local support group meeting for people who are blind and visually impaired, I was struck by the stories that people told. I noticed that these stories were unlike the stories I had previously heard about blind people. I had read stories about blind people performing superhuman feats of strength—like biking across the country or scaling a mountain. The stories people told at the support group meeting, however, were about everyday experiences. I wondered what would happen if these kinds of stories circulated outside the walls of the meeting room. I imagined starting a writing group and finding a way to publish these stories. Could everyday stories about disability change public perceptions of people who are blind and visually impaired?

But I immediately questioned myself—do I want to do this just because I am a writing teacher? Would it be purely self-fulfilling? Would I be turning these people into research subjects? Would I be stomping on this organization's territory? Although I was unsure about the convergence of my two identities—as a university writing instructor and as a visually impaired person—at the end of the meeting, I pitched the idea to the director of the program, and he was enthusiastic. I forced myself to try it.

In this essay, then, I reflect on my experience of starting a community- writing project for people who are blind and visually impaired. My goal is to explain how working with people on their disability narratives has shaped my understanding of writing and rhetoric, and in turn, my understanding of my role as a writing instructor. I draw upon two areas of scholarship—disability rhetoric and community writing—in order to critically reflect on my experiences.

DISABILITY RHETORIC AND COMMUNITY WRITING

First, I draw upon Jay Dolmage's theory of *métis* to make sense of the ways helping others write about disability has developed my own understanding of language. In *Disability Rhetoric*, Dolmage positions people with disabilities as "*makers* of meaning—rather than as surfaces reflecting the meanings of others, rather than as objects of knowledge" (95). In this essay, I reflect on how learning to see people who have disabilities as "makers-of-meaning," allowed me to expand my understanding of language. Dolmage proposes that *métis* can be used as a methodology for understanding disability meaning-making. He defines *métis* as "the rhetorical art of cunning, the use of embodied strategies, what Certeau calls 'everyday arts,' to transform rhetorical situations" (5). *Métis* is further described as cunning, embodied, and sideways moving rhetoric. In order to better understand what I have learned from people who write about disability, in this essay I begin to use *métis* as a lens through which to understand the rhetorical choices that people made when writing about disability.

Second, I reference conclusions from Tiffany Rousculp's *A Rhetoric of Respect: Recognizing Change at a Community Writing Center* to make sense of my role as a university writing instructor working within a community. In reflecting on her ten years of experience with the Salt Lake Community Writing Center (CWC), Rousculp explores what it means to cultivate a "rhetoric of respect" between Salt Lake Community College and the CWC. She explains that in many instances, her own and others' academic notions of what counts as "change" or "empowerment" limited their perceptions of the agency community writers gained through the project. Rousculp explains that she perceived some people to be in need of "a specific revision": "I measured them by how far they wanted to migrate into my environment. My interpretation required them to transgress their current identities rather than for me to pay attention to my own" (91). In this essay, I reflect on how my own identity as a writing instructor evolved throughout the community-writing project. I use Rousculp's concept of "rhetoric of respect" to demonstrate how I began to let my role change as I learned from the writers' own experiences of communicating about disability. Further, I touch on the tensions I experienced between the personal and the public—between personal and public identities and between personal and public writing—in order to demonstrate how and why I finally decided to study disability.

Transitioning from Writing Teacher to Community Writing Leader

At the outset, I was self-conscious about my role in the community writing project. As a university writing teacher, I never had to think too hard about my purpose. Because college students are required to write, my purpose always felt clear. In the initial stages of planning the community-writing project, however, I kept asking myself, "Why am I doing this? Do people who are blind or visually impaired even want to write about being blind or visually impaired?" Additionally, I felt conflicted about my own personal investment in the project. On one hand, I wanted the project to be purely personal—my purpose would be to learn more about my own disability identity, and hopefully, I would help others with their writing along the way. On the other hand, I was self-conscious about my personal investment and worried that I would be forcing my agenda upon people for whom writing might have little personal or public consequence.

To avoid going it alone, I applied for a small grant from my university. After receiving the grant, I began partnering with a local organization to solidify a plan. The organization's outreach coordinator convinced me that there are certainly people who are blind and visually impaired who want to write, but they may not have found an outlet. To align myself with the mission of the organization, they suggested that I recruit participants from across the state. I had originally conceived of the writing group as a group of people sitting in a room together, but when they explained to me that transportation is the biggest obstacle for getting people who are blind and visually impaired together, I had to reimagine my idea of a writing group. Together we concluded that phone conferencing would be the most accessible medium through which to communicate, and we would recruit participants through various low vision support outlets across the state. I sent out two different recruitment announcements. The first described the project as a "writing group" (a well-known term among writing instructors) and the second described the project as a "statewide storytelling project" with the goal of creating an archive of the life experiences of people who are blind and visually impaired in the state. The first announcement, which called the project a writing group, elicited almost no responses. The second recruitment announcement, in which I called the project a statewide storytelling project, elicited almost thirty responses. It was at this moment that I first realized I would need to continue revising my idea of a writing group by responding to the needs and desires of the community.

Knowing little about disability as an identity, the blind community, or community writing projects, I began by relying on what I know about writing instruction: I know that people need prompts, examples, exercises, feedback, and most of all, praise. I was not so sure, though, whether or not helping people write about disability would be different. Quite frankly, I had no idea what kinds of prompts would be appropriate for writing about disability, and I felt uncomfortable shaping the direction of people's writing. When I teach personal narrative in college composition courses, I strive to respect the integrity of students' personal stories, but in my role as a teacher, I do not hesitate to respond to their writing in a way that helps them meet the goals of the assignment. In the community, however, I was not quite sure how much of that "teacher" role I should play. In many ways, I didn't feel like I had the authority to lead people in writing about disability—I knew about writing and writing instruction, but I didn't know about disability, and I sure didn't know about writing disability.

So I decided to begin by asking the writers what they wanted to do. While I had a plan in mind, one not unlike the syllabus for a college writing course, I wanted to find out what the writers' actual needs and desires were. To my surprise, many of the group members immediately articulated the idea that they find storytelling to be central to communicating their experiences of disability. Many expressed that they see a need for greater visibility of stories about disability. They also described many different experiences with writing and relationships to it: some have published memoirs, others have written unpublished memoirs, others write for work or for

their church, others blog, and some have never written for work or pleasure at all. Feeling perplexed by how I would accommodate such a variety of experiences, I defaulted to imagining the community-writing project as a college writing course. I reverted to the plan I know best. I introduced the idea of drafting. I supplied a copy of Anne Lamott's "Shitty First Drafts." I started encouraging writers to give feedback. I supplied a "best practices for feedback" tip sheet. I asked writers to read their writing aloud. I gave short lectures about "showing versus telling" and the importance of communicating a message in a story.

After a few weeks, though, I started to feel like something was amiss. It wasn't the same feeling that I get when I sense that my students haven't done the reading. I sensed that something else was going on.

Renegotiating the Agenda

I soon realized that I would need to adapt my agenda, on both a conceptual and logistical level. When I asked a group of people who are blind and visually impaired to read their writing aloud over the phone, I quickly realized I would have to alter my strategy. Many of the writers were using screen readers so they couldn't look at the words on the page—they could only listen to them—and others were using screen magnifiers of various kinds, so reading aloud on the spot was not the easiest task. Because I wanted to stick to my strategy of having writers listen to each other's writing, I asked the writers if I could read their writing aloud for them (although I am visually impaired, I can read comfortably off a computer screen with specific accessibility settings). They agreed, and we found that this strategy was helpful for giving feedback over the phone. By reading their writing aloud in the moment, I was able to help the writers refresh their memories of each other's stories.

Later, I offered other pieces of advice about how to give feedback on writing, like "be specific," "point to specific pieces of evidence," and "direct the writer to specific lines and words." Again, I quickly realized that this kind of specificity is not always possible for many of the writers when we are giving feedback over the phone. I realized that when you are listening to writing rather than looking at it, it is much more labor-intensive to have to recall specific lines and words. Over time, we naturally shifted from giving feedback on the phone to giving feedback over email because it allows for more time to compose feedback immediately after listening to or reading the drafts.

I also had to figure out how to give feedback that would help writers tell their stories in the ways they wanted to tell them. Of course, I had encountered this challenge before when teaching undergraduates, but I felt even more of an obligation to respect the integrity of these writers' stories. I felt especially responsible because I was working in partnership with a local organization—I did not want community members to think of me as the know-it-all academic. I was very self-conscious about my role as an insider/outsider. I do share the experience of being visually impaired, but I believe that I have had a relatively privileged experience with disability—I have received the accommodations I need to study and work, and I am younger and far less visually impaired than many of the members of the writing group.

But when I realized that the participants did want to learn from me, I decided that the most useful thing I could teach them is what I know about how to tell a story. I noticed that in their initial drafts, many of the writers were not doing what I considered "storytelling"—they were writing about their experiences, but they were speaking about them in general terms, rather than by focusing on specific moments and events. This is something I see in student writing all the time, and I tell them things like, "Show don't tell" or "Slow down" or "Focus on specific moments." When I began using this language with my writing group members, I made sure to tell them that I am not giving this advice because of some arbitrary textbook rule—it is because I believe that we can communicate in more powerful ways if we tell stories that allow readers to experience our moments and our lives, if we let them into our realities.

Eventually I began to realize that my ideas about storytelling might change as I learned more about what it is like to communicate about disability. Soon the writers were teaching me about how to tell a story.

Learning to Narrate Disability

As we continued to compose our stories, I became more and more aware that my writing pedagogy wasn't holding up as well as it does with undergraduates. As I explained above, I advised writers to focus on specific moments to tell more powerful stories. I noticed that some writers were making these changes in their writing, but overall, many of the writers continued to write in what seemed to me like general terms, focusing on a specific dimension of their experience like cane training, grocery shopping, or self-advocacy. Many of the writers opted to be more instructive and pragmatic than dramatic and emotional when I had advised them to focus on specific moments and details in order to let readers into their experiences.

It started to become clear to me, though, that while I could teach these writers about how to tell a powerful story, they were beginning to teach me about how to write about disability. In retrospect, I see their writing processes as processes of exercising *métis*, or cunning, embodied, sideways moving rhetoric—a rhetoric that attempts to work with, through, and against myths and stereotypes. In the following section, I will use a couple of examples to demonstrate how the writers began to teach me about what it means to narrate disability, and I will end by explaining how these instances shaped my understanding of my role within the project and my relationship to disability studies as a scholar of writing and rhetoric.

A Few Examples of Métis in Action

I'll begin with one of my own writing challenges as a way to demonstrate the complex task of narrating disability. I began the writing group with a desire to communicate about the perspective I have gained, rather than lost, from the experience of losing vision. Andrew Solomon's book *Far From the Tree* inspired me to write about this aspect of my experience—Solomon describes his interviews with many parents of children with various disabilities who articulate the enlightenment and happiness they've gained from parenting special needs children. When I explained my story idea on the phone to the writing group, they all seemed to agree and understand the sentiment I was getting at. When I sat down to write the piece, however, I felt like it wouldn't be a simple task to communicate a feeling of gratitude and happiness. I knew I had to *show* rather than tell readers about the feeling, but I was stymied by the thought that disability is never considered a positive or happy thing. I was well aware that the idea of disability, especially the idea of vision loss, scares people. I worried that those fears would prevent my readers from understanding and believing my point about the affordances of living with a disability, so I ended up abandoning the topic. I had no idea how to write against or through the pervasive cultural narratives of fear and despair that shape perceptions of blindness and disability.

But other writers have taught me some navigation strategies.

One writer wanted to describe what she calls "the bubble of isolation" that surrounds people with disabilities. She expressed that she wanted to use her story to instruct people on how to socially approach people with disabilities, or as she puts it, "break bubbles." When attempting to turn the story into a short radio piece, she received feedback from a producer asking her to focus more on emotions and less on directives. The writer insisted that she needed to use directives because her experiences of being blind since birth and having been a clinical psychologist have taught her that directives help people figure out what to do in stressful situations.

I was fascinated by this interaction because I could have likely given this writer the same feedback—as a writing teacher, I often suggest that students focus on specific moments and let readers into those moments, a move that often involves engaging emotion. While this writer's story does focus on a few specific moments and does describe emotional reactions, she frames it with directives that instruct readers on how to approach people with disabilities. When the producer insisted that the writer use more emotional appeals than give directives, the writer stood her ground and explained why she thought directives would be more effective than emotions at changing behavior. The writer explained that from her experience of being blind since birth, she knows that clear directives help people change behavior and that engaging emotions, while moving, is not an as effective of a strategy for moving people to action. Even though the producer stood behind her theories about the pivotal role of emotion in radio storytelling, they met somewhere in the middle and finally recorded the story for broadcast.

As an observer of this interaction, I was fascinated by the deep-seated conflicts that emerged from these two approaches to communicating disability. What is more, I admired the writer's use of a rhetoric that departed from my own ideas about what makes a good story, as well as from the radio producer's own convictions about what makes a good radio story. Her rhetoric was in fact cunning—she deliberately chose to not make her story primarily emotional because she knew that an overly emotional story about disability could perpetuate stereotypes and she doubted its effectiveness in changing behavior. While I had initially read her drafts as "needing to focus on more specific moments," she later showed me that her directives and general language were intentional—she knew from her own experience of being a blind person that this is the kind of rhetoric she feels is necessary in order to cause change. This is an example of one instance in which my ideas about what counts as change or empowerment, as Rousculp puts it, were challenged. I began the project with the assumptions that people will want to write emotional stories, that writing emotional stories will result in empowerment, and that those stories will result in change, but this incident revealed to me alternate ways the writers might gain agency through the project.

Another writer wanted to write about going for walks by herself. In her initial drafts, she described one walk in which she has a near-collision with a bicyclist, gets lost, and asks for help from the same woman she ran into on a previous walk. The story was lighthearted, cheerful, and humorous, but from my perspective, it lacked narrative arc and a take-away message. I encouraged her to include more information about her vision loss, what this walk taught her, and how this walk fit into the trajectory of her own understanding of her disability (in other words, I asked her to write a book instead). She revised the story, taking some of my recommendations into account, but once again, I was left feeling like something was amiss. I was making suggestions in the same way I do with students, and I understood that these writers are more mature, and some of them are more experienced writers, but it felt like something else was happening in these exchanges. I could tell that these writers were making deliberate choices but not the ones I originally hoped they would. Numerous times this writer had emphasized her belief in the value of humor—she approached many of our conversations with a sense of humor, so it did not surprise me that she wrote her story with the same tone. While I have yet to ask this writer about her rhetorical intentions, I now see her use of humor as cunning—her lighthearted, upbeat tone is striking and unexpected, and the sense of humor she uses to approach and interpret the events of her life run contrary to narratives of loss and despair. Once again, I would not have originally seen humor or lightheartedness as a means of gaining agency through writing, but it has become increasingly clear to me how important it is to let individuals decide how they will exercise agency.

Further, these experiences caused me to revise my idea of a writing group. At first I would begin our phone conversations by discussing a specific writing strategy, but we would quickly depart from the subject of writing. Group members would launch into conversations about their personal experiences with stigma, technology, filing lawsuits, or whatever was going on in their lives relative to blindness. At first, I saw these conversations as tangential—I scrambled to find ways to bring the conversation back to the writing task at hand, but later I realized that connecting on these topics was serving as a means to discuss disability communication. Our conversations often focused less on the mechanics of telling powerful stories than they did on what kinds of rhetoric might be useful for telling our stories in ways that challenge stereotypes and cultural narratives. Now we spend our conversations connecting on issues and experiences relative to blindness and visual impairment, and after the conversation, I email a list of topics that were discussed and encourage writers to claim those topics for future blog posts. Many writers have expressed that they almost always leave the conversation with a story idea in mind. In other words, I shifted from imagining our phone conversations as a venue for talking about writing to viewing our conversations as a means of generating story ideas and rhetorical strategies.

WHY STUDY DISABILITY?

From this experience, I've learned why, as a composition and rhetoric scholar, I would study disability. Yes—it is true that part of my motivation for starting the community-writing project was because I am disabled, and yes, it is true that the experience has taught me a lot about myself. But what is more significant to me is that it has taught me about language. Whereas I once declared, "We just don't have the language to talk about disability in daily life" in my disability studies course, I am now beginning to understand why I felt that way, and I have learned that my hunch was not unfounded. As Dolmage articulates, we have failed to see people with disabilities as makers-of- meaning rather than as objects of meaning:

> From antiquity to the very present, disability has been seen as something simple to trope and frame. In this way, rhetoric has been used to mark out and stigmatize disability, thus providing us with limited means of interpreting and understanding the role of people with disabilities in rhetoric and in society. (83)

When I kept repeating my comment in class about the difficulty of communicating about disability, I may have been avoiding outing myself as disabled, but I also may have been steeped in a kind of rhetoric that "marks out and stigmatizes" disability. I was not aware how disability can be "the very possibility {and concurrently the uncertainty) of human knowledge" (124). This service project has taught me about the complex challenges of finding words to describe an embodied experience, particularly one that is so over- determined that the most common linguistic labels like "blind" or "visually impaired" ignite fear in the minds of readers and listeners. It has taught me about the challenges of writing through, with, and against large cultural narratives of despair, dependency, and deficit. It has taught me how a cunning, embodied, sideways moving rhetoric can shirk expectations and challenge norms. Most importantly, it has taught me to reimagine what it means to tell a powerful story.

It has also taught me to reimagine my role as a writing instructor, both within and outside university classrooms. As I have articulated, I learned to let go of my ideas of whatcounts as change or empowerment for community writers. I now realize that conventional ways writing instructors conceive of helpful approaches to the writing process (I.e. reading aloud, providing oral feedback) might not always be the most accessible means of engaging in the writing process. I now know that I should strive to provide as many options for engaging, and sometimes those options may not be immediately apparent. Further, my own life experiences do not suffice as the basis for understanding how storytelling, or rhetoric, works. Each individual's life experiences shape the way they approach communication, and teachers should facilitate exploration of those methods, rather than restrict them. And finally, I learned that if I truly listen to writers' own goals, rather than relying on my own plans and priorities, I might learn more about writing and rhetoric than I knew before.

And yet there is always more to learn. I am now interested in the process of learning how to write and communicate about disability. I am interested in how people with disabilities learn to approach the task of changing attitudes and behaviors. How do people with disabilities learn to make rhetorical moves? How do we learn to exercise cunning rhetoric in the face of dominant narratives? How do we learn to move sideways, against the grain of dominant narratives while also maintaining forward motion? How do we learn to use emotion without overdramatizing our experiences? My hope is that questions like these will expand our understanding of language and its abilities and inabilities to convey human experience. Dolmage writes that because

> *meaning* itself can be metaphorized as immobile, 'crippled,' delayed, in need of assistance... metaphor should be seen as the space within language where the breakdown of meaning is addressed not with correction or seamless substitution, but with something else: where the holes in language are plugged with squares and triangles, or where we recognize the inaccessibility of all meaning-making. (103)

It is those squares and triangles that I want to know more about. I want to know how those squares and triangles turn into powerful, conversation-changing stories. I believe that knowing more about the accessibility and inaccessibility of language will make me a better composition and rhetoric teacher—it will make me better at helping students plug their holes with squares and triangles. I now see that studying disability is one way for me to get there.

Works Cited

Dolmage, Jay. *Disability Rhetoric*. Syracuse: Syracuse University Press, 2013. Print.

Kerschbaum, Stephanie L. "On Rhetorical Agency and Disclosing Disability in Academic Writing." *Rhetoric Review* 33.1 (2014): 55-71. Print.

Rousculp, Tiffany. *A Rhetoric of Respect: Recognizing Change at a Community Writing Center*. National Council of Teachers of English, 2014. Print.

Solomon, Andrew. *Far From the Tree: Parents, Children, and the Search for Identity*. New York, NY: Scribner, 2012. Kindle.

Annika Konrad is a PhD Candidate in Composition and Rhetoric at University of Wisconsin-Madison, where she teaches undergraduate writing courses, works in the Writing Center, and is a TA assistant director of the first-year writing program. She received her M.A. in English from The Ohio State University in 2011. Her research interests include disability rhetoric, narrative, writing program administration, and literacy studies. As she describes in this essay, in 2013 she received a grant to launch a statewide storytelling project for people who are blind and visually impaired. She continues to grow the project and publishes stories on *The Outlook* from Here (www.theoutlookfromhere.wordpress.com). She also serves on the Board of Directors of the Wisconsin Council of the Blind and Visually Impaired and is a trainee member of the McPherson Eye Research Institute, which is a multidisciplinary community of scholars researching the science and art of vision. She is planning a dissertation on disability communication in which she will interview people about their experiences of learning to communicate about blindness and vision loss. She has published in *British Journal of Sociology of Education* and presents regularly at the annual Conference on College Composition and Communication. You can learn more about her work and find her contact information at www. annikakonrad.com.

COMMUNITY LITERACY JOURNAL

Community Literacy Journal is on the Web at http://www.communityliteracy.org/

The *Community Literacy Journal* publishes both scholarly work that contributes to the field's emerging methodologies and research agendas and work by literacy workers, practitioners, and community literacy program staff. We are especially committed to presenting work done in collaboration between academics and community members.

We understand "community literacy" as the domain for literacy work that exists outside of mainstream educational and work institutions. It can be found in programs devoted to adult education, early childhood education, reading initiatives, lifelong learning, workplace literacy, or work with marginalized populations, but it can also be found in more informal, ad hoc projects.

For us, literacy is defined as the realm where attention is paid not just to content or to knowledge but to the symbolic means by which it is represented and used. Thus, literacy makes reference not just to letters and to text but to other multimodal and technological representations as well.

Poetic Signs of Third Place: A Case Study of Student-Driven Imitation in a Shelter for Young Homeless People in Copenhagen

We admire Matthiesen's piece very much for its sensitivity and respect for young people in her story of what happened at a shelter for young homeless people in Copenhagen, where she offered writing workshops, while at the same time modeling for literacy researchers how we might understand the rhetorical skills and rhetorical capacities of young people. Matthiesen's work leads her to the conclusion that, drawing on Ray Oldenburg's "third space" — Oldenburg describes the third place as a place situated between home and work — that "paradoxically, the residents have no home and no work." Researchers and literacy practitioners will certainly benefit from Matthiesen's observation that "a third place may be far from what a homeless person really needs. Or maybe it is closer to it than we might think."

4 Poetic Signs of Third Place: A Case Study of Student-Driven Imitation in a Shelter for Young Homeless People in Copenhagen

Christina Matthiesen

During a series of writing workshops at a shelter for young homeless people in Copenhagen, I examined to what extent the literary practice of student-driven imitation with its emphasis on self-governance and a dialogical approach can engage marginalized learners in reading and writing. I found that student-driven imitation had the potential to engage different kinds of writers and that they adopted the practice with ease and confidence. In addition, I experienced that the residents' preferred genre was poetry and that they generally sought a neutral space with low attention to social status, characterized by dialogue and a homely feel. This space is comparable to Oldenburg's third place, and I suggest that poetry is a textual marker of this space.

> Reading, however, is free.
>
> —Quintilian (X.I.19)

Clearly, it began with an idea. Not an explicated need. Not an invitation or request. Actually, I ended up insisting, mostly out of curiosity, but some stubbornness might have been at play. My idea was cultivated from two interests especially: my exploration of imitation as delineated by Quintilian; and my attraction to the public turn of composition as scrutinized by Elenore Long and developed by Linda Flower and Paula

Mathieu, amongst others, as well as the ethnographic work of Ralph Cintron. My exploration of imitation as delineated by Quintilian had led to the development of a concept I call student-driven imitation (Matthiesen 5). Student-driven imitation foregrounds the choice and reflection of the individual student: "Which texts fascinate me, and what do I need or want to learn?"

Here, I will tell a story of what happened at a shelter for young homeless people in Copenhagen, where I held a writing workshop series of thirteen sessions based on student-driven imitation. My aim was to examine if, and to what extent, student-driven imitation has the potential to engage marginalized learners in reading and writing. These learners may be with or without learning disabilities, but typically have negative, or poor, educational experiences due to difficult life situations, and therefore may struggle with reluctance towards learning and low confidence levels.

Imitation exercises from the classical rhetorical tradition are seldom seen in community literacy projects, maybe due to their often restricted pedagogical scope, which focuses primarily on pattern practice (see D'Angelo; Glenn, Goldthwaite, and Connors; Terrill; and Fish). However, student-driven imitation foregrounds a practice based upon the students' own choices of text and an unrestricted interaction, in which mirroring is not the goal but process is. This practice, I claim, has the potential to engage marginalized learners in reading and writing, since it is highly inclusive of the experiences and reflective practice of the individual learner, and emphasizes the decision-making of the individual learner as a reader and writer, her preferences, goals, and manner of interaction.

Where imitation exercises generally build upon the reciprocally reinforcing relation between reading and writing (Nelson 437; Salvatori 659), as well as train dual attention to both the learner and the text (Terrill 297), student-driven imitation also strongly asserts the premise of dialogism, as developed by Bakhtin, naturally dependent and receptive to what has already been said and written (Bakhtin 276). This is reflected in the five dimensions of student-driven imitation: "1) Paying attention to FASCINATION", "2) Identifying QUALITIES WORTH IMITATING", "3) Carrying out CRITICAL REFLECTION", "4) Considering ACCEPTANCE", and "5) Exploring ways of INTERACTION" (Matthiesen 79-83). The dimension of interaction animates unrestricted interaction across genres, and situations: a blog post may stir up a poem, and the other way around. Maybe a perspective was found useful, maybe a metaphor, maybe just a word, maybe only if twisted or mocked. In this manner, student-driven imitation, as a literate practice, seeks to strengthen rhetorical agency: that is, both rhetorical skills (as restricted imitation exercises) and the ability to find or create rhetorical opportunities (Hoff-Clausen, Isager, and Villadsen 57), by becoming attuned to and grant agency of others (Geisler 15; Flower, "Public Engagement" 202). In Michael Warner's sense of what constitutes a public, self-organized attention to and reflexive circulation of discourse (Warner 419), the literate practice of student-driven imitation can be viewed as "a mode of public engagement" (Asen 191). Thus, student-driven imitation as a literate practice not only underscores the experience and goal-setting of the individual learner, but is based upon participation in public life through reading and writing. Hereby, the practice resembles key principles in Dewey's thinking on education: impulses, experiences, and goals of the learner are central and must be linked to concrete action, inquiry, interaction, and participation in public life (Dewey, "Democracy" 101, "Experience" 33). But student-driven imitation also contains an aspect of Freirean pedagogy, which seeks a dialogue not dominated by authoritarianism, alienating intellectualism, but instead animates a dialogue in which students hold power as subjects (Freire 67). This contrasts to "banking education," in which the teacher preserves knowledge (61). In the subject of rhetoric, language itself is the core content of the education, but in contrast to other educational content, language is free and renewable for everyone. Yet, as Deborah Brandt, inspired by Bourdieu, reminds us, language is often made scarce and hard to get (769). Student-driven imitation seeks to acknowledge and foster receptiveness to both the language and invention of the individual and of the other, "elite and street, canonical and vernacular" (Matthiesen 90). One cannot do anything wrong when working with student-driven imitation, and one can work with student-driven imitation on one's own, attuned to the individual talent in everyday life – all one needs is pen and paper. Thus the literate practice seeks to promote independence, confidence, and a sense of agency, important properties for all types of writers, especially those on the margins (Alberti 391). In addition, working with the concept does not depend, at least in the long run, on teachers, technical support, or funding. Once explained and tested, the student can work with student-driven imitation on her own.

As we shall see, student-driven imitation as a literate practice has the potential to include and engage writers on different levels, and is easily adopted. What I did not foresee, though, was the residents' preferred genre, poetry. Nor that they would generally seek a dialogue with me, and the other residents, characterized by a low attention to social status, playful moods and a homely feel, in which conversations about reading, writing, education, and politics could unfold, and conflicts and anger surface. This dialogic space is comparable to the sociologist Ray Oldenburg's third place. The concept of third place is bound to urban informal public spaces, such as the barbershop, the pub, the gym, or the street, places we seek between our first and second place, home and work. It is characterized by open, neutral ground, voluntary recurrent participation in, primarily, dialogue, low attention to status, playful moods and a homely feel (Oldenburg 22–38). In line with Dewey's view on communication in local communities (Dewey, "The Public" 153), Oldenburg sees great democratic potential in third places: here a community can take shape, connect, and built up, "give substance and articulation to group sentiment" (75), but he also underscores the personal benefits of the third place: it promotes "novelty," "perspective," and "spiritual tonic" (Oldenburg 44–55). I find Oldenburg's concept relevant here, because it emphasizes, besides dialogue, open, neutral ground, recurrent voluntary participation, and low attention to status.

The emergence of a space comparable to the third place was marked, I propose, not only by the nature of our physical recurring meetings in the shelter, but by the residents' preference for poetry, a genre of neutral ground and with low attention to status, as opposed to telling one's own story or writing job applications.

I begin with an account of the setting and set-up of the workshop. Then, I exemplify how student-driven imitation can work in relation to poetry and specify the residents' strategies for interaction. This leads to an illumination of the value of poetry in relation to student-driven imitation. Next, I point to other signs of engagement, from anger to conscientiousness and curiosity, which may have been triggered by the dialogic approach of the concept and workshop. Finally, I discuss how strengths of this open-ended version of the literate practice may also be a weakness and conceivably induce a feeling of lack of progress and purpose. This leads to an outline of strategies of possible value to future projects.

THE SETTING AND SET-UP

An often-used, informal term for young homeless people in Denmark is "sofa-surfers". This term points to the fact that young homeless tend to hide their homelessness and avoid the most obvious and often rough places sought by adult homeless, such as the most well-known shelters and street corners where they sell the homeless' newspaper. Thus, these young marginalized people often live a hidden life away from institutions, treatments, and social and educational activities. According to the social workers that I have been in contact with, this group of young people typically see themselves as simply lacking a place to stay, not as homeless people with all their accompanying connotations. Nor do they look like homeless persons in the sense of the stereotypical image: a homeless man with a dog and three plastic bags, sleeping on a bench in a park. This ought not, however, lead us to conclude that the lack of a place to stay is their only problem. Many suffer from the same problems as the majority of non-immigrant homeless in Denmark. Besides economic poverty, these problems include social, personal, and interpersonal problems, such as a general distrust of others; problems with attention and concentration; alcohol and drug abuse; intense angst, and, sometimes, psychiatric issues such as psychosis and schizophrenia. A fairly new initiative to meet these vulnerable, marginalized young people is RG60, a shelter and dwelling place for young homeless between 18 and 30 years of age, established in 2010, and located in the area of outer Nørrebro in Copenhagen.

To enter RG60, you must ring the bell and wait for one of the social workers to open the massive black door. A camera is placed above the door in a small gate. From the gate, behind a fence, you get a glimpse of the yard. RG60 is both a shelter and a social service offering accommodation for up to six months, sometimes longer. All residents can use the large living room, and unlike most shelters for homeless people in Copenhagen, the living room may be used 24 hours a day. When entering RG60, you immediately step into the front part of the living room. Here, you find table tennis, table football, two or three locked-in computers, and a small room for video games. The other part of the living room contains sofas, a TV, and a long table used for meals and house meetings. The walls are covered with paintings made by the residents, from dreamy blue flowers to graffiti-like patterns. Usually, the living room is not used until around 1 p.m. or later, when the residents either return to the house after having done errands or get out of bed. The vast majority of residents have no jobs or education.

RG60 was a relevant and compatible partner for many reasons: their focus on the growing number of young homeless people in Denmark; their guidelines, which give residents the possibility of staying, not only at night, but during the day, for periods of up to six months and sometimes longer; their allocation of funds to offer young homeless a place to stay and an action plan with contact to caseworkers but no regular in-house pedagogical activities. Finally, my project matched the founding principles of RG60: participation and self-government.

My initial meetings with the staff and the director were characterized by positive responses. It turned out that RG60 fairly often receives requests from institutions that wish to work with them. Most often these invitations are turned down, since they rarely point towards actually engaging and supporting the residents. Encouraged by this opening, I visited RG60 a couple of times to hang out and get a sense of the place and talk with the residents. Few of them showed any interest: typical responses ranged from "Who are you, don't you think we can write?" to "I do not like writing at all." Despite this apparent reluctance from the residents, I decided, with the director's approval, to explore what would happen if a workshop was actually set up. This decision was in part inspired by Flower's work with urban high school students with learning disabilities: "For them, rhetoric is an embodied act that opens them to being co-opted by the discourse of disability in which they become the object of its rhetoric, not a rhetorical agent" ("Going Public" 138). Of course, I could not presuppose that all residents had learning disabilities; some had, I knew. I did not meet the residents with questions about their baggage, but instead with an invitation to write. I wanted to get a chance to show the residents that this project sought to build upon and strengthen what people actually can do instead of what they cannot do, and to work with a rhetorical approach to reading and writing, that is a holistic, functional and purposeful approach, foregrounding meaning-making instead of teaching fragmented skills (Flower, "Going Public" 140).

Our plan ended up looking like this: nine writing workshops were to be offered in February 2011 at the long table in the living room each Monday and Wednesday, from 1 p.m. to 3 p.m. At the end, and upon request, we prolonged the workshop series with four additional sessions, of which no one came to the last two. Each workshop was setup to be based upon student-driven imitation and include related kick-about exercises of various kinds, dialogue, and response. Participation in the workshop series was not binding. The residents could drop in halfway through the workshop series, or in the middle of one workshop, and attend one or all workshops. At a subsequent house meeting, I presented the workshop. It was entitled *Strong words*.

The project was designed in an action oriented research manner, that is, grounded in dialogue, concrete action, and reflective practice, allowing all participants room for intervention in order to shape content, goals, and process (Lewin 38; Huang 99; Rönnerman 19), much in line with the pedagogy of Freire. As is significant for action research, the project was aimed at exploring and developing a new experience and a possible new practice for all participants: residents, staff, and myself as a writing educator with a special interest in the concept of student-driven imitation.

The material for this investigation is my logbook and workshop plan. Having my logbook as a source for the study gives the account an autoethnographic touch. I will present glimpses of the world of RG60 and the workshop series in order to tell, not the whole story, but an integrated and balanced one.

Initial Experience: The Blend of Public/Private and a Glimpse of the Third Place

On Tuesday nights, RG60 have their house meetings. Sometimes they last ten minutes, sometimes thirty. Updates are given. Disputes discussed. Afterwards they clean the house for about fifteen minutes. On such a house meeting, two weeks before the first session of the workshop series, I presented the workshop. The staff did not indicate that residents could sit still for very long, so my presentation had to be brief and engaging. With me I had a poster for the workshop series, a visualization of the concept of student-driven imitation, and pens, and post-it pads. Inspired by Andre Breton's surreal parlor game, my plan was to get them to write just one half-sentence each. Every other person is supposed to write an if-phrase, while the other half writes a so-phrase. Afterwards, the phrases are read aloud and combined into a sentence by the person sitting next in line. I wanted to explore if they would walk away from the task, as I had been warned, or actually write, and, if so, whether they would groan or feel excited. As is the case of student-driven imitation, Andre Breton's surreal parlor game is about connecting words and writers in a free manner. The surreal parlor game especially highlights chance and attentive listening, and often evokes unexpected creation of meaning and joy.

Eleven residents participated in the house meeting: Four girls, seven boys. Some smelled of alcohol. On the table was stale cake from the local bakery. "Please, have some cake," they said. Five minutes later, the floor was mine. With the poster in my hand, I presented the workshop series. "None of us escapes language," I said, "the language of others, the language of ourselves, therefore we should approach language with a conscious attitude and train our awareness and skills as readers and writers." I stressed that the workshop would combine reading and writing attuned to their interests and needs, from job applications to poetry. They seemed to listen. I was surprised by their attention. Then, one said, "Don't you have a poem with you?" In my bag I had a short poem by the Danish poet Lars Skinnebach, desperate and philosophical.

"Read it again," they say. Some of them want to see it. We talk about it, its meaning and words. Who is egocentric? A girl, F, wants to keep it. Shortly after, I present the visualization of student-driven imitation. Their attention, I feel, is more polite. Then, I hand out post-it pads and pens. Some look skeptical. Then they write. No one leaves the table. I am thrilled to see them all putting pen to paper. Then we combine their phrases. They listen to each other. Applaud. Laugh. They seem excited to read their own phrase aloud. One boy, B, has written several sentences, full of rhythm and rhyme. He is eager to read it aloud. It is beautiful and philosophical. Everyone seems surprised.

While they cleaned the house, I put up posters for the workshop. Quite a few spoke to me, stressing that writing is important, that Danish grammar is a struggle. They would like to work with songwriting and poetry, they told me. One wanted to work with job applications.

Between the house meeting and the first workshop session, I visit RG60. The residents are talkative. Two of them are painting. One comes by with a plate full of scrambled eggs. "Do you want any?" he says before he sits down and grabs the daily newspaper. The conversation turns from the other day's documentary on Egypt to personal stories about having no contact with relatives. When I unlock my bike outside the house, three of them are smoking a joint the size of my thumb. "See you Wednesday," they say, and look as if we have an appointment.

So, did they sit and wait for me, ready with pen and paper, five minutes to one on the day of the first workshop? Of course not. I did not expect them to, either. Three residents were in the living room; one is sitting at one of the two computers in the house, the other two, V and S, are watching a film with Charles Bronson. None of them wants to participate. Their turning away is polite and firm. After a while, they leave the room for a smoke. There I am, sitting in the sofa, wondering what to do. I look at the clock on the wall. It is 13.30.

Then, through the windows I get a glimpse of F. She is in the office talking to one of the social workers. Maybe she would like to participate? I will have to wait to find out. Energized by this, I move to the kitchen, just to have a look. There is K. He wants to participate. Meanwhile, S has turned up in the kitchen. He tells me about his experiences with school: about always behaving well, but not being able to concentrate. He does not know his age. He would like to sit with us and listen. We place ourselves at the long, worn wooden table in the living room. F is there now. She does not know whether she wants to participate or not, but she will sit with us and eat her lunch, rye bread with liver paste. It is two o'clock in the afternoon now. There are a handful of residents in the living room watching television. They do not want to participate, but they are paying attention to what is happening at our table. I have the feeling that they are paying attention even with the back of their heads.

K, S and F want to know where I am from. I tell them about my project, about rhetoric, its educational tradition. K wants to improve his song writing. He already has several drafts on his computer. He agrees to bring them to the next workshop. F wants to work with poetry. She admires the beautiful sadness of Tove Ditlevsen's poetry and the snug humor of Benny Andersen's. F makes us a cup of tea. Then, she goes to her room and returns with four notebooks. Somewhere in one of them, there is a poem that she would like to show me. It is a poem she has written some years ago. It is about a burning candle. A young man appears. He wants homework. All of us agree to bring a text with us to the next workshop. K a song. F a poem. I will bring both. The guy that wanted homework has walked away. F and I are shaking hands. She is looking forward to choosing a poem, but she is not sure if she can come to the next workshop because of the Super

Bowl. I will be here, I say. Hm. Are we on a roll now? And if so, how and where to?

These initial experiences show that the residents do have an interest in writing, an interest that does not seem apparent when they are asked point blank about writing, but which appears when they have writing presented to them. The house meeting as well as the first workshop session indicate that this interest in writing is fragile, easily ignited and just as easily forgotten or rejected.

Also, these initial experiences underscore the fact that a shelter is a mix of the private (a living room with remarks such as "have some cake") and the public (an institution with staff and rules), zones that the Western tradition commonly has understood as spatially distinct (Warner 26). The concept of student-driven imitation is a blend too, mixing and bridging private and public: the starting point of student-driven imitation is the fascination of the individual, but the texts are public, circulated and open to everyone. Likewise, the concept calls for personal reflection as well as interaction outside the home - see Warner's list (29). Certainly, it is not unique that private and public are intertwined: "Public and private are not always simple enough that one could code them on a map with different colors – pink for private and blue for public. The terms also describe social contexts, kinds of feelings, and genres of language" (Warner 27). Thus, they are merely hosts of norms and contexts that intersect, evolve and differ in culture and time, and are regularly challenged: in Western politics, for instance, by former counter publics such as women's and gay movements (Warner 51), in theory by such as Hauser's concept of vernacular rhetoric. Maybe we even have social contexts and genres of language where private and public not only blend, but actually merge. Such social contexts could be Oldenburg's third place. For Oldenburg, though, the third place is an open physical space: the pub, the street. But if, as Warner proposes, we instead link public and private not to space, but to social contexts, types of feelings, and genres of language, then I propose that private and public merge in the third place, and that an example of such a textual genre could be poetry, the residents' preferred genre, characterized by third-place traits such as an open neutral ground for dialogue, low attention to social status, playful moods, and a homely feel.

Poetic as in Poetry: Confidence, Dual attention, and Public Discourses

On a roll was certainly not the right expression. Particularly at the beginning of the first couple of workshop sessions, I started out with a tour around the house asking if anyone wanted to join the workshop. The number of participants fluctuated between one and five. Three participants became regulars: the girl F, and two guys, B and V. F, age 26, was a high school graduate with two years of additional education. B, age 20, had dropped out of high school more than once. V, age 22, had never entered high school. He had quite successful work experience as a telephone salesman. They represented three levels of literacy: F was a relatively skilled writer, accurate and with a talent for rhythm and suspense. V was untrained and unaccustomed to writing, but possessed basic formal writing skills. B, on the other hand, had problems with basic formal writing skills such as spelling and coherent sentence structure, but he had a copious vocabulary and was eager to communicate in general, and also in writing.

Increasingly, other residents would come by, sit down and listen, join the conversation, talk about reading and writing, education and politics, sometimes about family life and experiences at institutions. When asked directly about what kind of texts they would like to work with, the answer was poetry.

Poetry, as opposed to the telling of one's story, provides a neutral ground, with low attention to social status, where private and public merge. The writing space of poetry is both personal and universal: it is a genre that strongly stresses the individual temper and at the same time, with its implied fictional distance acquires a universal character. In this free writing space, inquiry and expression can unfold while escaping some of the demands of fiction and persuasive writing in terms of length, coherence, conventions, and grammar. Poetry per se is a right to shape your own language.

As inherent in the concept of student-driven imitation, the residents were themselves supposed to bring texts to the workshop, based on their fascination as readers and reflection as writers. This happened only once, when F brought a poem by a former fellow student at a boarding school, about a little girl in a children's home.

At the end of the third workshop, we agreed that for the next workshop I would bring ten different poems. I chose poems that differed in terms of theme and form. All of them were fairly short, one page, and written between 1920 and 2009 by Danish poets.

On the long table are ten poems. In turn, we, that is, B, F and I, pick a poem and read it aloud. We respond spontaneously to each poem. Meanwhile, V shows up. He wants to see what we are doing. "But I am not going to read it aloud," he says. The others pick a poem again and read aloud. Afterwards V, too, reads a poem aloud. They read aloud with care and concentration, shaping words in their mouth, some of which they are not familiar. They listen to each other and easily grasp and describe the emotions at stake in the poems – from Leth's poem about controlling the body, competition, and performance, to Hammann's poem about the trivial acts of a well-behaved person, foreshadowing not only frustration but an animal underneath.

After having read all ten poems aloud, they each pick a poem for student-driven imitation. We are going to work with the following dimensions of student-driven imitation: fascination, qualities worth imitating, and interaction. F sticks to the poem that celebrates love; V picks a surreal poem; and B picks the poem about the trivial acts of a well-behaved person. With a green marker they now underscore ideas, subjects, lines, and words that fascinate them. All words are shared and unfolded – from the idea of the lover as a surveyor and the word "life doubler" (F) to lines such as "do I fall out of society and into a dream" and "The stars are psychotic children" (V). Then, with a blue marker, they underscore ideas, subjects, lines, and words that they find worthy of imitation. Overlaps appear. Newfound aspects are valued. The findings are shared and unfolded. Subsequently, they start writing their own poem, inspired by the poem that they have worked with, and by their findings. I stress that they can do whatever they feel like: quote, twist, mock, choose to reuse the theme or just a word.

After a while, they read their poems aloud. V has interacted with the surreal poem in a *mimetic* way, reusing the theme and style in a loyal manner, even quoting a few lines, but adding rhyme at the beginning of the poem. F has interacted with the homage to a beloved person in an *inspirational* but independent manner, reusing the theme, skipping the surveyor metaphor, using a more straightforward style, adding rhyme throughout the poem, reusing the word "life-doubler" at the end as in the source text. B, on the other hand, has interacted with the poem about civilized behavior in an *antagonistic* manner, twisting the theme by underscoring the idea that comparing human to human is far more important than comparing humans to animals. B's poem goes even further and ends with a reflection on how the responsibility of man constantly increases.

These imitation strategies illustrate that the residents easily interacted with their poems in a free self-governed manner. They each independently found and shaped a strategy of imitation suitable for their individual temper and intention and expressed joy over their processes and results. They did not need a presentation of already listed strategies, as for instance *following, transformation, eristic*, all taken from literary imitation practice in the Renaissance (Bender 345). Immanent in the literary imitation strategies of the renaissance is the source text. This is the case too with the restricted imitation exercises in rhetorical education: memorization, translation, and paraphrase (Corbett 246; Sullivan 13; Terrill 305). The restricted imitation exercises may train both comprehension and sentence structure (rhetorical skills), but they allow little room for the individual temper, situation, and intention (rhetorical capacity). On the other hand, I argue that the fourth typical imitation exercise in rhetorical education, close analysis (Corbett 245; Sullivan 13) holds the potential to train both skills and capacity, at least if the source text is used in writing as a means of invention in relation to individual temper, situation, and intention. Here, mirroring is not an end in itself, inspiration is.

In line with Quintilian's notion of imitation and the concept of student-driven imitation, the crucial starting point is pedagogical, and the aim is inspiration. Thus, the outcome in relation to the source text can be more or less mimetic, more or less atomized, even to a degree where it is hard to trace the source text. Hence, an endless variety of imitation strategies can materialize.

As illustrated in the varied imitation strategies of the residents, the process of interaction came easily, naturally, and with unpredictable and diverse results, both in terms of invention and style. These strategies are far from pattern practice, even though pattern was studied. The strategies may overlap, as is the case for instance with the antagonistic and inspirational strategy. An outline of a typology is not within my scope here; instead, I would like to highlight fluctuation and hybrids as premises for student-driven imitation – as is the case with traditions of imitation generally (Muckelbauer 66; Warnick 128).

So, what value does poetry hold in relation to student-driven imitation, besides sharing and underscoring a need for a right to one's own language and a space that is both private and public, in which one can act independently, with confidence, and a sense of agency? I think two aspects are worth highlighting, 1) the dual attention and dialogic interaction of imitation in itself as valuable, and 2) the literary genre's potential to reflect, explore, and play with multiple public discourses, as delineated by Bakhtin (292).

Concerning the first, in all text-based imitation a dual attention of the student to both a public text and to herself and her own writing is fostered, thereby anticipating a democratic stance: "*Imitatio*, as a tenet of rhetorical pedagogy, is as central to the tradition as two-sided debate and strategic effacement, but less often noted as valuable for the crafting of democratic citizens" (Terrill 300). What Terrill highlights is the stance and movement of duality in imitation, not a specific discourse. Hence, the process of imitation in general is valuable, regardless of the choice of discourse, poetic or political, from the past or from the present. Especially, I argue, unrestricted imitation strategies, as opposed to the restricted strategies Terrill highlights, promote a dual attention with a rhetorical approach, in contrast to a technical.

Concerning the second, the literary genre's potential to reflect, explore, and play with multiple public discourses. I stress that poetry and fiction should not be set aside in relation to public discourses. Literary language can "unite in itself parodic stylizations of generic languages, various forms of stylizations and illustrations of professional and period-bound languages, the languages of particular generations, of social dialects and others" (Bakhtin 292). Only a few of the ten poems in our workshop happened to have such polyphonic traits of recurrent public discourses, but focusing to a higher degree on such poems could be worth exploring.

Poetic as in Imagination and Deep Feeling: Dialogue, Discovery, and Trust

Despite the fact that all three residents, B, F, and V, ended this session of student-driven imitation by selecting two poems each for future work with books by the poet whose poem they had interacted with, this kind of thorough work with student-driven imitation did not happen again. I naively envisioned us moving up a level towards some kind of mastery as if we had our feet on a ladder. I envisioned posters with their poems in the living room. A reception. But our feet were on slippery stones at the sea. And what I had not envisioned was anger.

At the following workshop, B and F participated. B's body was boiling. Legs pumping against the floor. He delivered a long, seemingly unstoppable monologue of frustration: over people in power, relativism in general as opposed to one religious truth, the written word as sacred, and untouchable, the workshop, the assumption that rhetoric could make a difference, democracy. I naturally wanted him to turn his words into writing. That would also force him to slow down and focus, as well as explore his ideas. B, being especially frustrated with the lack of justice in a democracy, became highly upset when I suggested he should write about it: "Do you want the Secret Service to come after me? I don't want to put anything on this subject to paper. Are you crazy?"

Generally, the workshop sessions at RG60 were unpredictable on every level. I did my best to adjust to the current situation and the residents' reactions and requests, from anger to a wish at the end for prolonging the workshop series. Repeating the moves from the fourth workshop did not appeal to them. Instead, I came up with exercises that supported the literate practice of student-driven imitation stressing self-governance and especially dialogue. Alongside this, F pursued through the workshop series her newly found interest in haiku poems, while V worked with descriptions of his hours at job activation. In both cases, I assisted with text examples and feedback. Below, I will describe three exercises that in different ways support the literate practice of student-driven imitation:

Connect to a Sentence You Come Across: 'You and Publics Around You'

Since I wanted to know more about their attention to whatever publics, and I wanted them to pay attention to words and texts around them as both readers and writers, I asked them to find sentences that somehow appealed to them or set their mind in motion and, in a free manner, use the sentences as starting points for their own writing. Between Wednesday and Monday, they were asked to find four sentences, write each sentence at the top of a paper, including its source, and then write their own text below. B did not choose sentences, but words: power, justice, love, and his interaction led to some well-written aphorisms. I was allowed to read but not to comment on his writing. F had found sentences in mainstream online newspapers, silly headlines that annoyed her, and her interaction lead to chatty elaborations of the silliness, as if she were talking directly to the media behind. This exercise supports the principle of self-governance in student-driven imitation as well as the dimensions of both fascination and interaction.

Collaborative Story Writing: 'You and I and Our Imagination'

In the middle of one of B's outburst of anger, for some reason—out of the blue, actually—I suggested we write a story together. He accepted this invitation. He wrote one passage; I wrote the next. A story of a wounded soldier took shape. This dialogic way of writing forced both of us to read, understand, and connect with the writing done by the other. In this manner, I found a pathway to comment on his writing, whenever I had a good reason, with regard to problems with grasping the meaning, typically because of missing words or misspellings. This exercise highly supports receptiveness to the words of another, a basic premise of student-driven imitation, as well as the dimension of interaction, stressing especially coherence and surprise.

Chreia: 'You and Your Expansion of Famous Quotes'

With the ambition to engage more residents and examine their reaction to a more directive set of rules, I introduced the classic progymnasmata-exercise chreia (Kennedy). I brought in quotes by Disney, Woolf, and Cohen, amongst others. In this session five residents participated, selecting their favorite quote, struggling with the elements in the chreia, from praise and paraphrase to example and testimony, all of them expressing both frustration as well as excitement over working with a strict form. The chreia was compared to a puzzle, releasing a feeling of fulfillment when every bit ended up fitting together. As in the case of student-driven imitation, the chreia cultivates the creation of meaning, investigation, and receptiveness in relation to the words of another, while at the same time cultivating the ability to connect to and develop the words of oneself. In addition, the chreia supports a systematic, thorough approach also available in student-driven imitation.

These dialogic exercises were accompanied with various emerging conversations on reading (Wikipedia, Harry Potter) and writing (in school, on facebook), education and institutions (turnover of teachers), democracy and justice, religion and family. Some days other residents would join us at the table, typically curious about our conversation and what we were doing. Sometimes, not mechanically, I suggested questions and feelings to be explored in writing, from journal writing to persuasive writing. I also suggested that we make posters with their poems. Only F was tempted by this idea.

These points of impact show that a group of the residents recurrently engaged in the writing workshop series in a curious and conscientious manner. Also, these points of impact signal that the workshop on some level ignited not only engagement in reading and writing, but also a wish to create, commit to, and nurture a dialogue comparable to Oldenburg's third place, the recurrent voluntary participation, the low attention to status, and the homely feel. This was reflected not only in their writing, but also in acts such as sitting still for two hours, often without a break or a smoke, making coffee, bringing biscuits, shaking hands at the end of a session, sending apologies in advance if they were unable to show up, and in the topics and nature of our conversations. Even the outbursts of anger can be seen as a wish to communicate and a sign of confidence, trust, and curiosity: "How can I dialogue if I am afraid of being displaced, the mere possibility causing me torment and weakness?" (Freire 71). These third-place traits may have been sparked or supported by the self-governed and dialogic approach of the workshop. Nevertheless, they are not an inherent consequence: the residents could have preferred to work individually with job applications and with a minimum of dialogue with regard to other matters. I came with the aim to examine whether, and to which degree, student-driven imitation could engage marginalized learners. I did not enter RG60 to manifest rules, but to come to know and match individuals and subject matter so that as many as possible could contribute (Dewey, "Experience" 56). Freire emphasizes:

> do not go to the people in order to bring them a message of "salvation", but in order to come to know through dialogue with them both their *objective situation* and their *awareness* of that situation …. One cannot expect positive results from an educational or political action program which fails to respect the particular view of the world held by the people. Such a program constitutes cultural invasion, good intentions notwithstanding. (76)

In regard to student-driven imitation, it is clear, though, that some kind of scaffolding and revised approach is needed. The residents did not bring in texts, and they apparently did not wish to repeat moves that they had already tried out. Various related dialogic exercises that supported the literate practice of student-driven imitation, on the other hand, were welcomed, including exercises that drew on their attention to publics, and exercises that trained a systematic, thorough approach to connecting reading to writing.

Student-Driven Imitation and the Third Place as Potentially Trans-formative

Student-driven imitation draws on and combines reading and writing in community engagement. The project at RG60 based upon student-driven imitation sought a Freirean dialogue where students hold power as individual readers and writers, but neither the project nor the concept holds a collaborative problem-posing agenda, as Freire promotes (Freire 60), and as we find today in community literacy think tanks (Flower, "Public Engagement" 65). Similar to the street theater projects with homeless people facilitated by Paula Mathieu (73), student-driven imitation has a strong focus on individual expression, but then no immanent public performative dimension. Instead, the project and the concept tried to highlight entering into publics via reading, not via publishing or performance. So, relevant metaphors to describe the project are a *cultural womb,* and partly a *gate*, establishing a dialogue between people, institutions and discourses who might not otherwise meet.

The metaphor of a cultural womb implies characteristics such as nurturing, preparing, and inspiring, and the metaphor of a gate implies creating access, connections, as well as room for conflicts to unfold (Long 23). The two metaphors describe the nature and function of the third place well. This space surely has its limits. It is not the ideal public as described by Dewey: a public aroused, as a reaction to and in contrast with specific government decisions, in order to change a policy or for mutual defense (Dewey, "The Public" 27–28). Dewey described this as an ideal, aware that the complexity of modern society, especially the character of mass communication and multiple publics, is a strong constraint (126). Therefore, Dewey strongly underscores communication, the give and take of language in public and across publics in the everyday, as the ground on which a community is built and from where a public can arise (154). The third place has similar potential, but whereas communication is a practice between people everywhere, the third place is a specific space, open, neutral, and characterized by recurrent voluntary participation in dialogue and low attention to status.

The writing workshop series at RG60 based upon student-driven imitation provides insight in relation to both marginalized young people as readers and writers and the literate practice of student-driven imitation. The writing workshop series signal that young marginalized people can and wish to engage in reading and writing, including writers with a low level of formal skills as well as more experienced writers. The writing workshop series indicate that poetry can be a preferred genre for marginalized young people: a free writing space of open neutral ground, with low attention to social status; a textual third place, in which they can act independently and with confidence. Specifically in relation to student-driven imitation, the writing workshop series at RG60 discloses that this literate practice has the potential to engage and include writers of various kinds, also those on the margins. The experience reveals that this literate practice is easy to work with independently with confidence.

In addition, the writing workshop series at RG60 indicates some challenges in working with literate practice of student-driven imitation and marginalized young people: a need to provide the participants with selections of texts, a crucial need to vary exercises instead of aiming at repeating all or a selection of the dimensions, and finally, I suggest, a need for strengthening reflection and progress. With regard to variation, working more exclusively with each dimension of student-driven imitation could provide not only variation, but also a deeper understanding of each dimension, including aspects such as subject shaping, reader relation and writer's presence. Related, dialogic reading and writing exercises can also be used to support the literate practice of student-driven imitation, from Andre Breton's surreal parlor game to the classic *chreia*. Finally, I anticipate that working with journal writing could strengthen and unfold the participants' reflection in relation to central questions, such as "what fascinates me as a reader?" and "what would I like to learn?". Thus, journal writing could help explicate and maintain purposes and goals, and potentially make progress more evident.

These are the results of working with student-driven imitation in a shelter with the aim to engage young homeless people in reading and writing. This open-ended approach is one way of working with student-driven imitation. Another way is working with student-driven imitation in relation to one specific discourse or genre, which partly compromises the concept's essential property of self-governance, but opens up several scenarios, from using student-driven imitation in traditional education, in projects aimed at collaborative problem-posing in public, e.g. news paper production, to using student-driven imitation in projects aimed at reaching personal goals, e.g., job applications or dispensations, which are projects of change within reach (Cushman 13).

The residents at RG60 engaged in student-driven imitation in an open-ended manner and formed a space and dialogue around reading and writing with traits of a third place, marked by the residents' preferred genre, poetry. Oldenburg describes the third place as a place situated between home and work. Paradoxically, the residents have no home and no work. Thus, a third place may be far from what a homeless person really needs. Or maybe it is closer to it than we might think.

Works Cited

Alberti, John. "Teaching of Writing and Diversity: Access, Identity, and Achievement." *Handbook of Research on Writing*. Ed. Charles Bazerman. New York: Lawrence Erlbaum, 2008. 387–397. Print.

Asen, Robert. "A Discourse Theory of Citizenship." *Quarterly Journal of Speech* 90 (2004): 189–211. Print.

Bakhtin, Mikhail M. *The Dialogic Imagination. Four Essays*. Austin: University of Texas Press, 1981. Print.

Bender, Daniel. "Imitation." *Encyclopedia of Rhetoric and Composition. Communication from Ancient Times to the Information Age*. 1st. ed. Ed. Theresa Enos. New York: Garland, 1996. Print.

Brandt, Deborah. "Afterword. The Real and Fake Economics of Writing." *jac* 32 (2012): 769–778. Print.

Cintron, Ralph. *Angel's Town: Chero Ways, Gang Life and Rhetorics of the Everyday*. Beacon Press, 1998. Print.

———. "The Timidities of Ethnography. A Response to Bruce Horner." *jac* 22 (2002): 934–943. Print.

——. "Wearing a Pith Helmet at a Sly Angle: Or, Can Writing Researchers Do Ethnography in a Postmodern Era?" *Written Communication* 10 (1993): 371–412. Print.

Corbett, Edward P. J. "The Theory and Practice of Imitation in Classical Rhetoric." *College Composition and Communication* 22 (1971): 243–250. Print.

Cushman, Ellen. "The Rhetorician as an Agent of Social Change." *College Composition and Communication* 47 (1996): 7–28. Print.

D'Angelo, Frank J. "Imitation and Style." *College Composition and Communication* 24 (1973): 283–290. Print.

Dewey, John. *Democracy and Education, an Introduction to the Philosophy of Education*. New York: The Free Press, 1966. Print.

——. *Experience and Education*. New York: Touchstone, 1997. Print.

——. *The Public and Its Problems*. Original Publication. Athens: Swallow Press/Ohio University Press, 1927. Print.

Fish, Stanley. *How to Write a Sentence, and How to Read One*. New York: Harper, 2011. Print.

Flower, Linda. *Community Literacy and the Rhetoric of Public Engagement*. Carbondale: Southern Illinois University Press, 2008. Print.

——. "Going Public - in a Disabling Discourse." *The Public Work of Rhetoric: Citizen-Scholars and Civic Engagement*. Ed. John M. Ackerman & David J. Coogan. The University of South Carolina Press, 2010. 137–156. Print.

Freire, Paulo. *Pedagogy of the Oppressed*. Trans. Myra Bergman Ramos. London: Penguin Books, 1996. Print.

Geisler, Cheryl. "How Ought We to Understand the Concept of Rhetorical Agency?" *Rhetoric Society Quaterly* 34 (2004): 9–17. Print.

Glenn, Cheryl, Melissa A. Goldthwaite, and Robert Connors. *The St. Martin's Guide to Teaching Writing*. 5th. ed. Boston: Bedford, 2003. Print.

Hauser, Gerard. *Vernacular Voices, the Rhetoric of Publics and Public Spheres*. Columbia, University of South Carolina Press, 1999. Print.

Hoff-Clausen, Elisabeth, Christine Isager, and Lisa S. Villadsen. "Retorisk agency. Hvad skaber retorikken? [Rhetorical Agency: What Makes Rhetoric?/What Does Rhetoric Make?]." *Rhetorica Scandinavica* 33 (2005): 56–65. Print.

Huang, Hilary Bradbury. "What Is Good Action Research?" *Action Research* 8 (2010): 93–109. Print.

Kennedy, George. *Progymnasmata: Greek Textbooks of Prose, Composition, and Rhetoric*. Atlanta: Society of Biblical Literature, 2003. Print.

Lewin, Kurt. "Action Research and Minority Problems." *Journal of Social Issues* 2 (1946): 34–46. Print.

Long, Elenore. *Community Literacy and the Rhetoric of Local Publics*. West Lafayette, Indiana: Parlor Press LLC, 2008. Print.

Mathieu, Paula. *Tactics of Hope: the Public Turn in English Composition.* Portsmouth: Boynton/Cook Publishers, 2005. Print.

Matthiesen, Christina. "Elevstyret imitatio: En retorisk skrivepædagogik i teori og praksis [Student-driven imitation: A Rhetorical Writing Pedagogy in Theory and Practice]." Diss. University of Copenhagen, Copenhagen. 2013. Print.

Muckelbauer, John. "Imitation and Invention in Antiquity: A Historical-Theoretical Revision." *Rhetorica: A Journal of the History of Rhetoric* 21 (2003): 61–88. Print.

Nelson, Nancy. "The Reading-Writing Nexux in Discourse Research." *Handbook of Research on Writing.* Ed. Charles Bazerman. New York: Lawrance Erlbaum, 2008. Print.

Oldenburg, Ray. *The Great Good Place.* 2nd. edition. New York: Marlowe, 1999. Print.

Peck, Wayne Campbell, Linda Flower, and Lorraine Higgins. "Community Literacy." *Collge Composition and Communication* 46 (1995): 199–222. Print.

Quintilian. *Institutio Oratoria.* Trans. H.E. Butler. London: Harvard University Press, 1998. Print.

Rönnerman, Karin. "Action Research: Educational Tools and the Improvement of Practice." *Educational Action Research* 11 (2003): 9–21. Print.

Salvatori, Mariolina. "Reading and Writing a Text: Correlations Between Reading and Writing Patterns." *College English* 45 (1983): 657–666. Print.

Sullivan, Dale. "Attitudes Toward Imitation: Classical Culture and the Modern Temper." *Rhetoric Review* 8 (1989): 5–21. Print.

Terrill, Robert. "Mimesis, Duality, and Rhetorical Education." *Rhetoric Society Quarterly* 41 (2011): 295–315. Print.

Warner, Michael. *Publics and Counterpublics.* New York: Zone Books, 2005. Print.

———. "Publics and Counterpublics (abbreviated version)." *Quarterly Journal of Speech* 88 (2002): 413–425. Print.

Warnick, Bryan R. *Imitation and Education: A Philosophical Inquiry into Learning by Example.* Albany: State University of New York Press, 2008. Print. SUNY Series, The Philosophy of Education.

Author Bio

Christina Matthiesen is an assistant professor at Aarhus University, Department of Education, in Denmark. She holds a MA and PhD in rhetoric from the University of Copenhagen, where she taught writing and theories of rhetoric and composition pedagogy from 2002-2012. In her dissertation from 2013 she introduces and investigates the concept and literate practice of student-driven imitation, reinvigorating Quintilian's progressive notion of imitation. She would like to give her thanks to Linda Flower for her invaluable assistance in the development of this essay.

COMPOSITION FORUM

Composition Forum is a peer-reviewed journal for scholars and teachers interested in the investigation of composition theory and its relation to the teaching of writing at the post-secondary level. The journal features articles that explore the intersections of composition theory and pedagogy, including essays that examine specific pedagogical theories or that examine how theory could or should inform classroom practices, methodology, and research into multiple literacies. *Composition Forum* also publishes articles that describe specific and innovative writing program practices and writing courses, reviews of relevant books in composition studies, and interviews with notable scholars and teachers who can address issues germane to our theoretical approach.

Composition Forum is on the Web at http://compositionforum.com/

Multimodality, Translingualism, and Rhetorical Genre Studies

Laura Gonzales argues that the translingual practices of L2 students can bridge connections and help develop pedagogical applications of multimodality and RGS, primarily by helping writing instructors teach genres as fluid and socially situated. In addition, Gonzales presents a methodology for analyzing the embodied practices of composition students, which can further expand how genres are theorized and taught in composition courses.

5 Multimodality, Translingualism, and Rhetorical Genre Studies

Laura Gonzales

Abstract: *This article situates one possible future for rhetorical genre studies in the translingual, multimodal composing practices of linguistically diverse composition students. Using focus group data collected with L1 and L2 students at two large public state universities, the researcher examines connections between students' linguistic repertoires and their respective approaches to multimodal composition. Students at both universities took composition courses that incorporate rhetorical genre studies approaches to teaching writing in conventional print and multimodal forms. Findings suggest L2 students exhibit advanced expertise and rhetorical sensitivity when layering meaning through multimodal composition. This expertise comes in part from L2 students' experiences combining and crossing various modes when they cannot rely on words alone to communicate in English. Through this evidence, the researcher argues the translingual practices of L2 students can bridge connections and help develop pedagogical applications of multimodality and RGS, primarily by helping writing instructors teach genres as fluid and socially situated. In addition, the researcher presents a methodology for analyzing the embodied practices of composition students, which can further expand how genres are theorized and taught in composition courses.*

Introduction

In their presentation at the 2014 *Conference on College Composition and Communication*, "Rethinking Difference in Composing Composition:

Language, Translation, Genre, Modality," Min-Zhan Lu, Anis Bawarshi, Nancy Bou Ayash, Juan Guerra, Bruce Horner, and Cynthia Selfe situated the future of writing instruction in translingual, multimodal practices and pedagogies. Bringing together key scholars in translingualism, multimodal composition, and North American Rhetorical Genre Studies (RGS), this panel highlighted the importance of pushing beyond what Selfe described as the "single language/single modality perspective" in writing instruction[1].

The emergence of multimodality and translingualism, and the connections between these concepts, Selfe and Horner explain, reflect "the development and increasingly global reach and use of new communication technologies and networks" as well as "the increasing and increasingly undeniable, traffic among peoples and languages" (4). Rhetorical Genre Studies, by "direct[ing] our attention to the sociality of discourse," highlights the movement between languages and modes outlined in translingual and multimodal scholarship (Coe, Lingard, and Teslenko 2). By putting multimodal and translingual composition in conversation, this paper situates one possible future for RGS in the multimodal, translingual composing practices of contemporary composition students.

Rhetorical Genre Studies and Multimodality

Rhetorical Genre Studies, developed in part through Carolyn Miller's seminal work highlighted in this special issue of *Composition Forum*, expands previous conceptions of genre to "fuse text and context, product and process, cognition and culture in a single, dynamic concept" (Paré 57). As such, RGS "encourages us [and potentially our students] to consider the complex interconnections" between "the full social and symbolic action of textual practice" (Paré 57). Rather than focusing on restricted types of genres (e.g., "argument" or "persuasive" essays) with bounded (monolingual/monomodal) rules and conventions, RGS illustrates "one of the stronger and most promising developments for comprehending the sociality of discourse while allowing discursive freedom and agency to individuals" (Coe, Lingard, and Teslenko 2).

Building on the discursive freedom and situated practice promoted by RGS, some North American RGS scholars interested in multimo-

---

1. For a continued discussion of the "single language/single modality perspective" outlined in this panel, see Selfe and Horner 2013.

dality are encouraging composition instructors to use RGS as a way to help students conceptualize genres in less bounded, more socially-situated ways (Arola, Ball and Sheppard 2014; Hawisher et al. 2013; Selfe and Horner 2013; Shipka 2011). For example, Arola, Sheppard, and Ball's recent *Writer/Designer: A Guide to Making Multimodal Projects*, is explicitly grounded in Rhetorical Genre Studies, using RGS to help students select the appropriate modes to rhetorically compose arguments through multimodal projects. This approach, the authors explain, is founded on an understanding "that texts and genres constantly shift in form, content, and meaning based on historical, social, cultural and other ideological contexts" (3). Similarly, Jody Shipka emphasizes the imperative for writing instructors to teach multimodal genres rhetorically, in order to help students continue functioning as "rhetorically sensitive individuals" who "understand that an idea can be rendered in multi-form ways" geared to various audiences (Shipka, "Including," 78).

Together, these scholars argue that multimodal pedagogies grounded in RGS "provide students with a much broader toolkit from which to function as rhetors in the world," helping them reconceive genres not as static forms that only exist in educational settings, but as socially situated heuristics developed to meet the needs of particular communities at specific times (Arola, Ball, Sheppard 2013). The aim of both RGS and multimodal composition is to understand writing in context and to leverage their rhetorical impact when communicating with various audiences. The goal of multimodal composition curricula using RGS as a framework, in turn, is to help students understand writing as socially situated rather than as static, rule-bound phenomena.

Translingualism: A Bridge across Languages, Genres, and Modes

Similar to the less-bounded conceptions of genres promoted by multimodality, proponents of translingualism suggest "communication always involves a negotiation of mobile codes," including languages, media, gestures, and other semiotic resources (Canagarajah "Translingual" 8). The translingual turn in composition seeks to highlight "practice-based, adaptive, emergent, multimodal, multisensory, multilateral, and therefore multidimensional" aspects of writing, further situating genres within social contexts (Canagarajah,

"Lingua," 924). According to Lu and Horner, translingualism treats semiotic modes and cultural/linguistic histories "as always emergent, in process (a state of becoming), and their relations as mutually constitutive," rather than "treating these as discrete, preexisting, stable, and enumerable entities" (587). Thus, translingualism offers a way to connect the socially situated conceptions of genres promoted by RGS with the flexible, audience-centered approach to teaching writing adopted by multimodal scholars.

The "translingual approach" to writing and writing pedagogy described by Horner, Lu, Royster, and Trimbur addresses "how language norms are actually heterogeneous, fluid, and negotiable," hence "directly counter[ing] demands that writers must conform to fixed, uniform standards" (305). By unbinding genres from static forms and encouraging movement across languages and modes, translingualism has "attracted the attention of scholars and teachers in writing studies at all levels," while simultaneously resulting in many adaptations that "fail to define the concept or use it consistently" (Matsuda 479). For this reason, any study that claims to use translingualism as a framework must provide a particular definition to be used in context of the data presented.

For the purposes of this paper, I will be using translingualism as a framework to analyze the fluidity and negotiation of language in various modes. That is, translingualism (as it is used in this paper) provides a lens by which to examine (and value) "how writers deploy [and combine] diction, syntax, and style, as well as form, register, and media" (Horner, Lu, Royster, "Language," 304). Translingualism, as I will be using the term, does not define or represent students' linguistic backgrounds[2]. Rather, translingualism gives us a framework for

---

2. In this paper, I draw a distinction between students who speak and write in English as a first language (L1 students/writers) and students who speak and write in English as a second language (L2 students/writers). While I adopt translingualism as a theoretical frame due to its fluid, emerging definition of language, I also acknowledge and account for concerns raised by a group of L2 writing instructors who recently published "Clarifying the Relationship between L2 Writing and Translingual Writing: An Open Letter to Writing Studies Editors and Organization Leaders." In this letter, L2 writing instructors "call attention to a problematic trend developing among writing studies scholars based in North America: a growing misunderstanding that L2 writing and translingual writing are somehow competing with each other or, worse yet, that one is replacing the other" (Atkinson et al., 1). Translingual-

understanding the fluidity of modalities and languages, a framework that we can use (as I intend to do in this study) to further understand how our students draw on their linguistic experiences to make meaning through their composing practices.

The study presented in this paper provides one illustration of how RGS, with its multimodal and translingual implications, is already being enacted by contemporary composition students who are continuously "shuttling" between languages and modes to make meaning, leveraging rhetorical resources to meet communicative needs in increasingly diverse contexts (Canagarajah "Translingual"). By presenting data from a study that explores linguistically diverse composition students' perceptions of multimodal genres, I will suggest one possible future for RGS lies in the multimodal, translingual connections already being made in our classrooms by students who, to varying degrees "regularly confront the challenge of working across languages" (Lu and Horner 585). In the sections that follow, I will present an anecdote to illustrate how students leverage rhetorical resources to cross linguistic and modal boundaries. I will then elaborate on the connections between multimodality, translingualism, and RGS to further foreground how students, and in particular student who have faced and continue to face broad linguistic transitions, can help RGS continue pushing composition scholarship beyond a "single language/single mode" model.

---

ism as a theoretical frame breaks "false binaries" such as "monolingual versus multilingual" by suggesting that "negotiation and change are inevitable" in all language acts (Matsuda 480). However, as Atkinson et al. further clarify, the fact that all language acts are inherently translingual does not discount the broad linguistic transitions and histories of L2 writers who had to shift from speaking and writing primarily in one language (e.g., Chinese, Spanish) to speaking and writing primarily in a second language (e.g., English). For this reason, as described by Atkinson et al., L2 or "second language" writing still stands "as a technical term that refers to any language other than the first language" adopted by an individual (2). In this paper, I use the term "L2 writer/L2 student" to reference a student who learned English as a second language, and the term "L1 writer/L1 student" to reference a student who learned English as a first language. All students in this study speak English as either a first or second language (with none of them speaking a third or fourth language).

Enacting Multimodality, Translingualism, and RGS: Nathalia's Story

Recently, in my first-year composition (FYC) class, I assigned a short reading response that asked students to respond to the following prompt: "Drawing on Deborah Brandt's definition of literacy sponsors, please identify some of Malcolm X's literacy sponsors." As my students came up to the front of the room at the end of class to submit their responses, one student, Nathalia, looking mortified, claimed, "I did this wrong. Can I please turn this in tomorrow?" as she handed me the drawing depicted in Figure 1.

Figure 1: Nathalia's Reading Response

When asked to "draw on" something to explain something else, Nathalia literally drew her responses. Most students provided a written, conventional print[3] response that reflected their understanding of Brandt's concept to describe how Malcolm X learned to read through his various interactions with the people, places, and things that sponsored his literacy. However, Nathalia accurately, albeit unconventionally, explicitly drew some of Malcolm X's literacy sponsors as they are described in "Learning to Read," a chapter from his autobiography that I assigned in class.

---

3. In this paper, I use the term "conventional print" to describe what Bowen and Whithaus call "the structure of using words on a page to be read as a text" (5). Conventional print genres (as I use the concept in this paper) are genres limited to alphabetic, printed (non-digital) representation.

In my assignment prompt, I used the phrase "draw on" with the assumption that students would perceive I was asking them to write about Malcolm X using Brandt's framework. In some ways, my assignment prompt was situated in a single language/single mode ideology, as I assumed all students would interpret the word "drawing" through an English-based, academic lens, and that these students would then respond to my prompt through a conventional print mode. Though the rest of my students did so, Nathalia interpreted my directions differently. In her reading response, she illustrates (quite literally) that time, Bimbi, the dictionary, and jail served as Malcolm X's literacy sponsors, which she understood as "agents....who enable, support, teach, model, as well as recruit, regulate, suppress, or withhold literacy" (Brandt 166). Through his interactions with these sponsors, Nathalia illustrates, Malcolm X developed different literacies, including reading and writing.

Though not immediately evident, I realized Nathalia's reading response was not an anomalous error, but rather a reflection of her ability to utilize a variety of semiotic resources when attempting to communicate her ideas. Several months after she turned in this drawing, Nathalia told me she learned to speak English as a second language, one she learned after moving to the US from Colombia, where she spoke Spanish. By combining her interpretation of the word "drawing" with illustrations and words describing Malcolm X's literacy sponsors, Nathalia's reading response was an act of translanguaging, as she "adopt[ed] interpretative strategies," to combine words and visuals in her multimodal reading response (Canagarajah "Translingual" 4). Rather than beginning with a conventional understanding of the "reading response" genre (one that I may not have clearly described to my students), Nathalia began to develop her response by thinking beyond conventional print, monomodal genres. Cued by her interpretation of the word "draw," Nathalia conceptualized ways to present her answer through pictures, combining colors, words, and images. She didn't have a template or pre-established generic idea for what this drawing was supposed to look like, but she knew the ideas she wanted to convey and managed to illustrate these ideas through her pictures. It wasn't until Nathalia saw other reading responses that she became alarmed by the genre conventions assumed by her peers (and by me as her instructor).

Though this story represents a single example of a translingual/ transmodal writing act performed by an L2 writer, experiences like Nathalia's prompted me to continue paying attention to the ways students who have crossed broad linguistic boundaries display rhetorical dexterity when conveying their ideas through multimodal projects. This rhetorical dexterity, I argue, can be directly related to students' experiences moving between semiotic resources to convey their thoughts. As Lachman Mulchand Khubchandani suggests, when L2 writers "*cannot* rely on a shared language or grammatical norms, they align participants, contexts, objects, and diverse multimodal semiotic cues to generate meaning" (31). The process of generating cues to develop meaning is not unique to L2 students (Lu and Horner 2013). However, as my study will further demonstrate, students who have a history of broad linguistic transitions may be especially adept at generating cues across languages and modes based on their extensive experiences code-switching (both linguistically, culturally, and often times transnational) in order to adapt to "the whole new system" of writing in English-dominant American classrooms (Seloni 48). For this reason, my study suggests that as composition studies moves beyond a single language/ single modality approach to writing by combining RGS, multimodality, and translingualism, we might learn from the experiences and strategies of L2 students who are already crossing and combining languages and modes to convey meaning in their daily communication.

Method and Rationale

As a preliminary exploration of how linguistically diverse L2 students interact with multimodality and translingualism, two focus groups lasting 1.5 hours each were conducted to understand how students' approaches to and conceptions of writing shift when composing print and multimodal genres[4]. Focus groups were used as a method to encourage dialogue between participants sharing specific characteristics, including languages and linguistic backgrounds (Krueger and Casey). Exchanges between participants and me as the focus group facilitator

---

4. The Institutional Review Boards at both universities approved the study and cleared the use of video recording and transcripts for publication. Additionally, students signed informed consent forms that allowed me to publish screen captures from the recorded footage.

were analyzed to account for the ways tacit assumptions about writing emerged through conversation. By conducting focus groups, I could trace not only how individual students discussed their writing practices, but also how students conversed about these practices as they recalled their experiences in similar composition courses.

Composition curricula at both institutions asked students to compose both conventional print and multimodal genres in the same semester. Students at both universities were asked to write a literacy narrative and rhetorical analysis assignment in a conventional print form, and were then asked to "remix" either the literacy narrative or rhetorical analysis through a multimodal genre. Composition curricula at both universities incorporated rhetorical genre studies approaches to teaching writing by encouraging and requiring that students identify, analyze, and compose a variety of genres appropriate to different rhetorical contexts. For example, the "remix project" assignment sheet used at one university asked students to "design a project that illustrates your awareness of the rhetorical choices you make." The purpose of the remix assignment as described in this same assignment sheet explains that students should be able to "Demonstrate the ability to locate, critically evaluate, and employ a variety of sources for a range of purposes" by adapting their previous assignment through the use of various media. In the course objectives for composition curricula at both universities, instructors explain they want their students to develop and demonstrate an understanding that writing is socially and culturally situated. In this way, composition curricula at both universities draws influences from RGS by teaching writing as rhetorically and contextually bound.

Students from various linguistic backgrounds were recruited for these focus groups, in order to understand if and how students' linguistic backgrounds influence their approaches to multimodal composing. Ten self-identified L2 writers and seven self-identified L1 writers at two large state universities who created multimodal projects in composition courses were recruited. While students were not separated into L1/L2 focus groups, they were asked to identify their linguistic backgrounds when agreeing to participate in the study. Asking students to describe their linguistic backgrounds allowed me to draw potential connections between students' linguistic repertoires and their approaches to multimodality.

Since all students took composition in English at universities in the US, learning more about my participants' linguistic and cultural transitions helped me better understand the extent to which they "regularly confront the challenge of working across languages" (Lu and Horner 585). In this way, I was able to explore how linguistic transitions, and the extent to which students navigate these transitions in their daily communication, may impact students' use of rhetorical resources in their writing classrooms. Including and highlighting L2 students in a broader discussion of RGS illustrates not only how L2s (who are already present in most of our composition programs) reflect the struggles of the first-year composition student body in general, but also how the L2 population can help the field understand composing processes (and challenges) more broadly.

Footage was analyzed and coded using ELAN video coding software (http://tla.mpi.nl/tools/tla-tools/elan/). Since most research about composition students is focused on what instructors say about students' writing practices or what the students say about their own writing practices, using video to capture the embodied and visual discussion taking place during the focus groups provides an additional layer of understanding (Hawisher, Selfe, Berry and Skjulstad 2012). As Hawisher, Selfe, Berry and Skjulstad explain in their justification for using video data to both collect and present narratives and interviews in *Transnational Literate Lives in Digital Times*, videos "add additional semiotic information and more to alphabetic representations of research." In order to adequately represent the "additional semiotic information" provided through the video analysis and coding of the focus groups conducted for this study, I will first expand on the software and methodology used to code focus group footage for this study, before elaborating on the analytical tools afforded through this method of analysis.

Background on ELAN Coding Software:

ELAN, developed by the Max-Planck-Institute for Psycholinguistics (MPI), is a transcription and coding tool intended to help researchers both transcribe video and audio data. As described by Brugman and Russell in their analysis of ELAN presented at the 2004 *International Conference on Language Resources and Language Evaluation,* the benefit of coding software like ELAN is that it allows coders to transcribe and then "add more and more analytic layers" through an iterative process (n. pag.). These layers, or "tiers," can be applied simultaneously to a specific section of video data, thus forming "complex referential structures" to code "speech and gesture modalities" simultaneously (Brugman and Russell n. pag.). For the purposes of this study, using ELAN's tiers allowed me to code both students' verbal and embodied responses to my questions about their experiences with conventional print and multimodal genres. This was particularly crucial for a study including students from various linguistic backgrounds, as these students used gestures to clarify ideas that may not have been communicated clearly through spoken English alone.

For example, Figure 2 is a screenshot of the coding sequence for one L2 student's response. In the previous scene, the focus group moderator asked, "Can you tell me what you did to create your multimodal project in your composition class?" The student responded by explaining that she made a video, where she used songs to make the video "more dynamic." As she said "more dynamic," the student used her hands to make circular gestures that ranged in size from large to small. She then continued by explaining that the songs she selected for her video allowed her to "zoom into" specific points she wanted to make in her video. The circular gestures in this case illustrated this student's movement from broader to smaller, more focused ideas as she "zoomed into" specific points through her video project.

As seen in Figure 2, ELAN's tiers allowed me to code this student's response as a verbal "answer" to the focus group facilitator's question, an embodied answer to the question as represented through the student's circular gestures, and a comment about multimodal composition. Additionally, ELAN's tiers allowed me to note this student identified her first language as Spanish. The question posed by the focus group facilitator, in addition to the students' verbal and embodied answers, represent a single "interaction," which is also accounted for in the tiers represented in Figure 2. Through this example, it becomes clear how ELAN's tiered system allowed for a rich contextualization of students' responses. This contextualization became increasingly important as students continued discussing their engagement with multimodal composition. To fully research how students enact RGS in their composing practices, and to account for how students translanguage through both their verbal and embodied responses, I needed to use a method of analysis that allowed me to code not only what students were saying in response to my questions, but also how they were responding through their words and gestures. In the following section, I will elaborate on the tiered categories used to code video data from both focus groups.

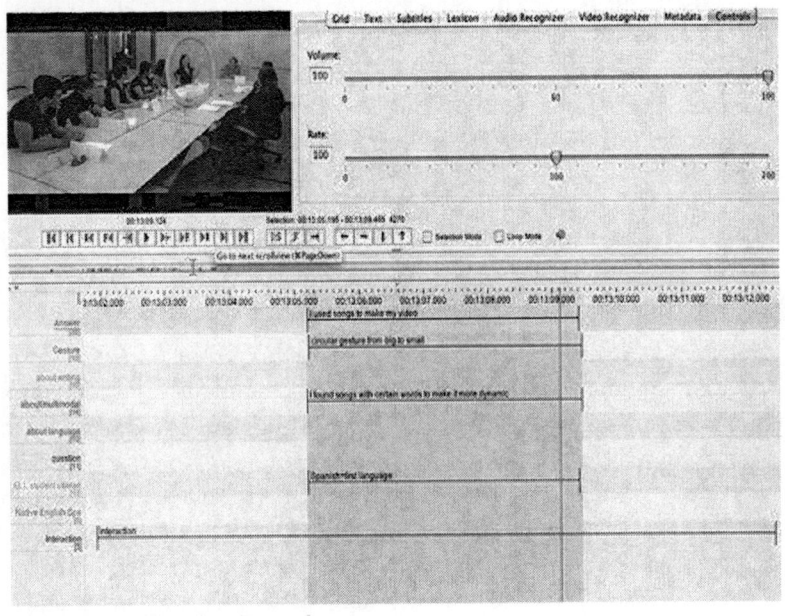

Figure 2: Tiered Coding Example

Coding Strategies

Using ELAN's tiered coding scheme, I coded all "exchanges" (Blythe 2012) between myself (the focus group facilitator) and focus group participants during the 230 minutes of video footage. I also coded exchanges among focus group participants. I used macro-level codes (e.g., questions, answers, exchanges) to first code all interactions, and then adopted axial coding strategies to create micro-level codes to further illustrate interactions (Saldaña). For example, I first watched the footage and noted each time the focus group facilitator or the participants asked a question, and each time the facilitator or the participants provided an answer. These broader categories represent the macro-level codes used in the first round of coding. After coding macro-level categories, I watched the footage again to develop micro-level codes *in vivo*, as I watched the interactions between focus group participants and the facilitator. I then watched all the footage a third time to specifically code for the micro-level categories developed during a previous viewing. These micro-level categories included: comments about multimodal projects, comments about conventional print papers, embodied gestures, and comments made about learning and navigating new languages.

The tiered coding scheme also allowed me to note when comments were made by L1 writers or L2 writers. As they discussed their experiences with writing, many participants shared stories regarding their experiences learning a new language, so this last category developed through grounded methodology (Oktay) as I coded the videos during the second viewing. Another affordance of the coding software was that rather than transcribing the entire focus group and then figuring out what was important, I could transcribe as I coded, focusing on transcribing the micro-level codes which are included in the results and discussion sections.

Table 1 provides sample codes for both macro and micro level codes. One utterance or comment could have up to three tiers of codes. Macro-level codes refer to questions and answers exchanged between the focus group facilitator and participants, and micro-level codes reference student projects or language identifications (L1 or L2 writer).

Table 1: Coding Tiers and Examples

Example/Utterance	Tier 1 Code(s)	Tier 2 Code(s)	Tier 3 Code(s)
"Do any of you speak a language other than English?"	Question, Exchange	statement about language learning/process	N/A
"Can you tell me about your process making your video or website? How did you put your ideas together?"	Question, Exchange	statement about multimodal project/writing	N/A
"When I write papers I have a lot of ideas, but I can't get them on paper"	Answer, Exchange	statement about conventional print writing	Statement from L1 writer

Example/Utterance	Tier 1 Code(s)	Tier 2 Code(s)	Tier 3 Code(s)
"When I write papers I worry about putting things in the right order"	Answer, Exchange	statement about conventional print writing	Statement from L2 writer
"In Thailand we don't use the same order of words like in English, so when I learned English I had to change the order of my words"	Answer, Exchange	statement about language learning/process	Statement from L2 writer
"I was born in China and learned to speak English when I was 18"	Answer, Exchange	statement about language learning/process	Statement from L2 writer
wave motions used when describing multimodal project	Answer, Exchange	embodied gesture, statement about multimodal project/writing	Statement from L2 writer

As evidenced in Table 1, micro-level codes are nonexclusive subcategories situated within the broader question, answer, and exchange macro-level codes. While this type of tiered coding allowed me to account for most utterances represented in the exchanges during the focus group, some utterances did not easily fall into the selected micro-level codes. For example, in one response, a student commented that "a video is more flexible than a paper." In this case, the student was making a statement both about multimodal and conventional print genres. For this reason, I coded this instance as both "statement about conventional print writing" and "statement about multimodal project/writing." In this way, the quantitative results of the analysis adequately reflect this particular statement. Additionally, though I coded for the linguistic background of the speaker making each utterance during the focus group ("Statement from L2 writer"/"Statement from L1 writer"), I removed these codes from the quantitative analysis when they were referencing the focus group facilitator.

After coding all exchanges between the facilitator and focus group participants, I used ELAN to count all instances of each code, calculating both numerical frequency and percentage of coverage for each category. The quantitative results are presented below in Table 2, followed by a discussion of relevant patterns and examples.

Table 2: Code Frequencies and Percentages

Code	Numeric Frequency	Percentage of Coverage
embodied response	43	6.5
Statement about conventional print genres/writing	79	12.0
Statement about multimodal project/writing	83	12.6
Statement about language learning/process	41	6.2
Statement from L2 writer	77	11.7
Statement from L1 writer	70	10.6
Question	65	9.9
Answer	147	22.4
Exchange	58	8.8
Totals	656	100.7

As evidenced in Table 2, L2 and L1 students had similar participation in the focus group discussions, accounting for 11.7% and 10.6% of coded utterances respectively. Additionally, the total percent coverage represented by all coded utterances extends slightly beyond 100% to 100.7%. This increase accounts for utterances that represented boundary codes, such as the statement that referenced both multimodality and conventional print writing described in the discussion above.

Results and Discussion

The 17 students in attendance during the focus groups had 8 different first languages: English, Chinese, Arabic, Spanish, Portuguese, Thai, Italian, and Hindi. There were a total of 656 coded strands, consisting of 58 exchanges (macro-level codes) made up of 65 questions and 147 answers between the focus group facilitator and focus group participants. There were also a total of 43 embodied responses coded during the discussion.

Although L1 and L2 students had similar concerns about composing conventional print texts, L2 writers discussed their multimodal composing practices differently than L1 writers. In the sections below, I will provide examples of how L1 and L2 writers represented at the focus groups described similar anxieties about writing conventional print genres. I will then move on to illustrate the differences between L1 and L2 students' multimodal composing practices, before drawing further implications for researching multimodality and RGS through a translingual perspective.

Students' Anxieties about Print Genres: "I just can't get my thoughts on paper"

When asked to describe their approaches and potential anxieties about composing conventional print genres such as the print version of their literacy narratives or rhetorical analyses, 12 of 17 students expressed similar concerns, stating that they had trouble translating their ideas into writing (the other 5 students gave less specific answers like "I've always hated writing" or "I don't know why I don't like writing). Tiffany[5], an L1 focus group participant from Ann Arbor, Michigan, explained, "I always know what I wanna say in my paper, but for some reason I just can't get my thoughts on paper." Similarly, Ramon, a student from Cuba who learned to speak English at the age of 8, explained, "What I struggle with always is transferring my ideas from my thoughts to the paper. Like, I know what I wanna say and what I wanna get across, but I can't get my thoughts on paper." None of the students seemed concerned with their ability to generate ideas for things to write, as they clearly knew what they wanted to say, but 12 of 17 students mentioned having at least some difficulty taking these thoughts from their heads to their papers.

While transferring thoughts from their minds to paper(s) is a common concern for both L1 and L2 students, the embodied gestures exhibited by 12 L1 and L2 students during this discussion provide additional insights into potential reasons for this particular concern with conventional print writing. As students moved from pointing to their heads where their thoughts and ideas are stored, to the table, where they presumably perceived the papers to be written, they made direct, linear gestures with their hands (see Figure 3). They tapped their heads

---

5. All students' names were changed to protect their identities

several times to explain they knew what they wanted to say (see Figure 4), and then made direct lines from their heads to the paper, demonstrating no room for flexibility or fluidity in the process.

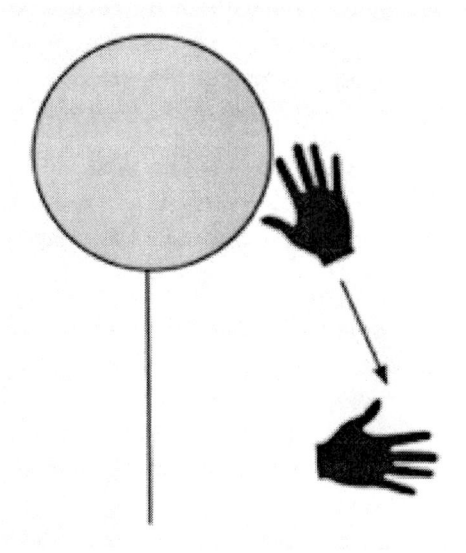

Figure 3: Students' linear perception of print genres

Figure 4: Ramon and Tiffany tap their heads to signal their ideas

Students' perceptions of conventional print writing, and their discussion of the perceived need to "transfer" thoughts to paper, signals a common (and problematic) construct about the one-directional movement students perceive to take place as they transform thoughts into writing. More specifically, 12 L1 and L2 students described a unidirectional move going from their heads to their papers (and not back to their heads) as they wrote conventional print genres. Their hands remained straight and flat throughout these gestures, signaling a bounded perception of what it means to write conventional print, mode-restricted genres.

Students' gestures, in conjunction with their verbal discussions, suggest a limited, linear perception of conventional print genres. As Tiffany continues discussing her experiences with conventional print writing, she references her previous writing courses, explaining:

> When I was taught to write it was like these are the types of assignments you have...like a memoir or a research paper. And it was like you write it like *this* and it's *this* way. And this is the type of assignment that it is so do it.

The trouble, then, according to Tiffany, comes when students attempt to represent their ideas through conventional print genres, those that, as Tiffany suggests, are perceived by students as written *this* one way. Tiffany recalls memoirs and research papers as "ways of classifying" the writing she was asked to do in college (Devitt, Bawarshi, and Reiff 550). Writing conventional print genres in college, Tiffany explains, requires an adherence to prescribed forms and guidelines, signaling the "genre effect" that takes place when "an illocutionary statement—an indirect statement that intends to induce action in an interlocutor—results in a perlocutionary effect or consequence" (Rounsaville "Selecting" 2012). In this case, when Tiffany is asked to write a conventional print genre in a college classroom, she reacts by following the same linear processes she has always used when writing college papers. That is, she identifies the "type" of assignment she is being asked to write, and she follows the guidelines she identifies as relevant to this academic genre. These guidelines for writing conventional print genres are not founded on the rhetorical situation in which she is writing, but rather rely on Tiffany's preconceived ideas of what she classifies as "memoirs" or "research papers."

Min, a student from Thailand who learned to speak English when she was 18, expressed similar concerns with and descriptions of conventional print genres, stating, "In Thailand we write in a different way. Like things aren't in order like intro and body conclusion so that's hard for me. I worry about getting that right when I write normal papers." Again, Min's conception of what makes a paper "normal" echoes a generic rigidity similar to Tiffany's conception that academic writing is written *"this* [same] way." Rather than perceiving conventional print genres as "stabilized for now" heuristics situated in their rhetorical contexts, students in both focus groups, representing radically diverse linguistic backgrounds, describe writing these papers as a linear, limiting process (Schryer 204). To them, conventional print genres continue to be governed by stable rules that apply across different courses and contexts.

Tiffany's repetition of "this" and "this way" in her discussion of conventional print genres, in addition to Min's comment that conventional print genres are always written in a particular "right order" suggests at least these 2 students believe there is a correct way to represent their thoughts in conventional print genres. According to students like Min and Tiffany, writing academic, monomodal genres represents a challenge in fitting ideas into generic containers or templates to be approved by their instructors. The challenge is not thinking or gathering ideas (evidenced by students' confident head tapping), but rather fitting these ideas into what students perceive to be rigid generic rules.

On Multimodality: "In a video you have...I don't know . . . more flexibility"

While 12 of 17 students (both L1 and L2) expressed similar concerns when discussing their processes and experiences writing conventional print genres, there were various differences in participants' approaches to multimodal composition. All 17 focus group participants raised their hands when asked, "Who would say they prefer making multimodal projects instead of writing print papers?" However, students' reasoning for this decision differed, especially between L1 and L2 participants. For L1 students, multimodality seemed to be another way to repeat the words and ideas they already had in mind. Five of 7 L1 writers described their multimodal projects as a way to "emphasize" their ideas or to "repeat" the thoughts they expressed in their written paper. In contrast, 8 of 10 L2 writers described their multimodal projects as a way to "expand on" ideas that were not easily conveyed through written forms. That is, L2 writers used multimodality to layer a multiplicity of meanings rather than to reiterate a specific idea.

For example, Anne, an L1 writer from Florida, explained,

> I knew what I wanted to say in my project, but making a video let me repeat my idea. I thought of the words I wanted to use,

and then found songs that had those *exact* words and added the songs to my video.

Anne explains making a video in her composition class to remix her conventional print literacy narrative. In her multimodal literacy narrative, she was describing "good feelings" she experienced during her composing process. Since she was thinking about the phrase "good feelings," she explained, she found Flo Rida's song "Good Feeling," and added this song to the background of the PowerPoint slides she was displaying in her video. Anne's multimodal composing process demonstrates some understanding of the affordances provided multimodal genres, as she found a song to emphasize her ideas. However, Anne's direct representation of the phrase "good feeling" with a song that is titled "good feeling" also echoes the concerns of scholars in multimodality. These scholars argue that linearly representing monomodal texts or ideas in digital form does not make adequate use of multimodal resources (Bowen and Whithaus; Lutewitte).

Rather than using various modes, such as beats in a song and images in a video, to represent different understandings of "good feelings," Anne only claims to have used the song "good feeling" because she was thinking about the phrase, "good feelings." In this way, Anne's multimodal project still reflects a "privileging [of] words, their sequencing, and rules of usage as the primary organizing system for articulating experiences" (Bowen and Withaus 5). Because Anne could rely on words to describe her literacy experiences as she was composing her multimodal project, her composing practices and genre conceptions remained bounded by alphabetic rules typically found in conventional print genres.

Another student, Camila, an L2 student who moved from the Dominican Republic where she spoke only Spanish to Florida to start college, also described the affordances of multimodal composing. She explained:

> Sometimes I don't have the right words to use on my paper, but when I don't have the right words and the teacher lets me make a video, I can use my video to better show my audience my idea.

Camila described a video rhetorical analysis project where she "remixed" a Coca-Cola advertisement. In this multimodal rhetorical analysis, Camila wanted to show that advertisements "usually only have one type of girl in them." Camila wanted to show other types of girls, so she found images of girls "with different styles, different clothes, and different hair" to use in her video. She then also changed the font of the original Coca-Cola advertisement, to "show the audience what I mean by different." She used multiple colors, diverging from Coca-Cola's traditional red and white logo, to indicate to her audience that she was talking about difference. Lastly, Camila explains, she added a song to the background of her video, because "a song can explain something for you through beats and sounds that you don't know how to say through words." While Camila wanted to illustrate the impacts of only showing advertisements with "one type of girl," by portraying "different girls" in her video, she wasn't quite sure how to represent difference through words.

Based on her discussion, Camila seemed to be interpreting and demonstrating conceptions of "difference" in various ways, relating to style, culture, and taste, and she leveraged a variety of semiotic resources to convey these ideas. She was enacting a rhetorical genre studies approach to multimodal composing by using various modes "to represent a topic in a way that adds meaning to [rather than repeats the ideas of a] text" (Arola, Ball, and Sheppard 52). Camila was using a "guiding metaphor" of difference to rhetorically illustrate her analysis through various modes (Arola, Ball, and Sheppard 52). Instead of relying on words to describe her ideas, Camila moved on consider how the various modes she was using could illustrate what she was thinking.

Camila explained she often doesn't "have the right words to use" in her writing, which directly contrasts with Anne's comment, "I *knew* what I wanted to say" in words. This example suggests students' perceived competence speaking English might influence their approaches to multimodal composing. When students can rely on a specific set of words to convey their ideas, they seem to be almost limited by these words as they draw on other semiotic resources (e.g., pictures, songs) to compose multimodal projects. Contrastingly, when L2 students like Camila are less confident in their use of specific words, they are pushed to merge (or translanguage) across modes as they think of different ways to convey their ideas. While L1 and L2 students translanguage to some degree, students who have had to cross drastic linguistic boundaries (such as having to learn English after speaking only Spanish for many years) have more experience translanguaging (and thus layering modes to convey meaning) across a wider range of contexts.

Xen, an international L2 student who had been speaking English for less than a year when he took his composition course, explained he had an "incredibly difficult" time writing conventional print papers for his composition class. When his teacher assigned a multimodal project that asked him to "remix" a literacy narrative paper he had written earlier in the course, Xen created a comic strip that illustrated the frustration he experienced when he first started taking college courses in the US. These frustrations, he explained, started when he had a 20 hour flight delay when he was flying to the US from China. In this comic, Xen combined words with his own illustrations, portions of which are depicted in Figure 8.

Figure 5: Portions of Xen's Comic submitted for a literacy narrative "remix" assignment

As depicted in Figure 8, Xen's illustrations are relatively simple, not initially suggesting a deep understanding of the affordances provided by multimodal composition. During his discussion, however, Xen explained that he liked having the opportunity to create a comic to illustrate his initial experiences coming to the US because in the comic, he "didn't have to worry about making words sound a certain way." When initially writing his literacy narrative in a conventional print form (without the comic illustrations), Xen said he "could not show what he meant" because he was worried about "using words the right way." In his comic, however, Xen said he used fewer words and drew "rage faces" to further illustrate how he was feeling during his long flight to the US. "Rage faces" reference "Rage Comics," "a series of web comics" with simple drawings "typically used to tell stories about real life experiences" (*knowyourmeme*). Using "rage faces" in his comic,

Xen explained, allowed him to illustrate his frustration in a way that was "way easier" than having to describe the way he felt through written words. With the opportunity to create a multimodal project, Xen was able to draw on his repertoire of "antecedent genres" by using "rage comics" to illustrate emotions in his remixed, multimodal narrative (Freadman; Rounsaville "Selecting"). While Xen's illustrations are not elaborate, and though he still relies on conventional print texts to some degree, his adoption of multimodality prompted him to use previous genre knowledge rhetorically to convey his ideas as he repurposed his literacy narrative into a comic.

As evidenced by Camila and Xen's purposeful layering of meaning in their multimodal projects (and Nathalia's drawing in the anecdotal example presented in the introduction), L2 students (or at least the 8 of 10 students evidenced in this study) practice translingualism by "re-contextualizing" and "reforming" semiotic modes and antecedent genres (Lu and Horner 588). Though 12 of L1 and L2 students describe experiencing some difficulty translating their thoughts to paper, when given the option to use other semiotic modes, 8 of 10 L2 students describe using multimodality to layer (rather than to repeat) meaning using various rhetorical resources. In some ways, students like Camila who purposely layer various modes and media exhibit "rhetorical sensitivity" that pushes them to "understand that an idea can be rendered in multi-form ways" (Shipka "Including" 78).

Through their translanguaging practices, 8 of 10 L2 writers in this study display an inherent rhetorical dexterity when developing strategies for composing multimodal projects, as they use multimodality to break from bounded, "container" models of genre often identified with conventional print texts. These different rhetorical strategies and fluid approaches to multimodal composing processes were also evident through students' embodied gestures as they described regarding multimodal projects and flexible genres, which will be discussed in the next section.

Describing Multimodal Genres Through Gestures

While the 7 L1 writers in this study did not use any consistent gestures when discussing their multimodal projects, 7 of 10 L2 students used what I describe as fluid or wave gestures as they discussed how they bring together various resources like images and sounds to convey their ideas through multimodal writing. These 7 students were in the same group of 8 L2 students who described using multimodality to extend (rather than repeat) their ideas. The other 3 L2 students did not use any consistent gestures.

In contrast to the linear, bounded gestures used by 12 of 17 participants (both L1 and L2) when discussing their difficulties transferring thoughts to print papers, 7 of 10 L2 students' embodied descriptions of multimodality were far less rigid. For example, Natalie, an L2 student from Paraguay, said she prefers multimodal projects to conventional print genres because, in a multimodal project, like the video she made for her literacy narrative in her composition class, "you are not limited. You have .. I don't know ... more flexibility." As Natalie said "flexibility" she moved her hands in various directions simultaneously, signaling the way she brought together various resources and ideas when putting her project together.

As Natalie spoke and moved her hands, you could see the way she was signaling the movement of various resources, including pictures, texts, beats, colors, and sounds in non-linear patterns that brought her audience through her argument. In Figure 6, we can see Natalie discussing the flexibility of multimodality through the waves she makes with her hands.

Similarly, Enrique, an L2 student from Brazil, made an up and down wave gesture with his hand when he described a music video he made for his composition class. In discussing his process, Enrique explained, "Making the video was hard because, you don't just have words and pictures, but you also wanna use the beat of the music to get your ideas across." As Enrique said "get your ideas across," he made waves with his hand, as evidenced in Figure 7.

As Enrique made the wave gestures when discussing the way he layered the beats of a song with the images in his video, he also moved his body up and down when saying the word "beat," further illustrating the complex meaning-making process in which he engaged during his multimodal composing process. To Enrique, a multimodal project provided him with various choices to make--rhetorical, unbound, choices that were carefully planned and articulated in his video and in his verbal and embodied discussion. Not having words to rely on, or rather to limit him, Enrique readily brought in other modes to illustrate his ideas, and he deliberately layered these modes to create his project. Like Camila's layering of colors, images, and sounds in the project she submitted to her instructor, Enrique layered his verbal discussion of the affordances provided by multimodality with the gestural movement of his hands in shoulders.

Figure 6: Natalie uses fluid, wave motions to discuss multimodality

Figure 7: Enrique Makes Hand Gestures When Discussing his Multimodal Project

Enrique's discussion of multimodality echoes the definition of multimodal composing provided by proponents of RGS approaches to multimodal composition. For example, these scholars explain multimodality includes composing through "videos, visual images, audio essays, video games, t-shirts (Odell and Katz, 2009) and even live dances" (Shipka, 2011), thus allowing for the combination of digital and embodied modes that Enrique exhibits both in the project he created and in his embodied discussion of multimodality (Arola, Ball, and Sheppard "Multimodality" n.pag.). Enrique and Natalie's embodied discussions of multimodality can help us understand "the complex and highly rigorous decision-making process student[s] employ while producing" their multimodal projects (Shipka, "Toward," 3). These embodied discussions further illustrate L2 students' enactment of RGS through multimodal composition, as students using gestures in this study display a rhetorically-situated understanding of how modes can be layered to convey meaning.

While students' verbal description of multimodality provided some insight into their approaches to multimodal composition, examining students' gestures also allowed for an additional layer of understanding. Conventional print genres were presented as linear by 12 of 17 participants, moving directly from the mind to the paper. Multimodal projects were far less rigid, described by 7 of 10 L2 writers through waves and recursive motions moving between students' ideas.

The flexible, unbounded gestures depicted in Figure 7 were only prevalent in 7 L2 students who appeared to have a rather complex, sophisticated understanding of multimodality. In addition, rather than perceiving their video projects as an opportunity to repeat their ideas (like Anne's repetition of the phrase "good feeling"), 8 of 10 L2 students verbally highlighted their ability to draw on a variety of semiotic resources to layer meaning through their multimodal projects. To L2 students, or at least the 8 L2 students represented in this study, multimodality allowed an opportunity to illustrate, through whatever means available, the ideas they felt to not "have the right words" to convey. Furthermore, having the ability to compose multimodal genres appeared to have an impact in shifting students' tacit constructs of genres more generally. For example, before leaving the focus group, Camila explained:

> I just want to say that making my video project was useful. Before, I used to think 'oh my God, I can't even understand myself when I write...how is a teacher every going to understand me?' But when I made my video, I could use pictures and colors that are...you know...like a universal language. A picture can say something for you that you don't know how to say. So now when I write my paper for my history class if I can't think of a way to explain something I'll use a picture if I can.

While Camila's statement reflects an isolated instance, it's interesting to note she connects creating a video project for her composition class with being able to draw on semiotic modes (like pictures) in other papers for her history class. By explaining that she uses pictures when she "can't think of a way to explain something" in her history class, Camila suggests she, after making her video project in composition, focuses on delivering meaning (rather than following static generic conventions) when writing for her other courses. By tying these experiences to her video project, stating, "I just want to say that making my video project was useful," Camila implies her experience with multimodal composition can be linked to her reconception of academic genres beyond static forms.

Camila's observation echoes the goals of scholars using an RGS approach to teach multimodality. As Arola Ball, and Sheppard explain, "One of the goals of a rhetorical genre studies approach is to teach students to transfer processes of genre analysis, composition, and revision into any kind of writing situation" (21). While Camila's isolated example does not provide enough evidence of the type of transfer described by Arola, Ball, and Sheppard, future studies examining translanguaging practices through multimodality and RGS could further explore the connections students like Camila may be making between multimodal composition and conceptions of genre both in and after first-year writing courses.

Focus group participants who viewed their multimodal projects as flexible seemed to understand the way genres are situated in context, once again suggesting a direct connection between multimodality, translingualism, RGS as they are adapted into composition pedagogies. Leveraging the translingual composing strategies used by L2 students when composing multimodal projects may useful to composition instructors and students from all linguistic backgrounds, and can significantly impact the way we combine multimodality, translingualism, and RGS in FYC.

Though it is not possible to generalize broadly from these results, based on the responses these focus group participants, a majority (8 of 10) L2 students exhibited a nuanced understanding of multimodality that could help instructors further explore how to teach genres in less bounded ways. This nuanced understanding stemmed from L2 students' experiences not having what they describe to be the "right words" to convey their ideas, a challenge that pushes students to use other, non-conventional print modes to make meaning. L2 students' discussion of multimodality reflected a complex ability to layer modes and meaning in their translanguaging practices. Eight of 10 L2 students used their multimodal projects as a way to demonstrate their rhetorical awareness and flexibility when conveying their ideas. They were aware of the ideas they wanted to convey and knew they had a wider array of semiotic resources available to them, enacting the fundamental principles of rhetorical genre studies by understanding how genres are situated, mediated, and delivered in context. More importantly, L2 students were keenly aware of how to leverage and layer these semiotic resources through their work, reflecting their extensive experience translanguaging or moving purposely between languages, media, and contexts.

By presenting L2 learners as experts in multimodal composition who readily enact rhetorical genre theory, we can continue moving away from the deficit perception of L2 learning that continuously plagues the academy. Acknowledging and highlighting the inherently dexterous, flexible, and rhetorical multimodal practices of L2 students may help us continue teaching students to leverage "the bandwidth of semiotic resources for communication in order to make available all available means of persuasion" (Selfe 2009). This leveraging of rhetorical resources, in turn, can help us build bridges between multimodality, translingualism, and RGS, in order to better account for the increasingly diverse backgrounds of students in our composition classrooms.

Limitations

Using ELAN's tiered video coding allowed me to "examine writing in relation to other salient semiotic resources" like students' embodied gestures, perhaps resulting in a broader understanding of "what writing does" and how students engage with writing through multiple modes (Leander and Prior 231). However, I limited my analysis of gestures to descriptive narratives rather than specific coded categories primarily to avoid making drastic generalizations about the embodied practices of a culturally and linguistically diverse group of students. While there were some patterns in students' gestures clearly evident through my descriptive notes and interpretations, I did not find it fruitful to adapt a more specific and prescriptive quantitative coding scheme to gestures at this time. While some students made grandiose, elaborate gestures in their discussions, others were much more reserved, gesturing under the table located in the focus group room. I assume there are cultural underpinnings grounding these various approaches to body language, and I chose to withhold my own judgment of these practices to avoid cultural overgeneralization or essentialism.

In using focus groups for this study, I aimed to encourage dialogue between students, and to provide an environment in which students who had shared composition curricula could recall similarities or connections between their experiences. While these conversations were undoubtedly fruitful, follow-up longitudinal, situated studies should continue to elaborate on the preliminary findings presented through the focus groups[6]. Individual interviews with students could help ex-

---

6. See, for example, Rounsaville 2014, which explores the transnational literacy practices and shifting genre conceptions of a self-identified "Third Culture Kid"

pand our understanding of how both L1 and L2 students arrived at their conceptions of and approaches to multimodality and RGS. Interviews and situated case-studies could be explored in future directions stemming from this project.

Conclusion

By using student narratives to analyze how rhetorical genre studies is enacted in the classroom, I traced a distinction between L1 and L2 students' conceptions of genres in composition. For 12 of 17 L1 and L2 students, conventional print genres are perceived as templates with strict, bounded guidelines. Approaches to multimodal composition, on the other hand, appear to be influenced by students' experiences with language acquisition and negotiation, with 8 of 10 L2 students describing multimodality (7 of 10 also using gestures) as an opportunity to purposefully layer meaning across modes in less bounded ways. In this way, while both L1 and L2 students exhibited translingual practices through their combination of modes when crafting multimodal projects, 8 of 10 L2 students described using multimodality to layer meaning as an affordance they could leverage when they did not have specific words available.

L2 writers, as evidenced by my focus group data, claim to not always have "the right words" when attempting to communicate in English, leading them to readily practice translanguaging as they leverage semiotic resources. The result is a complex, purposeful approach to multimodality illustrated through the narratives of L2 writers, an approach that could help begin to question how L2 students, as experts in multimodality, can help the discipline better understand how to teach and theorize the rhetorical nature of genres.

By highlighting students' experiences with multimodality, and by moving away from the linear, container-bound approach to writing, we might continue unbinding genres from rigid forms, languages, and classrooms, seeing and teaching them as ways of meaning-making across contexts. These ways of making meaning will continue to expand as languages and technologies keep shifting and as the field of rhetorical genre studies continues to account for and partake in these changes.

Disciplinary boundaries between multimodal composition, translingualism, and RGS are beginning to shift, moving the discipline away from the single language/single mode model that does not adequately account for the lived experiences of contemporary composition students (Canagarajah; Selfe and Horner; Lu and Horner). Additionally, cross-cultural, cross-lingual, and cross-disciplinary collaborations are already situated within the history of RGS (and other areas of genre studies), as evidenced in international genre conferences and publications such as the International Symposium on Genre Studies and the international genre collaborative hosted at www.genreacrossborders.org.

However, as North American Rhetorical Genre Studies continues to be adapted into contemporary composition curricula (e.g., Arola and Ball; Bowen and Whithaus), further emphasis on translingualism and multimodality can help RGS continue to reflect the diverse backgrounds and experiences of composition students. While some explicit links between multimodality and RGS are made in current composition pedagogy (Arola, Ball, Sheppard; Shipka, Bowen and Whithaus), studies like the one presented in this paper can continue to provide data-driven support for the affordances of expanding students' genre conceptions across various semiotic modes and contexts. Furthermore, leveraging L2 students' broad understanding of multimodal genres as "locations within which meaning is constructed" will help us continue viewing linguistic diversity as an asset rather than a deficit in our writing classrooms (Bazerman 19).

Works Cited

Arola, Kristin, Ball, Cheryl, and Jennifer Sheppard. "Multimodality as a Frame for Individual and Institutional Change." *Hybrid Pedagogy* (2014) n. pag. Web. 10 Jan. 2014.

Arola, Kristin, Sheppard, Jennifer, and Cheryl Ball. *Writer/Designer: A Guide to Making Multimodal Projects.* Boston: Bedford/St. Martin's, 2014. Print.

Atkinson, Dwight, et. al. "Clarifying the Relationship between L2 Writing and Translingual Writing: An Open Letter to Writing Studies Editors and Organization Leaders." Forthcoming in March 2015 issue of *College English.*

Bazerman, Charles. "The Life of Genre, the Life in the Classroom." *Genre and Writing: Issues, Arguments, Alternatives.* Eds. Wendy Bishop and Hans Ostrom. Portsmouth: Boynton, 1997. 19–26. Print.

Bazerman, Charles, Bonini Adair, and Debora Figueiredo. *Genre in a Changing World.* WAC Clearinghouse and Parlor Press, 2009. Web. 1 Nov. 2013.

Bawarshi, Anis. *Genre and the Invention of the Writer: Reconsidering the Place of Invention in Composition.* Utah State Univ. Press, 2003. Print.

Bowen, Tracey, and Carl Whithaus. *Multimodal Literacies and Emerging Genres.* Pittsburgh: University of Pittsburgh Press, 2013. Print.

Blythe, Stuart. "Coding Digital Texts and Multimedia." *Digital Writing Research: Technologies, Methodologies, and Ethical Issues.* Eds. Heidi McKee and Danielle Nicole Devoss. New York: Hampton Press, 2007. 203-28. Print.

Brandt, Deborah. "Sponsors of Literacy." *College Composition and Communication* 49.2 (1998): 165–85. Web. 2 March 2014.

Brugman, Hennie, and Albert Russell. "Annotating Multi-Media Multi-Modal Resources with ELAN." *Max-Planck-Institute for Psycholinguistics*, Wundtlaan: 2065-68. Web.10 March 2014.

Canagarajah, Suresh. "Lingua Franca English, Multilingual Communities, and Language Acquisition." *The Modern Language Journal* 91 (2007): 923-39. Print.

—."Negotiating Translingual Literacy." *Research in the Teaching of English* 48.1(2013): 40–67. Web.10 Feb. 2014.

—. *Translingual Practice: Global Englishes and Cosmopolitan Relations.* New York: Routlage, 2013. Print.

Clark, Irene, and Andrea Hernandez. "Genre Awareness, Academic Argument, and Transferability." *The WAC Journal* (2012): 65–78. Web. 10 Feb. 2014.

Coe, Richard, Lingard, Lorelei, and Tatiana Teslenko. *The Rhetoric and Ideology of Genre: Strategies for Stability and Change.* New York: Hampton Press, 2002. Print.

Coe, Richard, Lingard, Lorelei, and Tatiana Teslenko. "Genre as Action, Strategy, and Differance: An Introduction." Coe, Lingard, and Teslenko 1–10. Print.

Devitt, Amy. *Writing Genres.* Carbondale: Southern Illinois UP, 2004. Print.

Devitt, Amy, Bawarshi, Anis, and Mary Jo Reiff. "Materiality and Genre in the Study of Discourse Communities." *College English* 65.5 (2003): 541–58. Web. 5 July 2014.

Freedman, Aviva. "Interaction Between Theory and Research: RGS and a Study of Students and Professionals Working 'In Computers.'" *Rhetorical Genre Studies and Beyond.* Ed. Aviva Freedman and Natasha Artemeva. Winnipeg: Inkshed Publications, 2008. Web. 2 Feb. 2014.

Freedman, Aviva, and Medway, Peter. *Genre and the New Rhetoric.* Taylor & Frances, 1994. Print.

Genres Across Borders: An International, Interdisciplinary Network of Researchers, Theories, and Resources. North Carolina State University, n.d. Web. 5 July 2014.

Hawisher, Selfe, Berry, Patrick and Synne Skjulstad. "Conclusion: Closing Thoughts on Research Methodology." *Transnational Literate Lives in Digital Times*. Patrick Barry, Gail E. Hawisher, and Cynthia L.Selfe. Logan, UT: Computers and Composition Digital P/Utah State UP, 2012. Web. 2 Dec. 2013.

Khubchandani, Lachman M. "A Plurilingual Ethos: A Peep into the Sociology of Language." *Indian Journal of Applied Linguistics* 24.1 (1998): 5-37. Print.

Krueger, Richard, and Mary Anne Casey. *Focus Groups: A Practical Guide for Applied Research*. 4th ed. Thousand Oaks, CA: Sage, 2009. Print.

Leander, Kevin, and Paul Prior. "Speaking and Writing: How Talk and Text Interact in Situated Practices." *What Writing does and how it does it: An Introduction to Analysis of Text and Textual Practice*. Eds. Charlez Bazerman and Paul Prior. Mahwah, NJ: Erlbaum. Print.

Lu, Min-Zhan, et al. "Rethinking Difference in Composing Composition: Language, Translation, Genre, Modality. " *Conference on College Composition and Communication*. Indianapolis, IN. 21 March 2014. Panel Presentation.

Lu, Min-Zhan, and Bruce Horner. "Translingual Literacy, Language Difference, and Matters of Agency." *College English* 75.6 (2013): 582–607. Web. 5 July 2014.

Matsuda, Paul Kei. "The Lure of Translingual Writing." *PMLA* 129.3 (2014): 478-83. Print.

Meyer, Jan H.F., Ray Land, and Caroline Bailie. Editors' Preface. *Threshold Concepts and Transformational Learning*. Rotterdam: Sense Publishers, 2010. ix-xlii. Print.

Miller, Carolyn. "Genre as Social Action." *Quarterly Journal of Speech* 70 (1984): 151–67. Web. 2 Jan 2014.

New London Group. "A Pedagogy of Multiliteracies: Designing Social Futures." *Harvard Educational Review*. Harvard Educational Group, 1996. Web. 15 July 2014.

Oktay, Julianne. *Grounded Theory*. New York: Oxford University Press, 2012. Print.

Pare, Anthony. "Genre and Identity: Individuals, Institutions, and Ideology." Coe, Lingard, and Teslenko 57–71. Print.

"Rage Comics." *Know Your Meme*. Cheezeburger Inc., 2008. Web. 14 July 2014.

Rounsaville, Angela. "Selecting Genres for Transfer: The Role of Uptake in Students' Antecedent Genre Knowledge." *Composition Forum 26* (Fall 2012): n.pag. Web. 5 July 2013.

Rounsaville, Angela. "Situating Transnational Genre Knowledge: A Genre Trajectory Analysis of One Student's Personal and Academic Writing. Written Communication 31 (2014): 332–64. Web. 25 July 2014.

Rounsaville, Angela, Goldberg, Rachel, and Anis Bawarshi. "From Incomes to Outcomes: FYW Students' Prior genre Knowledge, Meta-Cognition, and the Question of Transfer." *WPA* 32.1 (Fall/Winter 2008): 97–112. Web. 1 April 2014.

Russell, David. "Rethinking Genre in School and Society: An Activity Theory Analysis." *Written Communication* 14.4 (1997): 504–54. Web. 13 Feb. 2014.

Saldaña, Johnny. *The Coding Manual for Qualitative Researchers*. 2nd ed. Thousand Oaks, CA: Sage, 2013. Print

Selfe, Cynthia, and Bruce Horner. "Translinguality/Transmodality Relations: Snapshots from a Dialogue." *The Working Papers Series on Negotiating Differences in Language and Literacy*. University of Louisville, 2013. Web. 5 July 2014.

Seloni, Lisya. "Academic Literacy Socialization of first year Doctoral Students in the US: A Micro-Ethnographic Perspective." *English for Specific Purposes* 31.7 (2012): 47-59. Web. 5 July 2014.

Schryer, Catherine. "Records as Genre." *Written Communication* 10.2 (1993): 200–34. Web. 10 Feb. 2014.

Shipka, Jody. "Including, but Not Limited to, the Digital: Composing Multimodal Texts." *Multimodal Literacies and Emerging Genres*. Eds.Tracey Bowen and Carl Whithaus. Pittsburgh, University of Pittsburgh Press, 2013. 73-90. Print.

Shipka, Jody. *Toward a Composition Made Whole*. Pittsburgh: University of Pittsburgh Press, 2011. Print.

Selfe, Cynthia. "Aurality and Multimodal Composing." *College Composition and Communication* 60.4 (2009): 616–63. Web. 10 Feb. 2014

Street, Brian, Pahl, Kate, and Jennifer Rowsell. "Multimodality and New Literacy Studies." *The Routledge Handbook of Multimodal Analysis*. Ed. Carey Jewitt. New York: Routledge, 2009. 191–200. Print.

X, Malcolm, Haley, Alex, and Attallah Shabazz. *The Autobiography of Malcolm X: As Told to Alex Haley*. New York: The Ballantine Publishing Group, 1964. Print.

JOURNAL OF SECOND LANGUAGE WRITING

The Journal of Second Language Writing is on the Web at https://www.journals.elsevier.com/journal-of-second-language-writing

The *Journal of Second Language Writing* is devoted to publishing theoretically grounded reports of research and discussions that represent a contribution to current understandings of central issues in second and foreign language writing and writing instruction. Some areas of interest are personal characteristics and attitudes of L2 writers, L2 writers' composing processes, features of L2 writers' texts, readers' responses to L2 writing, assessment/evaluation of L2 writing, contexts (cultural, social, political, institutional) for L2 writing, and any other topic clearly relevant to L2 writing theory, research, or instruction.

L2 Student–U.S. Professor Interactions Through Disciplinary Writing Assignments: An Activity Theory Perspective*

Fujioka's situated case study of a second language writer in a U.S. graduate course offers insight into the complex interactions among activity systems in advanced academic literacy. The semester-long study focuses on one Japanese student (Jun) and his professor in a graduate course in educational anthropology. Through an activity theory framework, Fujioka demonstrates how Jun and his professor mutually shaped, and ultimately transformed, one another's practices. This study contributes to scholarship on academic socialization and disciplinary literacy practices by highlighting the agency that learners have in transforming the communities in which they participate.

* Reprinted from the *Journal of Second Language Writing* 25 (2014): 40–58. © 2014, with permission from Elsevier.

6 L2 Student–U.S. Professor Interactions Through Disciplinary Writing Assignments: An Activity Theory Perspective

Mayumi Fujioka

Abstract: *This study aimed to explain the complexity involved in multiple agents' learning in interaction in graduate disciplinary writing contexts. Adopting activity theory (Engeström, 1999) as a guiding framework, I analyzed interactive experiences between an L2 English student writer and his professor regarding different writing assignments in a U.S. graduate course. Sources of qualitative data through one semester included interviews, a class observation, and written documents. The semilongitudinal nature of the study illuminated both participants' changes in their writing and teaching practices over time.*

Activity theory enabled the visualization of the participants' experiences with each assignment as an activity system. Moreover, the concept of interacting activity systems or activity system network offered a useful perspective to understand concurrent and multi-directional learning between the student and the professor, who mutually shaped and influenced each other's writing and teaching practices. The study's findings provide encouragement for L2 English students in terms of their potential power to bring change to their professors' teaching practices and their L2 disciplinary communities. Furthermore, through the lens of activity theory, the study offers future possibilities of exploring L2 graduate disci-

plinary socialization by investigating different genres as activity systems and learning in multiple directions among students.

INTRODUCTION

In graduate level second language (L2) writing studies, our notion of writing has been expanded beyond consideration of texts to that of writing as practice. The line of studies with this notion have focused on what students do, including interacting with disciplinary reading and producing texts, developing strategies to cope with the assignments, dialoguing with professors on their written texts, and responding to their comments in specific literacy contexts (e.g., courses, seminars, doctoral dissertation writing) (Angelova & Riazantseva, 1999; Belcher, 1994; Casanave, 1995, 2002, Chap. 3, 4; Dong, 1996; Prior, 1998; Riazi, 1997). These studies, mostly employing a naturalistic qualitative case study approach, helped enhance our understanding of graduate students' disciplinary socialization in their everyday literacy activity. Among those, Casanave's and Prior's rigorous documentations of both first language (L1) and L2 graduate students' literacy activities in U.S. disciplinary courses illustrated the individual, dynamic, and highly complex nature of disciplinary socialization to the extent that socialization encompassed students' resistance to various academic expectations of literacy activities in which they engaged. L2 graduate disciplinary socialization has been more recently explored in scholarly publication writing (e.g., Cho, 2004; Li, 2005, 2006, 2007) and genre knowledge development in different kinds of advanced academic writing (e.g., lab reports, Master's thesis, and conference papers; Tardy, 2005, 2009).

The view of graduate level disciplinary socialization through writing as concrete interactional activities in a local context is understood by the notions of "writing as situated social practice" (Casanave, 2002, p. 19) and writing as "participatory practice" (Casanave, 2008, p. 16), both of which were developed largely based on Lave and Wenger's (1991) notions of "communities of practice" and "legitimate peripheral participation" (LPP) (both on p. 30), in which novice members develop their expertise and professional identity with increasing participation in the social practices in the community comprising people with differing levels of expertise. In fact, many of the previous studies mentioned above adopted Lave and Wenger's view of learning as a guiding framework (e.g., Belcher, 1994; Casanave, 2002; Cho, 2004;

Li, 2005, 2006, 2007; Prior, 1998, Chap. 4; Tardy, 2005), applying it to graduate students as novices in their disciplinary communities learning from more expert members (e.g., professors, dissertation advisors) through participation in everyday discursive practices.

However, the original conceptualization of learning by Lave and Wenger (1991) and the subsequent adaptations of their analytical viewpoint to L2 graduate literacy development pose a problem in that they lack a concurrent and multi-directional perspective of learning among different people. Lave and Wenger noted that LPP does not refer to learning on the part of the novice only but the interaction between people and practice (p. 116), but their focus was still a unidirectional trajectory in which novices become experts. Their conceptualization of learning did not address multi-directionality in which more expert members in a particular community may experience change and transformation as a result of interactional experiences with less expert members. The change and transformation can also occur concurrently between and among the participating members in a community. Moreover, the community and the social practice may undergo change and transformation as a result of individual and collective changes brought by the participating members. However, this concurrent and multi-directional view of learning was not fully addressed in Lave and Wenger's framework.

Accordingly, the studies on L2 disciplinary socialization mentioned above appear to lack a perspective of learning taking place in multiple directions among different people. Those studies demystified the intricacies of graduate academic literacy practices between students and more experienced members in disciplinary communities (course professors, dissertation advisors, journal reviewers), including conflicts and negotiations over the executions and evaluations of particular writing assignments (Casanave, 1995, 2002, Chap. 3, 4; Prior, 1998), successful and less successful thesis/dissertation advising relationships (Belcher, 1994; Tardy, 2005), and accommodating to or rejecting journal reviewers' responses to manuscript submissions (Cho, 2004; Li, 2005, 2006, 2007). However, as a whole they did not document whether and how students' professors, advisors, or journal reviewers changed or transformed as a result of their interactional academic relationships with students, nor did they illustrate whether and to what extent students brought changes to the social practices in their disciplinary communities.

In the present study, I aim to offer an additional perspective to L2 graduate disciplinary socialization that includes a collective and multi-directional view of learning by focusing on disciplinary discursive practices of an L2 English graduate student and one of his professors in a specific graduate course. Through the narration of interactional experiences between the student and his professor, I illustrate how their interactions affected and contributed to individual and mutual changes in their writing and teaching practices within the course. As a theoretical framework of the study, I adopt activity theory (Engeström, 1999, 2001) because it depicts learning and development in multiple directions (Engeström & Miettinen, 1999) and it views learning as "both collective and individual" and "innovative and transforming" (Martin, 2005, pp. 143–144).

ACTIVITY THEORY: A COMPLEX AND DYNAMIC VIEW OF LEARNING

Activity theory is categorized as a branch of Sociocultural theory (SCT), traditionally defined in association with the work of Vygotsky[1] (e.g., 1978), central to which is the view of the human mind as mediated by both physical and symbolic tools (e.g., art, language, numbers; Lantolf, 2000). Based on Vygotsky's idea of describing the basic unit of human activity as a mediated subject (agent)–object (goal) interaction, Leont'ev (e.g., 1978 as cited in Kaptelinin, 2005) developed activity theory under a primarily psychological framework, emphasizing individuals' motives (underlying reasons) for specific behaviors (Zhu & Mitchell, 2012). Departing from Leont'ev's view of activity, Engeström (e.g., 1999) expanded the theory with a unit of analysis defined as "*object-oriented, collective,* and *culturally mediated human activity,* or *activity system*" (Engeström & Miettinen, 1999, p. 9, italics in original) (see Engeström, 2001; Roth & Lee, 2007, for the history and evolution of activity theory). In this study I adopt Engeström's version of activity theory because it encompasses elements pertinent to the social practice of graduate disciplinary writing, which is explained below.

Engeström (1987 as cited in Engeström, 2001) systematized activity theory with a graphic representation of an activity system, through

---

1. Prior (2008) provides a broader definition of SCT based on multiple interdisciplinary traditions, including Vygotsky's theories, anthropology, philosophy, and sociology in relation to writing research.

which observable aspects of human behavior become explicit. Taking a particular writing assignment in a graduate course, a term paper for example, a general description of the activity system of a student engaging in the assignment can be represented based on Engeström's diagram as follows (see Fig. 1).

The upper triangle represents Vygotsky's original proposal of subject (agent) working toward object/goal through mediational means[2] (Engeström, 2001). Possible mediational means for a student (agent) working on a term paper (object/goal) include language-based resources mostly, including class readings and discussions, and a model research paper, as language constitutes the primary mediational means.

In the lower section of the triangle, Engeström (1999, 2002 as cited in Wells, 2002) added three components (rules, community, division of labor) to show "the societal and collaborative nature" of specific actions (1999, p. 30), with the community consisting of multiple individuals sharing the same general object, the division of labor being understood as roles (task divisions, power, status) among the community members, and the rules including norms and conventions (both explicit and implicit) that regulate the interactions within the activity system. The application of these components to graduate student engagement in a term paper (see Fig. 1) is that a student is a member of the classroom community which operates by specific rules for writing a term paper (e.g., academic writing conventions in the particular field, instructional guidelines for the assignment, and grading for individual assignments and for the entire class) with division of labor (e.g., the professor assigning and grading student papers, and students executing the assignment, students consulting the professor and classmates for the assignment). The arrows between all the nodes in the activity system show "connections between all the nodal constitutive elements of the system, implying many forms of interdependence and mediating influence" (Wells, 2004, p. 74). Through all these mediating influences, the object/goal (a term paper) is transformed into an outcome (e.g., increased understanding of the topic and its application).

Despite being a static representation of a human activity, Engestrom's (1999) diagram is inherently dynamic; multiple individuals at a time serve as agents in a single activity system. Also, each element and the system as a whole undergo constant change (Roth, 2004;

---

2. Other terms such as *mediating artifacts, instruments*, and *tools* are also used in the literature, but in this study I use mediational means.

Wells, 2004). Moreover, a diagram can be expanded into two activity systems side by side with a potential shared object (Engestrom, 2001) or into an activity system network, a concept in which multiple activity systems interact with each other (Engeström, 2001). Another important characteristic of activity theory is that tensions and contradictions within and between activity systems potentially open a space for individual and collective change or development (Engeström, 2001; Wells, 2004). Those tensions and contradictions occur within or between components of an activity system or between interacting activity systems (Roth & Lee, 2007; Smith, 2010, pp. 25–26).

Activity theory has been gradually applied in L2 writing studies. The components of an activity system were used as an analytical tool for such areas as L2 English international students' learning to write in a first-year rhetoric and composition course in the U.S. (Nelson & Kim, 2001), pre-university English as a Second Language (ESL) students' writing development (Yang, Baba, & Cumming, 2004), college English as a Foreign Language (EFL) students' longitudinal change in L2 writing ability and motivation in relation to study-abroad experiences (Sasaki, 2009, 2011), and college EFL writers' use of writing strategies (Lei, 2008). More recently, Li (2013) focused on tensions in L2 English undergraduate writers' activity systems of academic writing based on sources. Beyond students' writing, Lee and Mak (2013) utilized activity theory in their analysis of two Hong Kong secondary school teachers' appropriation of peer feedback in their L2 writing instruction. Those studies adopted activity theory in order to situate L2 writing in the sociocultural context where it takes place. However, though they applied activity system components to individual writing/teaching practices, they did not address activity system networks (e.g., interactions between teacher's and students' activity systems). Thus, those studies appeared to miss the dynamic view of activity system as an interactive and collective endeavor.

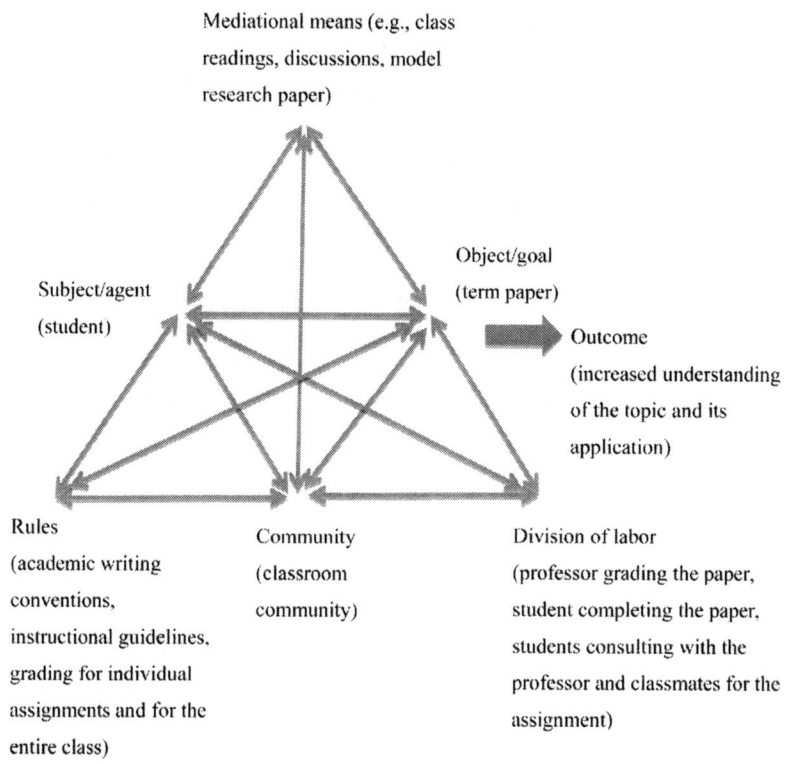

```
                Mediational means (e.g., class
                readings, discussions, model
                research paper)

                              Object/goal
Subject/agent                 (term paper)
(student)                                    ➤ Outcome
                                               (increased understanding
                                               of the topic and its
                                               application)

Rules                Community           Division of labor
(academic writing    (classroom          (professor grading the paper,
conventions,         community)          student completing the paper,
instructional guidelines,                students consulting with the
grading for individual                   professor and classmates for the
assignments and for the                  assignment)
entire class)
```

Fig. 1. Activity system of graduate student engagement in a term paper. Adapting Engeström's (1999) diagram.

In this study, I apply Engeström's (1999) representation of activity theory to investigate the interactions between an L2 English graduate student and one of his professors for disciplinary writing assignments, because activity theory's emphasis on collective practices (Smagorinsky, 2011) helps to see concurrent learning between different people and thus open possibility for multi-directionality of learning, as introduced earlier. For this purpose, I review existing data from a study I conducted earlier, the background and history of which I explain in the next section.

The Study

Background and research questions

The data of this study were drawn from the data pool of a larger study (Fujioka, 1999a) on the academic literacy experiences of a group of

American and Japanese graduate students in the U.S. Based on a social-constructivist view of writing (Bruffee, 1986), I investigated how students engaged in course writing assignments through interactions with their professors and peers. Among the cases I investigated in the study, the specific student–professor pair chosen as participants for this case study provided the clearest evidence of change in views of and attitudes toward classroom literacy practices. Although I reported aspects of this student's and other students' writing processes from the original study focusing on their cross-cultural literacy experiences (Fujioka, 1999b, 2000), learning strategies (Fujioka, 2002), and peer interactions (Fujioka, 2009), this focal pair sustained my interest over time, because I was unable to explain the individual and mutual changes they demonstrated until my encounter with activity theory. In addition to specific components in activity systems, the concept of interaction between or among activity systems was especially promising to interpret interactive experiences and mutual changes that participants demonstrated and thus may lead to understanding of the concurrent and multi-directional nature of learning between people. With a goal of explaining the complexity of multiple agents' learning in interaction, I revisited the original data with the following guiding questions:

1. How can the writing and teaching practices by this student and his professor within the course and their changes over time be represented by activity systems?

2. How can the mutual changes between the student and the professor be explained by interactive activity systems or activity system networks?

3. How do activity system networks help interpret participants' learning experiences beyond the course?

I conducted the original study in the School of Education at a large midwestern state university in the U.S, where I was a doctoral student at the time. The course for focus in this study was 5ZZ (a fictitious course number) "Educational Anthropology" (slightly altered from the original name), a 500-level graduate course offered in the Educational Leadership and Policy Studies Department. Of the 25 master's and doctoral students enrolled in the course during Fall Semester, 1997, there were 16 American and nine international students including four Japanese.

Method

Participants

The focal participants in the present study were Jun,[3] a Japanese student in the 5ZZ course and the course instructor, Professor Collins. Jun, whom I had known only briefly prior to the original study, accepted my invitation to Japanese graduate students majoring in education to participate in my research, and later Professor Collins, the instructor of 5ZZ, participated as the course instructor informant for whom Jun was engaged in completing various writing assignments. Though their data for this case study came from the time of the original data collection (September to December, 1997) and follow-ups (April and May, 1998), their latest information as of 2011 is provided in the epilogue. Jun, a 24-year-old, second year master's student, had completed his B.A. in political science in Japan and come to the U.S. for graduate work in educational policy studies at the institution where this study was conducted. During his undergraduate study, he had spent a year as an exchange student at another U.S. university. He had scored above 550 on the Test of English as a Foreign Language (TOEFL),[4] which his graduate school required at the time, and was admitted to graduate study without any ESL training. He was taking the 5ZZ course as a requirement in his major in the third semester of his master's study, upon completion of which he was planning to return to Japan to seek employment. Professor Collins, a young American professor in his thirties, was in his second year as an assistant professor in the Educational Leadership and Policy Studies Department in the School of Education. He had completed his doctoral degree in anthropology four years prior to the data collection of this study. He was teaching the 5ZZ course for the first time, which was also his first time teaching a graduate course in his academic career.

Besides Jun, another Japanese student from the 5ZZ course, Yumiko,[5] served as an informant to provide supplementary informa-

---

3. All names in this study are pseudonyms
4. At the time of Jun's application for this graduate program, TOEFL was only available as a paper version.
5. The data provided by Yumiko, who was in her first semester in the U.S.

tion in this study. All the participants signed informed consent forms, a required procedure for the original study to be approved by the University Human Subjects Committee.

Data sources and analysis

I employed salient components of a qualitative case study approach as discussed in the literature (e.g., Duff, 2008; Merriam, 2009), including triangulated data sources, member checks, and inductive analysis to identify emerging themes. Different data sources included a class observation, interviews, and documents. Two interviews in English with Professor Collins and three interviews in Japanese with Jun, conducted individually at different points in the semester, were open-ended with the following focus. I asked Professor Collins about his goals for the course, his expectations of the writing assignments, his experiences with students both in- and out-of-class interactions, and his reflections on the course after the semester was over. I asked Jun to describe his views of the course and the professor, his approaches to the readings and writings for the course, and his responses to the professor's comments on his written assignments. Documents included the course syllabus and handouts, some of the professor's email messages to the class about the assignments, Jun's drafts for the writing assignments, and his final submissions with Professor Collins's comments on them.

I made summative notes from the interviews and the observation recordings and transcribed portions of the focal participants' interviews that were critical for analysis. I translated the notes and transcriptions from the interviews with Jun to English. I then asked both Jun and Professor Collins to check the summative notes and transcriptions for accuracy and to make additional comments, and also for the translation accuracy in Jun's case. I also translated into English supplementary accounts provided by Yumiko in Japanese regarding specific course events.

For the analysis in the present study, I read the summative notes and transcriptions in both Japanese and English from the original study again. For accuracy and consistency, I repeatedly checked those sum-

---

at the time, were included in the data pool but eventually removed from the report of the original study (Fujioka, 1999a), due to my decision to focus on students who had completed at least one full semester in their U.S. graduate studies.

maries and transcriptions across the participants, as well as against the document evidence and partially against audio-recordings. Analysis involved two phases: composing a narrative (chronological accounts) and graphically representing the narrative based on Engeström's diagram (1999). The first phase started with my composing a narrative about interactional experiences between Jun and Professor Collins concerning the assignments and specific events in the course. I then added relevant excerpts from the transcriptions and portions from the other documents to the narrative. In the process of writing the narrative, I identified themes, most of which were in the form of straightforward phrases to describe participants' interactional experiences along with some elaborated statements.

In the next phase, based on the narrative, I represented both participants' experiences with writing assignments for the course as activity systems based on Engeström's diagram (1999), treating each assignment as a goal-oriented mediated activity. Following Swain, Kinnear, and Steinman (2011), who narrated a language teacher and her student's interactional experiences by visualizing both sides' perspectives based on the Engeström's diagram, I coded the elements in my narrative data and placed them in each component of the diagram (e.g., mediational means, rules, division of labor), repeatedly returning to the source readings on activity theory. Furthermore, I checked Jun's and the professor's diagrams over the same assignments and compared Jun's diagrams over different assignments to see how these activity systems were connected with each other and how their interactional experiences made sense as a whole.

Overview of the course

Here I introduce a brief overview of the course context for the participants' narrative. For Professor Collins, as a first time member of the graduate faculty, discovering the students' characteristics in the 5ZZ course was a major task. Having been trained as an anthropologist, he was slightly perplexed with the diversity of levels and background knowledge among the students, who ranged from beginning master's to advanced doctoral students and had varying degrees of background knowledge in anthropology, as well as varying interests in different fields of education. Due to this academic diversity among the students, he decided the main goal of this course should be to help students understand central anthropological concepts and apply them to their own areas of interest in education.

During a class observation, I found that, despite his casual demeanor, Professor Collins's lecture was somewhat difficult to understand due to his long, complicated sentence structures with dense information from the readings. Moreover, the entire class discussion on the readings was dominated by American students, causing me to consider the international students' difficulty with participating actively in the discussions and alerting me to the possibility of their also finding the writing assignments challenging.

There were four major writing assignments in the course, of which the descriptions and their percentages for the overall course grade were as follows:

(A) Reaction paper (5-page response to one week's assigned readings and summary of one related optional reading) 10%
(B) Notebook entries (summaries and notes of weekly required readings) 30%
(C) Mid-term take-home exam (responses to interrelated essay questions) 30%
(D) Term paper (12–15 pages) 30%

Among the assignments, questions and responses in the mid-term take-home exam were primarily based on and expanded from the reaction paper and notebook entries. In addition, neither Jun nor Professor Collins demonstrated changes in their views of or attitudes toward their writing/teaching practices over this assignment the way they did from the first (reaction paper) to the other subsequent assignments (notebook entries and term paper). For these reasons, I focus on the reaction paper, notebook entries, and term paper in the following narration of the participants' interactional experiences. In the following section, I present the narrative in the chronological order of the three assignments, under the themes which I identified, followed by the graphic representation of Jun's and Professor Collins's activity systems for each assignment.

Findings and Discussion

Challenging and defending positions

In the eighth week, Jun submitted his 11-page reaction paper based on four readings including a book chapter and an article written by Professor Collins. One of the points in his critique of the readings was a perceived gap between ethnographers' elitist attitudes in their use of abstract and complicated language in their writing and their mission to study local people in their everyday lives. He bravely named Professor Collins and another author, with a note at the end of the paper saying his argument was not meant as "a personal attack," and commented that their writing was excluding the readers who did not understand their language. He concluded his paper with his hope for future ethnographers' use of language that was more accessible to non-academics.

In his extended written responses to Jun's reaction paper, Professor Collins praised Jun's overall success in his effective summaries of the readings and acknowledged Jun's frustration as "legitimate and understandable." He pointed out, however, the misplacement of Jun's argument in that the articles Jun critiqued were written by ethnographers for an academic audience. He also argued for the usefulness of "complicated" language to express complex ideas or thought processes. At the same time, however, one of his comments revealed his relative novice status in the university faculty community; he emphasized the academic pressures placed on younger scholars to demonstrate an advanced level of writing to be recognized for tenure and promotion purposes. To summarize, the professor responded to Jun's challenge of the authority directed toward him personally by utilizing his disciplinary and academic writing expertise, but at the same time he defended his own writing style by revealing the behind-the-scenes struggles he was experiencing as a junior faculty member.

Clash of cultural expectations

Jun understood from the professor's comments that he needed to contextualize ethnographers' writing style, but he was offended by the last comment the professor made on his reaction paper, which said, "Meanwhile, readers prefer 'accessible' texts that don't challenge them to extend their vocabulary or conceptual stock. This is a problem, too." Jun interpreted this comment as the professor's prejudice against international students for their inability to understand advanced vocabulary or difficult writing in English due to their nonnative English speakers' status. His defensive view of the professor's comment was in fact related to the negative view of the professor he had held since the beginning of the semester. He detected a lack of understanding of international students on the part of the professor, Asian students in particular. He felt that Professor Collins was not including Asian students well in the entire class discussion or inviting their responses in non-threatening and non-coercive ways, as some of the senior professors at this graduate institution had previously demonstrated. He also heard that another Japanese student in the course protested against the professor's way of handling one of their Asian classmates, details of which I describe here.

According to Professor Collins, a Taiwanese student in the course, who he understood was struggling with the articles she was assigned to orally present to the class, expressed concern about pursuing this assignment in her meeting with him. Detecting extreme anxiety on the student's part, he decided to excuse her from the oral presentation in return for a more thorough written summary than those of her classmates one week before her scheduled presentation. In the following week, Yumiko, a Japanese student in the course, came to him and emotionally expressed her position that he should have encouraged the Taiwanese student to give her presentation and that he had slighted her by not requiring her to do so. He summarized Yumiko's perspective as follows:

> ... in sort of the kind of shared Asian culture that they have, that students may always be likely to kind of say how things are difficult and pressure the professor, but the professor should never give in, ... it was an insult in a sense for me to have let her [the Taiwanese student] off the hook ... because it was saying "Well, as a class, we wouldn't be that interested in your presentation anyway" and it got turned into a kind of insult like that.

Recognizing the student's reluctance to present as a sign of lack of confidence, Yumiko commented that she was angry with the professor because she did not think he was doing his job as a teacher when he did not encourage the student to follow through with the presentation. She further commented that she wanted the professor to learn about Asian students' ways of talking and thinking for the benefit of his future teaching. This incident, which Professor Collins took constructively, ended with the Taiwanese student's successful presentation through his encouragement and help.

Jun made a brief analysis of this incident without first-hand knowledge of the talk between the professor and the Taiwanese student. In his perspective, the source of the problem was Professor Collins's taking Asian students' remarks literally. He commented that Asians saying "I don't want to do this," which he assumed the Taiwanese student had said, was simply an expression "out of modesty," the same observation Yumiko made. He further said vehemently "since Asians always have respect for authority, we work hard for the class assignments because they are assigned by the authority [professors]." Along with his observations of the professor's interactions with students in the class, this particular incident added more evidence to Jun's belief that the professor lacked understanding about Asian students.

Clash of academic expectations

Receiving an A minus on the reaction paper, Jun visited the professor to ask him how he could improve this paper to an A standard. At the meeting, however, he was offended by the professor's comment that an A paper would be an exceedingly good paper, by which he felt that the professor was implying international students could not get an A. He also had complaints about the one-page two-sided handout titled "Writing Guidelines and Assignments" the professor had distributed to the class earlier in the semester, separately from a detailed nine-page course syllabus. The handout included passages about "Plagiarism," "Format" (e.g., clear organization, transition between paragraphs, and a topic sentence for each paragraph), and "Grading Conventions." To receive an A, for example, a paper should be:

> "well organized . . . and sentences are smooth and carefully crafted. There are virtually no errors in punctuation or spelling, grammar, or usage. . . .. The paper is tight, not wordy." (Quotes from "Walvoord, 'Helping Students Write Well,' MLA, 1986, p. 152" as stated in the handout). Evidence and/or supporting examples are carefully and judiciously employed, and the student shows a creative ability to bring original thought or experience to bear on the assignment.

Initially, Professor Collins felt no need to provide general writing guidelines for his students in the 5ZZ course. However, he found major problems including coherence, proper citations, and grammar in the American and the international students' early reaction papers. This experience prompted him to distribute this handout to the entire class, the information for which he had taken from the source above and the university writing-across-the-curriculum website.

Jun, however, found these writing guidelines "too general" to be helpful. He summarized what he had learned from the handout as "a paper should be consistent, coherent, with well-supported arguments," the expectations which Jun said "anyone doing graduate work here [in the U.S.] for one year would understand." Regarding the reaction paper, in the course syllabus, the professor stated that he would look for "coherence and insight," meaning that students should search for "connections and contradictions across the works and flesh these out." However, Jun felt that neither the writing guidelines nor the detailed course syllabus about each assignment helped him understand the professor's specific grading criteria for the writing assignments.

Jun's dissatisfaction with the professor's responses to his reaction paper also reflected his realization that the professor did not agree with his view that content should be evaluated over form. At the meeting, the professor told him to improve his writing, pointing out the corrections he had made in Jun's final submission including word-choices, definite and indefinite articles, third-person singular *s*, and careless misspellings. In fact, in his extended written comments on Jun's reaction paper, the professor wrote "Had you proofread the paper more closely and cleaned up some of the problems, it would have been an even more powerful statement."

Jun, however, felt that it was unfair for the professor to lower students' grades due to language problems, although he admitted he had not had his reaction paper read by anyone due to time constraints. He had missed the professor's mention of the need to have a paper proofread before submission stated in the course syllabus. On the issue of grading writing assignments, Professor Collins made the following comments:

> Maybe I'm too rigid or not understanding enough of international students, but I'm kind of strict about that [taking language issues into account for grading] because I feel that part of the process of coming to study in English is to really exert

oneself to master those phrasings and those expressions. So I need to kind of uphold that standard of excellence for what constitutes an A paper.

He further commented that he was still trying to figure out how to balance maintaining his standard of excellence and being supportive for students from different cultural and linguistic backgrounds.

The activity systems of Jun and Professor Collins: unsatisfying outcomes

The activity systems of Jun's engagement in the reaction paper and Professor Collins's assigning and grading the reaction paper are presented in Fig. 2.

In both activity systems, division of labor did not represent simple roles of the professor assigning and the student completing the assignment. Jun added respecting and challenging the authority to executing the assignment, as shown in his account of Asian student respecting the authority (professors) in completing an assignment in response to the Taiwanese student's problem with her class presentation, as well as his challenge of the intellectual authority in his reaction paper. Professor Collins, in his job of grading the assignment, activated his disciplinary and academic writing expertise but also revealed his stance as a junior faculty member struggling with the advanced level of writing demanded for his career trajectory. In other words, his disciplinary writing expertise and struggles in his present academic status served as mediational means that influenced his division of labor in responding to students' papers. Jun and Professor Collins seemed to work according to different rules in their activity systems related to the reaction paper. The notion of content over form in grading was an implicit rule for Jun; he felt that L2 English international students could receive an A based on the content and for that purpose their minor second language writing problems, such as grammar or spelling, could or should be overlooked. Professor Collins, on the other hand, emphasized form as an important grading criterion, as revealed in his written guidelines and interview comments, making his rules different from Jun's.

In both activity systems, tensions were experienced in the classroom community due to different cultural expectations between the professor and some students. Professor Collins's activity system was characterized by additional contradiction and tension[6] (as indicated in the note in Fig. 2). In his writing guidelines, for example, the short description of rules for an A paper made no reference to the course content. However, in his course syllabus he emphasized content ("coherence and insight") and his extensive written responses to Jun's reaction paper mostly concerned the insights Jun brought to ethnographers' writing styles. Furthermore, therewas a tension within the division of labor in that the professor realized his adherence to his "standard of excellence" may conflict with individual students' needed areas of assistance. The contradiction and tension resulted in unsatisfying outcomes in that the professor felt uncertainty about his grading while the student was dissatisfied with his grade and the professor's grading.

Changes in views of and actions toward the writing and teaching practices

Notebook entries, which lasted from the beginning of the semester until the eleventh week, turned out to be an opportunity for both Jun and the professor to change their views of and actions in the learning and teaching practices in this classroom community. This assignment consisted of students' summaries of and responses to a week's assigned readings, which on average comprised two or three journal articles and a book chapter. From the start, Jun felt making detailed reading notes was laborious and time-consuming and added the following comments in his first two weeks' notebook entry submission:

> I argue that this assignment is not much appropriate for a week-based task because 1) the amount of reading is so excessive that students are likely to have difficulty in finding its focus, organizing points and preparing some statements and 2) even though the certain guideline is given for the class, it still encompasses many aspects too broadly and questions are so demanding that students hardly can answer all of them within a week.

I think that more consideration should be taken especially for international students. What we can do in a week and what we expect for the class should be in many regards different than those of native

---

6. I used a symbol to represent contradiction and tension different from the one in Engeström (1999).

speakers or advanced graduate students. Some adjustment in reading assignments is truly hoped.

In response to Jun's request for making allowance for international students, Professor Collins wrote "Would this be fair? Should internationals have fewer demands placed on them?" In the end comments, however, he mitigated his tone of response and wrote:

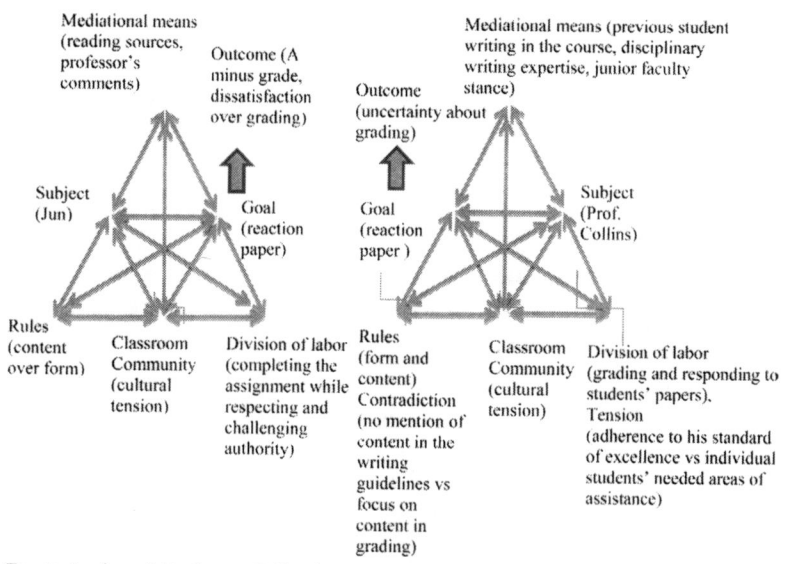

Fig. 2. Jun's and Professor Collins's activity systems of the reaction paper assignment. *Note*: The symbol — indicates "contradiction" and "tension."

> OK, point well-taken: I could have introduced this better and allowed more time, but the point was more to illustrate an approach than grapple with all the details. I need to make this clearer and give strategies for reading.

After all the students' first sets of notebook entries were submitted, Professor Collins started emailing guiding questions for each week's reading that were more focused than those from the previous weeks. In the hope that they would serve as prompts for students' improved notes, his revised questions called for the definitions of specific concepts described in particular readings and applications of those concepts to students' educational contexts.

Having learned that weekly readings would not be reduced, Jun changed his approach to making his reading notes for subsequent notebook entries. Rather than simple summaries, he formulated his responses based on the professor's guiding questions, adding direct quotes of important passages from the readings, making comments, and posing his own questions. Furthermore, in order to ascertain if he was on the right track, he started sending some of his notes to the professor by email, to which the professor made brief comments including the need for more careful reading or more condensed summaries of specific readings. After doing this for a few weeks, he felt his notes were gradually improving and decided to work on the rest without the professor's feedback.

On his accumulative final notebook entries, Jun received the score of 94 out of 100, with the following comments from the professor:

> Jun:
>
> This is outstanding work. You strike a nice balance between direct quotes, summary, and critical analysis. . .. You seem to have learned to move away from an exhaustive summary, which you attempted the first 2 weeks, to a more programmatic outline. Some of your observations are quite astute.
>
> Thanks for being a regular participant in class. I'm sorry I didn't create a more effective structure for all students to contribute to the discussion. I will take your comments to heart the next time I teach this course.

Jun was very satisfied with the professor's comments, as well as the progress he had made over the course of this assignment.

When asked to comment on the professor's appreciation of his efforts in participating in the class discussion, Jun smiled and said, "I was just sitting in class," probably "out of modesty" that he attributed earlier to his Asian cultural background. In the class I observed, however, he asked the professor a question about the term paper assignment without hesitation. Also he did not mention the difficulty contributing to the class discussion which Yumiko, the aforementioned Japanese student, continuously felt. She commented that most international students in the class including herself were silenced by a few dominating American students, an observation which was supported in Professor Collins's comment to Jun regarding the lack of an effective structure to invite all students' participation in class discussions.

Interconnectedness of two activity systems: signs of student and teacher enactment of agency

The activity systems of Jun's engagement in the notebook entries and the professor's teaching practices in regard to the assignment are characterized by various changes, in keeping with Roth's (2004) characterization of Engeström's triangle as "continuously undergoing change in its parts, in its relations, and as a whole" (p. 4). In addition to the internal changes, a change in one component in Jun's activity system affected another component and also brought about changes in the professor's activity system, resulting in further changes in Jun's activity system, as shown in Fig. 3.

In the initial notes, Jun was operating on the rules for making exhaustive summaries, the difficulty of which made him negotiate the assignment with the professor. This kind of explicit negotiation was observed in other studies of L2 English international students' literacy socialization (Prior, 1998, Chap. 2) and oral academic discourse socialization (Morita, 2004). In his negotiation over the assignment with the professor, however, Jun showed a contradiction in the node of division of labor from his previous activity system of the reaction paper, in which he advocated Asian students' respect for authority and capability to follow through on an assignment, but in his complaint about the notebook entries, he requested allowance for L2 English students in terms of the demands of work placed on them.

Although the negotiation failed, Jun's complaint about the assignment became part of mediational means for the professor in alerting him to the need for revised guidance on the reading notes (shown as curved arrows 1 in Fig. 3). Moreover, his revised guidance was first projected to the community (email guidance for the entire class), provoking Jun's solicitation for specific help on his notes, which became a new constituent in Jun's division of labor (curved arrow 2 in Fig. 3). His solicitation of help made the professor's division of labor include increased and individualized guidance (curved arrow 3 in Fig. 3). The changes in the professor's activity system, represented by the interconnected arrows in it, brought about clearer guidance on the reading notes as the outcome. This outcome served as effective mediational means for Jun in refining his notes (curved arrow 4 in Fig. 3), and, as shown in the internal arrows in his activity system, he began to operate on the new rules of critical analysis of readings. These internal changes in rules, division of labor, and mediational means in his activity system transformed Jun's notebook entries from meeting a simple goal of completing the assignment to developing improved strategies of reading and taking notes as the outcome. These interconnections in changes between Jun's and the professor's activity systems illustrate the idea of activity system networks (Engeström, 2001).

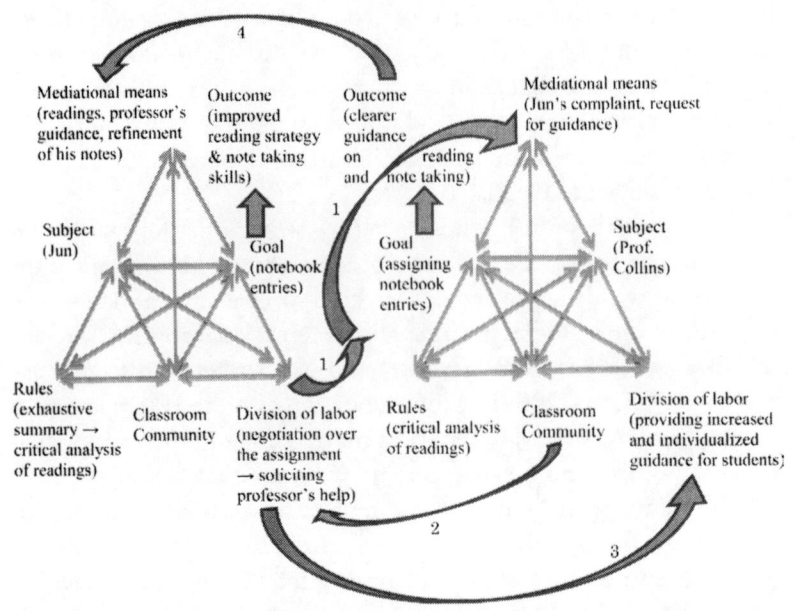

Fig. 3. Interconnectedness of Jun's and Professor Collins's activity systems of the notebook entry assignment.

Through these changes regarding the notebook entries, both participants demonstrated signs of agency, that is, "the power to act" (Roth et al., 2004, p. 51). With his negative view of the professor at the beginning and his doubts about the professor's grading procedures for the reaction paper, Jun could have taken an attitude of resistance by withdrawing from or selectively participating in the class activities, a choice made by some L2 international graduate students in Canada in Morita's (2004) study. Instead, he showed accommodation by taking advantage of the help offered by the professor, whose academic expectations he had resisted, and changing his approaches to the notebook assignment. In other words, he learned to change himself for his own benefit rather than continue to blame the professor.

Professor Collins also could have responded differently to international students' explicit negotiations for particular disciplinary assignments by reducing the reading load, as demonstrated by one of the professors in Prior's (1998) study, or providing no assistance (Morita, 2004). Instead, through his revised and improved guiding questions for the reading notes, he provided expert assistance to students, which, though assumed by many theories of socialization, Morita notes "may not always be readily available to all learners" (p. 598). In addition, Professor Collins acknowledged areas of improvement for his future teaching, for example, the need to develop effective structures for class discussion to facilitate all students' active participation, as he showed in his comments on Jun's notebook entries.

Professor Collins's changes in his attitude toward his current and future teaching practices indicate that classroom assignments provide opportunities for professors, as well as students, to enact their agency.

Final assignment: Jun's and professor's learning in and beyond the course

Jun was strongly determined to receive an A on the term paper, due partly to his failure to receive an A on the reaction paper and the midterm exam, but primarily to his desire to change the professor's perception of him as a student. Despite the successful experience with the notebook entries, Jun continued to hold a negative view of the professor, who he thought might be prejudiced against international students' intellectual capability due to their disadvantage in English. Thus, he decided to prove his intellectual competitiveness and try to "impress" the professor through quality work in the term paper.

In order to pursue his goal, Jun utilized his local knowledge, by which I mean the knowledge from their native cultures nonnative speakers utilize to pursue their goals in their target culture's educational practices (see Canagarajah, 2002, for detailed discussion on local knowledge). To meet the requirement of the term paper as a critical review of anthropological theories about the education of a specific cultural or ethnic minority group, Jun chose to apply anthropologist John Ogbu's framework of ethnic minorities to Korean residents in Japan. He had 26 reading sources altogether including some written in Japanese, half of which he had read in one of his previous courses.

In order to achieve the goal of receiving an A, Jun decided to employ three strategies. First, he took his notebook entry approach, that is, summarizing important reading sources and making notes of his responses to particular passages from the readings. This strategy was prompted by the specific requirement of a detailed summary of each of the readings and the synthesis of various sources in the term paper guidelines Professor Collins had provided in the course syllabus. Second, before composing a draft, Jun made detailed outlines of his paper, portions of which were reported in Fujioka (2000). He found that constructing outlines made his arguments consistent, which had been one of his major problems in drafting the term papers for previous courses.

Third, upon completion of his draft, Jun asked Ellen, an American student from the 5ZZ course, to read his paper before submission, in order to improve the overall quality of his draft. He and Ellen had been good friends, taking many courses together as part of the same major in educational policy studies, and he knew that she was a reliable reader. In fact, beyond grammar corrections and stylistic suggestions, she pointed out Jun's lack of argument and proper citations in his 5ZZ paper draft, which he highly appreciated. Some of the examples of Ellen's written comments on Jun's draft were reported elsewhere (Fujioka, 2009).

I found Jun's final product of the term paper, a 34-page text plus five pages of appendices and references, impressive. After a thorough literature review of educational issues of ethnic minorities, he astutely critiqued Ogbu's categorization of Korean residents in Japan as an involuntary minority group, with relevant sources of historical and current viewpoints. Moreover, he proposed his own view of ethnic minority issues based on an alternative theoretical perspective. Beyond its convincing argument and quality of writing, Jun's paper effectively communicated his strong commitment to and robust enthusiasm about his paper.

"All's well that ends well."

As he had earnestly aspired, Jun achieved his goal, receiving a final score of 95-A. Professor Collins congratulated Jun for his excellent work by writing the following comments on Jun's final submission:

> This is a remarkable paper in many ways. I know that you had done some of this work for another class, but I assume that some of your references, like Foley (1991), are new. If so, I congratulate you. Your incorporation of Foley's perspective is especially effective at the end.

> This paper is very thorough, perceptive, and notably well-written. It's an ambitious thesis which, for the most part, you support quite well. (Detailed comments follow about the content.)
>
> If it might serve your interests, this paper could be made worthy of publication with relatively little work.

He also orally congratulated Jun's local knowledge in that no scholars had previously attempted an inclusion of scholarly sources written in Japanese for the discussion of Ogbu's theory.

Professor Collins's comments truly surprised Jun, especially the mention of the possibility of publication, which was beyond his intent simply to prove his intellectual capability through a term paper. However, he decided not torevise this paper for publication as he had to finish the following semester before returning to Japan. After reflecting on the term paper and the course over the semester, Jun made the following comments:

> The professor's comments made me feel he evaluated me fairly and rewarded me for my hard work. Earlier I thought the professor did not give me an A because I was an international student, but I learned it was not the case. Although he has high expectations, he gives us an A if we work hard.

Furthermore, he was now grateful to the professor for including the notebook entries as a course assignment. He found that incorporating the notebook entry approach of making summaries and responding to readings, with which he had struggled in the beginning of the semester, worked especially successfully for the term paper.

After the semester was over, Professor Collins started developing ideas for modifications of his teaching strategies for 5ZZ in the future. For example, he learned about some students' difficulty coping with all the writing assignments in addition to thorough weekly readings and participation in the class discussions. Thus, he was conceiving an option of shorter writing assignments in the future in order to help students engage more in the required course readings.

Activity system network in and beyond the course

The activity system of Jun's engagement in the term paper, which is shown in Fig. 4, is characterized by his activity system networks.

It is noteworthy that for this assignment Jun utilized various mediational means acquired in this course and beyond. The means specific to this course included the professor's guidelines for the assignment, which also constituted rules; the course readings; and the reading and note-taking strategies he had learned from previous assignments in this course. Beyond the present course, his utilization of his local knowledge about the topic of the assignment, some reading sources, and the practice of detailed outlining, all came from his previous experiences, that is, his previous activity systems of past graduate literacy practices, which operated in specific communities under specific rules and division of labor, interacting with mediational means. All these previous activity systems along with the activity system of the notebook entry assignment in the course were incorporated into the mediational means in his present activity system, as shown in Fig. 4 (see also Barab, Barnett, Yamagata-Lynch, Squire, & Keating, 2002, for an object in an action nesting as a mediation tool in a subsequent action).

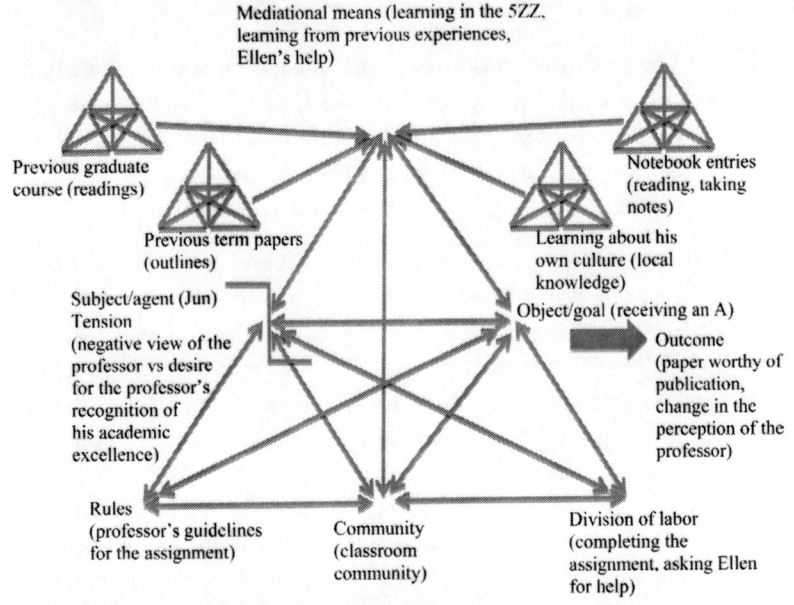

Fig. 4. Jun's activity system of term paper assignment. *Note*: Small triangles represent simplified versions of Jun's previous activity systems.

In Jun's activity system of working toward receiving an A on the term paper, he, as the subject, experienced internal tension between his continued negative view of the professor and his desire to be academically recognized by him. It is also noteworthy that asking Ellen, a member of the classroom community, for help constituted part of Jun's division of labor and, more importantly, through her critique of his paper draft, her help provided an important mediational means for him. All these constituents of each component in Jun's activity system (rules, division of labor, mediational means) transformed his goal of receiving an A for the paper into producing a paper worthy of publication as the outcome. Furthermore, his pursuit of an A resulted in another outcome, which was that he changed his perception of the professor, who he previously thought had underestimated L2 English international students' academic abilities, and accordingly his internal tension was resolved.

Professor Collins's activity system of the term paper assignment is shown in Fig. 5, but this diagram represents his teaching experiences in the course as a whole.

Although providing the instructional and writing guidelines for the class stayed the same in the rules, another part of his rules seemed to change from his initial ideas of equal demands on all students to more individualized structures of teaching for different students. In line with this change, he added more attention to students' needed areas of assistance to the division of labor of grading and responding to the assignments. More importantly, his various experiences with students in the course, students' writing, and their reactions to the assignments and class discussions all became mediational means for him. Through these mediational means, his original goal for the course, that is, helping students learn basic anthropological concepts and apply them to their areas of interests, provoked ideas for his future teaching as an outcome. As he continued to teach the 5ZZ course, some of the constitutive elements in each component in his activity system might stay the same, or change with different experiences with different students and different assignments, generating the activity system network of the 5ZZ course.

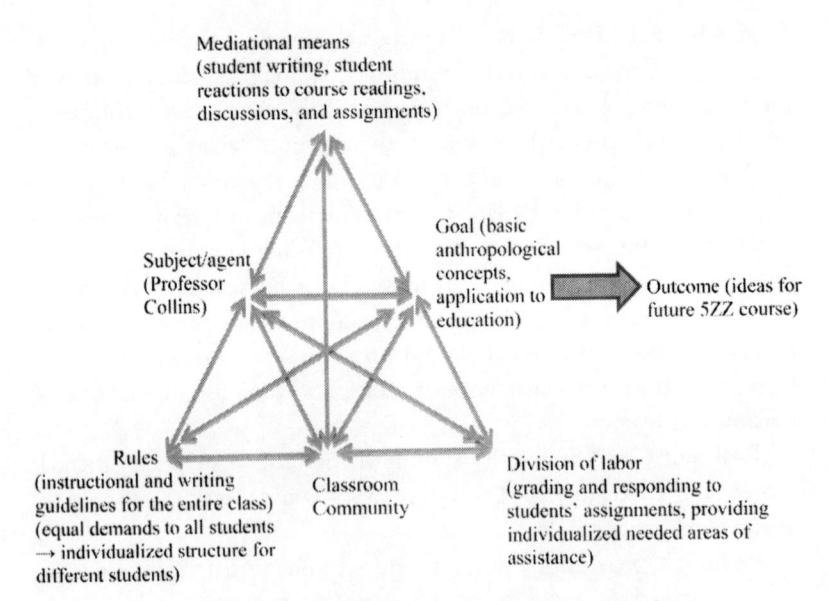

Fig. 5. Professor Collins's activity system of the 5ZZ course teaching.

CONCLUSION: ACTIVITY THEORY AND L2 DISCIPLINARY WRITING STUDIES

The present study echoed an important implication from previous studies for disciplinary literacy practices in that graduate students, at least at the course work level, engage in writing as a "game metaphor" (Casanave, 2002, xiv) by learning to write to meet the expectations of particular and different professors (Casanave, 2002, p. 114; see also Prior, 1998, p. 44). Jun's experiences in the course clearly showed his academic socialization within locally contingent literacy practices and, moreover, his professional socialization as a student through his transformation from a less secure to a mature learner with a balanced view of the professor in the end.

Beyond the student writer's literacy and professional socialization, this study adds to the literature by illustrating changes and transformations the writer brought to himself, his writing practices, his professor, and the social practices in his community. Jun's rigorous participation in the activity systems of multiple course writing assignments stimulated his professor's growth as a reflective teacher willing to modify his teaching practices, which ultimately contributed to

Jun's improved writing practices. Activity theory (Engeström, 1999) and Engeström-inspired representation of teacher-student activity systems in Swain et al. (2011) proved to be helpful for understanding concurrent and multi-directional learning between a student and his professor, who mutually shaped and influenced each other's writing and teaching practices. The theory was also useful for understanding how learning from previous activity systems was interwoven into the student's present activity system.

The power of activity theory to reveal multiple agents' learning and the interactions between their activity systems, leading to the concept of activity system networks, offers rich implications for graduate disciplinary writing studies. Specific graduate level writing activities are often connected with each other or developed into other writing activities, such as a term paper being developed into a thesis, a dissertation, a conference paper, or a journal publication as Professor Collins suggested for Jun's final paper, or a sequence of two or more of these. Thus, it may be worthwhile to investigate a graduate writer's engagement in genre-specific learning as an activity system, and, taking a view of systems of genre, which are "interrelated genres that interact with each other in specific settings" (Bazerman, 1994, p. 97), explore how one student's learning in different genres as activity systems are connected with each other, and how those activity system networks contribute to the student's overall disciplinary literacy development.

In line with the argument of genre systems, Russell's (1997, 2009) discussion on genre as a unit of analysis in relation to an activity system and Tardy's (2009) study on multilingual writers' longitudinal genre knowledge development in a writing course and their disciplinary contexts are revealing. However, in addition to individual writers' development of genre/activity system networks, activity theory makes it possible to see how activity systems of other participants in the writer's sociocultural context interact with the writer's activity system. Adding the activity systems of participants other than students themselves helps us expand or modify our knowledge of graduate disciplinary literacy development beyond the student–course instructor relationship examined in this study. Previous studies in the field investigated such areas as thesis/dissertation advisee–advisor (e.g., Belcher, 1994; Dong, 1996; Prior, 1998; Tardy, 2009) or student writer–journal reviewer (e.g., Cho, 2004; Li, 2007) relationships, and activity theory can offer a useful analytical framework to gain further insights into literacy practices based on these relationships. Or the theory could be extended to such relationships as graduate writer and peer or tutor, which have received limited attention in the field. Moreover, in light of professors', advisors', and journal reviewers' extensive involvement in the student's writing practices, their activity systems can be seen as those sharing or partially sharing the same object/goal as the student's (Engeström, 2009, p. 305), an instantiation of two interacting activity systems (Engeström, 2001, p. 136).

Another implication from activity theory that individuals can contribute to changing their and other activity systems (Roth, 2004) also helps to empower graduate students, L2 graduate students in particular, who learn to write in their disciplines in their target community. As shown in this study, Jun's view of himself as an L2 English writer and of L2 writers as a group was not stable over the course of the semester, moving from his emphasis on L2 students' academic capability at one point to a request for fewer academic demands on them at another time. Later on, however, his desire to prove L2 students' academic competitiveness to his professor became his driving force in the final writing assignment, which resulted in the professor's recognition of his academic excellence and his influence on the professor's attitude toward L2 students. Despite the tensions and contradictions Jun demonstrated in his activity systems, his eventual success and the change he helped bring about in the professor's activity systems of teaching practices provide encouragement for L2 graduate students.

Due to their nonnative speaker status operating in a community which is not their home environment, L2 international graduate students, a group to which I once belonged, may tend to think they have little to offer to their disciplinary classroom communities at least in their early stage of disciplinary socialization. However, by viewing their L2 literacy experiences through the lens of activity system, we recognize that they have the potential power to bring change to their contexts of learning, including those resulting from professors' increased awareness of effective teaching strategies and culturally appropriate teacher–student interactions. Since an activity theory approach suggests "ways to trace how people and their writing practices change, individually and collectively, as they move within and among various social practices" (Russell, 2009, p. 42), it may offer a great deal to the study of the advanced academic literacy of L2 writers, who make extended journeys between different languages, cultures, and also various writing contexts.

Future Study

It is my hope that this study has made a modest contribution to L2 graduate disciplinary writing studies by illuminating how synthesis of disciplinary socialization and an activity theory perspective of learning works to interpret the complexity involved in multiple agents' learning in their disciplinary contexts. Though this study focused on two agents, a student and his professor in a specific graduate disciplinary course, future study might explore different combinations of agents, including multiple students taking the same course and their interactional experiences among them and with the course professor. For example, Jun and Yumiko in this study, both L2 English international students from Japan, shared the same cultural observations about Asians' ways of verbal interactions as shown earlier, but they may have interpreted and approached the professor and the course assignments differently, due to their different levels of experience in graduate school, as being a newly starting first-year student (Yumiko) and as a more experienced second-year student (Jun). A comparison of their activity systems over course assignments in interaction with the professor's activity systems may reveal differences in each component of their activity systems (e.g., different mediational means for different students over the same assignment) and differences in tensions and contradictions (e.g., entire class discussions as a source of frustration for Yumiko while it was not for Jun).

Furthermore, as shown in the study, Ellen, an L1 English-speaking U.S. student in the course, provided an important mediational means for one of Jun's activity systems, but a question arises whether Jun or any other student in the course provided a mediational means for Ellen's activity system, in other words, whether there was a multi-directionality in learning among different students in the course. These further thoughts and questions could be explored by revisiting existing data from the original data pool of this study or by collecting new sets of data, through an activity-theory analysis, as activity theory "positions learning in the varied interactions between individuals" (Swain et al., 2011, p. 111).

Epilogue

In 2011, 14 years after the original data collection, I had a chance to visit Professor Collins at the same institution where the study was conducted. A young assistant professor back then was now a full professor still teaching the 5ZZ course. Due to technological changes over the years, the notebook entries were replaced by "inquiry notes," which students posted in an on-line forum so they could respond to each other's reading notes freely. The professor had also developed different instructional strategies in his teaching of 5ZZ over many years in order to facilitate all students' participation in class discussions, a goal for his future teaching which he had mentioned in his comments on one of Jun's papers. For example, he helped students build their confidence by participating in small group discussions, which he used increasingly, and inviting them to share their reading notes with their classmates. Through his experiences with international students, he had learned to understand the needs of those who were reluctant to speak voluntarily in class, and he now hoped he was responding to their concerns well.

Another major change in the course was the inclusion of more expressive writing assignments. For example, instead of a traditional term paper, a final reflection paper was now assigned in the form of a letter students wrote to themselves several years in the future in which they reflected on what they had learned in the course. The inclusion of nontraditional and more personal writing assignments was, according to Professor Collins, a result of his growth as a teacher and his confidence as an established scholar, who had become "a critic" of his own field and now advocated multiple forms of academic literacy for students, as he was now practicing in the 5ZZ course. These changes in Professor Collins's teaching practices over the years provided me a glimpse of the continuing evolution of the activity system of his 5ZZ course, in which "the past is carried into the present and modified in the light of current circumstances and future goals" (Wells, 2004, p. 73).

Professor Collins remembered Jun as one of the vocal and assertive students in his first-time teaching of the course. Although I would have liked to share with the professor updated information about Jun, unfortunately I had lost contact with him after a few email exchanges when he returned to Japan after finishing his studies in the U.S. If I had a chance to see Jun again, I would like to convey to him Professor Collins's words from our last meeting: "Jun would have enjoyed the course more now."

Acknowledgements

I would like to thank the editors and two reviewers of *JSLW* for their valuable and insightful comments, which helped me enhance my understanding of activity theory. I am also greatly indebted to Christine Casanave for her advice on activity theory and her ongoing encouragement in my writing process. I am also grateful to Carol Rinnert and Sharon Pugh for their careful reading of my manuscript. Last but not least, I would also like to extend my gratitude to David Squires and Yosuke Sasao for their assistance with the graphics for this study.

References

Angelova, M., & Riazantseva, A. (1999). "If you don't tell me, how can I know?": A case study of four international students learning to write the U.S. way. *Written Communication, 16*, 491–525.

Barab, S. A., Barnett, M., Yamagata-Lynch, L., Squire, K., & Keating, T. (2002). Using activity theory to understand the systemic tensions characterizing a technology-rich introductory astronomy course. *Mind, Culture, and Activity, 9*, 76–107.

Bazerman, C. (1994). Systems of genres and the enactment of social intentions. In A. Freedman & P. Medway (Eds.), *Genre and the new rhetoric* (pp. 79–101). London: Taylor & Francis, Ltd.

Belcher, D. (1994). The apprenticeship approach to advanced academic literacy: Graduate students and their mentors. *English for Specific Purposes, 13*, 23–34.

Bruffee, K. A. (1986). Social construction, language, and the authority of knowledge: A bibliographical essay. *College English, 48*, 773–790. Canagarajah, S. (2002). Reconstructing local knowledge. *Journal of Language, Identity, and Education, 1*, 243–259.

Casanave, C. P. (1995). Local interactions: Constructing contexts for composing in a graduate sociology program. In D. Belcher & G. Braine (Eds.), *Academic writing in a second language: Essays on research and pedagogy* (pp. 83–110). Norwood, NJ: Ablex.

Casanave, C. P. (2002). *Writing games: Multicultural case studies of academic literacy practices in higher education*. Mahwah, NJ: Lawrence Erlbaum.

Casanave, C. P. (2008). Learning participatory practices in graduate school: Some perspective-taking by a mainstream educator. In C. P. Casanave & X. Li (Eds.), *Learning the literacy practices of graduate school: Insiders' reflections on academic enculturation* (pp. 14–31). Ann Arbor: University of Michigan Press.

Cho, S. (2004). Challenges of entering discourse communities through publishing in English: Perspectives of nonnative-speaking doctoral students in the United States of America. *Journal of Language, Identity, and Education, 3*, 47–72.

Dong, Y. R. (1996). Learning how to use citations for knowledge transformation: Nonnative doctoral students' dissertation writing in science. *Research in the Teaching of English, 30*, 428–457.

Duff, P. A. (2008). *Case study research in applied linguistics.* New York, NY: Routledge.

Engeström, Y. (1999). Activity theory and individual and social transformation. In Y. Engeström, R. Miettinen, R.-L. Punama¨ki (Eds.), *Perspectives on activity theory* (pp. 19–38). Cambridge, UK: Cambridge University Press.

Engeström, Y. (2001). Expansive learning at work: Toward an activity theoretical reconceptualization. *Journal of Education and Work, 14*, 133–156.

Engeström, Y. (2009). The future of activity theory: A rough draft. In A. Sannino, H. Daniels, & K. D. Gutie´rrez (Eds.), *Learning and expanding with activity theory* (pp. 303–328). Cambridge, UK: Cambridge University Press.

Engeström, Y., & Miettinen, R. (1999). Introduction. In Y. Engeström, R. Miettinen, R.-L. Puna¨maki (Eds.), *Perspectives on activity theory* (pp. 1–16). Cambridge, UK: Cambridge University Press.

Fujioka, M. (1999a). *Genre as process: An examination of American and Japanese graduate students' writing of research papers in English.* Unpublished doctoral dissertation. Bloomington, IN, USA: Indiana University.

Fujioka, M. (1999b). Japanese students' academic literacy in English. In A. Barfield, R. Betts, J. Cunningham, N. Dunn, H. Katsura, K. Kobayashi, N. Padden, N. Parry, & M. Watanabe (Eds.), *The Proceedings of the JALT (Japan Association for Language Teaching) 24th Annual International Conference on Language Teaching/Learning & Educational Materials Expo* (pp. 160–165). Tokyo: JALT.

Fujioka, M. (2000). Japanese graduate students' development of academic writing ability in English: Their cross-cultural educational experiences in Japan and the U.S. *Hiroshima Journal of International Studies, 6*, 175–193.

Fujioka, M. (2002). Strategy development in English academic reading and writing: Two Japanese graduate students in the U.S. *The Proceedings of the 29th JACET (the Japan Association of College English Teachers) Summer Seminar 2001* (pp. 42–45). Tokyo: JACET.

Fujioka, M. (2009). Peer-author interactions in L2 disciplinary writing practices. *Kinki University Department of Language Education Bulletin, 9*(1), 21–48.

Kaptelinin, V. (2005). The object of activity: Making sense of the sensemaker. *Mind, Culture, and Activity, 12*, 4–18.

Lantolf, J. P. (2000). Introducing sociocultural theory. In J. P. Lantolf (Ed.), *Sociocultural theory and second language learning* (pp. 1–26). Oxford, UK: Oxford University Press.

Lave, J., & Wenger, E. (1991). *Situated learning: Legitimate peripheral participation*. Cambridge, UK: Cambridge University Press.

Lee, I., & Mak, P. (2013, March). *Appropriating mediation tools for written feedback: An activity theory approach*. Paper presented at TESOL 2013, Dallas, TX.

Lei, X. (2008). Exploring a sociocultural approach to writing strategy research: Mediated actions in writing activities. *Journal of Second Language Writing, 17*, 217–236.

Li, Y. (2005). Multidimensional enculturation: The case of an EFL Chinese doctoral student. *Journal of Asian Pacific Communication, 15*, 153–170. Li, Y. (2006). A doctoral student of physics writing for publication: A sociopolitically oriented case study. *English for Specific Purposes, 25*, 456–478.

Li, Y. (2007). Apprentice scholarly writing in a community of practice: An "intraview" of an NNES graduate student writing a research article. *TESOL Quarterly, 41*, 55–79.

Li, Y. (2013). Three ESL students writing a policy paper assignment: An activity-analytic perspective. *Journal of English for Academic Purposes, 12*, 73–86.

Martin, D. (2005). Communities of practice and learning communities: Do bilingual co-workers learn in community? In D. Barton & K. Tusting (Eds.), *Beyond communities of practice: Language, power and social context* (pp. 139–157). Cambridge, UK: Cambridge University Press.

Merriam, S. B. (2009). *Qualitative research: A guide to design and implementation*. San Francisco, CA: Jossey-Bass.

Morita, N. (2004). Negotiating participation and identity in second language academic communities. *TESOL Quarterly, 38*, 573–603.

Nelson, C. P., & Kim, M. (2001). Contradictions, appropriation, and transformation: An activity theory approach to L2 writing and classroom practices. *Texas Papers in Foreign Language Education, 6*(1), 37–62.

Prior, P. (2008). A sociocultural theory of writing. In C. A. MacArthur, S. Graham, & J. Fitzgerald (Eds.), *Handbook of writing research* (pp. 54–66). New York, NY: Guilford Press.

Prior, P. A. (1998). *Writing/disciplinarity: A sociohistoric account of literate activity in the academy*. Mahwah, NJ: Lawrence Erlbaum.

Riazi, A. (1997). Acquiring disciplinary literacy: A social-cognitive analysis of text-production and learning among Iranian graduate students of education. *Journal of Second Language Writing, 6*, 105–137.

Roth, W.-M. (2004). Introduction: "Activity theory and education: An introduction". *Mind, Culture, and Activity, 11*, 1–8.

Roth, W.-M., & Lee, Y.-J. (2007). "Vygotsky's neglected legacy": Cultural-historical activity theory. *Review of Educational Research, 77*, 186–232.

Roth, W.-M., Tobin, K., Elmesky, R., Carambo, C., McKnight, Y.-M., & Beers, J. (2004). Re/making identities in the praxis of urban schooling: A cultural historical perspective. *Mind, Culture, and Activity, 11*, 48–69.

Russell, D. R. (1997). Rethinking genre in school and society: An activity theory analysis. *Written Communication, 14*, 504–554.

Russell, D. R. (2009). Uses of activity theory in written communication research. In A. Sannino, H. Daniels, & K. D. Gutie'rrez (Eds.), *Learning and expanding with activity theory* (pp. 40–52). Cambridge, UK: Cambridge University Press.

Sasaki, M. (2009). Changes in English as a foreign language students' writing over 3.5 years: A sociocognitive account. In R. M. Mancho'n (Ed.), *Writing in foreign language contexts: Learning, teaching, and research* (pp. 49–76). Bristol, UK: Multilingual Matters.

Sasaki, M. (2011). Effects of varying lengths of study-abroad experiences on Japanese EFL students' L2 writing ability and motivation: A longitudinal study. *TESOL Quarterly, 45*, 81–105.

Smagorinsky, P. (2011). *Vygotsky and literacy research: A methodological framework*. Rotterdam, The Netherlands: Sense Publishers.

Smith, S. U. (2010). *Doctoral students' perceptions of learning in a blended research methods course: Three telling cases*. Doctoral dissertation. Available from ProQuest Dissertations and Theses data base (UMI No. 3432542).

Swain, M., Kinnear, P., & Steinman, L. (2011). *Sociocultural theory in second language education: An introduction through narratives*. Bristol, UK: Multilingual Matters.

Tardy, C. M. (2005). "It's like a story": Rhetorical knowledge development in advanced academic literacy. *Journal of English for Academic Purposes, 4*, 325–338.

Tardy, C. M. (2009). *Building genre knowledge*. West Lafayette, IN: Parlor Press.

Vygotsky, L. S. (1978). In M. Cole, V. John-Steiner, S. Scribner, & E. Souberman (Eds.), *Mind in society: The development of higher psychological processes*. Cambridge, MA: Harvard University Press.

Wells, G. (2002). The role of dialogue in activity theory. *Mind, Culture, and Activity, 9*, 43–66.

Wells, G. (2004). Discussion: Narrating and theorizing activity in educational settings. *Mind, Culture, and Activity, 11*, 70–77.

Yang, L., Baba, K., & Cumming, A. (2004). Activity systems for ESL writing improvement: Case studies of three Chinese and three Japanese adult learners of English. In D. Albrechtsen, K. Haastrup, & B. Henriksen (Eds.), *Writing and vocabulary in foreign language acquisition. Special Issue of Angles on the English-Speaking World*. Vol. 4 (pp. 13–33).

Zhu, W., & Mitchell, D. A. (2012). Participation in peer response as activity: An examination of peer response stances from an activity theory perspective. *TESOL Quarterly, 46,* 362–386.

Mayumi Fujioka is associate professor at Osaka Prefecture University, Japan. Her research interests include L2 academic literacy development, L2 writing center theory and practice, and interlanguage pragmatics.

WLN: A JOURNAL OF WRITING CENTER SCHOLARSHIP

> *WLN: A Journal of Writing Center Scholarship* is on the Web at https://wln-journal.org/

WLN: A Journal of Writing Center Scholarship (previous title: *Writing Lab Newsletter*), a peer reviewed publication with five issues per academic year, provides a forum for exchanging narrative and research-based studies of writing centers in high schools, colleges, and universities and addresses questions of the theoretical, pedagogical, and administrative work of writing centers. Articles illustrate how writing centers operate at the intersection of theory and practice, at once shaped by and producing innovative methods and scholarship. Authors reporting on research also describe programmatic models that can be adapted to other contexts. *WLN* aims to inform newcomers to the field as well as extend the thinking of those who are more knowledgeable and experienced. *WLN* also regularly includes a Tutors' Column of essays by and for tutors.

"Student Perceptions of Intellectual Engagement in the Writing Center: Cognitive Challenge, Tutor Involvement, and Productive Sessions"

Bromley, Schonberg, and Northway offer a study of student engagement that highlights the centrality of writing center work to the mission of the university. Their study, which surveys both private and public institutions, finds that writing center sessions provide students crucial opportunities for intellectual engagement in the forms of cognitive challenge and peer collaboration. Far from finding that students consider the writing center only as a product-oriented service, the authors have determined that "[s]tudents valued the experience of being cognitively challenged and collaborating well with their tutor, someone who was excited by their ideas and by them, both as writers and as people in the midst of a learning process" (5). Bromley, Schonberg, and Northway thus offer strong evidence supporting the idea of the writing center as an important site of knowledge-making on college and university campuses.

7 Student Perceptions of Intellectual Engagement in the Writing Center: Cognitive Challenge, Tutor Involvement, and Productive Sessions

Pamela Bromley, Eliana Schonberg, and Kara Northway

Student engagement and intellectual challenge are key to successful learning, according to widely circulated reports from the *National Survey of Student Engagement* (NSSE 36; Gallup-Purdue University). How student-writers engage and how they define and value engagement, however, is often missing from these conversations; in addition, the role of writing centers in engagement is often misunderstood. For example, the NSSE places writing centers only in one of four engagement categories—campus environment, as part of "support services"—separating writing centers problematically from two other NSSE categories, writing and learning with peers (NSSE 34, 45). Our empirical, multi-institutional study uncovers and evaluates students' definitions of intellectual engagement in their writing center sessions. First, most students report they are engaged. Second, students define "intellectual engagement" variously: as cognitive involvement; as affective social interaction; and further, as a collaborative process—not just a collaborative outcome—of problem-solving. Third, students are paying attention to, and valuing, both their own and their tutors' engagement, specifically whether consultants think and engage with them and their ideas, in contrast to the NSSE's assumption of one-way support implied in the language associated with campus support services. Finally, if students feel engaged, they are statistically more likely to report productive sessions. Simply coming in to talk about writing with a consultant (even an especially friendly one) is not always intellectually engaging or productive in and of itself.

The implications of our study speak to the place of writing centers within the knowledge-making communities that are our academic institutions. In light of the NSSE underreporting writing centers' work, our findings demonstrate that writing centers provide measurable engagement data in line with universities' missions. In combining quantitative and qualitative data, we illustrate the need to address students' multifaceted definitions of intellectual engagement formally and informally in pedagogy and research.

Methodology

Our study uses quantitative methods (administering the same exit survey) and qualitative methods (conducting focus groups) at three very different institutions: a small liberal arts college (SLAC); a medium, private, research university (MRU); and a large, public, land-grant university (LPU). In 2009-10, we collected over 2000 survey submissions, completed on computers immediately after sessions in each writing center. The survey included these two statements: "During the consultation, I felt intellectually engaged" and "I feel that my consultation was productive." We analyzed results at the 0.05 level using t-tests, defined by statisticians as a test that determines whether there is a statistical difference between data from two groups. At the 0.05 significance level, we are 95% confident that the differences observed are statistically significant and not the result of chance; at the 0.01 significance level, we are 99% confident that the differences observed are statistically significant.

Because we wanted to discover how students were defining "intellectual engagement" and to probe students' perceptions of their visits, we conducted focus groups in spring 2012 with writing center users. We had ten groups, totaling thirty-seven participants across all three schools. To train tutors to facilitate hour-long focus groups, we followed the protocol in Cushman, Marx, Brower, Holahan, and Boquet's 2005 WLN article, which outlines how to collaborate with tutors to conduct peer-to-peer focus groups by including information on moderator and participant selection, incentives, and recording and room set-up. Using our survey results, we created one set of questions for all campuses and then collaborated with tutors to adapt the questions for student populations. Our questions included 1) "For you, what does it mean to be 'intellectually engaged' in a writing center session? Can you give an example?" and 2) "Is it important that your session is intellectually engaging? Why?"

We note some potential study limitations. First, like many surveys, we did not pre-test the student survey to ensure validity; therefore, we were not able to confirm, in advance of administering the survey, that the language of all the questions was unambiguous to participants. Second, both the survey and the focus groups are subject to selection bias. With respect to the survey, tutors did not invite all students to complete it, and some students chose not to. With respect to the focus groups, students volunteered to attend and therefore may have been more likely to feel positive about their experiences, though some participants communicated negative experiences. Third, a potential exists for positive-response bias. Because students took the survey immediately after their appointments, a halo-effect may have occurred, in which students' initial positive perceptions of their visit to the writing center influenced their immediate survey responses (Bell 9). In addition, survey and focus group questions may have prompted students to give socially acceptable answers, something common in social science research (Podsakoff, MacKenzie, and Podsakoff 552). Finally, while the survey had 2000+ responses, the focus groups had only 37 participants, who could only share individual experiences. Limitations notwithstanding, investigating student engagement using mixed methods provides a fuller, more comprehensive picture than either method alone.

Results and Discussion

Identifying whether students believed they experienced intellectual engagement in their sessions was our first step. Our survey found that 83-95% of students agreed or strongly agreed that they did. While our surveys revealed that a large majority of students at all three schools felt intellectually engaged, our focus groups investigated students' understandings of what this meant to them, including whether students found such engagement productive. In responding to questions about their definitions of intellectual engagement, students reported a range of understandings that fell into two complementary categories: "intellectual engagement" in the writing center as cognitive challenge and "intellectual engagement" as tutor collaboration.

Intellectual Engagement as Cognitive Challenge

Students at all three schools indicated that intellectual engagement incorporated cognitive challenge, as shown in Table 1.

Table 1: Representative Definitions of Intellectual Engagement as Cognitive Challenge by Type of Institution—Focus Groups

SLAC	MRU	LPU
"Having my ideas challenged" "Actually making me think about whether or not what I was trying to say was worth saying"	"Challenge" "Just asking the questions and making you think about it in a new way and maybe try and help you engage in it"	"Being challenged" "Making you think"

Focus group responses at all three institutions were similar in that, without prompting, students defined "intellectual engagement" as "challenge." Students' responses from all institutions referred to being challenged and to "thinking," more explicitly:

> "Asking me questions about it until I know exactly what I am saying" (SLAC)
> "What I was thinking when I wrote that?" (sic) (LPU)
> "Pushing you beyond boundaries" (MRU)

Researchers in education and composition equate engagement with higher-order thinking, such as recognizing the necessity of making meaning out of information (Flynn 6-7; Manning and Hanewell 36). By promoting rhetorical awareness, tutors, like instructors, help challenge student-writers to draw conclusions from difficult and sometimes conflicting information. Our students' definitions of engagement diverge importantly from NSSE definitions. While the NSSE focuses on outcomes of educational experiences, students also find process valuable. As one can see from students' comments, the presence of a second party (the tutor) is what prompts intellectual challenge in the moment, through the give-and-take of conversation between the tutor and the student. Thus, cognitive challenge and thinking happen in, and because of, the writing center session, rather than exclusively through students' engagement with texts or content.

Intellectual Engagement as Tutor Involvement

In addition to perceiving "intellectual engagement" as cognitive challenge, focus group participants emphasized the necessity of their tutors' active involvement with their writing, thinking, and ideas. Students' reported understanding of intellectual engagement as thinking/challenge is tightly connected to tutors stimulating students' thinking. Intellectual engagement thus goes far beyond student-tutor rapport at all three institutions, as indicated in Table 2.

Table 2: Representative Definitions of Intellectual Engagement as Tutor Involvement by Type of Institution—Focus Groups

SLAC	MRU	LPU
"The [writing] fellow is thinking" "There is back and forth" "Things are clicking" "When my writing fellow doesn't tell me what they think of my argument, necessarily, but keeps asking me questions about it until I know exactly what I am saying"	"I like it when they're [the tutor is] just as excited about my work as I am" "Active communication" "The [tutor] I was talking to just got me interested. . . . The way he approached it I was like, 'Wow that could be a cool paper' where previously I was like, 'This sucks, I don't want to do this at all.'. . . And then I was really into it" "I just think [the tutor] has the power to spark your interest. . . . I feel like they're really good in the Writing Center about that. . . . [T]hey can gauge whether they feel like you're into the paper or not."	"Someone coming at you at the level you're at" "He or she is asking you questions, and it's making you think" "[The tutor] showing an interest. Then as an individual, clearly wanting [the writer] to succeed. Not just throwing words out"

Students notice whether consultants match intellectual challenge and excitement, revealing an understanding of intellectual engagement as a two-way street. Student-writers describe this engagement as centered not only in the writing, but also in the conversation and the individual writer and learner. In the focus groups, students reported a relationship between these features of intellectual engagement—cognitive challenge and tutor collaboration. As one student explained, "You have to use your brain because the only way you're going to understand any of the concepts or even begin to work on your paper, you have to be thinking on your feet, engaged in the conversation" (LPU).

Intellectual Engagement as Productive and Important

Having established the presence of intellectual engagement in writing centers and identified students' definitions of intellectual engagement, we can now ask: how does it affect students' impressions of how productive writing center sessions were? While some students in the surveys and focus groups noted that intellectual engagement was not linked to productive sessions, most students reported a strong, and even necessary, connection. Table 3 presents survey findings from all three institutions.

Table 3: Relationship between Intellectual Engagement and Productivity by Type of Institution—Survey Data

	SLAC	MRU	LPU
Of the students who felt intellectually engaged, the percentage of students who felt their consultation was productive	100%** (n=374/374)	99%** (n=1356/1369)	100%** (n=339/340)
Of the students who did not feel intellectually engaged, the percentage of students who felt their consultation was productive	67%** (n=10/15)	51%** (n=25/49)	18%** (n=5/28)

**At all three schools, a statistically significant difference exists when comparing the student productivity ratings in the first and second rows of the table ($p<0.01$).

If students agreed they were intellectually engaged, almost all of them also agreed sessions were productive (99-100%). Conversely, if students agreed that they were not intellectually engaged, they were much less likely to agree that their sessions were productive (18-67%). At all three campuses, t-tests reveal a statistically significant difference in students' productivity ratings depending on whether students are or are not intellectually engaged ($p<0.01$); there is a 99% probability that this finding is not due simply to chance. In short, student reports of intellectual engagement and productivity strongly overlap in the writing centers we studied.

While the survey data demonstrate the correlation between productivity and intellectual engagement, the focus groups showed a causal connection between productive, or successful, sessions and intellectual engagement. At all three schools, the majority of focus group participants connected intellectual engagement to productive sessions, as seen in Table 4.

Table 4: Relationship between Intellectual Engagement and Productivity by Type of Institution—Focus Groups

SLAC	MRU	LPU
"It is necessary" "Because I felt that my writing fellow was really thinking about my paper not just as a paper but as a statement, actually respecting it as some academic thought, as opposed to just a paper for a grade, which I found very helpful. It sort of got me to the place I wanted to be, and it also made the consultation really interesting and not just kind of something to sit through"	"It's hard to write a paper if you're not interested in it at all and you just really don't want to be doing it. . . . [I]f the person that you're meeting with is helping you get more involved with it or happy about writing it, then that's helpful. Because if they're not even interested in it, then you're not going to get anything out of that session"	"The only way you're going to understand any of the concepts or even begin to work on your paper . . . [is to be] engaged in the conversation you're having, so that way it can better benefit you" "Yeah, I believe so. That's the only way it's going to help you!"

Students noted not just the connection, but the necessity, of intellectual engagement for productive sessions.

There is a potential difference across institutions here. Very few students reported on the survey that they could have a productive session without being intellectually engaged, and students in all but one of the focus groups described intellectual engagement and productivity as wedded. Students in one of the five focus groups at the MRU did not believe that intellectual engagement was absolutely necessary for a successful session:

> "I don't think so"
> "It's not the tutor's job to be intellectually stimulated"
> "I don't have to be challenged to be productive"

These students were the minority in the focus groups both at the MRU and in general. This difference may be partially attributable to variations in campus cultures, such as the lack of an official mascot or central gathering place at the MRU.

Conclusions

Analyzing empirical data, we found that students who used our writing centers have a more nuanced understanding and appreciation of their own, and of their tutors', intellectual engagement. When students were intellectually engaged in the writing center, they believed their sessions were also productive. Students valued the experience of being cognitively challenged and collaborating well with their tutor, someone who was excited by their ideas and by them, both as writers and as people in the midst of a learning process.

That student-visitors valued their own intellectual engagement, that this engagement almost always led to productive sessions, and that tutors' engagement played a key role has two important implications. First, it causes us to reconsider tutor training. While scholars have usefully discussed the intellectual work of tutors and administrators (e.g., Hughes, Gillespie, and Kail 13, 26; Geller and Denny 115; Marshall 78), tutors need not only to consider their own intellectual work, but also to communicate it effectively. Because thinking is a difficult process to "see" in others, tutors need to be not only thinking during the session, as we already hope they are, but also making this thinking visible by actively engaging with students and their ideas. As the data make plain, the intellectual engagement of tutors, at its best, is seen by students as "clicking," "back and forth," "excited." This finding suggests that tutors should model thinking as a process of collaborative knowledge-creation. Making tutors aware that students notice how engaged tutors are suggests that, while we should not necessarily promote "performance" by tutors, we should explicitly encourage tutors to demonstrate more frequently and transparently their thinking processes and their personal engagement with every student-writer.

Second, our research changes how we communicate with the rest of the university in terms that are meaningful both to ourselves and to administrators concerned with student learning. Writing centers give students outside of the classroom a chance to practice intellectual engagement, something the national studies, campus administrators, and scholars report as essential to higher education. In conducting assessments for administrators and themselves, writing center practitioners can point to a statistically significant finding: that the more engaged students are in writing center sessions, the more productive students believe their sessions are. This finding on engagement, therefore, exemplifies one way that writing center missions dovetail with institutional missions—an expectation sometimes difficult for centers to make explicit. Such communication with campus administrators may help to articulate to the broader academic community the importance of robust writing center-based research to elucidate the complexities of student learning.

Works Cited

Bell, James H. "When Hard Questions Are Asked: Evaluating Writing Centers." *Writing Center Journal* 21.1 (2000): 57-78. Print.

Cushman, Tara, Lindsey Marx, Carleigh Brower, Katie Holahan, and Elizabeth Boquet. "Using Focus Groups to Assess Writing Center Effectiveness." *Writing Lab Newsletter* 29.7 (2005): 1-5. Print.

Flynn, Thomas. "Promoting Higher-order Thinking Skills in Writing Conferences." *Dynamics of the Writing Conference: Social and Cognitive Interaction*. Ed. Thomas Flynn and Mary King. Urbana: NCTE, 1993. 3-14. Print.

Gallup-Purdue University. Great Jobs, Great Lives: The 2014 Gallup-Purdue Index Report. *Gallup:* 2014. *Gallup Poll*. Web. 2 Sept. 2014.

Geller, Anne Ellen, and Harry Denny. "Of Ladybugs, Low Status, and Loving the Job: Writing Center Professionals Navigating Their Careers." *Writing Center Journal* 33.1 (2013): 96-129. Print.

Hughes, Bradley, Paula Gillespie, and Harvey Kail. "What They Take with Them: Findings from the Peer Writing Tutor Alumni Research Project." *Writing Center Journal* 30.2 (2010): 12-46. Print.

Manning, Carmen, and Heather Hanewell. "Creating More Effective Writing Assignments: The Challenge of Authentic Intellectual Engagement." *Journal of Teaching Writing* 23.2 (2007): 35-53. Print.

Marshall, Margaret J. "Sites for (Invisible) Intellectual Work." *The Politics of Writing Centers*. Ed. Jane V. Nelson and Kathy Evertz. Portsmouth: Boynton, 2001. 74-84. Print.

National Survey of Student Engagement (NSSE). *A Fresh Look at Student Engagement—Annual Results 2013*. Bloomington: Indiana University Center for Postsecondary Research, 2013. Print.

Podsakoff, Philip M., Scott B. MacKenzie, and Nathan P. Podsakoff. "Sources of Method Bias in Social Science Research and Recommendations on How to Control It." *Annual Review of Psychology* 63 (2012): 539-569. Print.

ACROSS THE DISCIPLINES

Across the Disciplines, a refereed journal devoted to language, learning, and academic writing, publishes articles relevant to writing and writing pedagogy in all their intellectual, political, social, and technological complexity. *Across the Disciplines* shares the mission of the WAC Clearinghouse in making information about writing and writing instruction freely available to members of the CAC, WAC, and ECAC communities.

Across the Disciplines is on the Web at http://wac.colostate.edu/atd

Instructor Feedback in Upper-Division Biology Courses: Moving from Spelling and Syntax to Scientific Discourse

Erika Amethyst Szymanski's essay is based on a limited study on a university campus with "a long-standing and well-regarded culture of writing but no formal WAC program independent of the general university writing program." Symanski considers current practices in teaching writing to science majors with an interest in instructor feedback on student writing within biology and science. A majority of professors in the first part of her study were revealed to focus their writing feedback on lower-order concerns, whereas a minority of professors focused feedback on how students could better enact the disciplinary writing conventions of the scientific genres. In the second part of her study, Szymanski interviews these professors. In support of much rhetorical genre studies research, she finds feedback that directs students to the scientific discourses and purposes of the disciplinary genres is most productive in helping students to understand writing in the sciences.

8 Instructor Feedback in Upper-Division Biology Courses: Moving from Spelling and Syntax to Scientific Discourse

Erika Amethyst Szymanski

Abstract: In this study, I present an analysis of instructor comments on assignments written for upper-division courses in the biological sciences as a window into current practices around teaching science writing to major students. My results demonstrate that, while the overwhelming majority of instructors respond primarily to lower-order issues of grammar and other surface mechanics, a minority comment primarily on concerns specific to scientific discourse with a corresponding decrease in focus on lower-order issues. What discriminates between these two groups is that the minority assign genres that closely mimic fully-developed professional writing in the appropriate field; the majority assign conventional undergraduate genres such as the research paper that do not explicitly reference the writing students who continue in the field can expect to perform following graduation. Interviewing several of the professors in this minority, I find that their attitudes toward teaching with writing are closely coupled with envisioning student writing as apprentice-professional work, suggesting that encouraging faculty in such attitudes may, in addition to other benefits, improve their feedback practices.

How and to what end instructors provide feedback on student writing is an area of explosive recent development in terms both of composition theory and praxis, and for good reason. Feedback on student writing is perhaps the most direct, specific, and personal way students receive writing instruction, a role not limited by the kind or context of the writing. And yet, the vast majority of study into feedback practice and efficacy, even in writing across the curriculum (WAC) contexts, has been situated in general education courses, leaving under-studied upper-division, major-specific courses. This deficit is particularly meaningful in the natural sciences where students are asked to write in specialized scientific discourses that can seem far removed from the writing they performed in first year composition and other lower-division general education courses.

In this study, I examine instructor feedback on assignments written for upper-division biology courses specifically to the end of investigating whether and how they use feedback to instruct students in scientific discourse. My results demonstrate that the majority of faculty in my sample comment not on issues pertinent to disciplinary writing but, disproportionately, on lower-order concerns. A distinct minority, however, focus their commentary on concerns specific to scientific discourse with a corresponding decrease in attention to superficial errors. That this minority explicitly ask students to write in apprentice-professional ways mimicking professional scientific work suggests a connection between assignments with explicit goals and more directed feedback. Interviewing several faculty belonging to this minority, I find that their attitudes toward teaching with writing are tightly tied to student writing as apprentice-professional work, suggesting that encouraging faculty to frame student writing experiences in this way may, beside other benefits, improve feedback practices.

Seminal work by Richard Straub and Ronald Lunsford's (1995) *12 Readers Reading* brought attention to the importance of instructor comments on student writing, proposed a taxonomy of comments, and offered a system for analyzing them within the context of an introductory composition course. Subsequent work has evaluated how students feel about the type of feedback instructors provide, the difference in quantity and quality of feedback provided by different kinds of reviewers, and the efficacy of various commenting protocols in improving student's understanding or in prompting effective revision. Toward the first end, Cho, Schunn, and Charney (2006) found that instructors provide mostly directive (calling for a specific change) as opposed to summative (restating points from the paper) or praise comments, while students reported that directive and praise comments were most helpful. A similar survey showed that composition students had decidedly mixed opinions on whether correction-oriented professor feedback was helpful or not (Lynch and Klemans, 1978). Evaluating the utility of non-corrective — that is, reader-based or coaching — feedback, numerous studies and commentaries cited in *12 Readers Reading* suggest that students learn more from this sort of more facilitative, less critical instructor commentary (Straub and Lunsford, 1995).

Importantly, the vast majority of these studies have been framed within composition and lower-division general education or introductory courses. Instructors in the natural sciences, especially in upper-division major courses, are faced with a different and perhaps more complex task than composition and general education instructors. Scientific discourse involves specific lexicons and genres that may differ dramatically from those used in the writing students produce in other contexts. To succeed as graduate or professional students and later in their careers, apprentice scientists must become proficient in what amount to new and foreign languages. Simultaneously, however, many undergraduate science majors continue to grapple with the foundations of effective writing: argument, organization, support, grammar, and surface mechanics, among other issues. These foundations become even greater challenges when coupled with the need to write in the specialized discourse of the student's major. How instructors are to handle providing feedback in this complex situation receives little attention in the literature.

Of several writing-intensive biology curricula proposed since the 1970's WAC revolution, none adequately address the criteria that are to be used in assessing student writing, how instructors are to be trained in writing assessment, or how the selected criteria relate to professional competencies. Alan Holyoak (1998) describes student writing assignments in detail, but makes no comment on instructor feedback or assessment. Margie Krest and Daria Carle's "content-based [science] writing course" focuses on "writing (style, grammar, mechanics), library research, and critical thinking," (1999, p. 224) but offers no suggestions on the relative weight or importance of these elements; furthermore, Krest and Carle place biology professors in the position of teaching style, grammar, and mechanics with no discussion of whether they need training in this arena or, if they do need it, how they are to obtain such training. Liberating science faculty from needing to attend to style concerns is equally unsatisfactory, as the line between what constitutes subject knowledge and genre or style knowledge when writing in disciplinary ways is far from definitive (Patchan, Schunn, & Clark, 2011). John Bean and colleagues come closest in offering science instructors a framework for assessing student writing (Bean, Carrithers, & Earenfight, 2005). Nonetheless, that so little attention is given to helping faculty negotiate the complex task of providing feedback on science writing qua science writing suggests that current instructor practices are likely neither coordinated nor optimized.

Larry Beason (1993) examined feedback and revision in four intermediate-level "writing-enriched" courses, beginning with the tacit assumption that students should be asked to write in the same way in classes across the curriculum. I begin with a very different assumption: that different disciplinary discourses "work" in different ways (Jones & Comprone, 1993) and that a primary function — indeed, *the* primary function — of writing in upper-division courses is to inculcate students in these unique discourses. Rather than evaluating the efficacy of feedback in generating understanding or revision, my goal is evaluating the extent to which biology professors use feedback to instruct students in the unique features of professional writing in the discipline that can only be addressed in these major courses.

I've chosen to examine feedback practices specifically in the biological sciences for three principle reasons. First, coming from a background in microbiology, these are the non-English disciplinary genres whose conventions I best understand. Second, undergraduate and graduate study in biology led me to suspect that purposeful, directive feedback was uncommon in the discipline. Coming to composition studies, the ideas of facilitative rather than directive feedback, of attending mostly to big-picture issues rather than minutia, and of using comments to strategically guide revision rather than to correct errors was all new to me; I had never seen these tactics appear on my own papers in biology. Third, programs of study in the biological sciences are often designed with the assumption that many students will continue with additional graduate or professional training in various schools of medicine, nursing, or physical therapy, research degrees, or professional certifications in agricultural or environmental sciences. When upper-division (that is, majors only) courses include writing, then, that writing should be frequently and even primarily aimed at teaching students the professional genres they will continue to see later in their studies and their careers.

Study methods

Teasing instructor practice away from instructor attitudes towards writing feedback is difficult without examining graded writing assignments directly. Towards that end, I catalogued professor comments on 237 individual writing assignments from upper-division undergraduate courses in biology-related disciplines at Washington State University (WSU). WSU hosts a well-developed writing program of which undergraduate and graduate writing centers, the writing placement program, and writing in the major courses are part. Though it has no independent WAC program as such, WAC functions are integrated under the general writing program umbrella. All students are required to complete two writing in the major courses, WSU's descriptor for upper-division writing-intensive courses across the curriculum. To receive the designation, a course must meet specific writing-related criteria including having course objectives related to writing, providing at least some opportunity for revision, and awarding a significant percentage of total course credit based on writing assignments. M-course syllabi are subjected to periodic review and writing pedagogy workshops are made available to the teaching community, but faculty who teach M-courses have not historically been required to participate in any particular faculty development program.

WSU requires all undergraduates to complete a mid-career writing evaluation — the Junior Writing Portfolio — consisting of three exemplary writing assignments from three different courses that may include essays, research papers, lab reports, creative works, or any other writing produced for course credit, plus two writing samples produced in a two-hour timed writing examination. The course instructor must agree that the student's response to the assignment is "acceptable" or "outstanding" for the course. Students are encouraged to complete the portfolio around the conclusion of their second year of study, though many fail to complete the process until well into their third or even their fourth year; thus, upper-division coursework is well-represented in the work collected for these portfolios. At submission, students are offered the option of making their portfolios accessible for research purposes and the writing program therefore houses a physical database holding thousands of student writing samples.

From this database I randomly selected 237 papers written between 2001 and 2011 (most between 2007 and 2011) for upper-division courses in biology, molecular biosciences, natural resource sciences, crop and soil sciences, horticulture, entomology, pharmacology, neuroscience, animal sciences, and zoology. Because WSU is a land-grant institution whose mission and structure emphasize the agricultural sciences, the writing samples I selected from disciplines under the general umbrella of biology were necessarily skewed towards applied plant and animal sciences. Some of the courses from which I drew samples, though by far not all, carry the writing in the major designation. Papers varied in length from single-page essays to project reports exceeding 20 pages.

For each paper, I catalogued all instructor comments as either "praise" or "criticism;" neutral comments proved insignificant in number. In addition, I classified each comment as related to "content" — a comment which could have been made only by someone with specific subject knowledge — "low prose" — pertaining to grammar or spelling within a single sentence — "high prose" — pertaining to grammar or structure across multiple sentences — or "scientific discourse" — pertaining to the use of terminology or the conventions of science writing (an extension of the comment classification system of Patchan, Schunn, & Clark, 2011, p. 378). Scientific discourse comments were operationally defined as those that would not have been made by someone outside the sciences or that would not likely have been marked were the paper written for an English composition course rather than a science course. Praise comments were sufficiently few in number and sufficiently vague — "good" next to a paragraph could be a comment on content, structure, or both, for example — to warrant consolidating all praise comments into a single category.

This taxonomy — topical, rather than functional — reflects distinctions in scope and purpose between lower-order concerns with surface mechanics and higher-order concerns surrounding such matters as argumentation, focus, organization, and development. Comments on content could function either on the lower order if, for example, a matter of a single mis-stated fact or an error in terminology, or the higher order in the case of major conceptual misunderstandings or theoretical gaps. While attempting to dissect content comments into these two categories might have been useful for understanding the extent to which instructors attend to large versus small issues, doing so would have required an impractically detailed understanding of both the course material and the instructor's understanding of that material. Moreover, content comments are most likely to stem from a need to correct conceptual misunderstandings and to reliably prompt correction, independent of their lower- or higher-order scope. Similarly, comments I classified as pertaining to scientific discourse — specific to the sciences, but *not* a matter of correcting content errors — could function either on lower or higher orders. A comment on the proper use of scientific terminology addresses a relatively minor genre convention with sentence-level ramifications (though one that still reflects a crucial and central feature of how biologists look at the world); a note on the need to frame a thesis as hypothesis-driven bears upon the structure and focus of the assignment as a whole. Separating out these comments from the low prose and high prose categories to which they would otherwise belong allows me to examine the extent to which professors are using feedback as an opportunity to provide students with instruction in the unique features of disciplinary discourse that can be taught only in these upper-division major courses.

Results and Discussion

Figure 1 quantitatively summarizes my observations. My corpus of 237 papers yielded 1950 comments in total: an average of 8.23 comments per paper. 44.15 percent of professors' comments concerned low prose issues of grammar, spelling, punctuation, and (non-scientific) word choice. 14.46 percent related to the conventions of writing scientific discourse: use of preferred terminology, citation style, appropriate level of detail, appropriate level of voice, and the like. 27.49 percent concerned errors in or issues with content. Very few comments — 6.00 percent — related to high prose issues of focus, organization, flow, transitions, etc. The remaining 7.9 percent of comments offered praise. I classified comments related to citation style — one of the most frequent occasions of professor commenting (or, more precisely, correction) — as scientific discourse comments, but counted all citation errors of the same type as a single comment per paper. Similarly, I counted correction of the same misspelled word multiple times throughout a paper as a single comment upon that paper because all of the comments represented only a single, specific issue. Thus, the 1950 comment total reflects the total number of discrete subjects of commentary per paper, but is less than the sum of all individual comments.

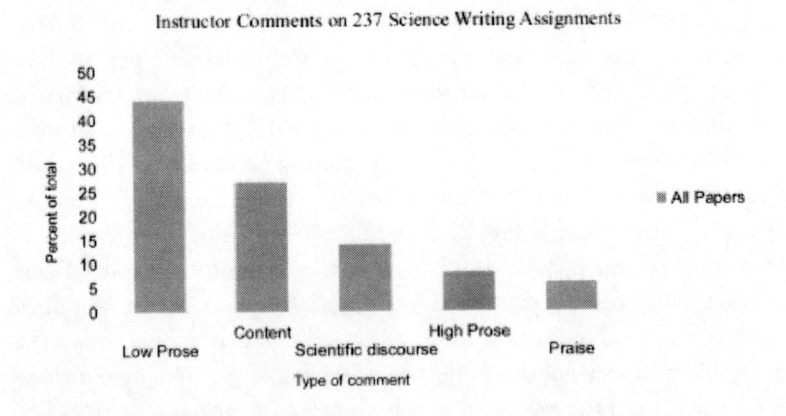

Figure 1. Instructor Comments on 237 Science Writing Assignments

While the percentages offer a useful summary, they mask the inconsistency in feedback practices I observed across papers. About 15 percent had few or no comments but were covered in the tell-tale red check marks of a skimmer searching for key words. At the other extreme, several different instructors edited heavily for style, marking both indisputable errors and non-erroneous stylistic preferences without distinction. Some professors marked sentences as awkward; others made no comment even on sentences that I was unable to parse even after several readings. Among papers with marginal comments, the number varied widely with as many as 100 distinct comments in the case of a mock-case report for an entomology course, 75 of which concerned sentence-level errors. Some professors clearly chose to ignore the bulk of errors when faced with papers strongly disfigured by spelling, grammar, and usage issues. In multiple instances of papers graded without rubrics, the only way I could make sense of a student's grade was by assuming that word choice, usage, and idiom as well as grammar and punctuation had been completely ignored; that is, the grade was very high while my reading of the paper was actively impeded by disfluency and sentence-level errors. Many professors did use rubrics for grading, and these rubrics were included as part of the portfolio submission. Some of these rubrics indicated as much as 27 percent of the total score assigned to issues of proofreading and mechanics. Most rubrics assigned credit to grammar, mechanics, and style in some form, though some did not. Considering that a majority of professors assigned one to six out of 20 to 100 total points for some version of "spelling/grammar/syntax" on grading rubrics, most then made a disproportionately large number of comments on an element worth so few points. With such a variety of practices, it seems no wonder that many undergraduates are confused about what constitutes "good writing" in the sciences.

Bean argues for commenting along "a hierarchy of concerns, descending from higher-order issues (ideas, organization, development, and overall clarity) to lower-order issues (sentence correctness, style, mechanics, spelling, and so forth" (2011, p. 322). Before addressing lower-order issues, it behooves professors to focus on higher-order issues. Both Haswell's (1983) study on "minimal marking" of student errors and Bartholomae's 1980 study on student's self-correcting behaviors when reading aloud suggest that a majority of students' surface errors arise from laziness or sloppiness, not from lack of knowledge. While few deny that these errors are still problematic, they do not necessarily reflect areas in which students need correction or instruction as much as, perhaps, convincing of the value of proofreading and professionalism, or revealing incidences of cognitive overload (Schwalm, 1985).

My limited survey suggests that science professors are spending a great deal of time and energy on lower-order concerns that distract from their ability to instruct on the higher-order issues of organization and reasoning and, moreover, issues of scientific discourse that can be taught uniquely in these classes. Important though clean surface mechanics are to professional science writing, they are not the areas in which students most need instruction in their upper-division major courses. Haswell's (1983) report on "minimal marking" famously showed that his students could locate and correct sixty to seventy percent of their surface mechanical errors when prompted to revise. I suspect that the percentage of self-correctable errors could be even higher in the papers I have studied, as students are increasingly likely to commit superficial linguistic errors when challenged with increasingly difficult and complex writing tasks (Schwalm, 1985, p. 631). Given the challenge of writing in an unfamiliar genre while employing complex scientific language and discussing difficult concepts, errors in language use and sentence structure are likely to increase as compared with a student's best efforts in a more familiar, less-specialized genre, but students are likely to recognize these "silly mistakes" as incorrect. In other words, if students are failing to understand something, it is almost certainly not low-prose language issues but scientific concepts and scientific discourse. And while the importance of clean mechanics is likely to be reinforced in lower- and upper-division classes across the curriculum, scientific concepts and discourse are not. Independent courses in science writing are becoming more common either as electives or requirements in undergraduate science curricula, but are far from universal; even were they universal, the expectation that students will learn the complexities of scientific writing in a single class is unfounded. Professors cannot assume that students will learn how to write as scientists outside of their upper-division major courses.

Several stand-out papers, notable first of all for the quality of the student's writing, led me to realize that not only were these papers unlike the majority, but they were like each other. Every assignment in my corpus could be classified as either a professional-genre or a student-genre paper. 215 out of the 237 papers I evaluated were written in the made-up genres that dominate undergraduate writing: the research essay (brief or long, with or without citations), student-styled lab reports — designed to demonstrate a student's understanding the function of a lab exercise rather than to present and interpret new findings, also brief or long, most often without citations — and short-answer homework questions. These genres disappear after graduation, whether students are headed for graduate school or industry employment. The remaining 22 papers — 9.28 percent — were deliberately constructed to mimic types of writing done by professional scientists: wildlife management plans, a case history written as for a medical journal, several manuscripts prepared exactly as for submission to the journal Genetics, and lab reports closely mimicking the style of a professional experimental report complete with an appropriate number of references, for example. (Anson and Dannels make a similar distinction, in their assessment of communication assignments in a food science department, between "industry simulation assignments" and "academic/graduate school preparation assignments," 2009.)

The comments on these few mock-professional assignments were by far the most interesting. A representative example amongst the mock-Genetics manuscripts showed evidence of the writer making a real effort to try on the scientist's role; though the writing suggested an undergraduate's still-incomplete conception of how to situate an experiment in the body of existing research, could have been better organized, and included some errors in terminology, it showed far more development in all of these areas than did even the best of the student-genre lab reports. Taking on the role of imaginary editor, perhaps, the professor focused feedback on those areas in which only an "expert insider" could comment. Out of 35 comments, five related to content, 14 to scientific discourse — matters of terminology, notation, formatting of figures, or organization of methods and results — and 14 to "low prose." Unlike the sentence-level comments on most papers, however, even these low prose comments largely concerned spelling and capitalization of species and gene names or proper italicization and similar style points germane specifically to scientific writing.

These observations correlating genre with style of feedback proved generalizable. Considering solely the 22 papers written in professional genres (Figure 2), the percentage of comments pertaining to scientific discourse doubles from 14.46 percent (for all 237 papers) to 28.13 percent, with a near-corresponding decrease in "low prose" comments from 44.15 percent to 23.75 percent and the remaining difference made up by modest increases in content and praise comments.

Figure 2. Instructor Comments on Science Writing Assignments by Assignment Type

Applying Beaufort's schema to the natural sciences, Patchan, Schunn, and Clark describe five types of knowledge necessary for effective science writing: "discourse community knowledge, subject matter knowledge, genre knowledge, rhetorical knowledge, and writing project knowledge" (2011, p. 166). Alaimo, Bean, and Nichols describe a similar set of knowledges germane to "discourse community knowledge" including "subject matter knowledge," "genre knowledge," "rhetorical knowledge," and "writing process knowledge" (2009, p. 18). The standard undergraduate lab report or term paper does little to prepare students in any of these areas save, perhaps, subject matter knowledge. While the format of an undergraduate lab report gives a nod to the formal scientific research article, the resemblance is superficial. Its content neither requires nor invites critical thinking about scientific literature, nor does it ask students to write for the scientific community: "the problem with lab reports is that they encourage students to think and write like students rather than like professionals" (p. 20). In a study of how public health students develop as professional writers, Clark and Fischbach observe that students are well-trained in writing for a student-teacher dynamic in which their job as students is to regurgitate information upon request (2008, p. 25). This writing is dramatically different from that of a public health professional charged, for example, with convincing a specific audience to exercise more or make dietary changes.

While it is tempting to imagine that qualities inherent in professional-genre assignments facilitate feedback higher on the hierarchy of concerns, nothing in my observations could explain why students and professors were responding differently to professional-genre versus student-genre papers, nor why professors were motivated to assign one versus the other in the first place. Professors who assign professional genres may be more inclined to offer higher-order feedback, independent of the genres they assign. They may spend more time coaching students or give students more time to write the professional-genre papers. Students may be more interested in writing these papers or be motivated, perhaps, by the idea of tongue-lashings from an imaginary journal editor. The uniformity of apparent purpose amongst these assignments — expressly asking students for apprentice-professional scientific work — strongly suggested that intentionality in assignment design carried over to intentionality in responding. Based on my catalogue data, however, I could only speculate on the attitudes and intentions of the professors whose assignments were represented in my sample. To investigate those attitudes and intentions more directly, I interviewed five of the professors who assigned professional-genre papers included in my corpus. What I found is that these faculty did indeed articulate a clear sense of intentionality and value toward how they teach with writing that connected their writing-intensive pedagogies with both their course objectives and their response strategies.

Interview Methods

I selected interview subjects via an email query sent to the professors for whom the papers I examined in the first part of my study were written. Though I addressed my query to every professor identified in my initial study still teaching at the university (a few had moved or retired), conspicuously, only members of the minority who assigned professional-genre papers responded positively to my request. I met with three in their campus offices; a fourth interview was held at a local pub and a fifth occurred via email. Interviews took approximately thirty to sixty minutes and were semi-structured: for the four in-person interviews, pre-determined questions served as guides and starting points for conversations that were largely open and driven by what the faculty members felt was worth discussing; for the email interview my initial questions provoked long narrative responses that extended beyond the boundaries of the questions. Two faculty members came from the department of natural resource sciences and one each from entomology, environmental studies, and the college of pharmacy. Interview responses were hand-coded for common themes.

Interview Results

Though the five professors I interviewed came from four different departments, taught entirely separate courses, were at different stages of their careers (from young assistant professor to full professor nearing retirement; all were tenure-track), and had all devised their approach to teaching with writing independently, several points of commonality emerged across interviews in terms of how they spoke about writing in their classes that ultimately relate to the feedback they offer students. The following five general principles emerged as common themes.

#1 — Writing is a process that incorporates revision.

> I'll tell the students I'll look at what they write and comment on them as many times as they'd like....If I had the opportunity I would re-give the students every opportunity to revise, and to rewrite, and to improve their writing skills.

> [I] start them early with a proposal around week five so that you know where you're going with this is not simple....What makes it successful is that they're starting very early, and they've talked about other projects in the same way.

All of these professors spoke of writing as a process that extended through the length of the course and involved multiple scaffolded elements. Four out of five professors spontaneously mentioned providing students with the opportunity to revise (the fifth mentioned revision when asked), even though only two of the four teach designated writing-in-the-major courses for which they are officially required to integrate revision. Bean notes that, in the many WAC faculty development workshops he facilitates, attendees tend to have one of two approaches toward providing feedback on student writing: the majority mark surface errors with an "editing orientation... the more numerous the errors, the less apt the teacher is to comment on anything else," while a minority make comments "oriented toward revision" (82). These are not overlapping philosophies; instructors tend to have one or the other. The professors I interviewed have clearly interiorized the revision orientation as a philosophy underlying their response to student writing including the feedback I analyzed.

#2 — Writing students do in class is connected to the writing professional scientists do in the field.

> The whole course is designed around professional development...so that you can walk the walk and talk the talk.

> My point is they need to have something — so it's a capstone class for our major, and it's required for graduate students — so they have an example of their writing that they can show to someone when they're trying to get a job.

> If you're a silviculturist and you can't write, you're never going to get your prescriptions accepted...writing is crucial

All of the professors clearly articulated that effective professional writing is important to their students' immediate and long-term future success and talked about communicating that point to their students. The persuasiveness with which these instructors made this connection and the passion with which they infused their assertions supports the hypothesis that students may indeed be motivated to invest more time and effort into the writing they produce for these instructors out of a belief that doing so will improve their ability to function as professionals. Moreover, the faculty are responding to student writing with apprentice-professional writing as an express outlook.

Susan Peck MacDonald argues that students move through four stages en route from high school to professional writing: first, "non-academic writing," then "generalized academic writing concerned with stating claims, offering evidence, respecting others' opinions, and learning how to write with authority" (which Bean argues is the goal of first year composition), thirdly "novice approximations of particular disciplinary ways of making knowledge," and finally "expert, insider prose" (MacDonald, 1994, p. 187; Bean, 2011, p. 228). These professors are transparent about presenting writing assignments to their students as an opportunity to work with "novice approximations" toward "expert insider prose," constructing writing as a bridge from college-level to professional work. They described employing problem-oriented writing assignments that expressly asked students to engage with "discipline-appropriate research questions" (Bean, 2011, p. 229) in a way that forces students to put on the role of apprentice-scientist rather than master student.

#3 — Good writing is connected to good thinking.

> I feel really strongly about the need for students to be able to express the ecological observations in writing...it seems to make a difference in how much the students actually develop and retain in the course.

> The process of writing consolidates your thoughts and helps to put them in order.

All five professors consistently discussed writing as an integral part of their teaching objectives, not a stand-alone or isolated element tacked on to their pedagogy. The three most senior professors indicated that they continued to emphasize writing in their courses not only because they see writing as an important professional skill, but also because they have seen student learning improve with student writing. Their feedback practices emerge, therefore, out of a strong ethic of valuing writing.

#4 — Writing assignments occupy substantial time and grade value.

> I give quite a bit of credit to students for their writing, and they seem to like that…they seem to think it's easier than taking an exam…I think that the writing reinforces their understanding better than exams.

> I feel that students should be writing on a weekly basis, or a semi-monthly basis to keep topics fresh in their mind and to keep writing — expressing.

All of the professors emphasized that their students are required to write frequently and consistently throughout the semester, either on multiple short assignments or on multiple stages of longer and more extensive assignments. They reinforce this message that writing is worthy of time and effort, both on the part of the students and on the part of the instructor, by allocating at least thirty percent of the total course grade — and as much as one hundred percent in the case of one senior capstone course — to writing assignments.

#5 — Feedback does not ignore low prose issues, but is primarily concerned with students' scientific thinking.

What I tell the students is this…I expect to see a paper with excellent spelling, punctuation, grammar…I simply expect that…I'm not going to go through and red mark all of that…I'm looking for conceptual understanding, organization…Students do tend to rise to that expectation.

[For otherwise good papers with lots of easily correctable surface errors, I'll give] really good scores, but I will comment on the surface error stuff.

I often use essay grading as a time to have a conversation with a student.

It is an academic commonplace that "science teachers are more willing than humanities teachers to excuse stylistic infelicities if the content is accurate," (Haswell, 2006) and yet matters of sentence construction comprised nearly half of the majority of science professors' comments in the corpus I examine above. When asked specifically about what types of feedback they provide on students' papers, the professors I interviewed attested that they comment on everything from content to scientific rhetorical devices to grammar and mechanics, but that grammar and mechanics are minor concerns. The consensus among these professors was that sentence-level errors are a problem and one for which they will lower a student's grade, but that they give higher-order concerns of content, support, and organization much more weight. One, quoted above, remarked that she simply expects students not to submit work marred by surface errors because she assumes that they have already mastered the skills necessary to do so. When pressed to say what she does when students don't "rise to that expectation," she insisted that only a handful of students in her multi-year tenure of teaching the course we discussed had turned in papers she deemed sub-standard. This professor also emphasizes peer-review and multiple drafts as students work on their writing over nearly the entire duration of the semester-long course.

Their responses suggest that all of these professors have independently generated a philosophy of commenting resembling Bean's "hierarchy of concerns, descending from higher-order issues (ideas, organization, development, and overall clarity) to lower-order issues (sentence correctness, style, mechanics, spelling, and so forth)" (2011, p. 322). Again, Bean argues that the utility of this hierarchy is that students are encouraged to revise for large-scale conceptual issues rather than focus on editing minutiae. Extrapolating, comments on scientific discourse should likewise focus students' attention on those concerns. While my initial data set provides evidence that this is, in fact, what these professors do, it was not a foregone conclusion that they would consciously articulate this philosophy. They do.

Implications for Using Writing in Upper-Division Science Sourses

Genres exist as repeated, similar responses to repeated, similar situations. Smith argues that the end comment to the first-year composition paper exists as a stable genre, and that this is so not because instructors have been trained to generate it, but because of the relatively stable repeated rhetorical situation of responding to student papers (1997). If professors in the natural sciences are highly divergent in their commenting practices, then, perhaps it is not because they have not been trained in effective response techniques but because they do not share a sense of how writing is being used and what it, and feedback, is intended to achieve.

While these data are far too limited to suggest any sort of causal relationship, they do point toward an association between asking students to perform apprentice-professional writing, feedback that supports that transition to discipline-specific writing by focusing on science writing-specific concerns, and attitudes congruent with — though developed independently of — contemporary composition theory. Perhaps this conclusion is not surprising. Condon and Kelly-Riley demonstrated in their 2004 study of the oft-assumed connection between writing and critical thinking competency that writing alone did nothing to improve the sophistication of students' critical thinking. Only when instructors assigned writing deliberately and consciously designed to improve critical thinking (as measured by a broadly-applicable, problem solving-based rubric) did students' writing exhibit corresponding improvements as measured by a corresponding rubric. Students are only likely to produce apprentice-professional scientific work when called upon to do so, and instructors' comments are part of the environment that asks for that type of work.

My study is limited by involving only one institution — a university with a long-standing and well-regarded culture of writing but no formal WAC program independent of the general university writing program. As a case study, however, it suggests that the benefits of working with science faculty to tailor writing exercises to disciplinary discourses — apprentice-professional writing rather than just writing in general — extend to a better environment for responding to student writing. Too, that some science faculty independently develop approaches to writing built around such principles as revision and writing as valuable and integral, expressly aimed at developing disciplinary discourse, offers evidence that this approach can be a good fit in biology.

Scholarly recommendations that professors attend to higher-order concerns above and before sentence-level errors, that they comment more through praise and reader-based observations than through criticism or direct corrections, and that professional genres be used to teach writing in the disciplines are not new — composition has been taking these recommendations seriously since at least the early 1980's and arguably earlier. Nevertheless, this exploratory study suggests that such recommendations are not being effectively communicated to instructors in the sciences even as these instructors are being encouraged by WAC initiatives to incorporate more writing into their teaching. WAC as a movement has directed its majority efforts toward encouraging a general culture of writing, with notable success. That so many papers in my corpus come from classes not officially designated as writing-intensive is encouraging: biology faculty are teaching with writing even when not compelled by the constraints of a course distinction. As a movement, however, it may not be equally successful in engendering a coherent sense of the purpose toward which that writing should be directed in the natural sciences, or engaged in the sort of collaborations that would improve understanding both by faculty in composition and in the disciplines of how writing works in disciplinary contexts. But more important than instruction or lack thereof in best practices, the lack of coherence in professors' commenting practices points toward the absence of a shared context for employing writing.

Telling science faculty to change their feedback practices makes feedback one more item on a list of things that composition faculty do "right" and science faculty do "wrong," one more opportunity to reinforce the much-bemoaned "missionary" model of WAC education (Bazerman, 1991; Condon and Rutz, 2012). Helping science faculty teach with writing aimed at disciplinary professionalization — through which more constructive feedback evolves — naturally moves toward a "consultancy" model through which engagement with WAC helps science faculty achieve their writing-related goals while recognizing them as experts in their professional disciplinary writing. Cataloguing comments from similar upper-division science courses at a university where such a consultancy model has been strongly espoused and where WAC programs focus on discipline-specific writing would be useful to test whether science faculty on a whole comment more on scientific discourse and whether the divide between student- and professional-genre assignments holds true.

References

Alaimo, Peter J., Bean, John C., & Nichols, Larry. (2009). Eliminating lab reports: A rhetorical approach for teaching the scientific paper in sophomore organic chemistry. *The WAC Journal*, 20, 17-32.

Anson, Chris M., & Dannels, Deanna. (2009). Profiling programs: Formative uses of departmental consultations in the assessment of communication across the curriculum. *Across the Disciplines*, 6. Retrieved from http://wac.colostate.edu/atd/assessment/anson_dannels.cfm

Bartholomae, David. (1980). The study of error. *College Composition and Communication*, 31(3), 253-269.

Bazerman, Charles. (1991). Review: The second stage in writing across the curriculum. *College English*, 53(2), 209-212.

Bean, John C. (2011). Engaging ideas: The professor's guide to integrating writing, critical thinking, and active learning in the classroom (2nd ed.). San Francisco: Jossey-Bass.

Bean, John, C., Carrithers, David, & Earenfight, Theresa. (2005). Transforming WAC through a discourse-based approach to university outcomes assessment. *The WAC Journal*, 16, 5-21.

Beason, Larry. (1993). Feedback and revision in writing across the curriculum classes. *Research in the Teaching of English*, 27(4), 395-422.

Cho, Kwangsu, Schunn, Christian D., & Charney, Davida. (2006). Commenting on writing: Typology and perceived helpfulness of comments from novice peer reviewers and subject matter experts. *Written Communication*, 23(3), 260-294.

Clark, Irene L, & Fischbach, Ronald. (2008). Writing and learning in the health sciences: Rhetoric, identity, genre, and performance. *The WAC Journal*, 19, 15-28.

Condon, William, and Kelly-Riley, Diane. (2004). Assessing and teaching what we value: The relationship between college-level writing and critical thinking abilities. *Assessing Writing*, 9(1), 56-75.

Condon, William, & Rutz, Carol. (2012). A taxonomy of writing across the curriculum programs: Evolving to serve broader agendas. *College Composition and Communication*, 64(2), 357-382.

Haswell, Richard. (1983). Minimal marking. *College English*, 45(6), 166-170.

Haswell, Richard. (2006). The complexities of responding to student writing; or looking for shortcuts via the road of excess. *Across the Disciplines*, 3. Retrieved from http://wac.colostate.edu/atd/articles/haswell2006.cfm

Holyoak, Alan R., (1998). A plan for writing throughout (not just across) the biology curriculum. *American Biology Teacher, 60*(3), 186-190.

Jones, Robert, & Comprone, Joseph J. (1993). Where do we go next in writing across the curriculum? *College Composition and Communication, 44*(1), 59-68.

Krest, Margie, & Carle, Daria O. (1999). Teaching scientific writing: A model for integrating research, writing and critical thinking. *American Biology Teacher, 61*(3), 223-227.

Lynch, Catharine, & Klemans, Patricia. (1978). Evaluating our evaluations. *College English, 40*(2), 166-170, 175-180.

MacDonald, Susan P. (1994). Professional and academic writing in the humanities and social sciences. Carbondale: Southern Illinois University Press.

McLeod, Susan H. (1992). Writing across the curriculum: An introduction. In Susan H. McLeod & Margot Soven (Eds.), *Writing Across the Curriculum: A Guide to Developing Programs* (1-11). Newbury Park: Sage Publications.

Patchan, Melissa M., Schunn, Christian D., & Clark, Russell J. (2011). Writing in the natural sciences: Understanding the effects of different types of reviewers on the writing process. *Journal of Writing Research, 2*(3), 365-393.

Schwalm, David E. (1985). Degree of difficulty in basic writing courses: Insights from the oral proficiency interview testing program. *College English, 47*(6), 629-640.

Smith, Summer. (1997). The genre of the end comment: Conventions in teacher responses to student writing. *College Composition and Communication, 48*(2), 249-268.

Straub, Richard, & Lunsford, Ronald F. (1995). 12 *Readers Reading.* Cresskill, NJ: Hampton Press, Inc.

HARLOT: A REVEALING LOOK AT THE ARTS OF PERSUASION

Harlot is a digital magazine and web forum dedicated to provoking playful and serious conversations about rhetoric—from reality television to public monuments, religion to pop music, and everything in between. Harlot's mission is to publish pieces that are relevant, interesting, and provocative to a wide range of audiences, not just academics or specialists in one field.

Harlot is on the Web at http://harlotofthearts.org/

"Emoji, Emoji, What for Art Thou?"

In this piece, Lebduska examines the history and usage of emojis to challenge assumptions that these graphic elements constitute a debasement of and danger to traditional literacy. Instead, she argues, emojis are "an emerging visual language of play" with its own affordances and constraints. Combining historical narrative, critical analysis, and writing theory, Lebduska's work exemplifies strong scholarship delivered in an accessible and engaging manner. Notably, this article has become a touchstone in conversations about emoji as communication. Referenced in Wired's "We're All Using These Emoji Wrong" and Washington Post's "Sleepy Face, Sad Face or Shocked Face: The Emoji Identity Crisis," the work is now cited in Russian, German, Spanish, Portuguese, etc. Such circulation confirms its critical value and particular success in relation to Harlot's mission.

9 Emoji, Emoji, What for Art Thou?

Lisa Lebduska

By providing a history and context for emojis, this essay argues that they are more a means of creative graphic expression than a threat to alphabetic literacy, and that their study contributes to a re-materilaizing of literacy. The essay acknowledges that in some instances emojis do help to clarify the intent or tone of alphabetic writing, but emojis, like alphabetic writing, are culturally and contextually bound. Emojis expand expression and in doing so open themselves to re-appropriation, interpretation and even misinterpretation, along with the affirming possibilities of artistic creation.

Emoji Keyboard

"We were just nerds, goofing around" (Fahlman qtd. in Garber). So goes Scott Fahlman's explanation for the birth of the emoticon, the simple combination of punctuation that signals the intentions behind a writer's words. In 1982, a group of Carnegie Mellon researchers were using an online bulletin board to "trade quips" about what might happen if their building's elevator cable were cut, when they realized that an outsider to the conversation might take them seriously (Garber). They developed the iconic :) to make sure everyone else was in on the joke. And the rest, as the saying goes, was history. Or were the emoticons word-devil spawn? Did they constitute an attack on language, yet another instance of the "erasure of language" (MacDonald) what

James Billington, the Librarian of Congress, described as "the slow destruction of the basic unit of human thought — the sentence" (qtd. in Dillon)?

Mary Pickford wearing a kimono

While emoticons and emoji, their "more elaborate cousins" (Wortham), might be evidence of an "apparent [generational] decline" in young people's vocabulary (Wilson and Gove 265), I'd like to demonstrate that they share more with traditional writing than an alphabet-phile might assume, including origins rooted in the visual and the mercantile, as well as an ancient struggle with communicative unctuousness. Emojis are not so much destroying linguistic traditions as they are stretching them, opening a gateway to a non-discursive language of new possibility and even responding to John Trimbur's call for a rematerializing of literacy (263), by reminding us that writing always had and always will have a visual component mediated by a material world. The narratives of emojis, then, are the narratives of writing itself.

Scholars have called out the myth of alphabetic literacy's transparency as a denial of writing's materiality and the role played by larger systems of production (Trimbur), as well as an assertion of Western superiority (Miller and Lupton). In response to this need to materialize writing, I wish to provide context for emojis, complicating these tiny stamps of humanity and unpacking some of the alphabetic resistances to them so as to position them as an emerging visual language of play, whose study will help us to think more visually and materially about writing and encourage us to experiment with the ludic potentiality of a non-discursive form.

Alternative emojis

Almost a decade after the Carnegie Mellon invention of emoticons, emojis (translated as "picture characters") emerged in Japan, consisting of both more fleshed-out versions of emoticons ☺ instead of :) for example), as well as a pantheon of objects, activities, and events ranging from cactuses to cash. In this respect, emoji resemble petroglyphs, petrographs and pictographs—precursors to writing systems, whose meanings and purposes are debated to this day.

Emoji origins in teen and commercial culture are indisputable. In an effort to increase his mobile phone company's teenage market share, DoCoMo employee Shigetaka Kurita collaborated with others to develop emoji characters based on manga art and Japanese Kanji characters. But senders and recipients had to use the same network in order for the characters to display properly (Marsden). Faced with the material constraints of the cell phone and their interest in having the networks communicate with one another, Japanese programmers

BABEL FISH

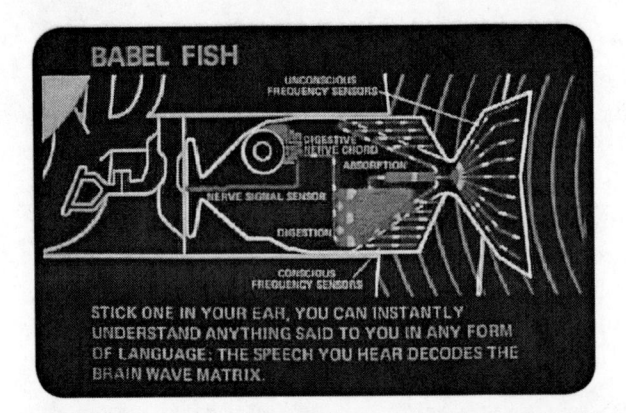

STICK ONE IN YOUR EAR, YOU CAN INSTANTLY UNDERSTAND ANYTHING SAID TO YOU IN ANY FORM OF LANGUAGE: THE SPEECH YOU HEAR DECODES THE BRAIN WAVE MATRIX.

reached consensus on computer codes for the emoji, which are now part of all mobile web and mail services in Japan. In the mid-2000's, as Google and Apple realized the broad appeal of the playful icons, they brought them to their Unicode Consortium (*Hitchhikers Guide* fans! Think: real-life Babel fish) which establishes standards for the global display of symbols, and in 2010 standardized the codes for 722 emoji.

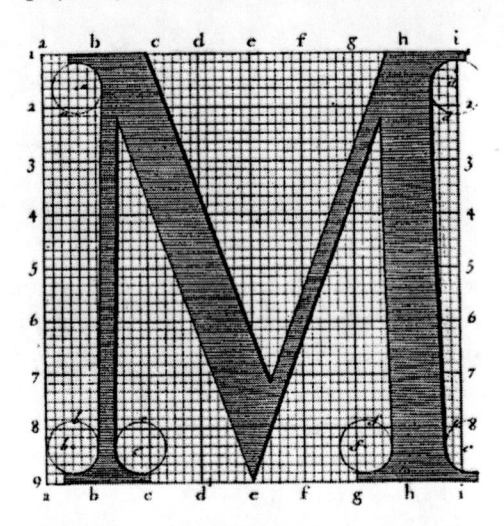

This move to standardize resembled the efforts of Louis the XIV to standardize typographic forms through the commissioning of the "roman du roi" typeface, which relied on an Academy of Sciences committee to map the typeface onto a grid, as opposed to previous typefaces which had evolved over time and which were hand cut. Trimbur sees the Sun King's commissioning of the committee as an attempt "to embody the authority of the scientific method and bureaucratic power" (266). Individual engravers would no longer have an influence on the emerging shapes and the sameness of every printed letter would be guaranteed through its adherence to a mathematically reproducible template. Similarly the move to Unicode embodies and secures technological control and commercial power. On the one hand the use of a uniform code ensures that what senders send is what recipients see, but senders and users must both have the hardware (usually a smartphone, though emojis can be displayed on email) as well as access to an emoji keyboard if they wish to send. Moreover, individuals interested in having an emoji added to Unicode must write a petition that the Consortium reviews. Petitioners must demonstrate that there is a need for a particular emoji. According to Mark Davis, president of the Unicode Consortium, the emoji "must be in the wild already" (qtd. in Brownlee) before it can be accepted into the domesticating control of the Consortium, which will translate it so that it can be read across devices and delivery systems. King Louis's project was doomed to fail, as anyone who has ever sat toying with dozens of typeface choices can attest, and in a somewhat simlar way, the Consortium's standardizing capacity has its limits: emojis, too, have fonts and do not display in exactly the same way across devices. Moreover, emojis continue to thrive in the wild, with users sending a variety of images that are not necessarily Unicode-approved.

Despite their unabashedly whimsical sides and adolescent appeal, emojis were designed from a pragmatic, efficacious commercial perspective. Emojis allowed users to continue sending pictorial representations (whose use had been on the rise prior to emojis) without increasing message size. Bandwidth did not need to increase and speed was maintained as each emoji counted as only a single character. Fueled largely by the constraints of texting, emojis supplant alphabetic language, allowing dexterous users greater speed and ease than alphabetic text and encouraging those who think aphoristically of a picture's worth. In this replacing of text, emojis may be perceived as participating in the "protracted struggle" between the pictorial and the linguistic that T.J. Mitchell observed, "the relationship of subversion, in which language or imagery looks into its own heart and finds lurking there its opposite number" (43). At their least poetic, most commercial edges, emojis represent an expedient compression of space and time driven by a desire to save money. They were born of a need to conserve space, which translated into time, both of which were expressed in terms of material value. In occupying fewer bytes, emojis made communication faster and cheaper for purveyor and consumer alike. And for this they got a bad rap.

Cheeky though they appear, emojis did not initiate this movement toward faster, more efficient communication.

Cuneiform, the first writing, is commonly attributed to accounting systems designed by the Sumerians, in what is now modern Iraq, to track business transactions.

We can imagine ancient poets and priests, even before Plato's famous Phaedrus invective against the memory-dissolving threat of writing, turning away in disdain from early cuneiform and its mercenary mission and what Craig Stroupe describes as a presumed "rhetorical instrumentalism" (629). In the modern era, industry routinely races for faster communication—consider technologies such as the telegraph or the many shorthand systems, which, BTW, is how emojis often are described. All communications—visual and alphabetic—serves multiple purposes, which are sometimes derailed purposefully, through re-appropriation and re-design and re-imagination, and sometimes derailed by accident, happenstance and the emergence of new forms.

Few of us now would recognize Sir Isaac Pitman's shorthand notation system of 1837:

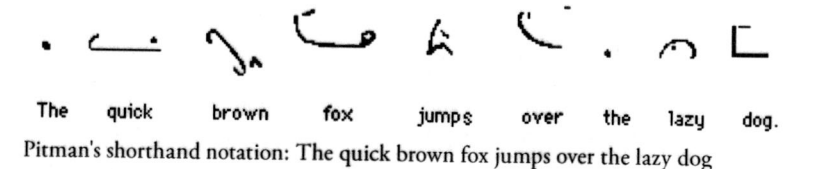

Pitman's shorthand notation: The quick brown fox jumps over the lazy dog

In their heydays, Pitman's approach and other shorthand systems such as Gregg's were understood by a small subset of professionals who had the proper training in them. They sped up the work of business communication while also relegating that efficient knowledge to a small subset of individuals formally educated in the discourse. Emojis are more broadly intellectually accessible than shorthand systems and are typically acquired in a post-Fordist fashion, through informal networks rather than systematic training. Only readers trained in Pitman notation would recognize the system's lines and squiggles; by contrast, readers without formal emoji training would recognize ☺. I will return to this issue of recognition and iconicity momentarily.

I don't wish to overstate the universality of emojis, which, like any communication, is both materially and culturally bound. Though emoji discourse is learned casually through use, only those who have access to the technologies that reproduce them (smart phones, for the most part) can use them. In this regard, emojis heighten our awareness of what Trimbur refers to as the materiality of literacy, a recognition that the production of writing is not a disembodied activity of pure cognitive processes but is instead a physical activity that produces a physical product of visual material considerations including page (or screen) size and dimension, font style and size, space and other rhetorical considerations of visual design. Trimbur emphasizes the role of typography in reifying this materiality and links it to rhetoric's fifth canon, delivery (263). As with a consideration of typography, a consideration of emoji encourages us to re-visualize writing and to think about how it is circulated, how it performs work in a world of class, race, gender, cultural and age relations.

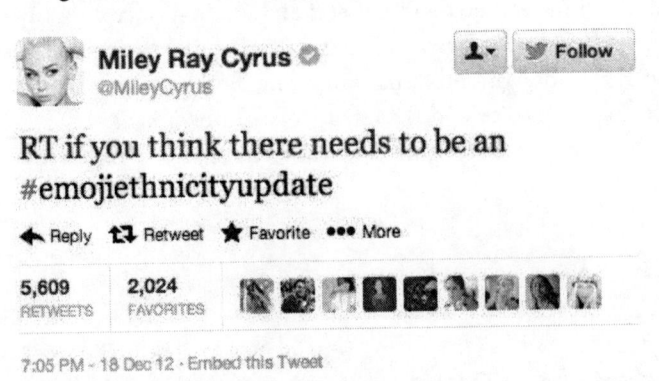

> **Miley Ray Cyrus** ✓
> @MileyCyrus
>
> RT if you think there needs to be an #emojiethnicityupdate
>
> ← Reply ↻ Retweet ★ Favorite ••• More
>
> 5,609 RETWEETS   2,024 FAVORITES
>
> 7:05 PM - 18 Dec 12 · Embed this Tweet

Miley Cyrus tweets

Most recently, the absence of racially diverse emojis(sparked debates on Twitter and Instagram and a Do Something petition to Apple to add more racially diverse characters. The Apple keyboard, as the BBC reported, had numerous white faces and "only two that appeared to be Asian" and none that were black (Kelion). The call for more diverse emoji was dismissed by some in the blogosphere, particularly when Miley Cyrus attempted a Twitter campaign to increase emoji diversity, but at the core of the debate was the construction of race by one of the fastest-growing modes of communication. White again was being represented as a universal, non-raced race. Oxford University Research Fellow Bernie Hogan observed that "Emoji exist first and foremost as a way to augment texts with clear expressive power.... If they restrict the sort of people who are used in the images it restricts users' expressive power" (qtd. in Kelion). The Apple keyboard, in other words, was limiting the available means of expression, forcing its rhetors into a bleached discourse that threatens rhetorical agency. Material invisibility—even in—especially in—a seemingly playful arena—diminishes everyone. Whether they were persuaded by the racial ethos of the petition or more inspired by the fact that 92% of African Americans own a cell phone and 56% own a smart phone (Smith), (constituting a powerful consumer base), is impossible to say, but Apple management has pledged to racially diversify its emoji options. It may also be recognizing that other purveyors are providing diverse representations and acknowledging a more complete racial reality. Oju, an African company aimed at "liberating Africans from digital exclusion" has developed an ojus app for Google, using the tagline "everyone smiles in the same language" and featuring brown-toned faces (Ouja Africa). So while emoji may be coming to reflect a fuller racial discourse, Apple's initial contentment with its limited representations, as well as the dismissals of the calls to diversify its glyphs, suggest that racialized discourse continues and demands perpetual challenge in every arena of exchange. Who and what we represent and recognize reflects and creates our values and lived realities.

Small though they may be, emojis resonate with populist power: Over 300 million images are shared daily by Facebook users; 45 million are posted through Instagram (Rock). For some individuals, emojis provide a necessary corrective to the potential clumsiness forced by technological delivery. Japanese author Motoko Tamamuro explains that the Japanese "tend to imply things instead of explicitly expressing them, so reading the situation and sensing the mood are very important. We take extra care to consider other people's feelings when writing correspondence, and that's why emoji became so useful in email and text – to introduce more feeling into a brevitised form of communication" (qtd. in Marsden). Tamamuro's concerns are similar to those early English-language adopters of emoticons—wary of language's missteps and interested in closing as many gaps between intended and received communication.

Emojis, like the earlier emoticons, sometimes are aimed at helping readers to interpret all the kinds of language that linguist John Haiman categorizes as "un-plain speaking," including sarcasm, "simple politeness, hints, understatements, euphemisms, code, sententiousness, gobbledygook, posturing, bantering jocularity, affectation and ritual or phatic language." Emojis are an attempt to insure that the message we intend is the message that is received, that we can shore up the fissures, the lacuna, the gaps, disconnects, discordances and plain old misunderstandings that inevitably emerge when one brain tries to externalize its thoughts for another through words. Emojis inherit a long tradition of enlisting visuality to do so.

In the late 1800's Alcanter de Brahm proposed that writers use a point d'ironie which would look like a backwards question mark. I sent this trivia to a colleague in the French department, who noted, with his own ironic and somewhat repulsed tone, "The whole point of irony is that it is not pointed out." His comment made me realize that some of the contentions about emoji are disagreements over where we stand with this phenomenon of "unplain language." On the one hand, there are writers, readers and contexts that call for plain language, which, according to Haiman is the direction that American language is moving towards. Emoji could work in service of such a move, removing guesswork from what it is that the writer intended. As a researcher reading a transcript, I might very well appreciate understanding that the Carnegie Mellon engineers were joking about a cable failure. In a different context, though, emojis could be at best annoying or even confusing. If I am in a crowded theater when a fire erupts, I do not wish to look up and see a sign that says, "EXIT ☺" or even "EXIT ☹." I feel the same way about the happy and sad smile faces that adorned my Rhode Island tax return, though I imagine the person who composed it assumed taxpayers might be charmed to see ☹ after "you owe this amount." Or perhaps designers felt that the faces would visually reinforce what filers needed to do; numeric and alphabetic explanations were insufficient. When I filed and saw the ☹ telling me that I owed money, the glyph neither clarified nor charmed; it simply sat as unappreciated adornment whose sad face served up a visual poke in the eye. Like most readers, I inhabit multiple interpretive contexts. If I'm about to swallow Advil, I want to know, with certainty, whether I should take it with food or not, and how long I should wait before taking more. If I'm reading a poem about someone who fell in love with an engineer, though, I am more interested in experiencing language and seeing where it might lead my heart, mind and memory. I take my emojis the same way.

Emojis occupy a both/and position. It is most likely that emojis—as with all attempts to stabilize—result in some magnanimous efforts producing both magnificent failures and stunning successes. So while some composers use emojis to clarify, others use them to mystify and neither necessarily succeeds all the time, because, at the end of the day, humans are what they are: wonderfully complex, connected and individuated creatures, forever striving to reach one another. Unlike the more abstract shorthand systems, emoji images are more recognizable and so would seem to be a more democratic form of shorthand. But communication is never that simple. Even if we were able to remove emojis from their material constraints—which we cannot—we would still encounter emojis as the smiling, frowning, winking poster children of Of Grammatology, challenging both the phonocentrism and logocentrism of de Saussure because they exemplify non-phonetic writing while signifying both absence and presence. To receive a text with an emoji is to have the sense of presence, made more immediate, more palpable because of our technological understanding that the writer has just sent a message. Emojis, like alphabetic words, always point somewhere else. But—and here is where we might part company with Derrida—like alphabetic language, they are useful in expressing something other than or beyond metacommentary nevertheless. Letters get received, rescued from their purloined places, and emojis, too, hit their marks, but in broad clouds, like electrons hovering around a nucleus of meaning.

More of our dear readers recognize ☺ as a smileyface than readers would have recognized Pitman's shorthand · as "the," probably even in Pitman's day. These readers, however, do not necessarily agree on its signification. The apparent iconicity of the ☺ is debatable. ☺ does not represent a word. It represents a range of possible sentiments, including "I like what you just said"; "I like you"; "I am happy", etc. Moreover, smiling itself is culturally dependent. The emoji is not insulated from the maddening or, some would say delightful soap-bar quality of all communication. Emoji Cro-Magnon might have intended the smiley first, foremost and ONLY to clarify the tone of a previous expression so that readers understood that the expression was not to be taken seriously, as in "I'm joking here," yet it has since been used to express a range of other sentiments, and may or may not be used to clarify the tone of a previous expression. The emoji ☺ may point us in the direction of lightheartedness, but even among speakers from similar cultures, irony and sarcasm are always possibilities. As ever, context is king.

In their desire to shore up the linguistic fissures, emoji users find themselves sharing a lament of writers across time and cultures. We might recall T. S. Eliot bemoaning the "shabby equipment, always deteriorating" available to the poet in "East Coker," or Italo Calvino observing that "The struggle of literature is in fact a struggle to escape from the confines of language; it stretches out from the utmost limits of what can be said; what stirs literature is the call and attraction of what is not in the dictionary" (qtd. in Gabriele 59). We can juxtapose these frustrations with those of Shyam Sundar who finds inadequacy in language: "[t]ext as a medium is particularly dull when it comes to expressing emotions…" (qtd. in Wortham). While Sundar's observation is expressed neither as a poem nor as a deep meditation on art, at its core, it joins with Eliot and Calvino in its exasperation with the limitations of the alphabetic language. But Sundar is neither poet nor novelist. He is co-director of the Media Effects Research Laboratory at Pennsylvania State University and his solution for escaping the language prison is neither poetry nor prose. Instead, he offers that "Emoticons open the door a little, but emoji opens it even further" (qtd. in Wortham). Admittedly, Sundar's reference to "dull text" might be enough to make a humanist or any lover of literature. . . .

Anyone who has ever wept or laughed or been stirred to action after reading would surely want scare quotes around "dull." For our entire lives, texts have been anything but dull. (Well, maybe a few.) But to be fair to Sundar, he's referring not so much to Shakespeare as he is to the quotidian texts sent by phone, the dozens or hundreds or thousands of messages sent every day by individuals when they are walking or waiting at the dentist or sitting in class or driving down the Interstate, often in front of me. He is, in a sense, seeking to liven the language of the everyday. Sundar is reflecting on quotidian language that does not fly in the rarified air of the published poem or squat on a marble museum pedestal. He wants to change the register of the daily exchange of Every Texter. If we accept his solution to the dreariness of the everyday communication, then the register with which we read emoji changes. For a brief Derridean moment, a friend's emoji-graced message, texted in the middle of the day, constitutes an always-in place meditation on words' shortcomings, a challenge to the limits of what we think is fundamental. That is, from the earliest age we are taught that to know the

ABC's of X, Y or Z is to possess a foundational knowledge. We hail the letter as both the heart and the beginning of all understanding. Placed in this context, the sending of a 👧, in its very presence, suggests "the ABC's of the matter are and always will be unfit for the task of communicating what I have to say to you." There is more to emoji than meets the glance. At the moment, these airy icons may prevent such a heavy interpretation. But it may be worth bearing in mind both that the sender of an emoji we cannot quite fathom is indeed attempting to express the inexpressible, to say that there is something he or she thinks or feels that is beyond the smooth gloss of letters. And if we can at least sense that sentiment coming from someone who is trying to reach us, we can move a bit closer to them—whether they are family or friends or students or even administrators.

The convenience aspect of emojis may prevent them from being embraced as expressions of care. We cannot deny the speed that emoji usage affords. It is much easier, for Nimble and Chubby Thumb alike, to press ✈️ than to use a cellular phone to type out all of the words, including a capital letter, in "My airplane is arriving." Indeed, the debut of this airplane arrival emoji, one of 270 emoji newly approved by the Unicode Consortium, prompted New Yorker writer Ian Crouch to observe, only slightly tongue in cheek: "it's difficult to imagine how we lived without [certain emoji characters] for so long." Within specific contexts, emojis offer instantaneous connection. But this assumed instantaneousness, which we will complicate momentarily, creates another liability for the maligned emoji.

Because of emoji ease, receivers of emoji text may take offense at receiving 👧 instead of a note, sharing the sentiment of President Obama who expressed relief that his daughter had chosen an alphabetic path to his affection: "Malia, to her credit, wrote a letter to me for Father's Day, which was obviously much more important to me than if she had texted an emoji, or whatever those things are" (qtd. in Walker). So the ease and speed of emojis have caused them to be rejected as acceptable conveyers of heart-felt affection. Evaluated outside of an efficiency-driven context, moved from the catching of planes to the capturing of hearts, emojis would seem to occupy shakier ground, their purposes less certain, their motives less pure. The daughter who casually pastes 👧 instead of reflecting, drafting and revising a heart-felt letter to her father in a callous quest for Beloved Child Points surely does not deserve the badge. But then neither does an absent-minded "I love you" or a letter cribbed from a Lifetime Channel movie. Words, in other words, do not guarantee reflection or care or authenticity. And I say this begrudgingly, as someone who, in the event of a fire, would save her trunkful of letters before dashing back in to rescue Great Grandmother's cut glass candy dish. But I say this also as someone who has dashed off a lazy "that's great!!!" (3 !!! indicating more effort than a lackadaisical!) in response to a friend's happy news. The medium is not necessarily *the* message; context counts. Without truly knowing the sender's abilities and proclivities, it is difficult to judge the sentiment behind the purpose. Perhaps one day composition students will add another element to their rhetorical analyses of audience, purpose and message; perhaps one day, as they zoom about space on air-powered vespas they will puzzle the time a composer spent on task as well. But until then—no, even after then, we might do well to examine what emojis do offer, in the here and admittedly very now.

Despite the very contemporary, post-Fordist zeitgeist into which the emoji has popped, it nonetheless links us to our earliest efforts at expression—pictograms, petroglyphs and petrographs. John Berger acknowledges the both/and quality of images as the earliest symbols, predecessors to the symbolisms of alphabetic language: "What distinguished man from animals was the human capacity for symbolic thought, the capacity which was inseparable from the development of language in which words were not mere signals, but signifiers of something other than themselves. Yet the first symbols were animals. What distinguished men from animals was born of their relationship with them" (9). Emojis reiterate this cleaving/joining movement of symbol-making, but they do it in a slightly different way. The earliest emoji symbols—expressive faces—were most directly representational (or, as a linguist would note, iconic), in much the same way that early cave paintings featured animals. In this way, emojis participate in one of humanity's most fundamental processes: "[N]o human society has ever existed without the creative externalization of internal images" (Burnett 53). Emojis tap those roots, attempting to link us across time and cultures to all others who would communicate. A monolingual speaker of English is more likely to understand a Finnish friend's ☹ than "kolkkous." Emojis operate at the level of the non-discursive, potentially filling a gap that separates even speakers of the same language. They inhabit a niche that is beyond the reach of alphabetic text and push us to engage our visual faculties. Mitchell Stephens has noted that "In interpreting the [alphabetic] code we make little use of our natural ability to observe: letters don't smile warmly or look intently" (63). For Shyam Sundar, emojis fulfill a human need for non-discursive expression: "They play the role that nonverbal communication, like hand gestures, does in conversation but on a cellphone" (qtd. in Wortham). Rather than having alphabetic text fly solo in conveying a message, emojis expand the possibilities of what might be expressed. Since their inception, emojis have been swept up by users with bigger ambitions for them, and in doing so have made the leap from being "users" to being "rhetors," joining a classic tradition that dates back to Ancient Greece and Rome. Catherine Hobbs explores a history of rhetoric tied to visualization, explaining that Greco-Roman law cases often depended on both the presentation of actual objects as well as orators' abilities to use visual imagery in persuading their audiences ("a scar, a wound, a bloody weapon or a toga") [58], a practice that continues in contemporary courtrooms, admittedly for better and for worse. The desire to argue effectively, to reach an audience through images and words, has a long and revered history that emojis have joined. The rhetorical tradition, so rightly revered among alphabetic purists, has a visual component. Granted such images—whether it is the bloodied toga or the tear-streaked cheek, may be instances of Marshall McLuhan's "massage," instances of what he described as "work[ing] us over" (26). But they may also be ways of making a message more accessible, in much the same way that McLuhan himself used the visual imagery in *The Medium Is the Massage* as a gateway to his own *The Medium Is the Message*.

Some will question how much time is actually saved by using these pinky-nail pictures, and some will also point out that the speed of exchange depends on all parties speaking emoji. If Nimble Thumb punches out ✈, but her friend doesn't understand and spends most of the morning puzzling out the possibilities that might mean, the message is purloined, composed but never received, the plane arriving but forever unmet. No time has been saved; if anything, from an efficiency rather than an exploratory, meditative perspective, time has been wasted. We are again faced with the importance of context and of discourse. Emoji efficacy works only if all parties speak the same emoji. Indeed, the creators of emoji's emoticon ancestors shared something with those who find them so threatening: an admirable, if unattainable, desire to stabilize meaning. Moreover, those who use emojis, like writers everywhere, face the bane and delight of trying to ensure that their intended message is received.

Kadomatsu emoji

Emojis are still in their language cradle. Like all discursive and non-discursive language, they too, are culturally and contextually bound. Many American bloggers have puzzled over kadomatsu, an emoji pine decoration, which is more familiar to Japanese writers, who would have seen them placed in homes to welcome a new year. In instances of cultural disconnect, those unfamiliar with the tradition have sent the *kadomatsu* as a sign of disrespect, mistaking it for a middle finger icon. While some images cross cultural borders, not all do. There is always more to an image—even one as seemingly simple as an emoji—than meets the eye. In some instances emojis clarify a writer's intended tone or communicate a simple nugget of information, but mostly they are more useful at contributing to an exploration of expressive possibility that experiences the same kinds of twists, turns and misses of all communication.

Consider Fred Benenson's rewritten version of *Moby Dick*:

ENGLISH: Call me Ishmael.

EMOJI:

Benenson's crowd-sourced, Kick-Starter-funded rewritten version of *Moby Dick*, *Emoji Dick*, was accepted into the Library of Congress in February 2013. As with any translation, Benenson's act was creative and subjective. (I still read that opening line as "phone, mustache face, sailboat, whale, ok.") Indeed, in an interview Benenson himself acknowledged the many interpretive choices he had to make during the translation: "I fully admit that there are large portions of the book that don't make any sense, and there are a number of reasons for that" (qtd. in Goldmark). We could view Benenson's efforts as an act of literary apostasy, but we could also see it as a work of art in its own right, a brave foray into challenging and unexplored literary waters in search of an elusive and formidable goal. While at least one Emoji Dick commentator predicted that the translation would lead to 💣 there seems to be evidence that emojis, if anything are opening paths of communicative exploration. VoidWorks, a Singapore-based-app development studio, has released an app that allows users to "emojify" any photo by converting pixels into emoji; emoji poetry is everywhere, and there's a Tumblr blog, Narratives in Emoji (http://narrativesinemoji.tumblr.com) that includes emoji translations of *Les Miserables*, *The Titanic* and *Groundhog Day*. Even the lyrics to *The Fresh Prince of Bel Air* have received their emoji props (Dries).

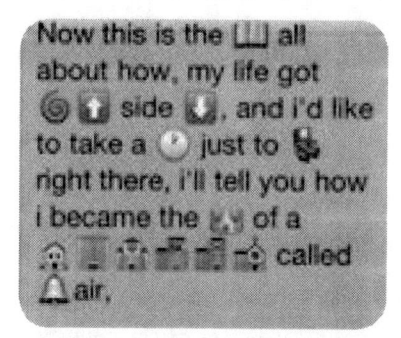

> Now this is the 🏫 all about how, my life got 🔄⬆️ side ⬇️, and i'd like to take a 🕐 just to 💺 right there, i'll tell you how i became the 🤴 of a 🏠🚆🚆🚆🚖 called 🔺 air.

The art world is also enjoying the fruits of emoji labors. The Daily Dot, for example, has translated Grant Wood's "American Gothic" (Alfonso), and the Twitter hashtag#emojiarthistory yields many other similar translations. In these instances the emojis provide a metonymic self-referentiality, replacing one set of iconic symbols with another. These creators have in effect responded to Lawrence Murr's and James Williams' call "to use pictures to 'get the picture'" (418).

In some instances emoji have themselves been subject to translation, as Justine on YouTube demonstrates in this aural representation of them:

Woman kissing compared to emoji kissing (https://www.youtube.com/watch?v=6B0NBVT6VP4)

In their visuality, their connection to gestures and their digitized form, emojis fit squarely in the social future called for by The New London Group in their 1996 "Pedagogy of Multiliteracies." An international collaborative aimed at developing new pedagogies that would respond to changing literacies brought by increasing globalization, cultural, social diversity and changes in technology, the group called for a literacy pedagogy of "available designs." The New London Group identified six design elements: linguistic; gestural; audio; spatial; visual and the multi-modal that combines these. Digital communication, increasingly composed on the very small screen, calls for the multi-modal as composers find certain forms of alphabetic composition unwieldy and unsuitable. In some instances, composers will be able to choose their medium, deciding if what they have to say is best expressed via the page, or if they need the more visual affordances of the computer screen or if they need the speed of texting via the tiniest screen of them all. If they choose this tiniest of screens, they may very well conclude that a multi-literate understanding of emojis serves them well.

Almost a decade prior to the New London Group manifesto, Murr and Williams would reason that "since language shapes our perception of reality it is clear that new concepts of language must be developed with the emergence of the visual culture. Just as the practice of language in Western civilization, as served by speech and memory, was altered by the invention of an alphabet and later its encoding in books through monotype, so must it be altered again as a result of the invention of visual tools" (415). Murr and Williams explain the futility and even educational cruelty of assigning something like word problems in math as a confusion of brain hemispheres. Science and math are right-brain activities: "it does not make sense to emphasize text-based descriptions of scientific phenomena in general, or mathematical phenomenon in particular..." (417). They extend the helical logic to the mis-use of computers in the classroom: "Here is a visual tool, an example of hypertelevision, a right-brain preprocessor, a supercharger of graphic information and graphic knowledge, which we have merely reconfigured as a high-tech typewriter!" (417). As antidote, they advocate a need for "some attention to graphic forms, drawing, painting and the visual arts, by raising our consciousness of symbols, by connecting text and graphics through the creation of language networks..."(418). Perhaps work with emojis will provide an entryway for such balance. Calls for the visual in the composition classroom have a long history. (See for example, Fleckenstein; George; Kress; Selfe; Stroupe; Yancey). The explorations that have already begun in classrooms are beyond the scope of this essay, but it is worth mentioning that emoji work has the potential to support the same kinds of rich learning experiences we seek in composition classes: a recognition of a multi-literate world; a platform for communicative play, experimentation and creativity; a basis for analysis of cross-cultural communication, identity and representations, and the threads of a re-materialized concept of composing.

Emojis have neither destroyed nor rescued words. We continue, as Megan Garber so beautifully puts it, to "MacGyver our way into language." At the end of the day, emojis are just as much a reflection of their creators as words, with just as much potential to express, explore, kvetch and ultimately connect us to others. Though in some instances they supplant words entirely, they also open up new vistas of exchange and creativity. They are in a sense, the words that got away, and then returned. As smiles and frowns and jetliners.

Lisa Lebduska teaches writing and directs the college writing program at Wheaton College in Massachusetts. Focused on the intersections and eruptions among composition, technology and people, her work has appeared in such publications as *WPA: Writing Program Administration, CCC, Narrative, Writing on the Edge,* and *Technological Ecologies and Sustainability: Methods, Modes, and Assessment.*

Acknowledgments: I wish to thank the Andrew W. Mellon Foundation for providing me with summer research support, including those allowing me to work with Hailey Heston (Wheaton Class of 2018), who found the Library of Congress images used here, and whose photoblog serves up many an image for thought.

Works Cited

Berger, Jon. "Why Look at Animals?" *About Looking.* New York: Random House, 1988. 1-28. Print.

Brownlee, John. "Where Do Emoji Come From?" *Co.design.* 30 June 2014. Web. 1 July 2014.

Burnett, Ron. *How Images Think.* Cambridge: MIT, 2004. Print.

Crouch, Ian. "New Emojis, but No Hot Dog." Culture Desk. *The New Yorker* 18 June 2014. Web. 20 June 2014.

Dillon, Sam. "In Test, Few Students Are Proficient Writers." New York Times. *New York Times*, 3 April 2008. Web. 20 July 2014.

Dries, Kate. "People Have iPhones and They're Not Afraid to Use Them." *Buzzfeed.* 5 February 2013. Web. 10 June 2014.

Eliot, T.S. *East Coker*. London: Faber and Faber, 1942. Print.
Fleckenstein, Kristie S. "Inviting Imagery into Our Classrooms." *Language and Image in the Reading Writing Classroom: Teaching Vision.* Eds. Kristie Fleckenstein, Linda T. Calendrillo and Demetrice Worley. Mahwah, NJ: Lawrence Erlbaum Associates, 2002: 3-26. Print.
Gabriele, Thomasina. *Italo Calvino: Eros and Language.* Fairleigh Dickinson P., 1994. Print.
Garber, Megan. "How to Tell a Joke on the Internet." *The Atlantic Monthly.* 24 April 2013. Web. 16 May 2013.
George, Diana. "From Analysis to Design: Visual Communication in the Teaching of Writing." *College Composition and Communication.* 54.1. (2002): 11-38. Print.
Goldfield, Hannah. "I Heart Emoji" *The New Yorker.* 16 October 2012. Web. 16 May 2013.
Goldmark, Alex. "Inside the Mind That Translated Moby Dick into Emoji" *New Tech City.* 27 February 2014. Web. 19 March 2014.
Haiman, John. *Talk Is Cheap: Sarcasm, Alienation and the Evolution of Language.* Oxford: Oxford UP, 1998. Print.
Hobbs, Catherine L. "Learning from the Past: Verbal and Visual Literacy in Early Modern Rhetoric and Writing Pedagogy." Ed. Fleckenstein, Calendrillo and Worley. 27-44. Rpt. in *Visual Rhetoric in a Digital World: A Critical Sourcebook.* Ed. Carolyn Handa. Boston:Bedford/St. Martin's, 2004: 55-71.
Holland, Jessica. "Emoji: A Tiny Graphic Can Be Worth a Thousand SMSes." *The National.* 7 April 2013. Web. 19 March 2014.
Kelion, Leo. "Apple Seeks Greater Racial Diversity." *BBC News Technology.* 26 March 2014. Web. 10 June 2014.
Kress, Gunther. *Literacy in the New Media Age.* New York: Routledge, 2003. Print.
MacDonald, Susan Peck. "The Erasure of Language." *College Composition and Communication.* 58.4 (2007): 585-625. Print.
Marsden, Rhodri. "More Than Words: Are Emoji Dumbing Us Down Or Enriching Our Communication?" *The Independent.* 11 May 2013. Web. 20 June 2014.
McLuhan, Marshall. *The Medium Is the Massage.* New York: Random House, 1967. Print.
Miller, J. Abbott, and Ellen Lupton. "A Natural History of Typography." Ed. Bierut, Michael, William Drenttel, Steven Heller, and D.K. Holland. *Looking Closer: Critical Writings on Graphic Design.* Vols. 1-2. New York: Allworth, 1994, 1997. 19-25. Print.
Mitchell, W. J. T. *Iconology: Image, Text, Ideology.* Chicago: U. of Chicago P., 1986. Print.

Murr, Lawrence E., and James B. Williams. "Half-Brained Ideas about Education: Thinking and Learning with Both the Left and Right Brain in a Visual Culture." *Leonardo* 21.4 (1988): 413-419. Print.

New London Group. "A Pedagogy of Multiliteracies: Designing Social Futures." *Harvard Educational Review*, 1996 66 (1), 60-92. Print.

Rock, Margaret. "From Talk to Telepathy." *Mobiledia*. 8 July 2013. Web. 1 July 2014.

Selfe, Cynthia. "Toward New Media Texts: Taking Up the Challenges of Visual Literacy." *Writing New Media: Theory and Applications for Expanding the Teaching of Composition*. Ed. Anne Francis Wysocki, Johndan Johnson-Eilola, Cynthia L. Selfe, and Geoffrey Sirc. Utah State P, Logan: Utah, 2004:67-110. Print.

Smith, Aaron. "African Americans and Technology Use: A Demographic Portrait." *Pew Research Internet Project*. 14 January 2014. Web. 6 June 2014.

Stephens, Mitchell. *The Rise of the Image, the Fall of the Word*. New York: Oxford UP, 1998. Print.

Stroupe, Craig. "Visualizing English: Recognizing the Hybrid Literacy of Visual and Verbal Authorship on the Web." *College English* 62.5 (2000): 607-632. Print.

Trimbur, John. "Delivering the Message: Typography and the Materiality of Writing." *Rhetoric and Composition as Intellectual Work*. Ed. Gary Olson. Carbonddale: Southern Illinois UP, 2002. 188-202. Rpt. in *Visual Rhetoric in a Digital World: A Critical Sourcebook*. Ed. Carolyn Handa. Boston: Bedford/St. Martin's P., 2004: 260-271. Print.

Walker, Hunter. "President Obama Is Glad He Didn't Get Emoji for Father's Day." *Business Insider*. 17 June 2014. Web. 2 July 2014.

Wilson, James A. and Walter R. Gove. "The Intercohort Decline in Verbal Ability: Does It Exist?" *American Sociological Review*. 64.2 (1999): 253-266. JSTOR. Web 20 July 2014.

Wortham, Jenna. "Whimsical Texting Icons Get a Shot at Success." 11 December 2011. *New York Times*. n.p.17 June 2014. Web.

Yancey, Kathleen. "Made Not Only in Words: Composition in a New Key." *College Composition and Communication*. 56:2 (2004): 297-328. Print.

IMAGES

Alfonso, Fernando III. "Reinterpreting Classic Works of Art with #emoji-arthistory." The Daily Dot. 13 February 2013. http://www.dailydot.com/culture/emoji-art-history-tate-getty/

Babel Fish Diagram. Hitchhiker Wiki. n.d. Web. 1 July 2014.

Cyrus, Miley Ray. "RT If You Think There Needs to be an #emojiethnicity Update." 18 December 2012, 7:05 p.m. Tweet.

Doctorow, Cory. "Crowdsourced Translation of Moby-Dick into Emoji." Boing Boing. Boing Boing, 21 September 2009. Web. 20 July 2014.
"Emoji Fortunes." Baker's Blog. 6 June 2013.
"Emojify: Turn Pixels into Emoji Emoticons to Make Unique Art Images." Appszoom. <http://www.appszoom.com/iphone-apps/photo_video/emojify-turn-pixels-into-emoji-emoticons-to-make-unique-art-images_hl-szh.html>
Heston, Hailey. "Light Bulb of Ideas." *Wandering, Wondering.* 29 March 2014. Web. 14 July 2014.
iJustine. "Emoji Emotions." YouTube. http://www.youtube.com/watch?v=6B0NBVT6VP4.
Kahn, Justin. "How to Get Emoji Keyboard on iPad." ipad *Notebook: Tips, Thoughts & Apps.* Web. <http://ipadnotebook.wordpress.com/2012/10/10/how-to-get-emoji-keyboard-on-ipad/>.
Lee, Eric. "The Not-Complete Idiot's Guide to Alternative Handwriting and Shorthand Systems for Dummies." n.d. Web. 10 June 2014.
Psar, Ira. "The Origins of Writing." In *Heilbrun Timeline of Art History.* New York: The Metropoitan Museum of Art. October 2004. Web. 14 October 2014.
Trahan, Heather. "A Composition in Film." http://vimeo.com/6902118.
"Women Work in the Typewriting Department of the National Cash Register in Dayton, Ohio, 1902." Library of Congress. Web.

Fair Use Statement

The purpose of all quoted material here is to quote and cite material within the bounds of academic fair use. I have attributed all authors and creators, providing a Works Cited.

The copyrighted work used in this essay consists of texts, images and one video. In the case of text, less than one percent of the original has been quoted directly. Images have been used in their entirety. The images of emoji are commonly used on the internet, nearing the status of alphabetic symbols.

ENCULTURATION

Enculturation was launched in 1996 by two graduate students. In twenty years it has never been affiliated with a press or organization and has only had minimal institutional support by one university. Currently it is hosted on an individual's server and supported with one RA through the University of South Carolina. Almost all of the managerial, editorial, and production work continues to be done by young faculty and graduate students in the field of rhetoric and composition. The mission of the journal has generally been to publish broader ranging interdisciplinary work related to rhetoric and composition that is more theoretical or media-oriented.

Enculturation is on the Web at http://enculturation.net/

Listening to the Sonic Archive: Rhetoric, Representation, and Race in the Lomax Prison Recordings

Sonic rhetorics and sound compositions are quickly emerging as predominant subfields in rhetoric and composition. Jonathan Stone's "Listening to the Sonic Archive" rightly points out that "we are not just dealing in scholarly fads, but in deep disciplinary grooves that require sustained attention if sound studies hopes to become as theoretically and methodologically integral to our work as visual studies has been." His work is a shining example of just what this sustained attention might look like. "Listening to the Sonic Archive" weaves together concerns for sound composition, historiography and archives, African American rhetorics, and an ethics of listening to show how historical sonic artifacts complicate our understanding of racial otherness through listening to history rather than reading it.

10 Listening to the Sonic Archive: Rhetoric, Representation, and Race in the Lomax Prison Recordings

Jonathan W. Stone

"Lightnin" Washington singing with his group at Darrington State Farm, Texas.

Introduction

In the opening paragraph of her August 2014 *enculturation* article, "Toward a Resonant Material Vocality for Digital Composition," Erin Anderson recounts, briefly, the development of sound studies as an interdisciplinary phenomenon and its growing influence in rhetoric and composition studies. As she notes, "sound studies scholars have made great strides toward highlighting the role of music, noise, and non-verbal sound as powerful modes of sensory experience, politics, and persuasion" (para. 1) Further, she observes that "scholars of sonic rhetoric have worked to carve out a space for sound as a subject of rhetorical analysis, a material for multimodal text production, and a methodological model for alphabetic writing practice." Given the contribution of Anderson's work and those she cites both within and outside of rhetoric and composition, it would seem we are at the genesis of a scholarly sonic boom.

Consider, however, the ways that Anderson's report on the status of sound in the field differs in tenor from another published only a few years ago by rhetorical studies scholar Greg Goodale. A guiding exigency in Goodale's *Sonic Persuasion* (2011) is his concern for sound's profound scholarly *neglect* in preference for visualist methods of knowledge making, not just in rhetoric, but within the entire Western tradition. As Goodale argues, this visualist attitude ramifies across intellectual history with particularly cacophonous moments during the Enlightenment in the development of scientific method and observation (both visualist practices) and then again during the nineteenth and twentieth centuries when print culture reached its apex. "Our captivation by visual culture," he concedes, "has produced a legacy that will take decades if not centuries to overcome" (5). He then calls us to the work.

Anderson and Goodale, working only a few years from each other, offer quite different perspectives on sound's relationship to rhetoric and its attendant fields. Surely, Anderson's assessment represents the kind of progress Goodale was advocating, but that progress is tempered by his reminder that we are not just dealing in scholarly fads, but in deep disciplinary grooves that require sustained attention if sound studies hopes to become as theoretically and methodologically integral to our work as visual studies has been. We can be encouraged, though, that the growing preponderance of new work in sound and rhetoric has precipitated an emergent scholarly community in rhetoric and sound studies not present in 2011 and one marked by increased opportunity for both conversation and critique. Before getting to the bulk of this essay, then, I trace few possible intersections for these emergent conversations (including my own potential contributions) as well as the questions and critiques they raise.

CULTIVATING AN ETHIC(S) OF LISTENING TO HISTORICAL SOUND

Like Anderson's "Toward a Resonant Material Vocality for Digital Composition," this article is also concerned with the sound of the recorded voice. Anderson's work toward developing a more robust understanding of what she calls the "futurity of voice" or "the possibility of remixing and rearticulating voices into new material assemblages" is a key advancement for sonic rhetoric (para. 24). Movement in our concern from *who* produced a voice to *what* that voice does apart from its originating body and "allowing [recorded voices] a valid existence beyond those bodies, even as bodies in themselves" shifts the rhetorical paradigm of the voice away from concerns about "protection" and "preservation" towards something entirely new (para. 18). So how do historians, especially those who work in and with archives—scholars for whom protection and preservation are important (and even ethically integral) components of their regular work—process and work within this paradigm shift?[1] One way, as we have seen in recent work from Jody Shipka, is to reimagine and recompose our understanding of the archive itself. When working explicitly with sonic archives,

---

1. Anderson is well aware of the importance of representational ethics, noting the "obvious liability" of efforts to intentionally defy the identity or property of individuals from which recorded voices originate. These concerns are particularly important to institutions like the Library of Congress where "protection" and "preservation" are part of its mission. Violations of these ethics are common, however. Two contemporary examples are worth mentioning: In 1999, the musician Moby had a hit record with "Natural Blues," which sampled Vera Hall's "Trouble So Hard" from a recording made by John and Alan Lomax for the Library of Congress archive. Similarly, Canadian artist Feist recently recorded a version of the traditional folksong "Sea Lion Woman," another Library of Congress recording. Moby never compensated Hall or her estate with a percentage of the monetary proceeds from the single and Feist claimed composition credit for "Sea Lion Woman" in the liner notes for her 2007 album *The Reminder*.

however, and particularly those within state or national institutional systems, remix and rearticulation can be applied as conceptual framings for exploring sound's useful disruption of *ideological* assemblages: gender, sexuality, and (of particular interest for this article) race and racial formation.

Another critique challenges work that seeks to isolate and bracket off single-sensory phenomenon for study. Steph Ceraso addresses this problem in her recent article "(Re)Educating the Senses: Multimodal Listening, Bodily Learning, and the Composition of Sonic Experiences," by arguing that listening should be understood as a multi-sensory practice. "Multi-modal listening," as she terms it, is a practice attuned to the ways that sonic experience involves a concert of sensory modes working together, and "moves away from organ-specific definitions and instead conceives of listening as a practice that involves attending not only to the sensory, embodied experience of sound, but to the material and environmental aspects that comprise and shape one's embodied experience of sound" (105). Thomas Rickert presses the critique a bit more intently suggesting in his recent work *Ambient Rhetoric* (2014) that the notion of "multimodality" itself emphasizes attention to parts rather than their sum and thus casts a discriminating shadow over the reality of our experiences within the complex ambience of the sensorium (142). The varying perspectives here remind us that even as we continue in our efforts to expand sound's theoretical potentials, a sustained scrutinizing of the sonic should lead to a more nuanced understanding of the multiplicities of rhetorical practice itself, across the sensorium.

It follows that the rhetorical practice of composing history stands to benefit from a variety of sonic inversions. Historiography, so often concerned with assembling the most effective methods for accuracy, precision, and preservation of a "true" historical narrative, finds in the sonic artifact the paradox of preserved uncertainty. Stepping away from the quest for certainty as a guiding principle in our work, allows us, in Christa Olson's words, to "learn, not teach, about the rhetorical histories we describe" (82). Olson answers the difficulty of working in a post-certainty age by inviting us to make that decentering part of our approach—to "build our histories on shifting sand yet find ways to make them stand" (82). She invites us to seek out and build "theories to slip" and to choose "conceptual frames that call tensions to the foreground" (96). Historical work, Olson suggests, offers an indispensable arena where we may begin working through the processes of a decentered approach to rhetoric. Historical work utilizing recorded sound, and particularly historical music, provides a conspicuous and auspicious place to begin the practice of what Gunn et al. call a new scholarly "ethic of listening" (477). Like Ceraso and Anderson, Gunn et al. encourage both critical engagement with sound scholarship across disciplinary boundaries as well as the disciplining of the physical body itself toward various listening practices. Compared to the traditional scholarly environment where academic practices have evolved and become engrained within visual practices (reading, skimming, and, of course, looking at the pictures), listening can be a different and demanding experience insofar as it requires of rhetoric scholars more time and patience (you cannot skim audio artifacts) in shaping potentially new sonic literacies. This in addition to the new (for many) experience of dealing in the indeterminate materiality of the sonic register itself which include modes not generally foregrounded in scholarly discourse: simultaneity, dissonance, and multiplicity.

In what follows, I bring together these conversations about the power of recorded voice, decentered rhetorical historiography, and an ethic of multimodal listening to study a shift in cultural history when technological development made a variety of sounds (and particularly music) more accessible to the public, thereby influencing the ways that sonic material culture could circulate and have influence. As mentioned, the emphasis here will be on musical artifacts—prison recordings—housed at the Library of Congress.[2] I examine the historical circumstances of the production of those recordings—the people who sing on them, their material and now digital "remains," as well as the field workers behind the recording machines—in order to better understand how sound as rhetoric decenters traditional approaches to and understandings of cultural history and historiography. Four case studies provide the bulwark for this study and will be supported by a

---

2. Many, if not all, of the recordings I present in this essay have been released in a variety of places, some sanctioned by the Library of Congress, others not. My selection of recordings, which are not yet a part of the public domain, have been graciously curated and sanctioned by the Library of Congress with the help of Todd Harvey, collections specialist and curator of the Alan Lomax Collection. Harvey's first response to me when I asked about publishing the songs was on the ethics of the process: "a good faith effort [should be made] to contact the rights holders." Unfortunately, no contact information is currently available for the estates of John Gibson, Mose Platt, or James Baker.

theoretical framework invoked above as well as by notions of rhetorical sound and voice provided by Eric King Watts and others. I conclude the essay with a discussion of how historical sonic artifacts such as those in my study productively complicate our understanding of racial formation and the ongoing racial project of reifying notions of racial otherness in the United States.

Most importantly, my study invites readers to stop reading history for a moment and listen to it. Listen to the archived voices and music of African-American men incarcerated in Southern labor camps and thus participate within and contribute to the ethics of listening described above.

I. Prison Moan

Listen: The Angels Drooped their Wings and Gone to Heaven
https://goo.gl/RTupqB

Sponsored by the Library of Congress, John A. Lomax and his son Alan traveled to eleven Southern African-American prisons during the summer of 1933 to record the "folksongs of the Negro[es]" incarcerated there. This music, John later wrote, was "in musical phrasing and in poetic content . . . most unlike those of the white race [and the] least contaminated by white influence or by modern Negro jazz" (Lomax 112). Both he and Alan understood the vernacular music of the isolated African American as a protected and preserved remnant of slave and, by extension, black culture—a mysterious world that, for most white citizens in the US, seventy years after Emancipation, was only just beginning to receive sustained scholarly attention. Their work that summer would produce over one hundred aluminum discs of recorded material, most of which the Library of Congress preserves, and now and then releases commercially.

Many of the recordings from the Southern prison stops, along with dozens of others collected from other sources during the trips, were carefully transcribed and published in the Lomaxes' *American Ballads and Folk Songs* (1934). Such publications were once relatively common and followed a similar production formula: a professionally trained musician worked with a vernacular musician to painstakingly transcribe a tune that would then be re-presented visually as sheet music within the text. *American Ballads* was among the first folk collections to be so compiled, using recordings instead of live performance as the source material. Re-presented in various stage-performances organized by the Lomaxes over the course of that decade, and then released in the early 1940s by the Library of Congress, the field recordings would eventually change how American vernacular music could be experienced, studied, and emulated by an expanding audience of both scholars and citizens. In its various phonographic releases, US vernacular music could be experienced beyond mere transcribed textual representation. The voices of the convicts, farmers, preachers, and many others, could at last be heard.

Listen: Black Samson - "Levee Camp Holler"
https://goo.gl/RTupqB

One voice was John Gibson's. When he first met John and Alan Lomax, Gibson had just begun serving a twenty-year sentence in the State Penitentiary in Nashville, Tennessee. Upon that meeting, Gibson (also known as "Black Samson") asked the Lomaxes to help facilitate his release (Lomax & Lomax 151). Perhaps that was why, despite his uneasiness, Gibson relented and allowed himself to be recorded for the Library of Congress archive. In December 1934, a little more than a year later, this report about John Gibson and the song "Levee Camp Holler" was published *American Ballads*:

> This song is the workaday of the Negro behind a team of mules. . . . Black Samson, whom we found breaking rocks in the Nashville State Penitentiary, admitted that he knew the song and had once sung it; but since he had joined the church and had turned away from the world, he no longer dared sing it. All our arguments were in vain. The prison chaplain protested that he would make it all right with the Lord. But Black Samson replied that he was a Hard-shell Baptist and that, according to their way of thinking, he would be in danger of hell-fire if he sang such a song. At last, however, when the warden had especially urged him to sing, he stepped in front of our microphone and, much to our surprise, when he had made sure that his words were being recorded, said: "It's sho hard lines dat a nigger's got to sing a worl'ly song, when he's tryin' to be sancrified; but de warden's ast me, so I guess I'll have to." And he did. But he registered his protest before the

Lord on an aluminum plate, now filed in the Library of Congress at Washington (49).

John Lomax's frankness about Alan's and his involvement in persuading Gibson is astounding, but the added detail of their having exerted pressure from ecclesiastical and institutional authority is dumbfounding. Obviously, such machinations were once tolerated, but there can be little doubt that the Lomaxes exploited John Gibson's desire for freedom by exhorting him, despite his pronounced and explicit reluctance to sing, an act of inducement that 80 years later we can readily call coercion.

A close listen of the field recording reveals more of interest in "Levee Camp Holler." The track begins with an introduction from John Lomax followed by a short protest Gibson: "Lord, this levee camp song is mighty bad to sing...." It is unclear why Gibson's words do not match up better with Lomax's published rendering. The track is also uncertain; there are starts and stops during the recording and another muted voice can be heard prompting Gibson with forgotten lyrics. He does not seem to know the song that well or acts as if he does not. Also, "Levee Camp Holler" cuts out abruptly during the middle of the ninth stanza—this compared to the 28 stanzas that appear in *American Ballads and Folk Songs*. The aluminum recording discs were cut in real time with a diamond-tipped needle and could only fit about fifteen minutes per side. Recordings frequently ended mid-song the way that "Levee Camp Holler" does, but those songs would usually be rerecorded on a fresh disc. Perhaps Gibson could not be persuaded into a second take.[3]

Though the dialectic is captivating, there is more to listen for on the recordings than the drama between present and muted voices. It is impossible not to notice the sound of the recording materials themselves—the scratch and glitch of technology's age and decay as well as the buttressing residues of preservation. There is the revolving swoosh

---

3. West Virginia University Press recently released "Levee Camp Holler" on *Jail House Bound* a collection of songs culled from the Lomaxes' 1933 prison trip. In the liner notes, they observe correctly that John Lomax often "altered the sequence of stanzas, changed words, or even compiled a version from several sources" for American Ballads and Folk Songs. He justified this from the standpoint of a curator. His goal was a comprehensive understanding of a song's variety, not the capture of a single performance, or a statement about a particular performer (even when one is implied).

of the original aluminum disc decipherable in an ebb and flow of static and a needle skip, caught and cut off quickly at the end. There is also evidence of the transfer by Library of Congress technicians, decades ago, from disc to magnetic tape. One can hear a hiccup in the audio—a faint echo of Gibson's voice as magnetic tape folds over onto itself momentarily in the mix. Finally, though much more difficult to detect, the song was transferred into the binary code of a compact disc where all previous imperfections codify forever in the digital version.

Here, compressed again as an mp3, "Levee Camp Holler" is available in ubiquity streaming on the Web (from iTunes to YouTube)—this song John Gibson never wanted to sing in the first place.

Gibson's travails were not atypical. Recording for the Lomaxes offered a unique opportunity, but one with spiritual and ethical consequences for both the subjects and Lomaxes themselves. These prison performances and the subsequent records offered a new if complicated rhetorical agency to a few of the musically talented convicts and also yielded lasting effects on how African-American culture circulated within the US. Portals to a remote, unfamiliar subculture, many of the songs that the Lomaxes archived would eventually contribute to African-American vernacular culture receiving a mainstream (largely-white) public reception that it had not yet enjoyed. Yet a tension emerges out of the knowledge that scholarly work arising out of the Lomax archive is scaffolded upon early 1930s social realities, realities that included a fascination with racial difference as well as concomitant objectification of the black subject/prisoner as historical material. Prejudice's power is, in this way, a paradox; it both motivates and constrains our ability and capacity for understanding and identification. The Lomaxes and other white scholars interested in cultural preservation shaped the reception of that history in profound, often problematic ways. The recordings thus remain a rich yet thorny resource for scholarly and popular inquiry to the extent that they indexed both black experience and the ongoing production of whiteness in the US.[4]

---

4. According to folklorist Patrick B. Mullen, it was John Lomax's southern paternalism that made the "idea that the white man was the hope of freedom for the black convict" so resonant within his worldview. In contrast, the growing leftist sentiment among the rising educated generation shaped Alan's ideals and contributed to his sense of "pity and desire to help" the African-American men and women he began to meet during his first field recording trip. Both Lomaxes "had their whiteness reinforced by contact with blackness and their own sense of freedom intensified by the lack of freedom of the prisoners they were recording" (84).

We receive the Lomaxes' project, then, within the dissonant complexity of both prejudice and progress. They understood themselves as part of a progressive initiative far ahead of their time. That time has long passed, however, and a contemporary point of view makes moral demands on the Lomaxes that may well have been incomprehensible to them. This, of course, is the paradox of progressive thought: it will be regressive soon enough.

The dissonances particular to the early 1933 and 1934 prison recordings are made more comprehensible through conceptual framings that lend themselves well to managing ambiguity. The first is a guiding principle of revisionist historiography—one cued to the both/and-ness of historical "fact" and music's power to capture the layers of that dissonance. Along with this notion of a conflicted representative historiography, another instructive dissonance reverberates instructively across the prison recordings: that of rhetorical voice. Voice as a theoretical concept already enjoys a rich literature within rhetorical and sound studies, which I will contextualize and expand upon below. I will trace three coalescing agencies of personal, communal, and political voice and describe the ways that traditional subject/object representative relationships within and among these agencies in the archive blend together within the sonic. Interested as I am in the agency of the prisoners—particularly the new agency that a chance to perform for the archive afforded a few of the most talented among them—I also wish to complicate the notion of agency to understand its inherently discordant contradictions.

Interlude: Listening Closely

We can begin to get a sense for the dissonance I mention above by listening carefully now to several field recordings from the prison archive. While the casual listening skills I have described above are a good place to start, deeper understanding of the music requires a more attentive ear. I have modeled what might be termed a "close listen" of the song "Levee Camp Holler" in the above "Overture," though there is a good deal more to say about the potential draw of such a listen. For example, I have mentioned sonic and non-musical clues of the material and historical conditions present during the recording (and after), but I have not yet addressed more traditional sonic components such as lyrics, tone, and melody (which are, perhaps, more intuitive). For now, permit me to emphasize the simple practices of care and attention. For example, it took several listens before I realized that someone was supplying John Gibson with the lyrics to "Levee Camp Holler." Sentient listening to this particular grouping of archival music can often be an affecting experience, but some recordings are more difficult to listen to. Their challenge results from the material conditions present at the time of the recording as well as the way that the wear and tear of technology's decay obscures their clarity. More poignantly, perhaps the most exacting difficulty in listening lies in the content of the recordings themselves. The prison recordings echo a despicable past of de jure segregation—resounding of evidence of oppressive injustice, systematic cruelty, and omnipresent prejudice. Each of these listening observations and experiences are significant and lend themselves to a more nuanced understanding of sound's rhetorical impact.

II. Dissonant Voices

Listen: Lightnin' Washington and prisoners, "Good God Amighty"
https://goo.gl/SFqHpe

After being refused admission to the Texas State Penitentiary in Huntsville and rebuffed by a negative experience at Prairie View state school for blacks (Now Prairie View A&M University), John and Alan Lomax made their first real headway in recording African-American prisoners when they visited the Central State Prison Farm in Sugar Land, Texas. At "Sugarland," the Lomaxes encountered two aging men who would become central to the prison archive. The first was seventy-one-year-old Mose "Clear Rock" Platt, who had been jailed for forty-seven years on a murder charge. The other, James "Iron Head" Baker was sixty-four and knew so many songs that John Lomax would later refer to him as a "black Homer." Platt, on the other hand, was a master improviser and could sing the same song with seemingly infinite variations and, just as easily, could make up new ones on the spot, making him, as John Szwed has written, "a folklorist's dream" (41). John Lomax recalls first meeting Platt and Baker in the hospital building on the complex while recording a convalescing man named Mexico in one of the large bedrooms there. Baker was watching the recording session with interest and said (in John's rendering), "I'se Iron Head, I'se a trusty. I know lots of jumped-up, sinful songs—more than any of these niggers" (Lomax 165). He recorded with the

Lomaxes for the rest of that night and throughout the next day, taking turns singing with his "pardner," Platt. The Lomaxes observed that the songs produced at Sugarland were of immense diversity. There were "rhythmic, surging songs of labor; cotton-picking songs; songs of the jailbird" as well as "songs of loneliness and the dismal monotony of life in the penitentiary; songs of pathetic longing for his 'doney,' his woman" (166). Above all, the Lomaxes averred the "words, the music, the rhythm, were simple" and the result of the "natural emotional outpouring of the black man in confinement" (166).

LISTENING AND VOICE: MOSE PLATT

In the following case studies, I move within the narratives that the Lomaxes collaborated on with Platt, Baker, and other prisoners to demonstrate sound's relationship to the oral/aural process of personal, communal, and institutional/political agency and remembering. Such processes can be understood as useful nuances of rhetorical voice. While voice as a theoretical concept has been employed to various (and sometimes disparate) ends, Eric King Watts usefully frames a way of understanding the theoretical potential of voice within the sonic mode.[5] Watts distinguishes a "middle road," between the "ontic and symbolic" potentials of voice, drawing out the tensions between "speech as a sensual, personal, and 'authentic' phenomenon and language as an abstract impersonal symbolic system" (180). These tensions are ever-present in the prison recordings and show up in the relationships and rhetorics at play in each level of the rhetorical situation. An example of such a tension can be heard in James Baker's singing voice, which, in concert with the material clues on the recording and the Lomax book excerpt, is a powerful reminder of his humanity and the reality of his

---

5. In his recent edited collection *The Sound Studies Reader* (2012), Jonathan Sterne curates a productive list of scholarship on the voice as the subject relates to the nascent field of sound studies. Among those whose work is important to the discussion of voice are Ferdinand de Saussure and his Course in General Linguistics, which situates the voice "as a fundamental modality of social enunciation"; Marshall McLuhan and Walter Ong, who "based an entire psychological theory of orality around ideas of the voice as presence"; as well as Jacques Derrida's critique of these positions as a misguided "metaphysics of presence" (491-2). Sterne's own positioning on voice is resonant with Derrida and his collection draws together several other works that complicate and expand upon traditional conceptions of voice.

subjugation. On the other hand, "Levee Camp Holler" was interesting to the Lomaxes as a *symbol* expressing African-American prison life and by extension an even more abstracted symbolic slave culture. Within such a paradigm, John Gibson himself is unimportant. For the rhetorical listener, the seemingly distinct ontic (or that concerned with *being*—in this case human being) and symbolic components of the recording merge. One cannot exist without the other, and indeed, the presence of a listener (us) opens up other possible meaning relationships between the recordings, the voices on them, and the institution that produced and distributed them.

In this way agency is both contingent to and emergent from the rhetorical situation that produced the recordings and has various meaning dependent upon which relationship is emphasized. Getting at this kind of rhetorical nuance was very much the point of Kenneth Burke's pentad, but I also find a recent framing from Thomas Rickert useful here. Following the work of Jenny Edbauer Rice and others, Rickert encourages an "ecologic" approach to rhetoric that embraces these complexities where "the interactions of numerous agents mutually form and condition a chaotically dynamic system" (xiv). For Rickert, rhetoric is ambient, and does its work "responding to and put forth through affective, symbolic, and material means, so as to . . . reattune or otherwise transform how others inhabit the world . . ." (162). Music performs this ambience well, particularly the ways that the affective, symbolic, and material aspects reveal tensions and dissonances within the rhetorical process which, in turn, requires an understanding of rhetoric in its complexity rather than as a tool for clear or incisive determinate persuasion.

An example of these various tensions and dissonances can be found in the voice of Mose Platt who, unlike Gibson, willingly participated in the field recordings. His voice can be heard on at least twelve distinct recordings, which include several solo performances as well as a number of collaborations with other prisoners, including Baker, his friend. Platt has a deep, distinctive baritone singing voice. His seemingly effortless vocal and pitch control indicate years of practice and performance. When other men join in singing with Platt, their ease and enthusiasm reveals participatory singing as part of a deeply embedded culture, not just a shared casual pastime among the prisoners.

Listen: Mose Platt – "Run Nigger Run"
https://goo.gl/Vfx3e1

I have selected two of Mose Platt's recordings for a close listen, both about slave escape and capture. The first, a song with the dubious title "Run Nigger Run," is presented here in preface to the second. "Run Nigger Run" evokes the long tradition of slave escape. In fact, a song with a nearly identical refrain can be connected to Nat Turner's slave rebellion in Southampton County, Virginia in 1831 (Lomax and Lomax 228). But listening to Mose Platt sing his version, it is difficult to mistake the enthusiasm in his voice as he performed it proudly for the Lomaxes, the warden, and an audience of his peers. Halfway through the recording (43), we even hear several voices encouraging Platt to keep singing. Clearly, a song about escape had meaning similar as well as particular to the tune's historical context. In a sense as much transgressive as comic, there is dissonance between these two renderings, one historical and symbolic, the other kairotic and salient to the moment. Platt had a dark sense of humor.

We see this dark humor again in another escape slave-escape song, called "Ol' Rattler." "Ol' Rattler" is a song named for its subject, a mythic prison watchdog. The dog's job was to chase and maul any escaping prisoner, a job presumably tied to a longer tradition of slave capture. For this example, I am interested in making the humanistic/symbolic dichotomy explicit by comparing recorded sound in varying shades of abstraction, from recorded vocal singing to its abstract visual/textual rendering. To make my point I will work backward—from most abstract to least. At the far end of that trajectory is Mose Platt and other voices on the recording which present a striking, unmistakably human contrast to the other representations. But in this most "present" and least abstracted space, I will pause to complicate the move toward championing the salience of the voice or its ability to access or understand deep humanity. A voice on an archival recording is still an abstraction and there is still an insurmountable distance between that recording and the people who made it.

In the excerpt (Figure 1) from *American Ballads and Folk Songs* (66), consider how race is represented discursively in the text of the sheet music through lingual dialect and in the short excerpted quote at the top from Mose Platt. Consider also how both textual and musical elements of this discursive artifact might have racialized the interpretation of the content. Lyrics rendered as dialect and grace notes in four of the five opening measures are each attempts to represent the sound of Mose Platt's voice, one approximating his vocal style; the other, seizing on the vocal nuances of his sung musical intervals. The lyrics to the song, printed on the opposite page, also approximate (and do not always match) with the recorded version. They do, nevertheless, depict a bleak reality of African-American prison life, one defined by its invisible and insurmountable rural borders. Ol' Rattler did not simply keep prisoners from escaping, for those who made the attempt would not survive his attack: "If I trip this time" one lyric relates, "I'll trip

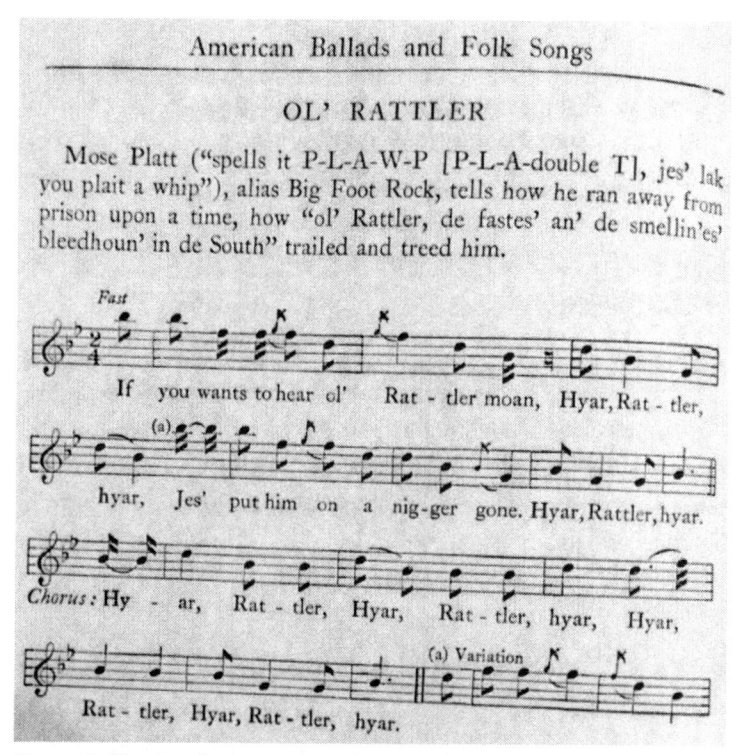

![American Ballads and Folk Songs — OL' RATTLER. Mose Platt ("spells it P-L-A-W-P [P-L-A-double T], jes' lak you plait a whip"), alias Big Foot Rock, tells how he ran away from prison upon a time, how "ol' Rattler, de fastes' an' de smellin'es' bleedhoun' in de South" trailed and treed him. Musical notation with lyrics: "If you wants to hear ol' Rat-tler moan, Hyar, Rat-tler, hyar, Jes' put him on a nig-ger gone. Hyar, Rattler, hyar. Chorus: Hy-ar, Rat-tler, Hyar, Rat-tler, hyar, Hyar, Rat-tler, Hyar, Rat-tler, hyar."]

Figure 1. Excerpt from *American Ballads and Folk Songs*.

no more." A close reading of the lyrical texts reveals several other elements, which, when paired with an analysis of other songs in the collection, reveal a complex association of fear, oppression, back-breaking labor, and the constant threat of death and violence—punctuated here and there with a cathartic line of comedy or bawdy tale of sexual conquest. The Lomaxes' meticulous inclusion of the lyrics allow for this careful analysis and, even in dialect, allow the interested reader an opportunity to reflect on the experience of captivity and the terror of attempted escape:

> Now I run till I'm almos' blin'
> I'm on my way to de long-leaf pine.
> I didn' have no time to make no thimpathee
> My nighes' route was up a tree.

The various visual, musical, and textual renderings of the transcription, however, contain several significant elisions. They tell us very little about Mose Platt. (We are fortunate to have his name at all given that many of the recordings are attributed merely to "unknown prisoner.") Platt is caricatured in the sheet music, with only his blackness, criminal status, eagerness to escape, and inability to do so represented in the song. Each of these subjectivities can then be re-inscribed and mythologized as representation stands in, ominously, for historical reality.

Listen: "Ol' Rattler" – Piano rendering
https://goo.gl/5KbFvz

In the above audio clip, I recorded a pianist's rendering of "Ol' Rattler" from the sheet music in *American Ballads and Folk Songs*. While the simple melody is also an abstraction of the actual vocal performance, it at least provides interested and musically literate readers with an approximated version of what the song sounds like. Scholars might use this melodic rendering in comparison to other folk melodies or it might even be appropriated by a jazz or blues musician and riffed upon in their own work.

Listen: Mose Platt -- Ol' Rattler
https://goo.gl/9833XM

Now, compare both the sheet music and the simple piano melody of "Ol' Rattler" with the Lomax recording. The differences are striking. Platt's voice is rich and expressive compared to the piano's monotones. Variations on the melody are noticeably present on the recording, even within the few verses captured. Platt's phrases sometimes garble together—just like they might in an everyday encounter; it is difficult to understand his every word. Also, his singing companions emerge as salient pieces of the song's arrangement while these parts go unmentioned in the text. In contradistinction to a prescriptive understanding of rhetoric as logical clarity in persuasion, the most powerful aspect of voice rendered here or anywhere else is not the clarity of its communicative potential, but its variety, nuance, and multiplicity.

Another powerful aspect of an "ontic" listening of recordings like "Ol' Rattler" is that it momentarily diverts attention away from the heroic white-savior narrative so prominent in Western culture and demands that attention be granted to the person's voice on the recording. Symbolic meaning is lain aside for a moment and we are reminded of Roland Barthes' characterization of the voice's uncanny ability to connect us with the human. For Barthes this human essence is the "grain of the voice," —or language "in its very materiality" (506). If, as John Durham Peters reminds us, "the voice is a metaphor of power," tied distinctly to the experience of embodied identity, then "[e]ach person's voice is a creature of the shape of one's skull, sinuses, vocal tract, lungs, and general physique. Age, geography, gender, education, health, ethnicity, class, and mood all resound in our voices" (n.p.). We hear each of these things in the recorded voice of Mose Platt—evidence of his distinct humanity, and even though incarcerated, his power and agency. However, and in line with Derrida's critique of the metaphysics of presence, the humanistic qualities of Platt can only reach out so far.[6] Eventually his voice gets lost in the mix of the earlier representations, and, under scrutiny, the recording also cannot bear the weight of a true *present*-ation of the subject. The recording—which has a grain all its own—reminds us of the disconnection and temporal distance between his human body and mechanized historical reproduction. And suddenly, Mose Platt becomes a ghost.

---

6. Joshua Gunn's work on speech, the voice, and, by extension, Derridian presence is instructive for further reading on the various material and theoretical tensions between sound and presence. See his 2011 essay "On Recording Performance or Speech, the Cry, and the Anxiety of the Fix," and his "Speech is Dead; Long Live Speech" from 2008.

Iron Head Blues: Secular and Spiritual Communion

James «Iron Head» Baker, Sugar Land, Texas

Platt's singing companion James Baker ("Alias: Iron Head" as he was wont to say on the recordings) had lived and worked as a prisoner in the Central Imperial Prisoner near Sugar Land, Texas. Tall and quiet, he had a reputation among fellow inmates as having a large repertoire of songs. Over several years of acquaintance, John Lomax got to know him well and would devote a whole chapter in his autobiography to Baker. As mentioned before, Lomax called Baker a "black Homer" because he knew hundreds songs of all varieties and his abilities for improvisation and on-the-fly composition may well have matched the genius of ancient epic poets. This comparison is more apt than even Lomax would have imagined. Baker's rhythmic facility contributed to his popularity with and also to his respect among fellow inmates. Baker said he got his nickname while on the Ramsey State Farm, a work prison in Angleton, Texas while cutting wood. A felled oak tree fell nearby and "Some of the limbs hit my head, an' it broke 'em off; didn't knock me down, an' it didn't stop me from working." So he became known as Iron Head.

On the other hand, Baker referred to *himself* as "De roughest nigger what ever walked de streets of Dallas. In de pen off an' on fo' thirty-fo' years" (Lomax 166). Calling himself, after six convictions, an "H.B.C.—habitual criminal, you know" (166). Lomax comments, however, that he did not really look the part. His dignity and tenderness far outshone any residual evidence of hardness in his face. By Lomax's description, Baker seemed a solemn and honest figure, one whom "unlike the other Negro convict[s] [. . .] confessed that he was guilty of other crimes than those that had put him in prison": "Mos' of de times dey didn't catch me" (168), he was said to say. Indeed, if anything, Baker had a familial relationship with other inmates. One night while he was recording for the Lomaxes, his colleagues crowded the room and shouted requests. One of those requests, Lomax writes, did cause a bit of a rise out of Baker. They urged him to sing "Shorty George" a song about "the short passenger train that ran from Houston to the farm once a month on a Sunday, bringing visiting wives and sweethearts" (168). They begged until Iron Head had to shout at them: "You niggers know dat song always tears me to pieces. I won't sing it," after which he walked away and stood in the corner shadows and motioned for Lomax. "I'll sing dat song low for you":

> Shorty George, you ain't no fren' of mine
> Take all de wimmens, leave de mens behin'

Listen: James Baker - Shorty George
https://goo.gl/CuKwLu

"It makes me restless to see my woman," he confided in Lomax. "I'se a trusty an' I has a easy job. I could run down one o' dem corn rows an' git away, any day. But when de law caught me, dey would put me back in de line wid de fiel' han's. I'se too ol' for dat hard work" (167).

In the spring of 1936 and after corresponding with Baker a few times, Lomax returned to Sugarland and arranged for Baker's parole. The conditions of his release were that he would work for Lomax as a chauffeur and as an ambassador in the prisons, "acting as a go-between with black musicians and demonstrating the kinds of songs Lomax was looking for" (Porterfield 375). After the recording trip concluded—and if Baker cooperated—Lomax would help him set up a business doing the work he had done in prison. Lomax tried unsuccessfully to teach him to drive, but Baker was more successful in his second role. "Feels sorta like home," he remarked after a stop at Parchman prison (Lomax 172). While they drove, Iron Head would often sing his favorite song, "Go Down Old Hannah," which was "one of the best known of the slow drag work songs sung by Negro prisoners in South Texas" (Botkin 5). Baker claimed to have first sung it in prison in 1908 "on long hot summer day when about three o'clock in the afternoon the sun (Old Hannah) seemed to stop and 'just hang' in the sky" (5). Unlike earlier examples, I have provided all of the lyrics for "Go Down Old Hannah" in order to call attention to the juxtapositioning of the sacred and secular represented there (which will be the focus of the next section).

Listen: "Go down, old Hannah"
https://goo.gl/k17ZWc

> Chorus:
>
> Go down, old Hannah,
> Won't you rise no more?
> Go down, old Hannah,
> Won't you rise no more?
>
> Lord, if you rise,
> Bring judgment on.
> Lord, if you rise,
> Bring judgment on.
>
> Oh, did you hear
> What the captain said?
> Oh, did you hear
> What the captain said?
>
> That if you work
> He'll treat you well,
> And if you don't
> He'll give you hell.
>
> Chorus
>
> Oh, long-time man,
> Hold up your head.
> Well, you may get a pardon
> And you may drop dead.
>
> Lord there's nobody feels sorry
> For the life-time man.
> Nobody feels sorry
> For the life-time man.

The inmates generally considered songs like "Go Down, Old Hannah" and "Shorty George" "sinful" and, like John Gibson, many refused or had to be persuaded to sing them. This, however, did not seem to be the case for Mose Platt or James Baker who sung them often and without much prompting, as often the anecdote above reveals, as part of the daily experience of living. "Sinful" songs are part of a rich tradition of secular African-American songs that, unlike the "negro spiritual," were sung for pragmatic rather than religious purposes. As a product of an antebellum African-American consciousness, Lawrence Levine writes, such African-American secular music was "occasional music" and "as varied, as narrow, as fleeting as life itself" (19). Spirituals, he argues, were the best source for understanding the black world-view during slavery because "slaves used it to articulate their deepest and most enduring feelings and certainties" (19). Despite these differences, Levine concedes that the two styles of music had unmistakable similarities: "In both the temple and the field, black song was for the most part communal song" (217).

This is the sense one gets listening to James Baker's songs in the Lomax archive. He was a master of both the secular and the sacred, and—in his case—the two styles often merge. It can be difficult to tell if a song is meant for working or worshiping. "Go Down, Old Hannah" is a prime example here. The song was a "slow drag work song" used in the field for laborious work with a hoe or other ground tilling implement. Listening to the song, the slow but intense rhythm of that work is manifest, but so also is the depth of the tune as an emotional petition to the sun, Hannah, to "rise no more." The song, despite its seemed secular content, is sung in a distinctly spiritual style and in the traditional call-and-response, or antiphonal, structure of sacred songs. This antiphony was intentionally communal and, as Levine and others have shown, residual of African life and sociality (33). In the case of "Go Down, Hannah," both the secular and the sacred are present. For Baker and his fellows, Hannah (the sun) is a source of both suffering and light. Her persistent rising and falling is a reminder of the rhythms of prison life, hard work, and the lack of hope for the "life-time man." Death-as-escape is welcomed and characterized here in the petitioning of the sun to "raise no more." However, the line "Lord if you rise, bring judgment on" could as easily be part of a hymnal. And the connections to the sacred may go even deeper than just style. Christians often see Hannah, the Old Testament mother of the prophet Samuel, as a type and shadow of Mary, mother of Jesus (see 1 Samuel 2). Like Jesus', Samuel's birth was miraculous; the rising and setting "sun" Baker sings of—one explicitly connected to judgment in "Go Down, Hannah"—is reminiscent of the other, homophonic, "son." In this case, the song has both a functional, practical communal purpose for the inmates as well as what sounds to be a more implicit, symbolic one. Still, the rhetorical complexity of the song makes it hard to classify as either secular or sacred. Instead, we can understand "Go Down, Hannah" as an amalgam of enmeshed rhetorical components, material, practical, spiritual, historical, and, for Baker, even sentimental.

LEAD BELLY AND THE SONIC POLITICS OF A PARDON

We have thus far explored the ontic and symbolic meshing of sound-as-voice as well as the rhetorical implications of such a meshing for personal and communal meaning making for incarcerated men in Southern Jim Crow prisons. We have seen—or *heard*— multi-vocal nuances within those two modes and I have sought to parse the ways that voice-in-song cuts across easily classifiable rhetorical ideals. Instead, those ideals are always in tension, always dissonant, and always decentered. So, even as voice is significant to personal identity, Gibson's, Platt's, and Baker's individual identities are easily subsumed by the symbolic in even the most carefully drawn attempt to focus in on ontological individuality. An intentionally symbolic understanding of voice, while a more familiar rhetorical positioning, is also complicated by this multi-vocality. Songs can be abstracted from their original voices and be given new meanings by external parties for specific institutional, nationalistic, or racial purposes, but the same music can also be richly symbolic for its originating users. Institutionalized or nationalistic symbolism codifies African-American experience (and race itself) into a reduced and simplistic monotone. To use a sonic metaphor from earlier in the essay, the institutionalization of the prison recordings has the same effect as their digitization: compression, distortion, and the codification of various imperfections. On the other hand, the sonic symbols at play within the vernacular context of the song itself—represented nicely in the antiphony of call-and-response—is that of community, sympathy, and shared struggle. The former symbolization is reductive, the latter productive.

In this final case study, I wish to discuss the political voice, which along with the personal and communal rounds out three agencies or rhetorical modes sonically discernable in the prison recordings. As I have asserted, the differences between these modes do not necessarily differ in the ways that they sound, rather they work together in concert and, depending on context, reach out to meet one rhetorical need or another, depending on what the moment offers up. This, perhaps, is one of the most exciting and frustrating elements of studying music rhetorically: it is rife with significance. Any one voicing can have a multitude of rhetorical implications. John Lomax understood this and used the music from the prisons (as well as the prisoners themselves when he could) to further his career. This was a part of the political environment of the prisons while the Lomaxes were on site making records. They were not just there to gather recordings, philanthropically for the greater good of the country. Occasionally, however, prisoners also recognized the political possibilities of their involvement with the Lomaxes and others from whom they could leverage privilege, and also took advantage.

In the above example, I mentioned that John Lomax helped to arrange James Baker's parole. Lomax then employed Baker as a traveling companion until their relationship and tolerance for one another dissolved and they parted company. Lomax encountered Baker a few years later in the Ramsey State Convict Farm where Baker was working on the garden squad. "I should have left him at Sugarland to weave from corn shucks horse collars and rugs for Captain Gotch and Captain Flanagan," Lomax later wrote (Lomax 177). As much as Lomax laments the ultimate results, Baker's release was a significant political triumph for both. Recall that John Gibson also hoped that his interaction with the Lomaxes would lead to his release. In a rhetorical situation where privilege is so unevenly distributed, the political agency of the incarcerated would be limited to the few things that might set them apart, like good behavior and cooperation. In Baker's case, when the Lomaxes arrived, his talent as a singer gave him sufficient agency to negotiate release—even though his freedom would not last long.

Baker's story is reminiscent, however, of the much more famous example of Huddie "Lead Belly" Ledbetter's release from Sugarland penitentiary in Texas in 1925. In January of 1935, *Time* magazine ran a headlining story in their music section titled "Murderous

Minstrel" that relates the story. Juxtaposed conspicuously alongside a more typical-to-form article about famed composer Igor Stravinsky, "Murderous Minstrel" was accompanied by the below verses and a photograph of a middle-aged African American man wearing worn overalls and strumming a patched 12-string guitar.

> I am your servant, composed this song;
> Please, Governor Neff, let me go back home
> I know my wife will jump and shout
> When de train roll up and I come steppin' out.
>
> Please, Governor Neff, be good an' kind,
> Have mercy on my great long time,
> I don't see to save my soul;
> If I can't get a pardon, try me in a parole [...]
> Please Governor Neff, be good and kind,
>
> And if I can't get a pardon, will you cut my time?
> If I had you, Governor Neff, like you got me,
> I would wake up in the mornin' and set you free.
> And I'm going home to Mary—po' Mary.

The article begins in a racially charged and sensationalized vernacular common to the day: "In Texas a black buck known as Lead Belly murdered a man." The statement, while crude and patronizing, was true enough. It referred to a 1918 incident that led to Lead Belly's imprisonment in Sugarland. The story continues, with a simplified account of the circumstances that led to his release in 1925 but then back into prison by 1930:

> [Lead Belly] sang a petition to Governor Pat Neff and was granted a pardon. Back in the Louisiana swamplands, where he was born Huddie Ledbetter, his knife made more trouble. He was in State Prison at Angola when John A. Lomax, eminent ballad collector, stopped by last summer and asked the warden if he could please hear Lead Belly sing.
>
> John Lomax arrived in Manhattan last week to lecture on ballads and with him was Lead Belly, wild-eyed as ever. The Negro had been pardoned again because Mr. Lomax had made a phonograph record of a second petition and taken it to Louisiana's Governor Allen.

This and many other reports of Lead Belly's *second* pardoning—a compelling but disputed detail related to the circumstances around his release from Angola prison—is part of a fascinating historical problem that, as both Lead Belly's and Lomax's biographers have acknowledged in different ways, remains "a central element of Lomax-Leadbelly lore" (Porterfield 331). In short, it never actually occurred, but Lomax and Leadbelly would both use the tale to advance their commercial and professional success.

The first pardon, however, is a fact of record. It is also a remarkable example of the ways that music became one of the few political tools afforded prisoners serving in the Southern African-American prison contexts at the beginning of the twentieth century. "Governor Pat Neff (Sweet Mary)" was the name of Lead Belly's sung petition. For it, Lead Belly drew on a number of rhetorical tactics to accomplish his goal of release. For example, Lead Belly knew Governor Neff was a Baptist and wished to appeal to his religious sensibilities. His girlfriend's name was Mary, but calling Mary his "wife" in the song was conflated powerfully with the symbolic Mary of scripture: "I put Mary in it, Jesus's mother, you know. I took a verse from the bible, around about the twenty second chapter of Proverbs, around the fourteenth verse: if you will forgive a man his trespasses, the heavenly father will also forgive your trespasses" (86). This compositional choice was part of a larger, more carefully composed process for Lead Belly. He didn't usually write down his compositions, but in this case he wanted to be precise. One of the better lines from the song, "If I had you like you have me, I'd wake up in the morning and set you free," is a good example of this precision. Listen here to the song in full, recorded out of its original context several years later, but maintained as an artifact of the pardon narrative in the Library of Congress.

Listen: Lead Belly – Governor Neff
https://goo.gl/MqHhm9

I will resist the temptation of a point-by-point analysis here—to do so would be to suppose that there is a determinable equation within the song that led to Lead Belly's release. Surely his musical talent, his persistence, his correct assessment of audience, his timing, and his lyrics were all contributing factors, but one cannot point casually to any one combination of those factors leading to his pardon by Governor Neff. This indeterminacy is part of the larger rhetorical decentering that occurs within a sonic rhetoric. A close listen paired with a careful historical analysis reveals several resonant and contributing details that point toward causality, but they also raise several unanswerable questions. Indeed, what is unknown about the release of Lead Belly from Sugarland in 1925 is as interesting as what is known. One question that looms large for this study, for example, is to what extent did Lead Belly pardon lore resonate within John Gibson, a captive of that same Sugarland complex in 1933, the year the Lomaxes arrived.

Conclusion: Toward a Sonic Rhetoric of African-American Vernacular Culture

To speak of "vernacular culture" is to consider how highly particularized experiences of quotidian folklife are everyday represented and codified both within that culture as a shared cultural identity and also as a means of presenting and differentiating that identity from other, sometimes competing, vernaculars. For Margaret Lantis, a more complete rendering of the idea might be the "vernacular aspect or portion of the total culture" which expresses the notions of "'native to . . .' or common of a locality, region, or, by extension, of a trade or other group: the commonly used or spoken as distinct from the written" (203). Vernacular culture, then, is more readily found in the currency of everyday experience (speech, and by extension song, but also in the "handmade" and material). The residue of tradition is represented within these practices, but the traditional need not mean antiquated. Indeed, Lantis's entomological analysis of the word reveals that the "Latin does not seem to suggest traditional or primitive but rather 'of one's house,' of the place. This is the connotation we want: the culture-as-it-is-lived appropriate to well-defined places and situations" (203). "Since speech is not only essential," she continues, "but an important essential of situationally structured behavior, it is quite all right if 'vernacular culture' suggests first speech, then an extension to other behavior" (203).

Though the Lomaxes were not necessarily the first investigators drawn to African-American study, their interest in collecting the musical vernacular artifacts of African-American prisoners is distinguished by their pioneering attempt to understand and give structure to an obscure, distinctly racial history of slave and postbellum culture through the study of recorded, speech-based vernacular artifacts in the study of African-American culture. Though the Lomaxes saw their work as one of cultural preservation—of locating and preserving a distinct and authentic African-American musical past—we can understand it as one exploring both racial difference *and* racial formation through the collection and distribution of African-American vernacular music. The proto-blues music that the Lomaxes and others recorded in the South carried with it vernacular evidence of what was taken by some to be a "new race" forged in the blending of African extraction and American emancipation/reconstruction. Amiri Baraka underscores this point by using this phrase in his influential study *Blues People*, arguing that the "African cultures, the retention of some parts of these cultures in America, and the *weight* of the stepculture produced the American Negro. A new race" (7, emphasis in original). Baraka makes music the "persistent reference" of his study because "the development and transmutation of African music to American Negro music (a *new* music) represents [. . .] this whole process in microcosm" (7-8). The Lomaxes' work, then, might be understood in terms of what Michael Omi and Howard Winant call a "racial project," which is "simultaneously an interpretation, representation, or explanation of racial dynamics, and an effort to reorganize and redistribute resources along particular racial lines" (56). Furthermore, "racial projects connect what race means in a particularly discursive practice and the ways in which both social structures and everyday experiences are racially *organized*, based upon that meaning" (56, their emphasis). Thus do Omi and Winant call attention to the linkage between social structure and representation in the processes of racial formation. These two elements can be understood in the same terms as the contrasting-but-linked elements discussed above related to voice where both internal/social and external/representative rhetorics are in circulation.

In the prison recordings the vernacular genres of African-American life on the sharecropping farms of the Jim Crow South help to understand distinct types of behaviors within African-American experience during that era and likely, as the Lomaxes suspected, much earlier eras as well. They also provide a keystone in our understanding of African-American music's progression from the 19th to 20th century. As well as presenting the rhythm of work life in the prisons in 1933, work songs such as "Levee Camp Holler" or "Pick a Bale O'Cotton" can be understood accurately enough as "the immediate predecessors of blues" (Baraka 18). Spirituals, as I have sought to show, characterize the merging of American and African superstitious/religious traditions; secular or "sinful" songs like "Ol' Rattler" or "Run Nigger Run" were expressions of sorrow, rebellion, sexuality, and playful levity. Each of these genres carry with them what Henry Louis Gates, Jr. has famously named "Signifyin(g)" elements.

Though dated, Gates's theory remains a poignant descriptor for African-American artistic, rhythmic, and poetic culture. Signifyin(g) is the "black trope of tropes, the figure for black rhetorical figures" (75) and can be found in the African-American linguistic stylings of (among others) trickery, half-truth, innuendo, boasting, and playful circularity. The manipulation of these "classic black figures of Signification" created African-American agency—the opportunity for "the black person to move freely between two discursive universes" (76) and help to understand Lead Belly's political petition. His music successfully Signified both African-American suffering and virtuosic creativity—a kind of masterful pairing of everyday black experience and white genre expectations. This both/and sonic rhetorical appeal allowed both he and James Baker to secure freedom from prison. Even when release was not the end result, all of the examples I have discussed above showcase vernacular African-American music's rhetorical power. We have heard this power in the voices of convicts engaged in everyday (and often personal) activities and emotions, in the symbolic cadence of community, and also as decontextualized representation of African-American culture appropriated by the powerful voice of institutional authority. Though we now see the cracks in the Lomaxes' methods and ideologies, their recordings would, for a time, have significant progressive impact on scholars' and later a (largely white) middle-class by nuancing previously held views of both racial difference through an increased understanding African-American experience during and in the decades immediately following slavery.

As a racial project, then, the Lomaxes' work within African-American prisons had two significant opposing ideological consequences, one expansive, the other, reductive. First, the sounds of toiling, worshiping, and otherwise Signifyin(g) prisoners would help to redraw the racially coded parameters of African-American vernacular culture for white audiences comfortable with paradigms drawn from other long-held black cultural representations.[7] Theorists within critical race studies call this process "rearticulation."[8] On the other hand, these representations would themselves become tropes of typical African-American life in the South —codified as the "African-American tradition"— and therefore limit and even re-essentialize public understanding of the complexities and always-evolving nature of African-American culture in the United States.

These ideas voice the ways that the study of vernacular music as rhetoric offers various possibilities for understanding cultural formation and difference. This is especially so when the vernacular is part of a racial project because of vernacular music's ability as a discursive practice to express multiplicity concisely. As I expressed in the introduction of this essay, the seeming paradox of concision/multiplicity should be a heralding attribute of a sonic rhetorical approach. In the prison recordings we listen to what seem to be a simple expressions of lived experience. But, as I have explored above, deeper listening reveals the ways interpretation, representation, and historical explanation of racial experience reveal the complexities inherent to racial dynamics in the US (Omi and Winant 56). Rhetorical meaning here is derived not

---

7. These representations include (but are not limited to) the highly influential and distinctly racist blackface minstrel show which permeated American culture from 1840-1940 and beyond, popular "race records" of "classic" city blues singers like Bessie Smith and others, and an increasingly whitewashed but popular jazz music of the day.

8. As Omi and Winant write, "Rearticulation is a practice of discursive reorganization or reinterpretation of ideological themes and interests already present in the subjects' consciousness, such that these elements obtain new meanings or coherence. This practice is ordinarily the work of "intellectuals." Those whose role is to interpret the social world for given subjects—religious leaders, entertainers, school teachers, etc.—may on this account be "intellectuals" (195).

through so-called *persuasion*, but from the difficult, often painful dynamics of working through and against difference—of both working towards a sustainable *understanding* of otherness and of working from the other side out of obscurity, discrimination, and subjugation and toward equality. In the 1930s, African- American vernacular music was beginning to be understood as more than a body of artifacts to be collected and indexed for the archive, but as a discourse engaged in changing understanding of race and racial difference itself. Indeed, during the interwar period, some began to realize, as Baraka argues, that African-American music was not just representative of black cultural experience "from slave to citizenship" but instead could be understood as being symbolic of American culture itself.

Works Cited

Anderson, Erin. "Toward a Resonant Material Vocality for Digital Composition." *enculturation: A Journal of Rhetoric, Writing, and Culture*. 18 (2014). Web. Jan. 2015. < http://www.enculturation.net/materialvocality>

Baraka, Amiri (Leroi Jones). *Blues People: Negro Music in White America*. New York: Harper Collins, 1963. Print.

Barthes, Roland. "The Grain of the Voice." *The Sound Studies Reader*, ed. Jonathan Sterne. London: Routledge, 2012. 504-510. Print.

Botkin, B. A., Ed. *Negro Work Songs and Calls*. Folk Music of the United States. Recording Laboratory, AFS L8. N.D. Print.

Ceraso, Steph. "(Re)Educating the Senses: Multimodal Listening, Bodily Learning, and the Composition of Sonic Experiences." *College English*, 77.2 (2014). Web. Jan. 2015.

Finnegan, Cara A. *Picturing Poverty: Print Culture and FSA photography*. Washington D.C.: Smithsonian Institution Scholarly Press, 2003. Print.

Gates, Jr., Henry Louis. *The Signifying Monkey: A Theory of African-American Literary Criticism*. New York: Oxford University Press, 1988. Print.

Goodale, Greg. *Sonic Persuasion*. Urbana: University of Illinois Press, 2011. Print.

Gunn, Joshua. "On Recording Performance or Speech, the Cry, and the Anxiety of the Fix." *Liminalities: A Journal of Performance Studies*. 7.3 (2011). Web. 29 Jun. 2014.

—. "Speech is Dead; Long Live Speech." *Quarterly Journal of Speech* 94 (2008): 343-64. Print.

Gunn, Joshua, Greg Goodale, Mirko M. Hall, Rosa A. Eberly. "Auscultating Again: Rhetoric and Sound Studies." *Rhetoric Society Quarterly*. 43.5 (2013): 475-489. Print.

Jackson, Mark Allan. Liner notes. *Jail House Bound.* West Virginia University Press, 2012. CD.
Lamp, Kathleen S. *A City of Marble: The Rhetoric of Augustan Rome.* Durham: University of South Carolina Press, 2013. Print.
Lantis, Margaret. "Vernacular Culture." *American Anthropologist.* 62.2 (1960), 202-216. Print.
Levine, Lawrence. *Black Culture and Black Consciousness: Afro-American Folk Thought from Slavery to Freedom.* New York: Oxford University Press, 2007. Print.
Lomax, John A. *Adventures of a Ballad Hunter,* New York: Macmillan, 1947. Print.
Lomax, John A. and Alan Lomax. *American Ballads and Folksongs.* New York: Macmillan, 1934. Print.
McLuhan, Marshall. *The Global Village: Transformations in the World Life and Media in the 21st Century.* New York: Oxford University Press, 1989. Print.
Mullen, Patrick B. *The Man Who Adores the Negro: Race and American Folklore.* Urbana: University of Illinois Press, 2008. Print.
"Murderous Minstrel" *Time Magazine.* 15 Jan. 1935: 50. Print.
Olson, Christa. "Places to Stand: The Practices and Politics of Writing Histories." *Advances in the History of Rhetoric* 15:1 (2012), 77-100. Print.
Omi, Michael and Howard Winant. *Racial Formation in the United States.* New York: Routledge, 1994. Print.
Peters, John Durham. "The Voice and Modern Media." *Kunst-Stimmen*, eds. Doris Kolesch and Jenny Schrödl. Berlin: Theater der Zeit Recherchen 21 (2004), 85-100. Web. 16 May 2014.
Rickert, Thomas. *Ambient Rhetoric: The Attunements of Rhetorical Being.* Pittsburgh, University of Pittsburgh Press, 2013. Print.
Shipka, Jody. "To Preserve, Digitize and Project: On the Process of Composing Other People's Lives." *enculturation: A Journal of Rhetoric, Writing, and Culture.* 14 (2012). http://enculturation.gmu.edu/preserve-digitize-project
Sterne, Jonathan. *The Sound Studies Reader.* London: Routledge, 2012. Print.
Szwed, John. *Alan Lomax: The Man Who Recorded the World.* New York: Viking, Penguin Group, 2010. Print.
Watts, Eric King. "'Voice' and 'Voicelessness' in Rhetorical Studies." *Quarterly Journal of Speech* (2001): 179-197. Print.

Songs (in the order of their appearance in the essay):

1. "The Angels Dropped their Wings and Gone on to Heaven." Sung by group of Negro convicts. Tennessee state penitentiary. Nashville, TN. AFS 00179 B02. John A. Lomax, August 1933.
2. "Levee Camp Holler." Sung by John Gibson (Black Samson). Tennessee state penitentiary. Nashville, TN. AFS 00179 B03. John A. Lomax, August 1933.
3. "Good God A'Mighty." Sung by group of Negro convicts with ax-cutting. State penitentiary, Huntsville, TX. AFS 00179 B03. John A. and Alan Lomax, November, 1934.
4. "Run Nigger Run." Sung by Mose Platt (Clear Rock). Central state farm, Sugar Land, TX. AFS 00196 A01. John A. and Alan Lomax, December, 1933.
5. "Ol' Rattler." Sung by Mose Platt (Clear Rock). Central state farm, Sugar Land, TX. AFS 00208 B01. John A. and Alan Lomax, April 1934.
6. "Shorty George." Sung by James Baker (Iron Head). Central state farm, Sugar Land, TX. AFS 00202 A02. John A. Lomax, February, 1934.
7. "Go Down, Hannah." Sung by James Baker (Iron Head), Will Crosby, R. D. Allen, and Mose Platt (Clear Rock). Central state farm, Sugar Land, TX. AFS 00195 A02. John A. and Alan Lomax, December 1933.
8. "Governor Pat Neff." Sung by Huddie (Lead Belly) Ledbetter with guitar. Wilton, Connecticut. AFS 00053 A. John. A Lomax, February, 1935. f.l. Nineteen hund'ed an' twenty-three, judge took my liberty away from me. Singer from Shreveport, La.

Enculturation is published under an Attribution-NonCommercial-ShareAlike Creative Commons License. Please see our copyright page for details.

PRESENT TENSE

Present Tense is on the Web at http://www.presenttensejournal.org/

Present Tense: A Journal of Rhetoric in Society is a peer-reviewed, blind-refereed, online journal dedicated to exploring contemporary social, cultural, political and economic issues through a rhetorical lens. In addition to examining these subjects as found in written, oral and visual texts, we wish to provide a forum for calls to action in academia, education and national policy. Seeking to address current or presently unfolding issues, we publish short articles ranging from 2,000 to 2,500 words, the length of a conference paper. For sample topics please see our submission guidelines. Conference presentations on topics related to the journal's focus lend themselves particularly well to this publishing format. Authors who address the most current issues may find a lengthy submission and application process disadvantageous. We seek to overcome this issue through our shortened response time and by publishing individual articles as they are accepted. We also encourage conference-length multimedia submissions such as short documentaries, flash videos, slidecasts and podcasts.

"An Annotated Bibliography of LGBTQ Rhetorics (Introduction)"

Matthew B. Cox and Michael J. Faris's "An Annotated Bibliography of LGBTQ Rhetorics," published in spring 2015 (Volume 4, Issue 2), is a monumental contribution to rhetoric and composition scholarship. Cox and Faris acknowledge that theirs is not the first bibliographic work in LGBTQ rhetorical studies, but they rightly assert that their annotated bibliography is distinct in its up-to-date entries that cross disciplinary boundaries and provide thorough, insightful annotations for researchers. Given the recent and much-needed growth of research in LGBTQ rhetorics, this annotated bibliography is an ambitious project and an invaluable resource for scholars.

We include here the introduction to the annotated bibliography as a whole. For the full bibliography, see https://goo.gl/jKY7ve or follow the QR code.

11 An Annotated Bibliography of LGBTQ Rhetorics

Matthew B. Cox and Michael J. Faris

INTRODUCTION

The early 1970s marked the first publications both in English studies and communication studies to address lesbian and gay issues. In 1973, James W. Chesebro, John F. Cragan, and Patricia McCullough published an article in *Speech Monographs* exploring consciousness-raising by members of Gay Liberation. The following year, Louie Crew and Rictor Norton's special issue on *The Homosexual Imagination* appeared in *College English*. In the four decades since these publications, the body of work in rhetorical studies within both fields that addresses lesbian, gay, bisexual, transgender, and queer (hereafter LGBTQ) issues has grown quite drastically. While the first few decades marked slow and interstitial development of this work, it has burgeoned into a rigorous, exciting, and diverse body of literature since the turn of the century—a body of literature that shows no signs of slowing down in its growth.

An annotated bibliography of rhetorical studies scholarship that addresses LGBTQ issues and queer theory would have been quite manageable only a decade ago. In 2001, Frederick C. Corey, Ralph R. Smith, and Thomas K. Nakayama delivered a compiled bibliography of scholarship in communication studies that addressed LGBTQ issues at the National Communication Association Convention. This bibliography compiled a list of 66 journal articles in communication studies published between 1973 and 2001 (Corey, Smith, and Nakayama; Yep 15) that revealed a slowly growing field.

The development of such a rich body of work in rhetorical studies, especially over the last decade, has warranted an annotated bibliography of rhetorical scholarship that addresses LGBTQ issues and incorporates queer theory. This bibliography is not the first in rhetorical studies to attempt to collect work that addresses LGBTQ rhetorical scholarship: We want to acknowledge previous bibliographic work, including Corey, Smith, and Nakayama's; Rebecca Moore Howard's; and Jonathan Alexander and Michael J. Faris's. While these bibliographies have been useful for scholars interested in LGBTQ rhetorical studies, they have quickly become outdated, are limited in their disciplinarity—either bibliographies in communication studies or in English studies—and do not provide annotations for readers.

This bibliography, then, is motivated by a series of exigencies. First and foremost is visibility and accessibility of research and scholarship in LGBTQ rhetorics. As Charles E. Morris III and K. J. Rawson note, while queer scholarship in rhetorical studies has been quite visible over the last decade and queer theory has been quite influential across the humanities and social sciences, "rhetorical scholars have been much slower in responding to the 'queer turn'" (74). This bibliography, we hope, can lend visibility to this body of work.

Thus, this bibliography serves a number of purposes. It should assist graduate students new to the field and researchers already far into their careers in understanding the rich history of sexuality studies and rhetorical studies, finding relevant scholarship, and developing exigencies in research that they can exploit for their own scholarship pursuits. While the field has been growing, it can be difficult to find queer rhetorical work dispersed across a variety of journals. If you had asked either of us as we began our graduate programs if there was much scholarship or even interest in queer issues in rhetorical studies, then we would have been able to reference a few articles—but not much else: Rhetoric studies seemed incredibly straight. And, in many ways, it still does. Graduate students are often encouraged to study heteronormative theory and, we might say, are trained to identify with it. Nakayama and Corey write, "Queer academics want to join the ranks" and do so through "idoliz[ing] heteronormative theories"—theories that have marginalized, ignored, and marked queer sexuality as deviant and abnormal (324). While the field is more inclusive of queer approaches than it was a decade ago when Nakayama and Corey published those words—thanks, in large part, to those cited in this bibliography—, many are still resistant to queer approaches. Professionalization in graduate school often discourages queering the field, as Alyssa A. Samek and Theresa A. Donofrio argue. This bibliography should be useful to graduate students—and to researchers already far into their careers—for understanding the rich work that has already been done in sexuality studies and rhetoric.

Additionally, we hope to encourage more engagement in rhetorical studies with sexuality from a variety of rhetorical approaches. This bibliography might also be useful to scholars looking to publish in queer rhetorics to identify journals that have been particularly open or hospitable to certain queer approaches.

Further, this bibliography should be useful for teachers of graduate seminars who want to incorporate sexuality studies or queer approaches to rhetorical studies in their seminars: Students in courses on feminist studies, identity and rhetoric, methodologies, historiography, public memory, composition studies, public rhetoric, public address, social movements, digital writing, and more can benefit from this bibliography.

Another important exigence of this project is the historical split along disciplinary lines between English studies and communication studies. We follow calls by Steven Mailloux, Michael Leff, and others to attempt to bridge the divide between these two disciplines. This divide goes back nearly a century, to 1917, when communication scholars left the National Association of Teachers of English to form the National Association of Academic Teachers of Speech, now the National Communication Association (Mountford 409; see Mountford for a discussion of this disciplinary split as well as attempts at and prospects for rapprochement). Mailloux notes—and we agree—that "[a] multidisciplinary coalition of rhetoricians will help consolidate the work in written and spoken rhetoric, histories of literacies and communication technologies, and the cultural study of graphic, audio, visual, and digital media" (23). Leff has encouraged us to "listen carefully and learn much more about the aspirations, idiosyncracies [sic], and anxieties of our rhetorical neighbors" (92). More recently, "The Mt. Oread Manifesto on Rhetorical Education," published in *Rhetoric Society Quarterly*, calls attention to our disciplines' "common interest" (2) to develop an integrated rhetorical curriculum. This disciplinary split is readily apparent in the scholarship listed in this bibliography: English studies scholars have shown a stronger interest in writing pedagogy (including in digital environments) and literacy whereas communication studies scholars have been drawn more toward studying popular culture, public memory, archives, and social movements (though these lists are neither exhaustive nor exclusive of each other). While these bodies of scholarship certainly speak to each other implicitly, explicit connections are few and far between.

Scholars in both fields, we believe, can benefit from the groundbreaking and recent work across rhetorical studies. Perhaps queer rhetorical studies can begin to serve as a model for bridging this disciplinary divide, as Roxanne Mountford notes feminist rhetoricians have done (419). Some of this work has already begun. For instance, the Rhetoric Society of America's 2009 Summer Institute featured a workshop on "Queer Rhetorics," led by Karma R. Chávez, Charles I. Morris III, and Isaac West, that drew participants from both sides of rhetoric.

In what follows, we provide a brief overview of queer theory for readers unfamiliar with this body of work, outline a brief history of how rhetorical studies has addressed and approached issues of sexuality and gender nonconformity, discuss our methods for compiling this bibliography, and preview the organization of the bibliography.

A Brief Introduction to that "Tinkerbell," Queer Theory

In the opening pages of Nikki Sullivan's *A Critical Introduction to Queer Theory*, she notes that queer theory often resists definition—and, indeed, it has become cliché to claim so. But such claims risk granting queer theory a "'Tinkerbell effect'; to claim that no matter how hard you try you'll never manage to catch it because essentially it is ethereal, quixotic, unknowable" (v). Here, we would like to provide a modest attempt at defining queer theory, understanding that the field is much more complex and rich than we can attest to in such a small space. In short, queer theory is a body of work—informed by a variety of methodologies and theoretical lenses—that examines and critiques discourses of sexuality with the goal of transforming society.

The term "queer theory" was first anachronistically applied to work in the late 1980s and early 1990s that did not explicitly claim to be queer theory. This work argued that social theory and feminist critiques were inadequate if they did not treat sexuality as its own category of analysis. We can briefly chart queer theory's genealogical roots in feminism, poststructural theory, vernacular theory from queer activism, and queer of color critiques. Feminists like Gayle Rubin, Eve Kosofsky Sedgwick, and Judith Butler, in now canonical texts, argued that sexuality warranted its own investigation separate from gender and that feminism could not successfully challenge patriarchy without radical changes in sexuality. As Sedgwick writes in *Epistemology of the Closet*, "an understanding of virtually any aspect of modern Western culture must be, not merely incomplete, but damaged in its central substance to the degree that it does not incorporate a critical analysis of modern homo/heterosexual definition" (1).

Second, queer theory is informed by poststructuralist theory, particularly the work of Michel Foucault. In *The History of Sexuality*, he denaturalizes assumptions about sexual identities and repressed desires. As a result, he provides a theoretical framework for the discursive construction of sexuality and the relationships between power, discourse, and sexuality. The third genealogical ancestor for queer theory is queer social movements like Queer Nation and ACT UP. In the 1990s, these movements advanced political and theoretical critiques of static gay and lesbian identities and questioned the relationship between sexuality, the nation, and citizenship (see Rand). Fourth, queer theory has been informed by queer of color critiques from scholars and activists like Gloria Anzaldúa and E. Patrick Johnson, who have argued for approaching identities as intersectional and attending to the particularities of lived experiences along axes of difference.

As Hanson Ellis summaries, "[q]ueer theory is the radical deconstruction of sexual rhetoric." Queer theory in many ways challenges the commonsense norms and assumptions most people think with (*doxa*) regarding gender and sexuality. It "attempts to clear a space for thinking differently about the relations presumed to pertain between sex/gender and sex/sexuality, between sexual identities and erotic behaviors, between practices of pleasure and systems of sexual knowledge" (Hall and Jagose xvi). Queer theory differs from gay and lesbian studies in a few ways. Michael Warner, in his introduction to *Fear of a Queer Planet*, calls for a new queer politics that rejects a "liberal-pluralist" approach to assimilating LGBT persons and concerns into a capitalist society (xxv-xxvi). Sedgwick's distinction between minoritizing logic and universalizing logic is useful in helping to understand queer theory. Whereas gay and lesbian approaches focus on the needs and interests of a minority—a minoritizing logic—a universalizing logic understands sexuality "as an issue of continuing, determinative importance in the lives of people across the spectrum of sexualities" (1).

Thus, queer theorists ask a variety of questions: How are identities constructed and validated, how do discourses about sexuality circulate and reaffirm or reassert power, how do queers or other marginalized sexual and gendered beings engage in "world-making" (Berlant and Warner 558)? This investment in world-making has meant that many queer theorists embrace anti-normativity. It is important to note that anti-normativity here is not embraced simply for the sake of anti-normativity itself but because, as Lauren Berlant and Warner explain, normativity continues to value statistical mass (and thus heterosexuality) and cramps spaces of sexual culture (557).

Methods for Building the Bibliography

Drawing from prior bibliographic work (Alexander and Faris; Corey, Smith, and Nakayama; Howard), citation-chasing, and searching the archives of over 60 journals in English studies and communication studies, we culled hundreds of citations down to the ones included in this bibliography. We tried to strike a balance of scope between comprehensiveness and accessibility. This balance necessarily meant being selective about what work to include.

Importantly, this bibliography is a bibliography of work by rhetoric scholars. We debated what sort of bibliography this should be: One that introduces queer theory to the field, or one that assists rhetoric scholars in understanding how the field has already been addressing sexuality over the last 35 years. Initially, it seemed unthinkable to put together a collection on queer rhetorics and not include the queer theorists whose volumes we had so many times turned to across publication, teaching, and conference presentation work. A queer rhetorics bibliography without Foucault, Butler, Sedgwick, Warner, David M. Halperin, Anzaldúa, José Esteban Muñoz, and J. Jack Halberstam? And yet, we also reasoned that many readers interested in the work shared here would have a working awareness of these scholars as LGBT and queer scholars, and even those readers who did not have this awareness would notice here the repeating nature of references to these foundational works in the rhetoric-oriented works we did cover. (Readers not familiar with queer theory can reference our discussion above and our Works Cited as a resource.)

And so, ultimately we decided to narrow our focus solely to scholarship in rhetorical studies, despite the rhetorical nature of queer theory. Indeed, we contend, along with Jonathan Alexander and Michelle Gibson that queer theory is "intimately *rhetorical*" (7).

Bibliographic work is in many ways disciplinary work, attending to and demarcating the boundaries of "what counts" as rhetorical, as related to sexuality, and as queer. Despite rich histories of LGBTQ scholarship in media studies and performance studies within communication departments, we have chosen not to include much of that scholarship (with a few exceptions), in part to make this project more manageable for readers. Additionally, what sort of research counts as rhetorical and as queer can be hotly debated. Certainly, due to both our disciplinary trainings (Michael in a rhetoric and composition graduate program in English and Matt in a stand-alone rhetoric and writing studies program), there will be gaps and unintentional exclusions, which we can only attribute to our "trained incapacities" (Burke 7).

Sketching Out Approaches and a History to Sexuality Studies in Rhetoric

It would be disingenuous to claim that rhetorical studies has one singular, coherent approach to studying sexuality and rhetoric. And indeed, creating a comprehensive heuristic for even the multiple, various, and sometimes even conflicting approaches within rhetorical studies is a difficult task, given the variety of scholarship conducted in English studies and communication studies over the last four decades. However, Sedgwick's distinction between minoritizing logics and universalizing logics (discussed above) is useful in understanding two distinct styles of approaches to incorporating sexuality into rhetorical studies. We identify three "stages" to scholarship in queer rhetorics, though by no means are these stages meant to be discrete. Indeed, minoritizing logics are still at play in more recent scholarship, and some early work took universalizing approaches.

Early work in the field largely took a minoritizing approach to sexuality, focusing on gay and lesbian identities (and occasionally transgender or queer ones, though rarely bisexuality). This work focused on visibility, coming out, identifying homophobia, and incorporating LGBT perspectives and rhetoric into teaching and scholarship.

A second stage of queer rhetorical work began to draw on queer theory and take a more universalizing approach to sexuality, understanding that sexuality is an aspect of all our lives, is present (though usually unnoticed) in pedagogical practice and theory, and is an approach useful to all rhetorical studies. These approaches turned to heterosexuality and heteronormativity as discursive constructions and began to critique and challenge rhetorical theory.

The third, most recent stage of queer rhetorical studies is the move to speak to other disciplines, including queer theory. That is, rather than solely import queer theory into rhetorical studies, scholars are beginning to show how queer theory and other disciplines can learn from rhetorical theory. This approach is not novel: As early as 1996, Robert Alan Brookey was arguing that while queer theory has insights for rhetorical studies, rhetorical studies can also contribute to queer theory because of its approach to "the particular" (45). But while Brookey made this claim nearly two decades ago, it is not until much more recently that queer rhetorical scholars have taken up this charge seriously. Isaac West's *Transforming Citizenship* provides an example of this approach. In critiquing queer theory's radical anti-normative stance, he offers rhetorical studies as an approach to mediate decontextualized queer theory resistances to "the norm." West understands rhetoric's focus on "contingency" as an opportunity to provide nuance and situatedness to rhetorical action and agency. "Without this awareness of contingency," he writes, "the anti-essentialist qualities of queerness are lost to a predetermined and fixed sense of radical anti-normativity incapable of accommodating anything other than facially recognizable acts of being against something, most notably, *the* norm" (25-6).

Again, this brief tour through the history of the field oversimplifies but provides one heuristic (among many) for approaching queer rhetorical studies.

Navigating this Bibliography

As with so many tasks around compiling this bibliography, organizing the work defied an easy answer or taxonomy. We have chosen two organizational schemes for this bibliography: chronological and thematic. The first section shares work from 1973 to 1995. We were able to see a visible increase in LGBT rhetorical work throughout the 1990s, and 1995 served as a somewhat arbitrary year to distinguish earlier work from later work. 1995 saw the publication of Harriet Malinowitz's *Textual Orientations*, which served as a touchstone for composition studies. Shortly afterward, in 1997, Jonathan Alexander published "Out of the Closet and into the Network" in *Computers and Composition*, one of his first publications in LGBTQ composition studies. In communication studies, 1996 marked the publication of Charles E. Morris III's "Contextual Twilight/Critical Liminality," an early contribution to queering methodologies. Additionally, Corey C. Frederick and Thomas K. Nakayama published their controversial "Sextext" in *Text and Performance Quarterly* in 1997. Thus, we see the mid-1990s as a "turning point" or "ramping up" moment for queer rhetorics—one among other possible points of departure.

The remaining ten sections of the bibliography are organized thematically, according to broad and admittedly overlapping categories. The bibliography, then, is organized according to the following eleven sections:

> Section 1: LGBTQ Perspectives: 1973-1995
> Section 2: Disciplinary Boundaries and Methodologies
> Section 3: Pedagogical Practices and Theories
> Section 4: Composition Studies
> Section 5: History, Archives, and Memory
> Section 6: Publics and Counterpublics
> Section 7: Rhetorics of Identity
> Section 8: Rhetorics of Activism
> Section 9: Discourses of HIV/AIDS
> Section 10: Popular Culture and Rhetoric
> Section 11: Digital Spaces

Because these sections overlap, we have also provided tags for each annotation; readers seeking to find related work can search through the bibliography for related tags. A list of tags is below.

A Final Note

It has been incredibly rewarding to read such a diverse array of scholarship that has approached sexuality and queered rhetorical studies over the last four decades. Even as we researched, wrote, compiled, and organized, we saw concurrently just how useful this resource is. It is, to say the least, reassuring to know that we have created something that seemed to us so useful.

It is important to us to note that we see this bibliographic work as a kairotic space—a first for rhetoric studies in its comprehensive nature, but by no means a canonical text. We hope this bibliography is productive for scholars who hope to continue to challenge the field in terms of methods, methodologies, epistemologies, and modes of publishing—digital and print.

Tags

ACT UP
Activism
Affect
Age
Agency
Allies
Archives
Bodies
Camp
Citizenship
Class
Closet
Collective Identity
Coming Out
Composition
Confessional
Counterpublics
Daughters of Bilitis
Desire
Digital
Disability
Disciplinarity
Drag
Ethics

Etiology
Ex-Gay
Feminism
Futurity
Gay Rights
Gender
Heteronormativity
Histories
HIV/AIDS
Homophobia
Identity
Immigration
Intersectionality
Legal
Lesbian
Literacy
Literature
Materiality
Media
Medical
Memory
Misogyny
Queer Nation
Passing
Pedagogy
Performativity
Politics
Popular Culture
Privacy
Psychoanalysis
Publics
Public Address
Race
Regionalism
Religion
Representation
Safe Spaces
Sextext
Silence
Technical Communication

Tolerance
Violence
Visibility
Visual Rhetoric

Works Cited

Alexander, Jonathan, and Michael J. Faris. "Issue Brief: Sexuality Studies." *National Council of Teachers of English.* 2009. Web.

Alexander, Jonathan, and Michelle Gibson. "Queer Composition(s): Queer Theory in the Writing Classroom." *JAC* 24.1 (2004): 1-21. Print.

Anzaldúa, Gloria. *Borderlands/La Frontera: The New Mestiza.* San Francisco: Aunt Lute Books, 1987. Print.

Berlant, Lauren, and Michael Warner. "Sex in Public." *Critical inquiry* 24.2 (1998): 547-566. Print.

Brookey, Robert Alan. "A Community like *Philadelphia*." *Western Journal of Communication* 60.1 (1996): 40-56. Print.

Burke, Kenneth. *Permanence and Change: An Anatomy of Purpose.* 3rd ed. Berkeley: U of California P, 1984. Print.

Butler, Judith. *Gender Trouble: Feminism and the Subversion of Identity.* New York: Routledge, 1990. Print.

Chesebro, James W., John F. Cragan, and Patricia McCullough. "The Small Group Technique of the Radical Revolutionary: A Synthetic Study of Consciousness." *Speech Monographs* 40.2 (1973): 136-146. Print.

Corey, Frederick C., Ralph R. Smith, and Thomas K. Nakayama. *Bibliography of Articles and Books of Relevance to G/L/B/T Communication Studies.* Paper presented at the annual meeting of the National Communication Association, Atlanta, GA. Nov. 2001.

Ellis, Hanson. "Gay Theory and Criticism: 3. Queer Theory." *The Johns Hopkins Guide to Literary Theory and Criticism.* 2nd ed. Eds. Michael Groden, Martin Kreiswirth, and Imre Szeman. Baltimore, MD: Johns Hopkins UP, 2005. Web.

Foucault, Michel. *The History of Sexuality: An Introduction. Volume 1.* Trans. Robert Hurley. New York: Vintage, 1990. Print.

Hall, Donald E., and Annamarie Jagose. Introduction. *The Routledge Queer Studies Reader.* Eds. Donald E. Hall and Annamarie Jagose, with Andrea Bebell and Susan Potter. London: Routledge, 2013. xiv-xx. Print.

Howard, Rebecca Moore. "Lesbian, Gay, Bisexual, and Transgendered Language, Discourses and Rhetorics." *Rebecca Moore Howard: Writing Matters.* 2014. Web.

Johnson, E. Patrick. "'Quare' Studies, or (Almost) Everything I Know About Queer Studies I Learned from My Grandmother." *Text and Performance Quarterly* 21.1 (2001): 1-25. Print.

Leff, Michael. "Rhetorical Disciplines and Rhetorical Disciplinarity: A Response to Mailloux." *Rhetoric Society Quarterly* 30.4 (2000): 83-93. Print.

Mailloux, Steven. "Disciplinary Identities: On the Rhetorical Paths Between English and Communication Studies." *Rhetoric Society Quarterly* 30.2 (2000): 5-29. Print.

Morris, Charles E., III, and K. J. Rawson. "Queer Archives/Archival Queers." *Theorizing Histories of Rhetoric*. Ed. Michelle Ballif. Carbondale: University of Illinois, 2013. 74-89. Print.

Mountford, Roxanne. "A Century After the Divorce: Challenges to a Rapprochement Between Speech Communication and English." *The SAGE Handbook of Rhetorical Studies*. Eds. Andrea A. Lunsford, Kirt H. Wilson, and Rosa A. Eberly. Los Angeles: SAGE, 2009. 407-422. Print.

"The Mt. Oread Manifesto on Rhetorical Education 2013." *Rhetoric Society Quarterly* 44.1 (2014): 1-5. Print.

Nakayama, Thomas K., and Frederick C. Corey. "Nextext." *Queer Theory and Communication: From Disciplining Queers to Queering the Discipline(s)*. Eds. Gust A. Yep, Karen E. Lovaas, and John P. Elia. Binghamton, NY: Haworth, 2003. 319-334. Print.

Rand, Erin J. *Reclaiming Queer: Activist and Academic Rhetorics of Resistance*. Tuscaloosa: U of Alabama P, 2014. Print.

Rubin, Gayle. "Thinking Sex: Notes for a Radical Theory of the Politics of Sexuality." *Pleasure and Danger: Exploring Female Sexuality*. Ed. Carole S. Vance. Boston: Routledge, 1984. 267-319. Print

Samek, Alyssa A., and Theresa A. Donofrio. "'Academic Drag' and the Performance of the Critical Personae: An Exchange on Sexuality, Politics, and Identity in the Academy." *Women's Studies in Communication* 36.1 (2013): 28-55. Print.

Sedgwick, Eve Kosofsky. *Epistemology of the Closet*. Berkeley: U of California P, 1990. Print.

Sullivan, Nikki. *A Critical Introduction to Queer Theory*. New York: New York U P, 2003. Print.

Warner, Michael. Introduction. *Fear of a Queer Planet: Queer Politics and Social Theory*. Ed. Michael Warner. Minneapolis: U of Minnesota P, 1993. vii-xxxi. Print.

West, Isaac. *Transforming Citizenships: Transgender Articulations of the Law*. New York: New York U P, 2014. Print.

Yep, Gust A. "The Violence of Heteronormativity in Communication Studies: Notes on Injury, Healing, and Queer World-Making." *Queer Theory and Communication: From Disciplining Queers to Queering the Discipline(s)*. Eds. Gust A. Yep, Karen E. Lovaas, and John P. Elia. Binghamton, NY: Haworth, 2003. 11-59. Print.

COMPOSITION STUDIES

Composition Studies is on the Web at http://www.uc.edu/journals/composition-studies.html

The oldest independent periodical in the field, *Composition Studies* is an academic journal dedicated to the range of professional practices associated with rhetoric and composition: teaching college writing; theorizing rhetoric and composing; administering writing related programs; preparing the field's future teacher-scholars. We welcome work that doesn't fit neatly elsewhere.

A Plea for Critical Race Theory Counterstory: Stock Story versus Counterstory Dialogues Concerning Alejandra's "Fit" in the Academy

Martinez's article models and argues for the value of employing counterstory as a powerful method for representing marginalized peoples' experiences and perspectives in rhetoric and composition. Counterstory, as Martinez eloquently and persuasively describes, lays bare the workings of racism on people's lives and thus offers a framework for validating researchers' embodied experiences. This method also prioritizes narrative as an effective means by which to foreground racism and its effects on people of color. This article was selected because the author represents voices and experiences that continue to figure too minimally in composition journals.

12 A Plea for Critical Race Theory Counterstory: Stock Story versus Counterstory Dialogues Concerning Alejandra's "Fit" in the Academy

Aja Y. Martinez

This essay in counterstory suggests a method by which to incorporate critical race theory (CRT) in rhetoric and composition, as a contribution of other(ed) perspectives toward an ongoing conversation in the field about narrative, dominant ideology, and their intersecting influence on programmatic and curricular standards and practices. As a narrative form, counterstory functions as a method for marginalized people to intervene in research methods that would form master narratives based on ignorance and on assumptions about minoritized peoples like Chican@s. Through the formation of counterstories, or those stories that document the persistence of racism and other forms of subordination, voices from the margins become the voices of authority in the researching and relating of our own experiences. Counterstory serves as a natural extension of inquiry for theorists whose research recognizes and incorporates, as data, lived and embodied experiences of people of color. This essay argues it is thus crucial to use a narrative methodology that counters other methods that seek to dismiss or decenter racism and those whose lives are affected daily by it.

My story is grounded in research and experience acquired through my 28-year academic journey. I am Chican@,[1] student, professor, and am embedded in the academy. However, because I am Chicana[2], my path has been riddled with pain, anguish, and what Tara J. Yosso refers to as "survivor's guilt." Why me? Why did I "make it" out of the Southside of Tucson when so many of my classmates were left behind? "Why her?" is what I have painfully come to know others—peers, family, and colleagues—have wondered about me as well. During my time in the academy, I have met barriers of institutional racism, sexism, and classism in courses I have taken, courses I teach, and through interactions with colleagues and professors. Granted, prior to my time as a graduate student and as a faculty member in higher education, I was surely not beyond the reach of these various "-isms"; however, I have been awakened to an awareness of them through a combination of maturing into adulthood, taking courses in which literatures about social injustice and post-colonialism have been provided, and unrelenting experiences in the institution in which my race is continually targeted by colleagues, students, and professors as a personal and professional deficit when I struggle, and as an unfair advantage when I succeed.

I am compelled to describe these experiences coupled with knowledge provided by other scholars who have found it necessary to speak from marginalized spaces like mine. And because I come from a culture in which the oral tradition as taken from lived personal experience is valued as "legitimate knowledge" (Delgado Bernal and Villalpando 169), I must write this essay as testimony because I cannot continue to forge an academic career without documenting the persistence of racism in the field of rhetoric and composition and in the academy at large. Through a method of storytelling that "challenges mainstream society's denial of the ongoing significance of race and racism" (Yosso 10), this essay illustrates a composite portrait told through counter-story (a methodology of critical race theory (CRT)) to inform our field as it faces a major demographic shift. I focus my work on Chican@s because this is the fastest growing population in the academy (U.S. Department of Education), a group from which I feel I can draw upon my "cultural intuition" (11). However, the theoretical, pedagogical, and methodological strategies based on CRT can certainly be adapted to assist other historically marginalized and underrepresented groups in the academy.

THE PIPELINE: REASON FOR CONCERN

According to the 2010 United States Census, roughly fifty million or 16% of the United States population is Latin@ (Ennis et al.). Since the 2000 Census, the Latin@ population has grown 43%, with the largest growth occurring in the Chican@ community, which increased 54%. Currently, 65% of the now 16% United States Latin@ population are Chican@, making people of Mexican origin or decent the largest Latin@ population in the United States. College enrollment for Latin@s has jumped 65% since 2000; however, completion of degrees in higher education do not reflect this growth (U.S. Department of Education).

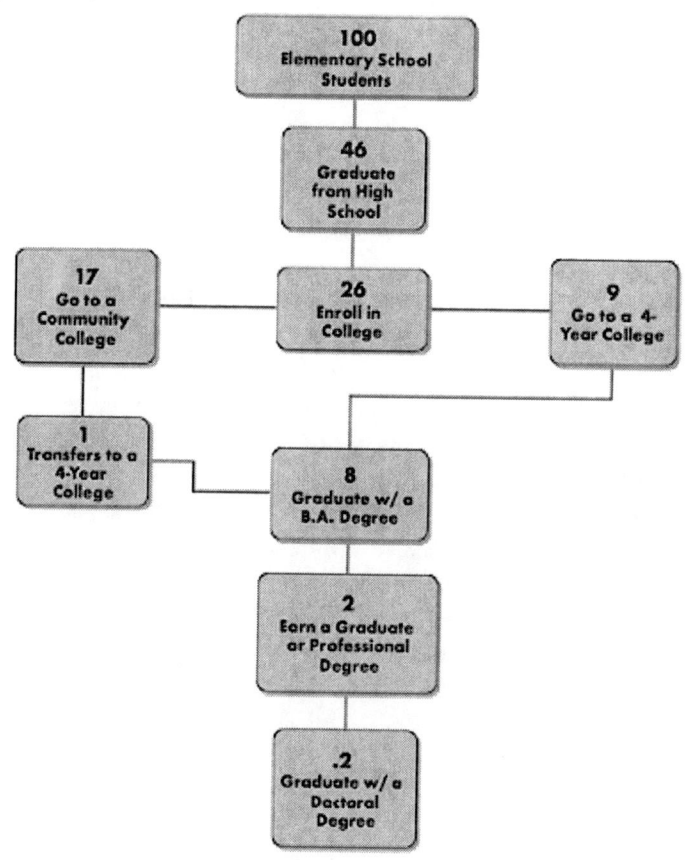

```
                    100
              Elementary School
                  Students
                      |
                      46
                   Graduate
                   from High
                    School
                      |
    17               26                9
  Go to a         Enroll in         Go to a 4-
 Community         College         Year College
  College
    |                                  |
    1                 8                |
 Transfers to    Graduate w/ a ────────┘
  a 4-Year        B.A. Degree
  College
                      |
                      2
                 Earn a Graduate
                 or Professional
                     Degree
                      |
                     .2
                 Graduate w/ a
                   Doctoral
                    Degree
```

Fig. 1. The Chicana/o Educational Pipeline illustrating low academic outcomes at each point along the educational pipeline in 2000. (From Tara J. Yosso and Daniel G. Solorzano, *The Chicano and Chicano Educational Pipeline,* CSRC Policy and Issues Brief No. 13. Los Angeles: UCLA Chicano Studies Research Center Press, 2006).

In "The Chicana and Chicano Educational Pipeline," Tara J. Yosso and Daniel G. Solórzano illustrate the Chican@ educational pipeline as gathered from the 2000 United States Census (specific to the category "Hispanic," and disaggregated to account for Chican@s, see fig. 1). According to the 2000 Census, only 9% of Chican@s enroll in four-year colleges, 8% graduate with a bachelor's degree, and less than 1% of the latter graduate with a doctoral degree. In 2010 the United States Department of Education's National Center for Education Statistics released a report on enrollment and completion trends based on the 2010 United States Census. Eight percent of Latin@s completed bachelor's degrees in 2010, compared to the 6% of Latin@s who completed them in 2000, translating to a 2% increase in ten years. Three percent of Latin@s completed doctorates in 2000 compared to 4% in 2010. If this data were disaggregated to account for Chican@s as an isolated category, the 2010 data would likely not reflect a significant increase in completion reflective of enrollment trends.

In "On the Rhetoric and Precedents of Racism," Victor Villanueva cites field-specific numbers concerning Latin@s/Chican@s in rhetoric and composition. Villanueva reports that in 1995, 26 of the 1,373 individuals who earned doctorates in English language and literature were Latin@, which rounds out to 2% (651). In 2010 there were a total of 1,334 doctorates in this discipline with 40 earned by Latin@s, thus representing only 3% of the degrees conferred, so in all, a 1% increase in fifteen years (U.S. Department of Education). As a more representative sample of the demographics specific to rhetoric and composition, Villanueva details the break down of CCCC membership, reporting that in 1999 Latin@s accounted for 1% of all members. As of 2012, Latin@ membership has risen to 2%, reflecting a 1% increase in approximately 10 years (Suchor). If I were to break down any of these statistics further, I am sure that someone like me—a first-generation Chicana, single mother resulting from a teen pregnancy—is an anomaly. Because of the numbers reflecting enrollment of Latin@s that are disproportionate to their success and completion rates, institutions and individual programs urgently need to examine the disconnect preventing entire fields from serving this burgeoning student demographic. The statistics on Latin@ student success and retention, and my own personal experience, reflect the fact that higher education, and particular to this study, rhetoric and composition, are in need of theory, practice, and methods that better serve individuals from underrepresented backgrounds.

A Call for CRT

In "Working with Difference: Critical Race Studies and the Teaching of Composition," Gary A. Olson calls for greater attention in the field of rhetoric and composition on CRT so as to assist writing programs and their instructors to become better prepared, pedagogically and administratively, for underrepresented student populations (209). Olson contends that CRT provides our field with the tools by which to interrogate the effects of racial bias that actively impede success and retention in rhetoric and composition for marginalized students. Despite important contributions from scholars such as Keith Gilyard, Shirley Wilson Logan, and Jacqueline Jones Royster, Latin@s in this field have but two influences significantly referencing a theory on race scholarship concerning Latin@s—Gloria Anzaldúa and Victor Villanueva. Even so, as Olson suggests, "[rhetoric and composition] has witnessed no sustained examination of race, racism, and the effects of both on composition instruction and effective writing program administration" (209). Like Olson, I suggest we turn to CRT, but I extend this argument to focus on methodology, counterstory, in our field's pursuit of actively challenging the status quo with regard to institutionalized prejudices against racial minorities that proliferate in United States institutions of higher education.

Particular to CRT's counterstory, this method of research has potential for producing scholarship and informing pedagogy and mentorship in the field of rhetoric and composition. As an interdisciplinary method, CRT counterstory recognizes that the experiential and embodied knowledge of people of color is legitimate and critical to understanding racism that is often well disguised in the rhetoric of normalized structural values and practices. In this essay, I employ CRT counterstory as a hybrid form of scholarly inquiry and specifically rely on composite counterstorytelling as a writing genre. This form of counterstory differs from fictional storytelling by critically examining theoretical concepts and humanizing empirical data while also deriving material for counterstory's discourse, setting, and characters from sources. These include but are not limited to statistical data, existing literatures, social commentary, and professional/personal experiences concerning the topics addressed. As a writing form and a rhetorical methodology, I argue that counterstory has applications for both scholarly publication and craft in the composition classroom. However, the biggest hurdle to overcome in the present racialized era resides in programmatic and institutional recognition and acceptance of the ideology responsible for structural forms of inequality alive and well in the academy. In an effort to humanize this reality, this essay illustrates, through two tellings, a "stock story" and a counterstory, which serve as tellings of Chican@ experience along the educational pipeline, with a focus on the 0.2% completion rate of Chican@ PhDs. In an effort to provide talking points for our field to engage in pedagogical as well as programmatic planning (including admissions/hiring practices and mentoring), my counterstory contributes a perspective that expands dialogue and understanding as to why this completion rate of doctoral degrees for Chican@s is nearly non-existent.

Richard Delgado and Counterstory versus Stock Story

In his foreword to Richard Delgado's *The Rodrigo Chronicles,* Robert A. Williams, Jr., calls Delgado's stories outsider stories. Williams says these stories "help us imagine the outside in America, a place where some of us have never been and some of us have always been, and where a few of us...shift-shape, like the trickster, asking the hard questions... without answers, questions about what it means to be outside, what it means to be inside, and what it means to be in-between in America" (xii-xiii). Delgado characterizes counterstory as "a kind of counter-reality" created/experienced by "outgroups" subordinate to those atop the racial and gendered hierarchy. While those in power, or as Delgado offers, the "ingroup," craft stock stories to establish a shared sense of identity, reality, and naturalization of their superior position, the "outgroup aims to subvert that ingroup reality" ("Storytelling" 2412-13). Delgado describes stock stories as those that people in dominant positions collectively form and tell about themselves. These stories choose among available facts to present a picture of the world that best fits and supports their positions of relative power ("Storytelling" 2421). Stock stories feign neutrality and at all costs avoid any blame or responsibility for societal inequality. Powerful because they are often repeated until canonized or normalized, those who tell stock stories insist that their version of events is indeed reality, and any stories that counter these standardized tellings are deemed biased, self-interested, and ultimately not credible. Counterstory, then, is a method of telling stories by people whose experiences are not often told. Counterstory as methodology thus serves to expose, analyze, and challenge stock stories of racial privilege and can help to strengthen traditions of social, political, and cultural survival and resistance.

Delgado outlines several generic styles counterstories can take: chronicles, narratives, allegories, parables, and dialogues ("Storytelling" 2438). In this essay I extend his discussion of counterstory by crafting dialogues, with a nod to sophistic argument, that present two tellings of the same event. As a theoretical device, the dialogue is more than familiar in the field of rhetoric and composition and has been most notably employed by Plato to aid philosophical inquiry. Victor Villanueva reminds us that Plato's "writing is significant by virtue of its genre, an attempt at representation of dialogue, of storytelling...not as logocentric discourse but as representation of discourse *in action*" ("*Memoria*" 16; emphasis added). Also, Patricia Bizzell and Bruce Herzberg note the value Plato places on depicting oral exchanges because of their ability to respond "flexibly to *kairos,* the immediate social situation in which solutions to philosophical problems must be proposed" (81). Likewise, Delgado's specific method of placing two dialogues side-by-side provides him the opportunity to develop his ideas through exchanges between characters that represent and voice contending viewpoints on contemporary social issues. The audience is invited to first experience a version of the events from a status quo point of view, which in the case of this article's stock story represents that of the institution. Following the stock story, a counterstory is then presented to develop my marginalized viewpoint and to critique the viewpoint put forth by the stock story while offering alternative possibilities for the audience to consider. I call this method of placing two dialogues concerning the same events side-by-side "stock story versus counterstory."

Beyond the styles of counterstory outlined by Delgado, Tara J. Yosso also explains these styles as generally composed in the autobiographical, biographical, or composite genre (10). For this essay, I compose my counterstories as composite dialogues, and an important feature of composite counterstory is the composite character. Composite characters are written into "social, historical, and political situations that allow the dialogue to speak to the research findings and creatively challenge racism and other forms of subordination" (Yosso 11). Because these characters are written as composites of many individuals, they do not have a one-to-one correspondence to any one individual (Delgado, *The Rodrigo Chronicles* xix). In many cases, and as is the case for this particular stock story versus counterstory, the composite characters are abstractions representing cultural or political ideologies, and could mistakenly be read as overly-stereotyped depictions of certain ideologies and politics. However, in the case of Delgado's work, and mine as well, composite characters in stock stories and counterstories represent more than just a single individual and are intentionally crafted to embody an ideology, such as institutional racism or a Chican@ academic identity. Accordingly, the stock story and counterstory crafted in this essay feature dialogues conducted among composite characters that represent university professor stocktypes, Chican@ students, and parents of underrepresented students.

A Stock Story Discussing a Chicana Graduate Student's Status as Qualified to Proceed in Her PhD Program

In the particular graduate program providing the setting for this story, a qualifying exam is conducted to assess students' potential for joining the professional conversation in the field of rhetoric and composition. This exam consists of a meeting between students and the program director during which the director engages in an assessment of each student's record in the program and the writing in her/his portfolio. The materials in the portfolio are meant to provide the director with a detailed sense of the student's analytical and writing skills. Aspects of the student's scholarship in the portfolio are evaluated based on a reflective essay and other academic writing (seminar papers) by the student. These writings indicate whether the student can step back from her/his writing and recognize her/his strengths and weaknesses as a scholarly writer and whether the student has developed a research trajectory indicative of her/his ability to perform graduate level work. In this story's program, the qualifying examination is intended as a mentoring opportunity for the student and program director to have useful conversations about the student's possibilities for writing and research. This particular step in the graduate school process was chosen because it serves a programmatic gatekeeping function for graduate students and can be especially problematic for underrepresented students, like the student discussed next.

The Stock Story

Setting. The program director and two professors are in a department conference room to discuss Alejandra Prieto, a Chicana graduate student who has failed her qualifying exam. In this program, as in others, if a student does not pass the qualifying exam, then a committee of professors will discuss the student, her portfolio, and her ability to continue in the program. The committee in this stock story consists of the program director and two professors, all of whom are white. The program director, D. Mosley, is male, from a middle class background, and tenured. One of the professors, F. Hayden, is male, from a working class background, and untenured, and the third professor, J. Tanner, is female, from an upper-middle class background, and tenured. Alejandra has completed her first full year of the PhD program after entering the program with a BA in sociology. The reasons for the committee's meeting are to discuss the student's failed attempt to pass her qualifying exam and faculty concerns about the student's research interests, writing ability, and an assigned final grade of C in a core program course (Cs in this graduate program constitute a failing grade; two Cs can result in expulsion.)

Mosley: Thank you for finding the time to meet today. I know the beginning of the semester is a busy time for us all, so I'm glad we could all decide on a time at last. Now I know you are unfamiliar with this sort of meeting, but it's official procedure after a student has failed his/her qualifying exam.

Tanner *[teasing]*: Yes, Mosley, I went ahead and double-checked the program handbook to see that this meeting was a legitimate way to proceed, considering we've *never* experienced a student failing her qualifying exam, at least not in the sixteen years I've been program faculty, not to mention the four additional years I served as chair.

Hayden: Well, that's not exactly true; I recall other faculty saying some students have been of questionable qualifying status before, but I hear they usually leave the program before we have to come to this stage of committee discussion.

Mosley: Either way, Alejandra's progress and status in the program have become a concern for those of us in the room today. After reviewing her course schedules for the past two semesters, I see that she's taken all but one of her courses from each of us, all courses in rhetorical theory and one in composition pedagogy with Dr. Burton. Of the four courses she's taken so far, Alejandra's grades are three A's, and one C, which Tanner assigned her. Now I met with Alejandra earlier this week regarding her qualifying exam and let her know concerns had been raised about her performance in class and her writing. I also had specific questions for her about the C she earned in your class, Tanner, to which she did not have an adequate answer. So I guess I'd like to start there with what happened in your class; what's your assessment of this student?

Tanner: Well, to be honest, she's a sweet girl, she really is. You know she even brought some sort of Mexican cake to class one day to share with everyone. Sweet girl. However, as I recall, I raised a major concern about this student when we were in committee meetings about new admits, and it's the same concern I'm raising now: Is this student a good fit for this program? You both served on the program admissions committee with me back when we were forming Alejandra's cohort and you both...

Hayden: Yes, Tanner, we remember how you objected to her admission because she would be starting the doctoral program with only a BA in what you deemed an unrelated field. But I also remember that she was one of a very few minority applicants that year, and, as an undergraduate, had impressive experience documented on her CV as a research assistant on nationally funded projects. Plus, with the direction our field needs to go concerning the changing demographics of student and faculty populations, it couldn't hurt to admit a student whose focus is on social issues related to race and education, rather than the mostly literature and creative writing folks we usually get. We need to be more interdisciplinary, you know that.

Tanner: That aside, Hayden, we're a top-five-ranked program, and we demand a lot from our students. Our curriculum is rigorous, and our students need to be the best and the brightest *in our field*, and it does nobody any favors to admit students who can't even tell you who and what the major theorists and journals of our time are!

Mosley: Okay, there's no reason to raise our voices. What we need is to return to the reason for this meeting, Alejandra's status as a student in this program. Talking about whether or not she should have been admitted is pointless because she's here, she's in the program, and we need to move forward and decide whether she should remain or go. Now, when I met with Alejandra for her qualifying exam, she was pretty emotional and not able to coherently discuss her progress in the program to this point. She even asked me outright if we admitted her as some sort of "affirmative action" recruit!

Tanner: [*mumbles something incoherent under her breath*]

Hayden: She didn't really ask that, did she? What did you say?

Mosley: She most certainly did, and I denied it, of course. This program, because of its ranking and rigor, is strictly merit-based, and I told her as much. Curiously she somehow knew she wasn't a first priority admit and was on our second list of admits.

Hayden: Well, I always thought it a bad idea to have grad student reps on admissions committees. They gossip too much, and sometimes damaging information falls into the ears of those never meant to hear it.

Mosley: Yes, well, back to the original question: Tanner, what happened in your class that resulted in this C on Alejandra's record?

Tanner: Right, well, did you ask her?

Mosley: I did, but I'd like to hear your perspective on the issue as well.

Tanner: Well, as I've said, again and again, Alejandra is just not a good fit for this program. She rarely spoke in my class, and the few times she did, her comments always drew the material back to her comfort zone of social oppression, particular to race. I mean sure, race is an issue, but it's all she wants to talk about! And then her writing! Her seminar paper was just not on par with the rest of the students, not in content or quality. She tried, in my opinion unsuccessfully, to tie everything she read and studied in my course back to what I feel are likely recycled papers from sociology courses or projects. That aside, this attempt she makes to fuse her old discipline and ours comes across as awkward, at best, in her prose. It's just not clear writing; there's no focus and no connection or contribution to the field. Plus, she doesn't even use MLA and seemingly makes no attempt to do so. I stand my ground and still contend she is not a good fit for this program. She *earned* that C in my course.

Hayden: Ouch, Tanner, a C may as well be an F in this program, but I hear what you're saying regarding her participation in class. I experienced the same thing in the course she took with me. She rarely ever spoke, which made me begin to question whether or not she read and, more so, if she even comprehended the material. I mean she was practically silent the whole semester.

Mosley: Did she ever miss class?

Tanner and Hayden: No.

Mosley: Yeah, she never missed a day of my course either, but I recall her silence as well. So Tanner, did you ever speak to her regarding your concerns about her classroom performance or her handling of course materials?

Tanner: She knew as well as any other student that I hold an open door policy. I am *always* happy to assist students in any way possible, and I set office hours and appointments with students whenever needed.

Mosley: Yes, I asked her during our meeting whether she ever visited you concerning her progress in your course or if she ever discussed her grade with you. She said she hadn't.

Tanner: No, she didn't, and as I've said, my door is *always* open to students.

Mosley: Well as the handbook states, the official purpose for this meeting is for us to discuss whether the student has made satisfactory progress, maintained a 3.5 grade point average, or had other problems in the program. We need to assess Alejandra's potential for joining the professional conversation in our field, and this is based on her record in the program, her writing in coursework, and her meeting with me as program director. After hearing both of your concerns, I'm pretty sure she shouldn't continue on toward the PhD. I'll be meeting with her again next week for a follow-up to her exam, and she and I will discuss a plan of what she should do next. I'm thinking it'll be in *her* best interest to just take the Master's and go. Are there any last topics either of you would like to discuss?

[*Tanner shakes her head no.*]

Hayden [*tentatively*]: You know, Mosely, I feel as if I'm pointing out the obvious, but I'm surprised this hasn't come up and that you're already considering she not continue in the program; despite Alejandra's C in Tanner's course, she did earn three A's in yours, mine, and Burton's courses. Does this not count as satisfactory progress? And come to think of it, for all the lack of contributions she made to course discussions, she did write really thoughtful, provocative reflection essays each week to the assigned reading in my course, so it was wrong of me to say and assume she didn't read or comprehend course material. And from what I remember, her seminar paper, while rough, was not any worse than those written by other first-years who came in with their BAs and, in fact, wasn't too far off the mark from what some MAs turn in. But Tanner, I think what makes her work...what's the word... difficult? Yes, I think her work is difficult for us to wrap our minds around because it's unconventional, probably by and large due to the fact that she approaches it from a perspective we're not trained in or accustomed to...

Mosley: Yes, Hayden, I hear exactly what you're saying. In fact, she did speak at least once in my course, and it was to ask what the "Eastern canon of rhetoric" is? [*laughing*] Different perspective indeed!

Hayden: So then, maybe it's not that she doesn't show potential for joining the professional conversation in our field, but perhaps it's that she has potential to say things we're uncomfortable with because her research interests are beyond our areas of expertise and her approach is something we've just not experienced before. Potential...I think she has it but just requires a better investment in mentoring—on our part.

Mosley: Tanner?

Tanner [*shrugs*]: I'm just not interested in her work. I don't understand it. And to be perfectly honest, I feel we've all done the most we can to help this student be successful. Her difficulties and failures in this program are hers, not ours. And Hayden, for all the positives you point out, do they in all honesty outweigh this student's shortcomings? Are you seriously suggesting we all, as faculty, shoulder the responsibility of teaching her *how* to be a student, a scholar, and a professional in *our* field. It's a little late in the game for her to play catch up in that regard, and I'm not paid enough to take on this task. You're either ready or not. You're a good fit, or you're not, and from what I've seen, she's not prepared to jump in and be the graduate student our program has such a successful record of bringing to degree and placement. So what does taking on Alejandra's lack of preparedness mean for us? More work. You, Hayden, of all people should be wary of this situation, what with your teaching load and the fact you still have quite a publishing quota to meet before you go up for tenure in a couple years. Do you honestly have the time it's going to take to mentor an underprepared student like Alejandra? Can you truly commit to mentoring this individual and showing her the ropes of this profession while also juggling the responsibilities you have to your own career and to the students who *are* prepared and *truly* need you? A student like Alejandra is unfair to us as professors who are pressed for time as it is. As I've already said, I'm not paid enough to teach someone how to be a student, and even if I were, I just don't have the time, none of us do.

Hayden: I never really looked at it that way…but how about if we…

Mosley [*interrupting*]: Good points Tanner, I believe Hayden and I hear you loud and clear [*winks at Hayden*] [*Hayden shrugs, shakes his head and looks down*], and we share your concerns. There's never quite enough time or money, now is there? [*chuckles*] Okay, I'd like to thank you both for taking the time to meet with me, and I'll take what you both have to say into serious consideration before meeting with Alejandra next week.

A Counterstory in which a Chicana Graduate Student and Her Mother Discuss her Status as Qualified to Proceed in Her PhD Program.

Setting. Alejandra has just left the office of D. Mosley, program director, after their follow-up meeting. The meeting consisted of Mosley recounting various talking points from the committee meeting (described in the stock story) and asking for Alejandra's response to the concerns raised by each professor in that meeting. The meeting lasted nearly an hour and resulted in Mosley suggesting that Alejandra consider finishing the program with the MA and perhaps seeking the PhD in another program or field. Tearfully, Alejandra calls her mother to discuss the meeting.

Alejandra: *¿Hola Mami, como estas?*

Mami [*concerned*]: *Bien. ¿Estás llorando mija? ¿Qué paso?* Was it your meeting?

Alejandra [*defeated*]: Yes…

Mami: Why, what happened?

Alejandra: He told me I should just take the Master's and go—

Mami: What?! And go? Go where? *¿Qué te dijo?*

Alejandra: I don't even know if it's worth getting into because he's right. I don't think I'm cut out for this program, maybe not even for grad school, I don't know…

Mami: Bullshit. *No es cierto mija.* You've worked too damn hard to start telling yourself "no" now…

Alejandra: I'm not telling myself "no" Mom; they are.

Mami: You have every right to be in that program, and no *pendejo* has the right to tell you that you can't…

Alejandra: But they're kicking me out.

Mami: Kicking you out? What exactly did he say?

Alejandra: Well, Dr. Mosley met with two of my professors to discuss my "progress and potential" in the program.

Mami: Which professors?

Alejandra: I've only taken four courses so far, and Dr. Burton is in Brazil for the semester, so beside Dr. Mosley, it had to be Dr. Hayden and Dr. Tanner.

Mami: Tanner? That *babosa* who gave you a C?

Alejandra: Yes, her…

Mami: Oh great.

Alejandra: So anyway, he said they all talked about my work in the program, and he told me they all "really like me as a person," and mentioned that Dr. Tanner had said how sweet I was because I brought Mexican cake to class one day to share with everyone...

Mami: That's nice *mija*, you did that?

Alejandra: No, I didn't; it was left-over cornbread from a barbeque place I went to the night before. And you raised me not to waste food, so I brought it in to share rather than throw it away.

Mami: What?! And because you're Mexican she assumes it's "Mexican cake"? Didn't you tell me once she's from the South? How can she not recognize cornbread when she sees it?

Alejandra: I don't know *Mami*; I think Dr. Mosley was just trying to give me a compliment before dropping the bomb.

Mami: Okay, so besides the cake, what else did he have to say?

Alejandra: He said each professor had specific concerns about my writing, my research interests, my classroom participation, and my overall "fit" for the program.

Mami: "Fit," what do they mean by that?

Alejandra: I don't know. Dr. Mosley's concerns about my research interests were really confusing. First, he asked how I think the fields of sociology and rhetoric and composition are related, but before he let me answer, he asked, "Do you really think the discussion of 'race' *still* has a place in this field?" Which I guess was his way of saying this field has already discussed race?

Mami: And so by "fit," is he saying your research interests in "race" aren't a fit for this field?

Alejandra: I don't know, but if you remember, one of the most racist things that ever happened to me was in Dr. Mosley's class.

Mami: *¿Qué?* Refresh my memory...

Alejandra: He gave us a list of fifteen theorists from this book called *The Rhetorical Tradition*, for the fifteen of us in the class to choose from and present to the rest of the class on their major contributions to our field. I don't know if people of color gravitate toward likeness, but the two of us in Dr. Mosley's class (me and this guy from St. Lucia) sat in the back corner, and by the time the list got to us, we looked at who was left and then both looked at each other with ironic grins. Guess who was left for us "colored" folks to choose from?

Mami: Who?

Alejandra: Frederick Douglass and Gloria Anzaldúa. You know who Douglass is right?

Mami: *Sí*, the black abolitionist, but I've never heard of Anzaldúa. *¿Es Mexicana?*

Alejandra: *Tejana*, and she identifies as Chicana, but isn't that crazy?

Mami: I know you're brown and got the *Tejana*, so does that mean the person who got Douglass is black?

Alejandra: Yep, Chev looks like what we'd classify as "black," but he's not African American. He's from the Caribbean, and me, well, I'm definitely not *Tejana*, and I've never called myself Chicana…

Mami: Right, you're Mexican. Your dad's Mexican, I'm Mexican, so you're Mexican.

Alejandra: Well, so I thought, but funny enough it was Dr. Mosley who called me "Chicana" today during our meeting. He said, "with your working class Chicana identity, you should have a wealth of cultural experiences to share and write about."

Mami: Why did he assume you're working class? If brown, then poor?

Alejandra: I know Mom; that's my point—it's all about assumptions in this program. No one bothers to ask me anything; they all just assume to know things about me, and it's like they all speak above me or around me, like I'm not here, as if it's easier for them to ignore me, unless I'm "sharing my wealth of cultural experiences"…

Mami: Like the Mexican cake?

Alejandra [*chuckles*]: Yeah. Exactly.

Mami: So let me get this straight: Mosley doesn't want you to talk about race as it relates to his classroom or the field, but instead prefers that you talk about your culture? What's wrong with this picture? Only talk about race if it has to do with happy topics like *tamales*, *mariachi*, and *folklórico*? *No cambian las cosas.*

Alejandra: I feel like my presence makes the professors and students uncomfortable.

Mami: Okay, so I can see *they* don't understand the "fit" of your research interests, but what was all this *cagada* about your participation being a concern?

Alejandra: Oh that. Dr. Mosley said the faculty is worried because I never speak up in class.

Mami: You don't speak in class?

Alejandra: No, not really, but here's why: in Dr. Tanner's course, for example, I genuinely tried to engage the material because I really identified with the gender and socioeconomic class issues brought up by the theorists she had us read, but when I would ask in class why race wasn't part of the discussion, since I know race, class, and gender are so interconnected in this country, Tanner would shut me down, every time. She'd say things like "well that's not really rhet/comp material you're referring to," when I'd cite sociologists who discussed the same issues but with race as a focus. I felt unwelcome in her class, like the knowledge I brought with me, from sociology and from my personal perspective concerning race, was always automatically dismissed, because, according to her, I wasn't really using a rhet/comp perspective.

Mami: So you didn't feel like you could make a contribution to the conversation? But I thought they brought you into the program because of your sociology background, because it was—what was the word?

Alejandra: Interdisciplinary. Right, that's what I was told too, but now Dr. Mosley's saying they're unsure if I'm a good "fit." And maybe I'm not a good fit. In Tanner's class I just felt defeated. So silence became my refuge; it seemed like my only immediate option for survival.

Mami: Mija, I'm sorry, that sounds terrible, I had no idea...

Alejandra: It's alright, *Mami*. But what I guess I don't understand about the students I'm in class with is this constant chatter they engage in—and that, according to Dr. Mosley, they're expected to engage in. But it happens in every class I take, so I guess I understand the professors' concern that I don't speak, but Dr. Mosley actually asked if my silence was due to the fact that maybe I had trouble comprehending the material?

Mami: What?! What a terrible assumption to make!

Alejandra: *Mami*, to them silence equals lack of comprehension. And it wasn't that I didn't "get it"; I just wasn't prepared to contribute to half of the discussions taking place because I'm new to the field. I'm still learning. And the few times I did speak, I was either shut down or given strange looks as if I said something disturbing. So I decided silence would be my best strategy for the time being. It's as if there's some cultural standard in grad school that I don't understand and am completely out of place in.

Mami: It sounds more like a foreign country than just school, but what I don't fully understand yet is how you got to the point in the conversation where Mosley said you should take the Master's degree and go.

Alejandra: Oh right, well, he brought up the C in Dr. Tanner's course and said Dr. Tanner claimed I never spoke to her about it and never sought her out during the semester for help in the course. But I basically told Dr. Mosley I'm terrified of Dr. Tanner, that she was so hostile, unwelcoming, and discrediting toward me in her class that the last thing I wanted to do was put myself in a vulnerable position like office hours with her, especially after the heinous grade she assigned me. *Mami*, a C in this program is pretty much an F, and an F-U, for that matter. I hope never to work with her again and will avoid her at all costs.

Mami: So what did Mosley have to say about that?

Alejandra: Well, Mosley didn't like that I haven't attempted to resolve this grade issue with Dr. Tanner and pretty much concluded the meeting with his recommendation that I finish the Master's and perhaps look into other programs for doctoral work.

Mami: And how do you feel about his recommendation? I've noticed you're not crying anymore...

Alejandra: Well, to be honest *Mami*, now that I've had the opportunity to talk about it, I don't feel sad anymore. I'm kinda pissed. It makes me mad that these professors would rather be rid of me than face working with a student who is unconventional and is then what? Scary? Threatening? A waste of time? What is it they dislike about me?

Mami: It's not that they dislike you; they don't *get* you.

Alejandra: And I guess that would make sense; it's not like there are any other Latina/os or Chicana/os in the program, not as students or faculty, so their discomfort has to be about more than just the fact that I come from another field. I think it's because I'm the first Latina/Chicana/Mexicana they've ever had in their program, and they don't know what to do with me.

Mami: Yes, as if accepting you into their program was all the work they needed to do to diversify. But what about making sure you succeed? No, apparently your success is not their problem and helping you succeed is definitely not what they're prepared to do.

Alejandra: I'm not gonna let them tell me "no." I'm going back to Dr. Mosley's office tomorrow for another meeting. We need to discuss what it's going to take for me to succeed in this program. I'm going to talk about race, I'm going to be interdisciplinary, and I'm going to make these people *see* me.

Mami: Good *mija*, that's what you need to do—get mad and get to work. Call me tomorrow to let me know how it goes; I've got to hang up and get *cena* going...

Alejandra: Mmmm, what are you making?

Mami: *Pues*, "Mexican cake," of course!

A Plea for Narrative: A Place for Counterstory in Rhet/Comp

When commenting on the conventions of academic discourse, Victor Villanueva notes the strength of *logos* but the pronounced weakness of *pathos* in academic exchanges ("*Memoria*"). This leaning toward logic and reason to best communicate "serious" thought, and the pitting of logic against the assumed unreliability and volatility of emotion reaches far back into Aristotle's original suspicions that a too-heavy reliance on *pathos* leads the audience away from truth—the kind verifiable by facts and "proof." But as Villanueva argues, the personal, too often tied to emotions beyond logic and reason, "does not negate the need for the academic; it complements, provides an essential element on the rhetorical triangle, an essential element in the intellect—cognition *and* affect" ("*Memoria*" 13-14; emphasis in original). For people of color, the personal as related through narrative provides space and opportunity to assert *our* stories within, and in many instances counter to, the hegemonic narratives of the institution.

Solórzano and Yosso characterize these hegemonic narratives as "majoritarian" stories that emerge from a legacy of racial privilege and naturalize racial privilege (27). These stories privilege whites, men, the middle and/or upper class, and heterosexuals by naming these social locations as natural or normative points of reference. A majoritarian story distorts and silences the experiences of people of color and others distanced from the norms such stories reproduce. A standard majoritarian methodology relies on stock stereotypes that covertly and overtly link people of color, women of color, and poverty with "bad," while emphasizing that white, middle and/or upper class people embody all that is "good" (Solórzano and Yosso 29).

Narratives counter to these majoritarian or stock stories, then, provide people of color the opportunity to validate, resonate, and awaken to the realization that we "haven't become clinically paranoid" in our observations and experiences of racism and discrimination within the institution (Villanueva, "*Memoria*" 15). In fact, as Villanueva points out, it is almost shocking to realize in the academic institution, where the sheer numbers of people of color are as exceptional as they are, how "our experiences are in no sense unique but are always analogous to other experiences from among those exceptions" ("*Memoria*" 15). What's more, as these experiences are narrated through spoken and increasingly written and published work, people of color come to realize not much by way of diversity and inclusiveness in the institution has changed. Thus, my work in narrative counterstory within this essay is inspired by narratives specific to rhetoric and composition, such as Anzaldúa's *Borderland/La Frontera*, Villanueva's *Bootstraps*, Gilyard's *Voices of the Self*, Vershawn Ashanti Young's *Your Average Nigga*, and Frankie Condon's *I Hope I Join the Band*. Each of these scholars uses a narrative voice to relate racialized experiences, and as a necessary function of counterstory, these narratives serve the purpose of exposing stereotypes, expressing arguments against injustice, and offering additional truths through narrating authors' lived experiences. My work extends this narrative trend already in use in rhetoric and composition by crafting counterstory, but deviates from more familiar forms of autobiographical or biographical narrative through using a composite approach to the formation of these narratives, an approach most notably employed by critical race theorists Derrick Bell, Richard Delgado, and Tara J. Yosso, and constitutes the methodological basis for my greater body of work (Martinez "Critical Race").

As noted in my reference above to Condon's work, whites can and do tell counterstories, and people of color in contrast, can and do tell majoritarian stories (Bonilla-Silva 151; Martinez, "The American Way" 586). The keepers and tellers of either majoritarian (stock) stories or counterstories reveal the social location of the storyteller as dominant or non-dominant, and these locations are always racialized, classed, and gendered. For example, Ward Connerly is African-American, from a working class background, male, and a prominent politician and academic. From his racialized position, Connerly is a minority, but speaks and represents himself from dominant gendered and classed locations. From the position of an upper class male, Connerly crafts stock stories to argue against affirmative action and to deny racial inequities. Alternatively, Condon's work narrativizes embodied whiteness and individual responsibility as a white ally. Although Condon is white, she is also a woman who speaks from a non-dominant social location, while as a white ally, she uses her dominant racialized location to craft critical race narratives that disrupt "discourses of transcendence" often responsible for leading audiences of white antiracists to believe they are somehow "absolved from the responsibility of doing whiteness" (13).

Condon makes an especially powerful case for the necessity of narrative by stating, "We need to learn to read, to engage with one another's stories, not as voyeurs but as players, in a dramatic sense, within them, and as actors who may be changed not only by the telling of our own stories, but also by the practices of listening, attending, acknowledging, and honoring the stories of our students and colleagues of color as well" (32). In my crafted dialogues above, I take up Condon's call to write and invite audiences into a dramatic engagement with these dialogues in hopes that through the detailing of the stock story versus counterstory, my audience will locate their own subjective identities within the characters and thematic focuses of the text. Although I write the above narratives to commune with an audience of people of color whom I assume will identify with and have academic experiences similar to those of Alejandra, this audience in not my primary target. My primary audience is the audience Condon herself identifies as the more difficult to persuade: "academics...who hope to join in the work of antiracism [who] need to stop minimizing the complexity and significance of narrative, stop depoliticizing the personal, and start studying the rich epistemological and rhetorical traditions that inform the narratives of people of color" (33).

Thus, I position my work in counterstory within social scientific interests with an active Humanities perspective, maintaining three main objectives: First, raise awareness of issues affecting the access, retention, and success of Latin@s in higher education, particularly in rhetoric and composition. Second, I hope this work will motivate discussion of strategies that more effectively serve students from non-traditional backgrounds in various spaces and practices, such as the composition classroom, mentoring, and graduate programmatic requirements so as to *achieve* access, retention, and success. And third, I offer this demonstration of stock story versus counterstory as a guide for counterstory not previously theorized by CRT, but which I believe will resonate with scholars in rhetoric and composition who are familiar with narrative forms spanning from Plato to contemporary scholars, and who seek options and variety in narrative forms to employ in the composition classroom and to publish work about these important issues.

As a narrative form, counterstory functions as a method for marginalized people to intervene in research methods that would form master narratives based on ignorance and on assumptions about minoritized peoples like Chican@s. Through the formation of counterstories or those stories that document the persistence of racism and other forms of subordination told "from the perspectives of those injured and victimized by its legacy" (Yosso 10), voices from the margins become the voices of authority in the researching and relating of our own experiences. Counterstory serves as a natural extension of inquiry for theorists whose research recognizes and incorporates lived and embodied experiences of people of color (Solórzano and Delgado Bernal 314). It is thus crucial to use a narrative methodology that counters other methods that seek to dismiss or decenter racism and those whose lives are affected daily by it. I have used personal stories as counterstory throughout this work to raise awareness about ongoing and historic social and racial injustices in the academy, combining reflection on lived experiences with literature and statistics (Yosso 10). This essay in counterstory suggests a method by which to incorporate CRT in rhetoric and composition, contributing to ongoing conversations in the field about narrative, dominant ideology, and their intersecting influence on programmatic and curricular standards and practices. I offer this essay as an argument for using narrative in our field, and as an invitation to those who would continue the story.

Acknowledgments

I want to thank Jaime Armin Mejía, Cruz Medina, Adela C. Licona, and the Smitherman/Villanueva Writing Collective for providing feedback and encouragement with this essay through its very many various stages and drafts. I want especially to thank my mother, Ana Patricia Martinez, who took the time to sit with me and co-craft the Mami-Alejandra dialogue. The voices of the mother-daughter exchange would not/could not be genuine without my mother's touch.

Notes

1. @: Sandra K. Soto states that her use of the "@" ending in Chican@ "signals a conscientious departure from the certainty, mastery, and wholeness, while still announcing a politicized collectivity" (2). This "@" keystroke serves as an expression of the author's "certain fatigue with the clunky post-1980s gender inclusive formulations" of the word and announces a "politicized identity embraced by man or woman of Mexican descent who lives in the United States and who wants to forge connection to a collective identity politics" (2).

It also serves to unsettle not only the gender binary but also the categories that constitute it.

2. Chican@ and Chicana/o are used in my work synonymously with Mexican-American. These terms are used in my work to refer to women and men of Mexican descent or heritage who live in the United States. According to Yosso, "Chican@ is a political term, referring to a people whose indigenous roots to North America and Mexico date back centuries" (16). Also see Acuña for more on the history and origins of this term.

WORKS CITED

Acuña, Rudolfo F. *Occupied America: A History of Chicanos*. 7th ed. New York: Pearson Longman, 2010. Print.

Anzaldúa, Gloria. *Borderlands/La Frontera: The New Mestiza*. 3rd ed. San Francisco: Aunt Lute, 2007. Print.

Bell, Derrick. *And We Are Not Saved: The Elusive Quest for Racial Justice*. New York: Basic Books, 1987. Print.

—. *Faces at the Bottom of the Well*. New York: Basic Books, 1992. Print.

Bizzell, Patricia, and Bruce Herzberg. *The Rhetorical Tradition: Readings from Classical Times to the Present*. 2nd ed. New York: Bedford/St. Martin's, 2001. Print.

Bonilla-Silva, Eduardo. *Racism without Racists: Color-Blind Racism and the Persistence of Racial Inequality in the United States*. 2nd ed. Boulder: Rowman & Littlefield, 2006. Print.

Condon, Frankie. *I Hope I Join the Band: Narrative, Affiliation, and Antiracist Rhetoric*. Logan: Utah State UP, 2012. Print.

Connerly, Ward. *Creating Equal*. San Francisco: Encounter Books, 2000. Print.

Delgado Bernal, Dolores, and Octavio Villalpando. "An Apartheid of Knowledge in Academia: The Struggle over the 'Legitimate' Knowledge of Faculty of Color." *Equity and Excellence in Education* 35.2 (2002): 165-80. Print.

Delgado, Richard. *The Rodrigo Chronicles: Conversations about America and Race*. New York: New York UP, 1995. Print.

—. "Storytelling for Oppositionists and Others: A Plea for Narrative." *Michigan Law Review* 87.8 (1989): 2411-41. Print.

Ennis, Sharon R., Merarys Ríos-Vargas, and Nora G. Albert. "The Hispanic Population: 2010." U.S. Department of Commerce: Economics and Statistics Administration, U.S. Census Bureau, May 2011. Web. 19 Dec. 2011. <http://www.census.gov/prod/cen 2010/ briefs / c2010br-04.pdf>.

Gilyard, Keith. *Voices of the Self: A Study of Language Competence*. Detroit: Wayne State UP, 1991. Print.

Logan, Shirley Wilson. *"We Are Coming": The Persuasive Discourse of Nineteenth-Century Black Women*. Carbondale: SIUP, 1999. Print.

Martinez, Aja Y. "'The American Way': Resisting the Empire of Force and Color-Blind Racism." *College English* 71.6 (2009): 584-95. Print.

—. "Critical Race Theory Counterstory as Allegory: A Rhetorical Trope to Raise Awareness About Arizona's Ban on Ethnic Studies." *Across the Disciplines* Fall (2013). Web. 12 Nov. 2013. <http://wac.colostate.edu/atd/race/martinez.cfm>.

Olson, Gary A. "Working with Difference: Critical Race Studies and the Teaching of Composition." *Composition Studies in the New Millennium: Rereading the Past, Rewriting the Future.* Eds. Lynn Z. Bloom, Donald A. Daiker, Edward M. White. Carbondale: SIUP, 2003. 208-21. Print.

Royster, Jacqueline Jones. *Traces of a Stream: Literacy and Social Change Among African American Women.* Pittsburgh: U of Pittsburgh P, 2000. Print.

Solórzano, Daniel, and Dolores Delgado Bernal. "Examining Transformational Resistance Through Critical Race and LatCrit Theory Framework: Chicana and Chicano Students in an Urban Context." *Urban Education* 36.3 (2001): 308-42. Print.

Solórzano, Daniel, and Tara J. Yosso. "Critical Race Methodology: Counter-Storytelling as an Analytical Framework for Education Research." *Qualitative Inquiry* 8.1 (2002): 23-44. Print.

Soto, Sandra K. *Reading Chican@ Like a Queer: The De-Mastery of Desire.* Austin: U of Texas P, 2010. Print.

Suchor, Kristen. "FW: CCCC Demographics." Message to author. 14 Dec. 2011. E-mail. U.S. Department of Education, National Center for Educational Statistics. Integrated Postsecondary Education Data System. "Completions Survey." Washington: US Department of Education. 2010.

Villanueva, Victor. *Bootstraps: From an Academic of Color.* Urbana: NCTE, 1993. Print.

—. "*Memoria* Is a Friend of Ours: On the Discourse of Color." *College English* 67.1 (2004): 9-19. Print.

—. "On the Rhetoric and Precedents of Racism." *CCC* 50.4 (1999): 645-61. Print.

Williams, Robert A., Jr. "Forward." *The Rodrigo Chronicles: Conversations about America and Race.* New York: NYU P, 1995. Print.

Yosso, Tara J. *Critical Race Counterstories Along the Chicana/Chicano Educational Pipeline.* New York: Routledge, 2006. Print.

Yosso, Tara J., and Daniel G. Solórzano. "The Chicana and Chicano Educational Pipeline." *CSRC Policy and Issues Brief* 13 (2006): 1-4. Print.

Young, Vershawn Ashanti. *Your Average Nigga: Performing Race, Literacy, and Masculinity.* Detroit: Wayne State UP, 2007. Print.

LITERACY IN COMPOSITION STUDIES

LiCS
Literacy in Composition Studies

Literacy in Composition Studies is on the Web at http://licsjournal.org

Literacy in Composition Studies is a refereed open access online journal that sponsors scholarly activity at the nexus of Literacy and Composition Studies. We foreground literacy and composition as our keywords, because they do particular kinds of work. Composition points to the range of writing courses at the college level, including FYC, WAC/WID, writing studies, and professional writing, even as it signals the institutional, disciplinary, and historically problematic nature of the field. Through literacy, we denote practices that are both deeply context-bound and always ideological. Literacy and Composition are therefore contested terms that often mark where the struggles to define literate subjects and confer literacy's value are enacted.

Teaching While Black: Witnessing and Countering Disciplinary Whiteness, Racial Violence, and University Race-Management

When the editors at LiCS got the call to nominate articles for this collection this year we already knew we wanted Carmen Kynard's "Teaching While Black" to be one of our nominees. This piece strikes us as being a crucially needed intervention in the discipline of Composition/Rhetoric. In this article Kynard calls on all of us in our discipline to "understand and rupture whiteness, racial violence, and the institutional racism of our disciplinary constructs." We particularly note the crucial importance of Kynard's point that our field's "central knowledge-making industry—both its journals and the processes of selecting its editors—reproduces racist logics" (3). Using stories from her personal experiences to "bear witness" (4), Kynard vividly illustrates how racist (il)logics underwrite actions of white faculty who, despite their claims to theoretical sophistication, are active agents of racism. This is an article that deserves wide circulation and attention.

13 Teaching While Black: Witnessing and Countering Disciplinary Whiteness, Racial Violence, and University Race-Management

Carmen Kynard

Imagine a department where there is only one black professor, a common occurrence across universities and colleges today. She is the first black professor in the history of the department there and certainly the first to be tenured. After many years, she finally sees a graduate student complete her dissertation, a young black woman who is also amongst the first black females to graduate with a doctorate from this program. And while there are plenty of ancestors and kinfolk across states, countries, and even continents celebrating this achievement, some of the white faculty are not as ecstatic. In fact, a few white junior professors, self-proclaimed feminists who teach first year writing, both stunningly under-achieving in their fields, begin to tell people that the professor wrote the dissertation for this black female graduate student, with the full support of staff/administration in spreading this Untruth. In the parlay of black youth culture, yes, we can call that: *haters gon hate*. While fully acknowledging all *that hateration*, let's also dig deeper.

It would seem that any researcher or scholar in the academy would know that you cannot possibly present at conferences, give keynote addresses, publish your own articles, review other articles for peer-reviewed journals, work on your own book manuscripts, review other people's manuscripts and books in print, work on grant-funded projects, and then also *write someone else's dissertation for them*. It seems safe to say that it is a huge task to even make time to read drafts of advisees' dissertations. This event is just one of many that show how white faculty and staff can be deeply invested in the illogic of their racism. This story, along with the many other stories that I will tell here, will serve not as micro-instances of campus racism but as macro-pictures of political life in American universities. I intend for these stories to offer a context for the ways in which we must understand and rupture whiteness, racial violence, and the institutional racism of our disciplinary constructs in composition-rhetoric as central to the political work we must do.

Tangled Webs: Racist Processes Seen, Heard, and Felt

Like any good theorist of race and racism in the academy today, I dutifully acknowledge that race is socially constructed and, therefore, a product of social relations and not biological/genetic difference. This does not mean, however, that I promote the general post-modernist zeitgeist and angst that would suggest that race is illusory or peripheral to social organization, past or present, or that our identities are so multiple and complex that race can evaporate as a social category (Roediger). The institutional racism in which students and faculty must daily think and act is always very real and moving according to the specificity of two directions: the local situation and the national tenor of the moment.

Zeus Leonardo's work particularly challenges much of our current research and discourse, especially when theorized solely from the location of white privilege, which, as Leonardo argues, only offers a passive description of white racial domination as if racial domination happens without active agents, making whiteness *a state of being dominant* rather than a calculated and calculating series of racist *processes*. Leonardo's focus on active agents is a compelling mode of analysis that I believe most scholars of color are discouraged from pursuing. While much of our work that has chronicled the multiple literate lives of students of color has been embraced, it is not clear that the work has actually *been mobilized* to change classrooms for students of color in schools and colleges. It is much safer for us to unfurl the specialized, disciplinary methodologies and vocabularies in which we have been trained rather than turn our analytical gaze onto our institutions and its actors that have maintained calculatingly repressive environments, policies, and climates for students and faculty of color. This is a kind of intellectual activist-work that is quite distinct from the organizational work that we do at bourgeois professional conferences and the scholarship that we most often pursue.

If we truly understand ourselves as social actors and not lone individuals, then we can move past a bourgeois liberal orthodoxy that would imagine the professors, staff, and administrators of my opening narrative as merely individuals in one department at one college and, instead, begin to see and name an entire constellation of actors and processes. There are tangled webs of authorizing, credentialing, and sanctioning that have gotten these very actors to the university positions that they occupy and that have created the kinds of academic departments and disciplines in which we do our work. In fact, my opening narrative is not particularly spectacular but highlights just another day on the job as I can tell countless stories just like it. It is what bodies of color must negotiate in white university spaces, even when those university spaces represent student populations that are majority of color (the only kind of university where I have ever worked). I have not worked at any single institution, to date, where I have found as many as even three other colleagues who notice, much less speak out, against these kinds of everyday racist microaggressions that I have described despite everyone's seeming incessant discussion of critical theories from postcolonialism/decolonization to intersectionality. The theories can become merely the stage for an academic performance, not a way of engaging the world and oppression in it.

The story gets even more complicated with these actors in my opening narrative. The web of connections is, indeed, quite complicated. We have to begin to ask, for instance: what does knowledge in this field look like and do when overwhelmingly white editors have published the work of white scholars about students of color, and when those very same white scholars would so casually and calculatingly defame the only black female professor and graduate on their campus? What might it mean that our publications about students of color emanate from racist roots and what does it mean when a publishing apparatus affirms that? From where I stand, I see a field whose central knowledge-making industry—both its journals and the processes of selecting its editors—reproduces racist logics. The very theoretical paradigms in which we work often operate from a space that requires the displacement and denigration of black women. While I understand how and why so many of my colleagues have the privilege of ignoring these "slippages," many of us do not have the luxury of overlooking such violence because we are its targets. In more pessimistic terms, many of us unknowingly contribute to a kind of "race-management science" if we accept academia's (our home institutions and our field) embrace of our scholarship on race but do not speak or write against the ways our institutions actively reproduce inequality.

Racism, institutional and structural, is not about some kind of general and generic racially divided world somewhere out there over the rainbow. There is never any moment when racism is subtle or exists as some kind of fine mist that is out there but that I cannot fully see on campus. We need to stop talking about racism and institutions this way in our writing and to our students. Oppression could never work if it were invisible, unarticulated, or unfelt by those it targets. Bonilla-Silva's work on today's college undergraduate students' unwavering reproduction of color-blind racism seems everywhere replicated in our field. A misplaced faith in the progress of the field, shifting demographics at our colleges, or a naturally-occurring expiration of racism have left us inert and unconscious of our own race-reproducing tendencies.

Deep Histories and the Complicatedness of Everyday Life: Teaching Narratives Defined and Refined

I am starting with the narrative of a black female graduate student and myself because I am suggesting that it is a critical context in which to understand the space in which black college students and faculty must write and carve out their (literate) being in colleges today. We face a resistance and questioning of our intellect that oftentimes looks no different from what Phyllis Wheatley faced when white colonists found it difficult to believe that Wheatley had written her own poetry (Carretta; Doak; Langley). She had to defend her authorship in a Boston court in 1772 to a group that included the then governor of Massachusetts (Gates). It was only when she provided "proof" that they signed the documents verifying her authorship, which was included in her *Poems on Various Subjects, Religious and Moral* published in 1773 (in London, not the U.S.) While the adage that history repeats itself is much too simple to capture social complexities under race and gender in the United States, a historically situated understanding traced back to the first book of poetry published by a black woman, Phillis Wheatley, does offer critical understanding of the continuum of racial barriers.

The late Critical Race Theorist, Derrick Bell, argued that we must see racial progress as cyclical, sometimes regressing in catastrophic ways and, at other times, incrementally moving forward (Bell; Delgado). He called this position Racial Realism and saw it as the most hopeful and pragmatic theoretical lens and praxis to do anti-racist work. His reminder of the importance of Racial Realism seems a portent for today given the brutal murders of Trayvon Martin, Jordan Davis, and Michael Brown, the treatment of Rachel Jeantel's court testimony about Trayvon's murder, the nationwide protests that have animated young activists, the military-state brutality against protesters in Ferguson, Missouri, the discursive somersaults that law enforcement and state institutions continually maneuver to justify racial profiling, and the obvious and constant reminder that to be black in the United States is to be the target of a ruthless racial violence. As central to my own theoretical grounding here, I stick most closely with Sylvia Wynter's "'No Humans Involved': An Open Letter to My Colleagues." Written in the midst of the Los Angeles uprising of 1992, Wynter passionately urges us to decode our disciplinary sense-making that is ideologically wedded to the very same violence waged against Rodney King and South Central Los Angeles. I propose to take up Wynter's charge here: 1) that, we begin to *notice* the violence in the classrooms and research that we sustain, and; 2) that, we question the disciplinary apparatus that makes it possible that racially subordinated students of color will experience racial violence at the site where they are supposed to be democratically educated. I'm talking about the kind of social and political processes that we need in order to prevent racist logics as viable membership in this community that we call composition-rhetoric and I am calling these racist logics of the same order of violence as the murders of Trayvon Martin, Jordan Davis, Michael Brown (and countless others), the dismissal of Rachel Jeantel, and the brutal targeting of Ersula Ore who was assaulted by campus police. Wynter was always sure that undoing racial violence is an intellectual and epistemological task, but only if we see the work in front of us.

I am offering my own personal experiences and stance of bearing-witness as more than just one individual's observations, but an indication of the levels of systemic racism that we do not address. General discussions about moral and philosophical principles of equity, equality, or diversity are no longer good enough so I take up the tools that Allan Luke privileges: the tools of "story, metaphor, history, and philosophy, leavened with empirical claims," all of which Luke argues are as integral to truth-telling and policymaking as field experiments and meta-analyses (368). I take up these tools in the context of myself as a writer and researcher of black language, education, and literacies and use narratives to offer stories of institutional racism that compositionists —and thereby, our field— have maintained. These narratives offer a place to decode the symbolic violence that is encoded into our disciplinary sense-making and move towards what a theory of Racial Realism might entail for our classrooms and discipline.

The series of stories that I tell here, beginning with my opening narrative, are intentionally crafted as method for organizing, presenting, and politicizing textual arrangement in scholarship (Coulter and Smith; Barone). Narrative as the form of my telling means that I am conscious of the ways that I use stories to understand and present the lives and literacies of students of color where my own cultural role as a black female storyteller enacts its own critical inquiry (L. Richardson, *Fields of Play*, "Getting Personal," "Poetic Representations," "Writing"; Gonick and Hladki).

Teaching While Black: Teaching Narratives Further Unfurled

In a graduate course that I once taught about New Literacies Studies, a white male student objected to Elaine Richardson's claim that women of color, with particular emphases on black women, are hyper-sexualized. In an extensive reading response that he wrote, Richardson's claims are unwarranted since "those women" are simply "promiscuous" and he placed "i.e., slutty" in parentheses after the word promiscuous, presumably because I might not know what such a word with so many letters might mean. He was, of course, not alone in his sentiments. More than a few white men in the class wrote about the ways we African Americans and Latin@s are no longer really challenged by racism; it is our laziness that keeps us behind since we just complain instead of working hard. Latin@s and African Americans are not the only group who have gotten some heat in my graduate classes.

I have read numerous accounts from white graduate students in my courses about how Asian scholars, especially Morris Young and his book, *Minor Re/Visions: Asian American Literacy Narratives as a Rhetoric of Citizenship*, were simply misinformed when thinking they were offering any pertinent information to anyone who has taught Asian students. In such examples, the numeric over-representation of one racial/ethnic group on a campus is akin to knowing about and respecting them. One might wonder, given this logic, why systems like slave plantations and European colonies, peopled mostly by brown and black bodies, were not oases of freedom, too. This idea that a teacher need not learn about Asian bodies because having their presence in a classroom is enough becomes fraught with problems. Two white female students once even visited my office to inform me, given their history of having taught many African American students, that Elaine Richardson (and myself since I upheld Richardson's position) do not fully understand how much better schools are for black people now and, as such, Richardson and I were distorting the truth. These two women even claimed to relate better (than Richardson and me) to African Americans given their Italian and Irish backgrounds, since they, after all, have experienced the same discrimination as blacks.

I have checked more than a few graduate students who never seemed to get the pronouns accurate on any Asian compositionists we read. It was obvious to me that they were unfamiliar with Asian names, like Min-Zhan Lu, who students often referenced with: "he argues. . . ." To deal with this, a group of white MA students decided to proclaim a new, radical gender politics for composition studies: they would exchange he and she pronouns for all authors since gender is, after all, only a social construction. And while that could be an interesting practice, this new radical experimentation was only waged on Asian bodies in the field: white scholars weren't subjected to these new experiments in she and he, his and hers.

I could go on and on like this. My narrative over-indulgence is meant to serve a specific rhetorical purpose here: rather than represent these examples as an exhaustive overview of my specific encounters, I intend to show these examples as casual, everyday occurrences. The responses that I have described are quite typical in the classrooms of black and Latina female professors, especially when your course centers the scholarship of folk of color and issues of race, class, and gender (Alfred; Sadao and Johnsrud; Thomas and Hollenshead). The prevalence of such racist backlash against faculty of color seems such a steady data stream that we will continue to have a thriving research literature (Stanley et al.; Stanley). Many of us are even taught how to account for negative student responses in classes that deal with race, class, and gender when we submit tenure files (Cleveland; Fenelon; Turner). The continuum is quite wide: depending on the school, black and Latina professors can expect calculated protection from offices like Minority or Multicultural Affairs; benign neglect in departments who don't seem to realize that their mentees say such things to faculty and peers of color (only the public expressions of "anger" by black students are noticed); or, at the extreme opposite end, we can expect departments to privilege white students' racist evaluations (Gutiérrez y Muhs, et al). At a National Women's Studies Association conference, for instance, there was significant discussion of one prominent university who validated the evaluations of students who wrote things about black female professors like: "this woman should never be a college professor; she needs to go back to the kitchen where her kind belong." Many of us know that this is what we must confront as the daily-ness of being a black or Latina female faculty member in white institutions. To imagine that changing such sentiments in white college students is an easy task is to ignore centuries of racial oppression and the current race-protest moment in which we live.

In the field of composition-rhetoric, however, we have an altogether different set of issues. For *each and every single* graduate student who I have described, *each and every single* one of them has been hired to teach writing on a university campus. These students are now adjuncts, contract faculty, or tenure track faculty; some work on campuses, especially those who are hired in the tri-state New York area where I teach, where the students are predominantly students of color. That young man who thinks all we blacks and Latin@s are lazy got hired to teach them by a team of compositionists who have been talking and writing up their programs in the field as offering important literacy opportunities for their students. That man who thinks all black and Latina women are "i.e. slutty" is *teaching them right now*. In some cases, some of these students are even proposing to conduct research about students of color. My anecdotes do not compose the story of an isolated, individual campus, but the wider culture of our field. Though I am an obvious member of the campus and program where these graduate students did their degree work, no compositionist or administrator has ever contacted me with questions about these graduate students' capacity for teaching students of color, questions for which I can surely supply a litany of responses. The only phone calls that I ever receive are when a graduate student of color is the job candidate and the one question that marks each conversation is about the collegiality of these young scholars of color: *do they play well with others?* I have seen no evidence, across dozens of programs, of any interest in white candidates' ability to work in classrooms with students or color, only an interest in whether or not young scholars of color will accommodate whiteness. When we talk about institutional racism as it impacts composition-rhetoric classrooms, the field, and college writing programs, we need never feel at a loss for seeing very specific, local iterations.

When discussions about race, culture, and whiteness go down in my graduate classrooms, it is often students of color who challenge white students, rarely other white students though many of them claim to do critical literacy teaching, anti-racist advocacy, and research amongst students of color. I am reminded of what Bell described when he protested Harvard's refusal to hire a black female law professor: white faculty agreed with him behind closed doors when they visited him in his office but they never spoke up or out in any public setting (Bell, *Faces*). In one particular dissertation proposal seminar, one white female graduate student, someone who is "researching" students of color, spoke at length in a class about how she felt the program was better before the "angry black man" joined; some faculty expressed the same sentiment to me in the hallways, never once problematizing white students' racism. In this kind of culture where we groom our graduate students, it is students of color who will take the heat, much like Bell did, all alone, when he stood against the racism of his peers. Graduate classrooms rarely award those white graduate students who choose to defy majority-white peers and yet, white students' silence is hardly liberatory for them either. More importantly, such silence puts white faculty and graduate students at risk of losing real collegial relationships with and trust from people of color, who will be few and far between on their campuses as it is.

Malea Powell's 2012 Chair's Address seems all the more pertinent here: the call that we *decolonize* our pedagogies, classrooms, and epistemologies. We need to know the deep histories and contemporary realities about racially subjugated groups before we can have something to say about teaching them (Ladson-Billings and Tate; Dixson and Rousseau; Yosso, Parker, Solorzano, and Lynn). The violence of seeing black and Latin@ people as lazy or promiscuous (i.e., slutty), the same as Irish or Italians, or too angry is the context of the classroom that, by my count, hundreds of black and Latin@ college students are sitting in this week, this month, this semester, this year; and, in each case, it was a compositionist who co-signed this placement into the field, position, or program.

If we politically and historically contextualize these narratives and anecdotes that I have provided, we have a very unique intellectual opportunity. I am not suggesting that our students with racist attitudes will not challenge their thinking somewhere down the line, but I am questioning how and why faculty of color experience such classroom events as routine and must do the bulk of the exhausting, debilitating, and non-value-added work of redressing students' racial wrongs, often without any support or acknowledgement from the departments, programs, schools, or fields in which they work. What I am also suggesting here is that we take advantage of an oft-missed opportunity: we can really see how racism works in our field if we ask when, where *and if* such graduate students' racism is ever challenged and re-directed outside of faculty of color's classrooms. I like to think of such students as a kind of dye into the field, like the kind medical doctors use: the dye that gets injected into your internal organs so that you can see where the problem areas are. We are not standing on the outside of racial violence in our discipline; we ourselves are encoding racial violence in how we constitute knowledge about people of color and how we are enacting racism with the people we hire and privilege as composition faculty.

There are, of course, position papers, policy statements, and white papers that we could design that need to address: guidelines for the awards granted to writing programs that explicitly communicate goals for culturally relevant literacy curricula offered to students of color; dispositions, research experiences, and practices to privilege when interviewing candidates to teach multilingual and multiracial students; articulations of PhD programming in the context of theory and praxis related to teaching multilingual and multiracial students towards radical, anti-racist ends; definitions of ethics of practitioner research and qualitative studies for scholars who research in communities of color but do not represent or live in them. However, this kind of policy-building cannot replace simultaneous ideological analysis. I am talking about the kind of work that Wynter was asking of us in 1992: namely, that we interrogate the horizon of understanding that induces the collective behaviors of so many sites in the field where racist teachers carry forth composition classrooms and racist editors stamp new forms of knowledge-making.

Borrowing from Foucault's notion of the episteme, Wynter reminds us that race is a "classificatory logic," albeit fictional since it is a social construction that gets elaborated by our disciplinary paradigms. Wynter describes teachers and "universally-applicable" researchers as the "grammarians" of our order, those men and women who are able to directly reflect the frameworks, systems of value, and cognitive model that the discipline most desires (what she might call a sociogenic code) (*Do Not Call Us Negroes*). There is a discursive and pragmatic power, however, in the counter-narratives and counter-epistemologies that color-conscious compositionist-rhetoricians can use to rupture this horizon of desires. It is the work that Wynter was asking us to do in 1992 and 1994: the most dispossessed amongst us must turn the tide and become the intellectuals who (re)write the sociogenic codes of the discipline that currently bind us.

ANOTHER DAY IN THE LIFE OF INSTITUTIONAL RACISM: A FINAL TEACHING NARRATIVE

Vickie, a young black woman and former student, a summa cum laude biology major and McNair scholar, was sent to her department's medical school advisor in her senior year of college. The advisor took one look at her, asked what her GPA was, and when she said 3.7, he told her she had no chance of going to medical school. He went on to explain to her that medical schools no longer accept "unqualified blacks" like her as they did in the 1970s and 1980s; that he only knew "one black girl" at the college who had ever gotten herself ready enough to get into medical school on her own "merit"; and that she probably wasn't going to do the same as "that other black girl." Other young black women shared similar stories about their "advisory" meetings: one woman was told that it was good she is Haitian because she will need Voodoo to pass her course; another was reluctantly told that she might, after all, actually make it into medical school since she was "only" applying to "those" medical schools at historically black colleges and universities. These are not things that happened years ago, but a few semesters ago, a seeming shock to many people who continually remind me: *yes, but look at Michelle Obama.*

When I have told this story to white audiences, many see each professor's attack as simply one, individual act of meanness, not systemic racism that structures black opportunities. And yet, it is the privilege under whiteness that only imagines such romantic individuality while Vickie and her peers are continually reminded on college campuses that they are *just black girls*. Vickie, however, cannot afford to understand this advisor as one, lone individual actor that the rest of the world won't replicate; and, at the same time, she can't let this man and that world eat away at her spirit and the triumphant woman she already is, has been, and is becoming. These ways of reading the world, far more complicated than any skills-set we teach in our writing classrooms, are what we must imagine as central to college education today.

Though Vickie's university was among the three most "diverse" universities in the country, its "epidermic" diversity is mostly a historical accident, not one of the "intentionally figured counter-hegemonic discourse communities" that Theresa Perry describes when she looks at the history of HBCUs (Kynard and Eddy). This epidermic diversity has little, if anything, to do with understanding or rupturing institutional racism. In fact, diversity rhetoric works *alongside* institutional racism in the ways that corporate management schemas use diversity as mostly a marketing tool. "Lower-tiered universities" will especially promote their epidermic variability as their only competitive advantage in the food chain of college ranking scores. Current tropes of educating for diversity neither examine nor rupture the premises and beliefs of a social order that negates the poorest/of color segments of our population. Instead, paradigms of (especially linguistic) diversity trek relentlessly toward the creation of a multiple-languaged but standardized-English-speaking rainbow coalition of multiethnic consumers who can function in a homogenized (and collapsing) marketplace. Multiple "peoples of color" can be incorporated, via schooling, into the criterion reference of the middle class without sabotaging or contradicting the aims of current modes of capitalism. Legal scholars have especially shown how this appropriation and disconnection of diversity from race has resulted in color-blind law *while* de facto and de jure racial discrimination continue (Bell; Guinier; Orfield; Moses and Chang). Ladson-Billings ("Is The Team All Right?," "Preparing Teachers") and many other educational scholars, from Darling-Hammond to Swartz, have critiqued a set of teaching and learning practices under the hubris of diversity that work to actually block true inclusivity by: coding and lumping historically marginalized groups into one single-massed "other"; removing group identities, cultures, and political needs from view; obscuring racism, homophobia, and sexism; serving the interests of capital; and amassing add-on content to predesigned forms and models. The college that manages brown and black bodies by photographing them as happy smiling faces for corporate ad campaigns but then promotes the campus actors who denigrate them is well-aligned with what "diversity" means and achieves in this era. If we understand that we all work in managed universities in the way Bousquet has so brilliantly outlined for us (too many of us still don't want to really account for and notice the ways that we exist in the most corporatized versions of higher education ever seen), then we need to understand that capital and "management" in the U.S. have always reproduced racial hierarchies in distinct, powerful ways. Economically managed universities are no exception to this rule.

But this story gets better.

I was asked to serve on a panel for "teaching multicultural student populations" at the college and accepted the offer, thinking I would get in where I fit in, and used the moment to talk in great detail about Vickie's experience and what it means to alienate future black female doctors from a health care system that has stunningly failed to improve the health and mortality of black women. After describing Vickie's encounter on that campus, I asked what I thought might be some good questions:

- What if the discourses—those ways of speaking, writing, and thinking—that we teach to students in schools are, in and of themselves, flawed and racist, or at least, problematically racialized? We can't really think that language and words do not matter, that language and words do not have consequence and material effect, can we?
- Can it really be a surprise that Valerie's advisor and his family are the dominant members of a system (both the medical profession and college campus) where African Americans have higher rates of avoidable hospital admissions,[1] where nearly 35 black women die per 100,000 births as opposed to 9 white

women, **where** heart disease was 50% higher among black women than white women in the 1980s and has increased to 67% now?
- **What are the connections between how Vickie is treated on this campus and a larger paradigm of structural racism where as a black woman, she** has twice the cervical cancer mortality rate compared to white women, is 28% more likely to die of breast cancer than white women, and—as if all that wasn't enough—will live roughly five fewer years than white women?[2]

I am not suggesting here that white faculty's racism is the center of gravity for such a system of unequal health disparities. My point with listing so many health disparities was not to chronicle the ways that black women die at the expense of noticing our lives. Instead, my point here was to ask a different kind of question for those interested in the educational life of someone like Vickie: **how is the macro-racism that Vickie faces** *off campus* (see "Income and Poverty in Communities of Color: A Reflection on the 2009 U.S. Census Bureau Data") **different from the world she must navigate** *on campus*? Our language and epistemology on campus are not innocent, benign, or socially non-determinant.

In my brief moment on the panel, I argued that, as faculty, we needed to adopt an activist stance where we challenge colleagues who endanger our students' daily lives with what Critical Race Theorists call racial micro-aggressions. I also argued that we must challenge the overt, off-campus racism our students also encounter, like our Muslim students who can never drive home on break without being stopped by the NYPD or fly home without going through multiple searches at the airport. I questioned the desire to create tried-and-true lesson plans for every ethnic group, the pedagogical version of an ethnic food court, and instead asked that we not make students of color the smiling/happy objects of marketing's corporate ads but actual bodies with histories of racial subordination that they are living out, both on and off campus. That to me would be the definition of teaching racially and ethnically diverse student populations. But it all seemed to fall on deaf ears.

In the Q&A session, a white female professor waxed on prophetically on how she works with students to make sure they do not wear big earrings in the business world, pointing at me and my earrings, and right when I thought I would go in on her, I was just even more stunned: without even a pause about my earrings, she went on to discuss how she had to learn to teach "the Chinese girls" who do not know how to talk or think, fully deploying "Chinese" as the code name for Asian students on the campus, though our Asian student population was not made up predominantly of Chinese-American communities. And, as always, though the room was heavily populated by white, senior tenured faculty, it was me, the most junior and the only woman of color, who challenged her. Since that day, this white woman has been promoted to dean; and Vickie's race-perpetrator is still the medical school advisor and has been promoted to director of scientific reasoning by a white male administrator who was sitting in the very audience of the panel discussion (given my description of her advisor and his long tenure at the university, he knew exactly who I was speaking of). As if that weren't enough, Vickie's perpetrator also directs the IRB office, which means he oversees all research on exactly the kinds of bodies he is utterly unable to value and humanize.

What I am suggesting here is that Vickie's experience, particularly under this corporate rubric of diversity, is routine, systematic, and systemic. None of these promotions are accidental or coincidental and for those who think I am simply a conspiracy theorist, I remind you of David Gillborn's argument that racism has never needed a conspiracy to be operational. As I have already iterated, I do not believe that *some* universities do not operate under these kinds of white supremacist cultural logics; whiteness doesn't require that we will all see or notice racism. What I am suggesting then is that in Vickie's routine experience, we see a crucial lens into the ways in which universities maintain white supremacy as a structure of both formal and informal rules where norms for the distribution of resources, benefits, and burdens are actively maintained.

It seems that in institutions where formerly white colleges and universities have experienced a browning and blackening of their student populations, not by conscious/deliberate action like with HBCUs but by geographic accident, racial anxieties actually increase for the most powerful, campus white stakeholders. The policing of black and brown bodies and minds gets escalated, a fate too many of us in the field do not readily challenge since many of us discuss racially subordinated students from university spaces that do not enroll many of them and, therefore, can often fetishize practice rather than engage the equally tangible and necessary work of interrogating the distinct kinds of institutional racism that still bar students of color from the very universities that enroll the largest number of them. Our inability to explicitly situate and name the acts of everyday institutional racism that are always inherent to teaching and to the literacies of our students seems stunningly related to James Gee's critique that what we have called our social turn—and its focus solely on the social processes of learning—was never really political enough. We never really interrogated systems of power, though we may have certainly improved learning structures. In this absence of a deliberate critique of power, we ourselves created the very possibility that progressive philosophies of education could be completely co-opted by neoliberalism such that even corporate mechanisms under current standardization regimes sometimes sound like us: *we may have supplied a much too-neutral language.*

But this story gets better still.

While I was on the "multiculturalism panel," being schooled on the kind of earrings I need to wear, learning how "stupid" "Chinese girls" are, and hearing just how inaudible the suffering of black women and Muslim students is, I had numerous voicemail messages waiting for me as well as a barrage of emails. I was being called to campus security for something a student was claiming he wrote in my advanced, undergraduate composition class: *could I really be teaching about race theory?* was the question.

In the class, one student, who I will call Sammy, elected to write an essay that uses his own experiences as a multiracial young man to interrogate America's neo-racism. Sammy is biracial (A Caribbean black father and white-skinned Latina mother) which, in his case, means he "looks Arab," with features that he describes as "a long, pointy nose, protruding ears, long eyelashes, tan skin and bushy eyebrows"—all of these racial descriptions are the student's.) As someone who is most often labeled as Muslim, Islamic, or Arab, based solely on his appearance, Sammy is routinely subjected to stops and searches: when he is driving, every time he goes to the airport, at the subways and at every major transportation setting. His writing red-flagged the campus security office when he printed his assignment on a campus printer. While I was, quite literally, presenting on a panel about educating our multicultural student population, Sammy was called into security headquarters and interrogated about his writing. Not even 10 minutes after my panel presentation, I had to phone in and assure the campus-homeland security that Sammy had indeed completed this assignment for me.

I never talked about this moment publicly with anyone other than my undergraduate students. There were so few faculty of color on that campus, less than any other campus I have ever visited, taught at, or myself attended, that we see each other very little and amongst those who do have a critical race perspective (there are even fewer), well, let's just say that we had our plates full. There was no single white ally anywhere on the campus, as was the case when I spoke up against a female faculty member's racist targeting of our only black male student in the grad program. I had already witnessed what Thomas Ross describes as the perpetual twinning of white innocence with black abstraction: white perpetrators of racial violence look back with shame while the assault on black bodies gets completely divorced from very specific, centuries-old experiences of racism. White faculty, especially junior members, eventually found a way to fault the black male student as it protected their tenure trek or, rather, their whiteness; meanwhile, white graduate students distanced themselves altogether from the issue, though they are writing dissertations on race theory (Linda Smith's work seems relevant here where she argues that Indigenous people have been the most researched subjects in western science but that has meant very little, if anything at all, for their liberation or the ease or end of their suffering.) No post-colonialist, no critical theorist, no African Americanist, and no queer theorist thought anything of this situation because they counted on white supremacy to let them sit on the sidelines and observe violence, racially mark the black male student as "difficult"; racially mark me as angry and inappropriate (I never seemed to pick the "right time" to discuss race with white people); and racially mark the white woman as "innocent" and "victim." With a white male faculty and staff running to protect her moral and pedagogical virtue, this white woman was simply someone who had intended no harm, the usual escape hatch for racist perpetrators, enlivening a black counter-narrative that might aptly be traced back to Ida B. Wells's *A Red Record* (one might wonder what an intentional racist act might look like if this is what white educators do when they are not acting intentionally.) With that kind of racial memory at an institution that shamelessly pimps its students' epidermic diversity when it serves white corporate interests, I knew very well that the campus homeland security, all former NYPD, would have impunity in demonizing both Sammy and me.

On this Typical Day at a university campus, after relaying Vickie's story about a man who would be eventually promoted, after being told that my earrings are inappropriate and that "Chinese girls" are stupid by someone promoted to upper level administration, after dealing with the campus homeland security, I had to go teach my race theory class. I got there five minutes late and the students had already started the class without me, with Sammy leading, who, smarter than myself, had recorded the entire conversation with campus-homeland security. The students then basically directed a discussion with Sammy and myself where we uncovered that Sammy and I basically walked into our interrogation with the same focus and goals, though we did not talk to one another beforehand: 1) we were both told lies about one another that we automatically knew were concocted stories; 2) we referenced and quoted the same critical race scholars; 3) we walked in with a conscious decision to not bow our heads and act like good, scared Jim Crow Niggras; 4) we guessed our white male interrogator's questions beforehand; 5) we both used trickster, signifying motifs and answered all questions with questions. From that point on, if and when students wrote "dangerous" texts, they gave me a USB drive and I printed/read it from my computer at home or they took it back to the Old Skool: they hand-wrote their texts. It seems ironic that while brown and black bodies across the country use social media and technologies for subversive means, at this college, the most subversive technology for students to discuss race was paper and pen.

While the hyper-criminalization of Arab bodies in the context of a university that celebrates its diversity and multiculturalism seems a contradiction, it is actually a logical aftermath if we see that the ideological apparatus under diversity and multiculturalism sustains and propels racism. I am reminded here of Wynter's 1990 work in *'Do Not Call Us Negros:' How Multicultural Textbooks Perpetuate Racism* where she shows how new "code words" of minority, diversity, and cultural pluralism replace the terrain of race and only further marginalize the centrality of both black and Indigenous groups to the instituting of America.

The Narrative Arc: A Happy Ending

It is worth explicitly stating here that when my racially subordinated students were writing texts that fused and infused their experiences with critical analyses of race, their bodies, experiences, and voices posed enough of a threat that we had to communally design counter-surveillance textual productions to actually do racial analyses. I had printed out hundreds of articles by compositionists on campus printers. And while I may have *thought* those readings were radical, I have been never called into campus security for them. It wasn't until students did the racial analyses themselves in their own writing classroom that campus homeland security came *literally* calling for them and me. None of these academic texts for academic audiences that we imagine to be so socially transformative has held as much of a threat as when racially marginalized college students counter-narrated their own experiences with white supremacy on and off campus. I just assume that anything perceived this dangerous in the hands of young multiracial, working class, first generation college students *has got to be right*. It would seem to me then that this is a first order of business on a to-do list for a complete dismantling of the hegemony of diversity discourses in higher education that operationalize racial assaults on the bodies of students of color.

I want to return here to Leonardo's reminder that critical analyses of race have to begin with the objective experiences of racially subordinated masses, since it is not in the interest of such groups to mystify the process of their own dehumanization. This seems critical to me in the field where even the texts that address race/anti-racism parade mostly white authors with an obligatory nod to the celebrity minorities of the field, allowing yet another publication of a white text by white authors who have often themselves perpetrated exactly the kinds of white supremacist violence that I have talked about in this piece. We need what LaNita Jacobs-Huey has described as *the natives "gazing and talking back"* in ways that explicitly interrogate *the daily operation of white supremacy in our field and on our campuses* rather than more performances of psychologically-internalized black pain for the white gaze (a practice that garners white attention and consumption, but never social change). I am not talking to or about those scholars seeking celebrity status, acceptance, or more face-time; this is work that requires you to make people *uncomfortable*. *Some folk gon need to get called out.* As Leonardo argues, in the least, this kind of focus on the objective experiences of racially subordinated masses as the frame for understanding the dynamics of structural power relations would finally move us away from always ONLY imagining a white audience when we write about race, literacy, life, and schooling. We only chokehold racial understanding and change when we proceed at what he so aptly calls the "snail's pace of the white imaginary" (Leonardo 80).

Insomuch that the stories I am telling here can have a happy ending, I will tell you that Vickie was accepted into each of the nine medical schools to which she applied with full scholarship. Sammy is at a MFA program that will allow him to focus more fully on racial experiences. The success that I see in Vickie's and Sammy's final endings is not in their material accomplishments but in their consciousness and ability to both navigate and *counter-narrate* the white supremacy they have faced and will continue to face, both on and off campus—two sides of the same coin. We need to follow their lead and counter-narrate the mainstream assumptions on which far too many have built their ideas about literacy and action in higher education.

Coda

In this coda, I am offering a serious of contemplative questions. I imagine two audiences here: 1) marginalized faculty/graduate students who are in the midst of or will soon experience antagonistic racial encounters on their campuses; 2) folk who want to better understand what I am talking about and how it impacts my critiques of and frustrations with both the academy and our field. By centering questions, I am asking readers to insert themselves into and experience a sense of urgency about the issues I have discussed. There are no *right or wrong* answers here, but you MUST come up with answers. Treat these questions as a lens onto a landscape that many may not have looked at closely before *but as promises of what is coming in the very near future for YOU.*

1. Think back on the excerpt about Vickie. Imagine that Vickie comes to you in tears about what her medical school advisor has told her. What will you say to her? What will you say, in that moment, such that when she walks out of your office, you will contribute to the humanity that she has been denied? What's *your* script? Now, imagine that this is the kind of exchange you have in your office at least once a week. What will

you do to rejuvenate *yourself* so that you can return each week without feeling depleted? To borrow from Wynter's notion of disciplinary sense-making: how does our field make sense of (i.e., explain, theorize, research, discuss, etc.) such routine interactions on our campuses?

2. Vickie is now in medical school. However, the professor who racially marked her as inferior is still at the university, with an even more privileged post than he had before with access to even more students of color. What will you do to counter his impact? You should assume, as is the case in this story, that no other administrator supports your concerns (*yes, you MUST STICK with this fact; do not retreat to your privilege and assume that when you talk, you will be heard*). Who will you talk to? What will you do? What is your role as a teacher? As an activist? As a WPA? To borrow from Wynter's notion of disciplinary sense-making: how does our field make sense of (i.e., explain, theorize, research, discuss, etc.) such routine promotions on our campuses?

3. Visit Dr. Yaba Blay's website and read her post about Tiana Parker, the seven-year old girl in Tulsa, Oklahoma who was dismissed from school in 2013 because she wore dreadlocks (http://yabablay.com/a-care-package-for-tiana-locs-of-love/). What is the college version of your "care package" for black girls like Vickie? To borrow from Wynter's notion of disciplinary sense-making: how does our field make sense of (i.e., explain, theorize, research, discuss, etc.) such experiences of black girls in schools?

4. Imagine that the one and only black, Arab, or Latino male in your class creates a writing portfolio where he has extensively researched police brutality and racial profiling and has also included his own personal experiences. Campus security reads the work since it was printed on the university server and so questions you about your class and your curriculum. What will you do? What will you say? What will you say to the student about his writing in the context of his campus experience? What is your role? For those of you who will simply prevent the one and only black, Arab, or Latino male in

your class from writing about such issues, how do you describe your curriculum, teaching philosophy, and writing politics given this prohibition? To borrow from Wynter's notion of disciplinary sense-making: how does our field make sense of (i.e., explain, theorize, research, discuss, etc.) such routine experiences for black, Arab, or Latino men on our campuses?

5. You are at a new university and you represent a marginalized group there (in terms of gender, race, sexuality, class, religion, size, ability, there is no one else in the department like you). Every semester of your graduate course, students write about this marginalized group of which you are a member in denigrating terms. Every. Single. Semester. You are the only person in your department facing this dilemma. What will you do? Assume that there is no willing mentor on your campus, who will you talk to (*yes, you MUST STICK with this fact; do not retreat to your privilege and assume that you always have supportive colleagues*)? Where will you go in the field—in the publications or at the conferences—where you can find intellectual work that addresses these issues? If you don't find a wide range of such publications or conferences, what do you think accounts for this silence? To borrow, one last time, from Wynter's notion of disciplinary sense-making: how does our field make sense of (i.e., explain, theorize, research, discuss, etc.) racism in education, inside and outside of classrooms?

Notes

1. (i.e., hospitalizations for health conditions that, in the presence of comprehensive primary care, rarely require hospitalization) Go to http://www.ahrq.gov/qual/nhdr03/nhdrsum03.htm

2. See www.blackwomenshealth.org

Works Cited

Alfred, Mary. "Reconceptualizing Marginality from the Margins: Perspective of African American Tenured Female Faculty at a White Research University." *Western Journal of Black Studies* 25.1 (2001): 1-11. Print.

Barone, Thomas. "Narrative Researchers as Witnesses of Injustice and Agents of Social Change?" *Educational Researcher* 38.8 (2009): 591-597. Print.

Bell, Derrick. "Diversity's Distractions." *Columbia Law Review* 103 (2003): 1622-1633. Print.

—. *Faces at the Bottom of the Well.* New York: Basic Books, 1993. Print.

—. "Racial Realism." *Connecticut Law Review* 24.2 (1992): 363-79. Print.

—. "Racial Realism in Retrospect." *Reason and Passion: Justice Brennan's Enduring Influence.* Eds. Joshua Rosenkranz and Bernard Schwartz. New York: W.W. Norton and Company, 1997. 199-206. Print.

—. *Silent Covenants: Brown v. Board of Education and the Unfulfilled Hopes for Racial Reform.* New York: Oxford UP, 2004. Print.

Black Women's Health Imperative, 2002. Web. 15 July, 2010.

Blay, Yaba. "A Care Package for Tiana: Locs of LOVE." *Dr. Yaba Blay: Professor, Scholar Producer.* 6 Sep. 2013. Web. 6 Sep. 2013.

Bonilla-Silva, Eduardo. *Racism Without Racists: Color-Blind Racism and the Persistence of Racial Inequality in the United States.* New York: Rowman & Littlefield, 2006. Print.

Bousquet, Marc. *How the University Works: Higher Education and the Low-Wage Nation.* New York UP, 2008. Print.

Carretta, Vincent. *Phillis Wheatley: Biography of A Genius in Bondage.* Athens: U of Georgia P, 2011. Print.

Cleveland, Darrell. *A Long Way to Go: Conversations about Race by African American Faculty and Graduate Students at Predominantly White Institutions.* New York: Lang, 2004. Print.

Coulter, Cathy, and Mary Lee Smith. "The Construction Zone: Literary Elements in Narrative Research." *Educational Researcher* 38.8 (2009): 577-590. Print.

Darling-Hammond, Linda. "What Happens to a Dream Deferred? The Continuing Quest for Equal Educational Opportunity." *Handbook of Research on Multicultural Education.* Eds. James Banks and C. McGee. San Francisco, CA: Jossey-Bass, 2004. 607-30. Print.

Delgado, Richard. "Derrick Bell's Racial Realism: A Commentary on White Optimism And Black Despair." *Connecticut Law Review* 24 (1992). Print.

Dixson, Adrienne, and Celia Rousseau. *Critical Race Theory in Education: All God's Children Got a Song.* New York: Routledge, 2006. Print.

Doak, Robin S. *Phillis Wheatley: Slave and Poet.* Minneapolis: Compass Point Books, 2007. Print.

Fenelon, James. "Race, Research, and Tenure: Institutional Credibility and the Incorporation of African, Latino, and American Indian Faculty." *Journal of Black Studies* 34.1 (2003): 87-100. Print.

Gates, Henry Louis Jr. *The Trials of Phillis Wheatley: America's First Black Poet and Her Encounters With the Founding Fathers.* New York: Basic Civitas Books, 2003. Print.

Gee, James. "The New Literacy Studies: From 'Socially Situated' to the Work of the Social." *Situated Literacies: Reading and Writing in Context.* Ed. David Barton, Mary Hamilton, and Roz Ivanic. Psychology Press, 2000. 180-196. Print.

Gillborn, David. *Racism and Education: Coincidence or Conspiracy?* New York: Routledge, 2008. Print.

Gonick, Maria and Janice Hladki. "Who Are the Participants? Rethinking Representational Practices and Writing with Heterotopic Possibility in Qualitative Inquiry." *International Journal of Qualitative Studies in Education* 18.3 (2005): 285–304. Print.

Guinier, Lani. "Admissions Rituals as Political Acts: Guardians at the Gates of Our Democratic Ideals." *Harvard Law Review* 117.1 (2003): 113-224. Print.

Guinier, Lani and Gerald Torres. *The Miner's Canary: Enlisting Race, Resisting Power.* Cambridge, MA: Harvard UP, 2002. Print.

Gutiérrez y Muhs, Gabriella, Yolanda Flores Niemann,, Carmen G. González, and Angela P. Harris, eds. *Presumed Incompetent: The Intersections of Race and Class for Women in Academia.* Logan, UT: Utah State University Press, 2012. Print.

"Income and Poverty in Communities of Color: A Reflection on the 2009 U.S. Census Bureau Data." Center for Research and Policy in the Public Interest, 2010. Retrieved Summer 2010. PDF file.

Jacobs-Huey, LaNita. "The Natives are Gazing and Talking Back: Reviewing the Problematics of Positionality, Voice, and Accountability among 'Native' Anthropologists." *American Anthropologist* 104.3 (2002): 791-804. Print.

Kynard, Carmen, and Robert Eddy. "Toward a New Critical Framework: Color-Conscious Political Morality and Pedagogy at Historically Black and Historically White Colleges and Universities." *College Composition and Communication* 61.1 (September 2009): W24-W44. Print.

Ladson-Billings, Gloria. "Preparing Teachers for Diverse Student Populations: A Critical Race Theory Perspective." *Review of Research in Education* 24.1 (1999): 211-47. Print.

Ladson-Billings, Gloria. *Crossing Over to Canaan: The Journey of New Teachers in Diverse Classrooms.* San Francisco: Jossey-Bass, 2001. Print.

—. "Is the Team All Right? Diversity and Teacher Education." *Journal of Teacher Education* 56.2 (2005): 229-34. Print.

Ladson-Billings, Gloria and William Tate. "Toward a Theory of Critical Race Theory in Education." *Teachers College Record* 97.1 (1995): 47-68. Print.

Langley, April C. E. *The Black Aesthetic Unbound: Theorizing the Dilemma of Eighteenth-Century African American Literature.* Columbus: Ohio State UP, 2008. Print.

Leonardo, Zeus. *Race, Whiteness, and Education.* New York: Routledge, 2009. Print.
Luke, Allan. "Generalizing Across Borders: Policy and the Limits of Educational Science." *Educational Researcher* 40.8 (2011): 367-77. Print.
Moses, Michele and Mitchell Chang. "Toward a Deeper Understanding of the Diversity Rationale." *Educational Researcher* 35.1 (2006): 6-11. Print.
National Healthcare Disparities Report, 2003. Agency for Healthcare Research and Quality, 2003. Retrieved Summer 2010.
Orfield, Gary. "The Access Crisis in Higher Education." *Educational Policy* 19 (2005): 255-61. Print.
Powell, Malea. "Stories Take Place." *College Composition and Communication* 64.2 (2012): 383-406. Print.
Richardson, Elaine. *African American Literacies.* New York and London: Routledge, 2003. Print.
Richardson, Laurel. *Fields of Play: Constructing an Academic Life.* New Brunswick: Rutgers U P, 1997. Print.
—. "Getting Personal: Writing Stories." *Qualitative Studies in Education* 14.1 (2001): 33-38.
—. "Poetic Representations of Interviews." *Postmodern Interviewing.* Eds. Jaber Gubrium and James Holstein. London: Sage, 2003. 187-201. Print.
—. "Writing: A Method of Inquiry." *The Handbook of Qualitative Research. 2nd Ed.* Ed. Norman Denzin and Yvonna Lincoln. Thousand Oaks: Sage, 2000. 923-48. Print.
Roediger, David. *How Race Survived U.S. History: From Settlement and Slavery to the Obama Phenomenon.* New York: Verso, 2008. Print.
Ross, Thomas. "The Rhetorical Tapestry of Race: White Innocence and Black Abstraction." *William & Mary Law Review* 32.1 (1990): 1-40. Print.
Sadao, Kathleen, and Linda Johnsrud. "The Common Experience of 'Otherness': Ethnic and Racial Minority Faculty." *Review of Higher Education* 21.4 (1998): 315-42. Print.
Smith, Linda Tuhiwai. *Decolonizing Methodologies: Research and Indigenous People.*Zed Books, 1999. Print.
Stanley, Christine. *Faculty of Color: Teaching in Predominantly White Colleges and Universities.* Bolton: Anker, 2006. Print.
Stanley, Christine et al. "A Case Study of the Teaching Experiences of African American faculty at Two Predominantly White Research Universities." *Journal of Excellence in College Teaching* 14.1 (2003): 151-78. Print.
Swartz, Ellen. "Diversity: Gatekeeping Knowledge and Maintaining Inequalities." *Review of Educational Research* 79.2 (June 2009): 1044-1083. Print.
Thomas, Gloria and Carol Hollenshead. "Resisting from the Margins: The Coping Strategies of Black Women and Other Women of Color Faculty Members at a Research University." *Journal of Negro Education* 70.3 (2002): 166-75. Print.

Turner, Caroline. "Incorporation and Marginalization in the Academy: From Border Toward Center for Faculty of Color." *Journal of Black Studies* 34.1 (2003): 112-25. Print.

Wynter, Sylvia. *"Do Not Call Us Negros": How Multicultural Textbooks Perpetuate Racism*. San Francisco: Aspire Books, 1990. Print.

Wynter, Sylvia. "'No Humans Involved': An Open Letter to My Colleagues." *Forum N.H.I.: Knowledge for the 21st Century* 1.1 (1994): 42-72. Print.

Wynter, Sylvia. "'No Humans Involved': An Open Letter to My Colleagues." *Voices of the African Diaspora: The CAAS Research Review* 8.2 (1992): 13-16. Print.

Yosso, Tara, Laurence Parker, Daniel Solorzano, and Marvin Lynn. "From Jim Crow to Affirmative Action and Back Again: A Critical Race Discussion of Racialized Rationales and Access to Higher Education." *Review of Research in Education* 28 (2004): 1-26. Print.

Young, Morris. *Minor Re/Visions: Asian American Literacy Narratives as a Rhetoric of Citizenship*. Carbondale: Southern Illinois UP, 2005. Print.

About the Editors

Brian Bailie is Assistant Professor of English specializing in rhetoric and composition at the University of Cincinnati, Blue Ash College. He has served as an associate editor for *Reflections: A Journal of Writing, Service-Learning, and Community Literacy*; published in *Reflections, Composition Forum*, and *KB Journal*; and is currently the interviews editor at *Composition Forum*. In collaboration with Chris Wilkey of Northern Kentucky University, the Peaslee Neighborhood Center, and the Greater Cincinnati Homeless Coalition, his current project is working with writers/artists from Cincinnati's historic Over-the-Rhine (OTR) neighborhood to document the changes in OTR due to gentrification.

David Blakesley is the Campbell Chair in Technical Communication and Professor of English at Clemson University. He is also the publisher and founder of Parlor Press. A Fellow of the Rhetoric Society of America, his books include *The Elements of Dramatism, The Terministic Screen: Rhetorical Perspectives on Film*, and *Writing: A Manual for the Digital Age*. His articles have appeared in journals such as *WPA: Writing Program Administration, JAC, Rhetoric Society Quarterly, Composition Studies, The Writing Instructor, First Monday*, and *Kairos*. He founded the Rhetorical Philosophy and Theory series with SIU Press and currently serves as editor of *KB Journal*.

Romeo García is Assistant Professor in the Department of Writing and Rhetoric Studies at The University of Utah. He focuses on critical approaches to working with marginalized students in institutional spaces. His research is attentive to meaning-making practices that are constellated, embodied, and practiced in spaces and places.

About the Editors

Kate Navickas is the Director of the Writing Centers and teaches writing and TA training courses in the Knight Institute for Writing in the Disciplines at Cornell University. She's recently taught classes on civic writing and protest, language discrimination, and archival research. Her research in feminist pedagogy focuses on the role of writing assignment texts in the invention process and fostering classroom relationships. More broadly, her interests include feminist rhetorics, affect and emotional labor, composition pedagogy and history, and WPA and writing center work. She is currently co-editing a collection titled *The Things We Carry: Strategies for Recognizing & Negotiating Emotional Labor in Writing Program Administration* and completing an interview with Minnie-Bruce Pratt for a special issue of *Pedagogy* on ideology in the classroom.

Adela C. Licona is Associate Professor of English, Director of the Institute for LGBT Studies, and Vice Chair of Social, Cultural, Critical Theory Graduate Minor at the University of Arizona. She has published in such journals as *Antipode, Transformations, Journal of Latino-Latin American Studies, Sexuality Research and Social Policy, Annals of the Association of American Geographers* and *Critical Studies in Media Communication*. She is the author of *Zines in Third Space: Radical Cooperation and Borderlands Rhetoric* (SUNY Press, 2012) and co-editor of *Feminist Pedagogy: Looking Back to Move Forward* (JHUP, 2009). She co-founded the Crossroads Collaborative, a think-and-act research, writing, and teaching collective, and Feminist Action Research in Rhetoric (FARR), a group of progressive feminist scholars committed to public scholarship and community dialogue. Adela serves on the editorial and advisory boards for *Feminist Formations, Women's Studies in Communication, QED: A Journal of GLBTQ Worldmaking, Spoken Futures and the Tucson Youth Poetry Slam*, and for the Ohio State University Press' exciting new book series *Intersectional Rhetorics*.

Steve Parks is Associate Professor of Rhetoric and Writing at Syracuse University and serves as Editor of Studies in Writing and Rhetoric. His most recent publication is *Writing Communities: A Text with Readings*, a book designed to enable instructors and writing programs to develop community-oriented classrooms.

CPSIA information can be obtained
at www.ICGtesting.com
Printed in the USA
FSOW01n1140191017
39921FS